SUFFERING VICTORY

A volume in the NIU Series in

Slavic, East European, and Eurasian Studies

Edited by Christine D. Worobec

For a list of books in the series, visit our website at cornellpress.cornell.edu.

SUFFERING VICTORY

SOVIET LIBERALS AND
THE FAILURE OF
DEMOCRACY IN RUSSIA,
1987–1993

GUILLAUME SAUVÉ

NORTHERN ILLINOIS UNIVERSITY PRESS
AN IMPRINT OF
CORNELL UNIVERSITY PRESS
Ithaca and London

Copyright © 2025 by Cornell University

All rights reserved. Except for brief quotations in a review, this book, or parts thereof, must not be reproduced in any form without permission in writing from the publisher. For information, address Cornell University Press, Sage House, 512 East State Street, Ithaca, New York 14850. Visit our website at cornellpress.cornell.edu.

Originally published as *Subir la victoire. Essor et chute de l'intelligentsia libérale en Russie (1987–1993)* © Les Presses de l'Université de Montréal, 2019

First published 2025 by Cornell University Press

Librarians: A CIP catalog record for this book is available from the Library of Congress.

ISBN 9781501781032 (hardcover)
ISBN 9781501781049 (paperback)
ISBN 9781501781056 (epub)
ISBN 9781501781063 (pdf)

Contents

Acknowledgments vii

Notes on Transliteration and Translation ix

Introduction: The Strange Fate of the Soviet Liberal Intelligentsia — 1

1. The Moral Challenge of Perestroika — 15
2. Liberal Moralism in the USSR — 34
3. Opinion and Truth — 52
4. A Reluctant Opposition (1989) — 72
5. Modernization and the Iron Fist — 112
6. The Dilemma of the Democratic Movement (1990–93) — 140
7. Forgotten Democratic Opposition Projects — 168

Conclusion — 186

Notes 195

Bibliography 225

Index 239

Acknowledgments

This book constitutes a translated and expanded edition of the work originally published in French in 2019 by Presses de l'Université de Montréal. In addition to expressing my gratitude to all those acknowledged in the original edition, I would like to extend my sincere appreciation to those who have contributed to enhancing the text. Ryan Perks rendered invaluable assistance in refining the English language of this work. Furthermore, I am indebted to the insightful discussions with Timur Atnashev, Morvan Lallouet, Marlène Laruelle, and Paul Robinson.

A special acknowledgment is due to James Krapfl for his guidance through the Anglo-American publishing process, accompanied by his encouragement and profound insights into central and eastern European politics in 1989, which I found to strongly resonate with the predicament of late Soviet liberals. However, it is important to note that while these individuals provided invaluable advice, they bear no responsibility for the final outcome.

I also wish to express my gratitude to *Europe-Asia Studies*, *Revue d'études comparatives Est-Ouest*, and *Slavic Review* for granting permission to include previously published material in this book.

Notes on Transliteration and Translation

Since this work is aimed primarily at non-Russian speakers, I have sought above all to produce a text that will be familiar to Anglophone readers. The result is a slight variation in the spelling of names in the main text versus formal source citations. In the former, I have maintained the common English spellings of Russian names, while in the latter I have kept to the Library of Congress system—the standard guide for the romanization of Cyrillic script in scholarly contexts. So, for example, I refer to Afanasyev in the main text and Afanas'ev in subsequent citations. I trust this will not be unduly distracting.

Unless otherwise noted, all translations are my own.

SUFFERING VICTORY

Introduction
The Strange Fate of the Soviet Liberal Intelligentsia

At the end of the 1980s, Russia found itself at the epicenter of a shock wave that would upend the country and change the face of the world.[1] Mikhail Gorbachev, general secretary of the Communist Party, had recently launched a vast program of reforms known as "perestroika," which initiated a transition to democracy and a market economy, gave freedom to the satellite countries of the Eastern Bloc, and brought about the end of the Cold War. But in so doing, Gorbachev unwittingly opened a Pandora's box from which all the contradictions of the Soviet state would subsequently emerge: economic backwardness vis-à-vis the capitalist West, secessionist movements, a revolt against the privileges of the *nomenklatura* (party elites), and more. In the end, the USSR was dissolved in December 1991 after a bitter political struggle, to the great surprise of many Soviet citizens and foreign observers. From the ruins of a socialist empire that many had considered immutable, a new Russia emerged, groping to join the community of capitalist democracies.

One of the most remarkable outcomes of this tumultuous period was the spectacular rise of the Soviet liberal intelligentsia in Russian public life and its precipitous fall at the end of perestroika. To understand the significance of this development, it is necessary to take a longer view, as it turns out to be exceptional from both a political and an intellectual perspective. After decades of severe censorship, the gradual opening up of the Soviet public sphere gave rise to a wave of hope and a thirst for new ideas. Gorbachev encouraged the intelligentsia to speak candidly about the country's problems in order to gather support for his efforts at reform and to weaken the position of his opponents. This was the beginning of a flourishing period for Soviet intellectuals, who became the darlings of newspapers, journals, and television programs. The literary scholar Georges Nivat, a longtime observer of Russian society, testifies to this opening: "The intelligentsia had found its ideal regime in perestroika, . . . television and big journals competed for [its] favor. It was a time when I recognized friends from the Moscow intelligentsia on the screen every day."[2]

From 1987 onward, the main beneficiaries of this newfound attention belonged to what is commonly called the "liberal intelligentsia," its representatives so described because they defended a vision of socialism that incorporated many liberal ideas: representative democracy, human rights, the rule of law, and the market economy, among others.[3] Many of these liberal intellectuals, whose influence had previously been confined to a narrow circle of insiders, suddenly became famous; their articles appeared regularly in major national media, and they were invited to speak at conferences throughout the country and abroad. Their influence on public opinion at that time was formidable enough to make their Western counterparts green with envy. Indeed, incredible as it may seem, it was common during the era of perestroika to see Soviet citizens lining up in front of newsstands—on cold, snowy mornings, no less—in the hope of getting their hands on the latest issue of *Novyi Mir* or *Znamia*, austere intellectual journals that offered lengthy articles in tiny black-and-white print.

How to explain such intellectual fervor? The reason is simple: these journals offered previously forbidden literary texts and polemical articles that pushed the limits of acceptable debate in Soviet society, which had undergone decades of severe censorship. From Kaliningrad to Vladivostok, the crimes of Stalin, the advent of democratization, and soon even the fundamental errors of Lenin and the Communist Party itself became topics of open discussion. With this new openness, the liberal intelligentsia rallied to its cause large numbers of the urban and educated Soviet population, many of whom would henceforth prove to be politically active. Indeed, these intellectuals did not limit themselves to the field of ideas. As soon as the first semidemocratic elections were held in the spring of 1989, several of them became involved in more nakedly political pursuits. The fame these individuals had acquired in the previous years allowed them to take the reins of the democratic movement in its successful opposition to the Communist Party.

This movement organized demonstrations among the largest in the country's history and contributed to the rise to power of Boris Yeltsin, who would become one of the main protagonists in the USSR's dissolution and then the first president of post-Soviet Russia.

Suffering Victory

For many liberal intellectuals, however, the victory over communism was a Pyrrhic one insofar as their unconditional support for Yeltsin had created the conditions for their own marginalization. After encouraging the concentration of power in the hands of a strong president, they were pushed aside, along with all other potential sources of competing power. It was in this powerless state that they witnessed the outbreak of a bloody war in Chechnya. Larisa Bogoraz, a veteran anti-Soviet dissident, would later express her regrets at these developments: "It's all our fault. We were so sick of the Soviet regime that we thought it should be destroyed by any means. So we supported Yeltsin, making him think he could do anything."[4] In the end, the liberal intelligentsia was largely discredited by its association with the authoritarian aspects of Yeltsin's regime and by the course of economic reforms, which plunged much of the population into poverty.

As rapid as its rise during perestroika, the decline of the liberal intelligentsia in the early 1990s was much more profound than the conservative backlash that inevitably follows any revolution. In several other eastern European countries, such as Poland and Lithuania, the liberals lost elections but returned to power a few years later. In Russia, by contrast, the decline of the liberal intelligentsia was both deeper and longer-lasting. In the decade following the end of perestroika, liberal parties in Russia saw their electoral support decline to the point of irrelevance, while nationalist and conservative ideas gained considerably in popularity. The relative freedom of the 1990s, and the influence of some liberal economists on the government's subsequent course of action, should not obscure the fact that the liberal intelligentsia as a whole was discredited, rendering it relatively powerless in the face of President Vladimir Putin's efforts to restore state power after the turn of the millennium.

From their tremendous rise in 1987 to their vertiginous fall after the adoption of the superpresidential Constitution of 1993, Russia's liberal intellectuals were the victims of a strange fate: their success against the Communist Party came at the price of their own decline in the post-Soviet era. As the economist Otto Latsis, himself a liberal intellectual, would say, "We suffered victory" (*poterpeli pobedu*).[5]

From Triumphalism to Disillusionment

It is easy to think of these events as belonging to some distant era. Today's readers, stumbling upon an older map of the world, may even be surprised to discover a country covering one-sixth of the earth's landmass, typically pictured in red, and bearing the now incomprehensible name of Union of Soviet Socialist Republics. And yet perestroika is a very recent event, as illustrated by the fact that most of those who have written about it are either protagonists or direct observers. Absent the calming effect that often comes with the passage of time, the tone and conclusions of these analyses are highly polarized, and they have undergone many changes since 1991, as Russia's transition to democracy came to seem more and more like an unfulfilled promise.

Among the various accounts of the rise and fall of the liberal intelligentsia, I distinguish two main historiographical trends: triumphalism, whose proponents celebrate the conversion of Russia's intellectuals to Western liberal ideas, and disillusionment, whose representatives denounce the supposed errors and illusions of the intelligentsia.[6]

The various triumphalist interpretations have in common a strong enthusiasm for the cause of the Soviet liberal intelligentsia, whose spirit of freedom and emancipation from Soviet dogma they celebrate. For this reason, they interpret the rejection of the sacred symbols of Marxism-Leninism as a sign of Russian liberals' conversion to the ideas of the opposing side of the Cold War—namely, that of the Western liberal democracies. The pioneering works in this vein appeared soon after the onset of perestroika. In response to those who saw these reforms as just another Soviet propaganda campaign, these scholars hailed perestroika as a genuine expression of the yearning for individual freedom and democracy of a rising portion of the Soviet population who enjoyed the benefits of urbanization and advanced education.[7] The emergence of democratic and liberal ideals among these Soviet citizens was thus seen as a precursor to the type of modernization already experienced by the citizens of the Western countries. This interpretation fed on a widely presumed similarity between Soviet and other developed societies: at the time, it seemed a matter of course that the democratic movement in the USSR "sought change in the direction of liberal or social democracy as these terms are commonly understood in the West"[8] or that it could be designated as liberal "in the classic European sense."[9] Indeed, Soviet liberal intellectuals were the darlings of their counterparts in the advanced capitalist countries, who could recognize themselves in these thinkers and who encouraged the dissemination of their ideas outside the USSR, giving rise to an abundant literature translated into English, French, Spanish, Italian, German, and Japanese, among other languages.

This triumphalist vision was so deeply rooted in the collective imagination that it survived unscathed in the writings of some authors—even after the many bitter disappointments of the 1990s,[10] as many of the most optimistic prognostications espoused by the Soviet liberal intelligentsia failed to translate into concrete action, and the discrepancy between the professed principles and the real-world policies of those who claimed to be "democrats" became all too obvious. And yet, since the rise to power of Vladimir Putin, most proponents of the triumphalist interpretation have felt compelled to explain why Western liberal ideas, despite their apparent triumph during perestroika, have subsequently been sidelined, if not discarded altogether. The most common explanations invoke the moral corruption of the Soviet population, Russian cultural atavisms, or structural factors related to the challenge of a simultaneous transition to democracy, market economics, and the nation-state.[11] In any case, the alleged causes of the liberal intelligentsia's rapid rise and subsequent fall are mainly considered exogenous and therefore do not affect the basic assumption of its conversion to Western liberalism.

In the 1990s, as Russia found itself mired in a deepening economic recession and facing the steady erosion of democracy, the optimistic vision of the liberal intelligentsia as the vanguard of Western modernity became the subject of growing skepticism. Several disillusioned scholars, many of whom were former supporters of the Russian democrats, did not hesitate to put the liberal intelligentsia on trial, accusing it of having perpetuated certain attitudes that were thought to have disappeared with the rejection of Soviet ideology: authoritarianism, intolerance, paternalism, and corruption. Without denying the importance of the structural factors impeding the establishment of democracy in Russia, these scholars insisted on assigning endogenous causes for the failure of the liberal intelligentsia.

Looking more closely at the various threads of disillusionment, I distinguish two distinct variants: the *negativity* thesis and the *inversion* thesis. The negativity thesis asserts that the liberal intelligentsia did not champion any particular ideals or specific political projects beyond the rejection of communism. In this perspective, the struggle against the existing system was motivated by a kind of diffuse and inarticulate moral protest. Rather than a conversion to Western liberal ideas, what took place was the mere abandonment of Soviet ideology, or even of ideology in general. In Russia, many liberal intellectuals display in retrospect just such a skeptical posture in response to perestroika, as a way to distance themselves from its ideals, which are now largely out of fashion in the country.¹² The negativity thesis is also advanced by several scholars who denounce the inability of liberal intellectuals to propose a new, positive vision of the world that could have cemented the role of democratic political parties, thus leaving the field open to the blossoming of a nostalgia for an idealized Soviet past.¹³

The most elaborate argument in favor of the negativity thesis can be found in the writings of the historian Timur Atnashev, drawing on his doctoral dissertation on the transformation of political discourse during perestroika, which remains unpublished.¹⁴ Echoing the writings of the historian John Pocock on the "Machiavellian moment" that marked the birth of modern political thought in the West,¹⁵ Atnashev describes the end of perestroika as an "anti-Machiavellian" moment characterized by the rejection of the legitimacy of human action in favor of an unquestioning faith in the natural and inherently positive evolution of history.¹⁶ According to Atnashev, this "subjective incompetence" helps to explain the peaceful course of regime change in the early nineties and also the weakness of the resulting political society, which was inherently conservative—including on its liberal wing—in its distrust of any conscious and voluntary project of political transformation.

The inversion thesis, by contrast, represents a direct response to the main premise of the triumphalist interpretation—namely, that the fall of the Soviet system resulted in the abandonment of official Marxism-Leninism and a genuine conversion to Western liberal ideals. The proponents of the inversion thesis claim that the relationship of the two poles is actually characterized more by continuity than by rupture. The liberal intelligentsia, they argue, would have inherited from Soviet ideology a voluntarist and intransigent political maximalism that forbids the compromises that are necessary for the practice of democracy and justifies all abuses in the name of the imperatives of modernization. The attitude of the liberal reformers has thus been referred to as "market Bolshevism," "Leninist liberalism," or "neo-Leninist hubris,"¹⁷ terms that convey the image of a messianic elite assuming for itself the responsibility of imposing progress on a backward majority.¹⁸

Perhaps the best-documented iteration of the inversion thesis was formulated by the political scientist Alexander Lukin in *The Political Culture of Russian "Democrats."*¹⁹ In that book, Lukin argues that the political culture of Russia's self-styled democrats essentially takes for granted the presuppositions of Soviet ideology, whose signs it merely reverses: the imperialist West becomes the "civilized world," while the socialist camp becomes the imperialist "totalitarian world"; the USSR is no longer ahead of its capitalist counterparts but instead lags behind; true democracy is liberal, while Soviet democracy is only a mask for class domination. This debt to Soviet ideology,

Lukin concludes, explains why Russian democrats have been unable to establish a truly liberal democracy, or even to fashion a functional state.

In today's Russia, the belief in the late Soviet liberals' alleged revolutionary hubris is widely accepted across the political spectrum, extending even to liberals. This assumption serves as another illustration of the inherent radicalism attributed to the Russian intelligentsia and the dangers associated with mass mobilization when it is not effectively kept in check by an enlightened leader.[20] This commonly held "historical lesson" from the perestroika era significantly contributed to shaping the antirevolutionary sentiment characteristic of contemporary Russia, which revolves around the idea that "even poor order is better than its destruction":[21] a sentiment later deliberately nurtured by the regime of Vladimir Putin to counter the specter of "color revolutions."[22]

Breaking Out of the Cold War

The main benefit of the disillusionment theses of the 1990s is that they challenged the widespread presumption of similarity that mistakes the global diffusion of liberal ideas for a sort of ideological mimicry.[23] The weakness of these interpretations, however, lies in their tendency to explain the political engagement of the liberal intelligentsia by way of an overarching ideological disposition, be it "negative" or "Bolshevik," that loses sight of internal complexities. In order to arrive at a more refined understanding of the political and intellectual life of perestroika, I believe it is necessary to go beyond the Cold War interpretive framework that, in Russia as elsewhere, approaches political thought in the second half of the twentieth century through the prism of binary ideological opposition.

This framework is obviously present in the triumphalist interpretation, which as we saw speaks of a wholesale conversion to Western ideas, but it can also be found in the disillusionment interpretation, and specifically in the inversion thesis, according to which Russian intellectuals' superficial embrace of Western liberalism reveals a lingering, if unconscious, attachment to its opposite—namely, Soviet ideological tropes. In this sense, while the negativity thesis goes beyond the binary alternative, it nonetheless remains dependent on its general framework: political thought that is not formalized in a clear-cut political doctrine or a full-fledged ideology, like Marxism-Leninism or liberalism, is treated as a type of pragmatic apoliticism.

Of course, the interpretative framework of the Cold War is grounded in history; it corresponds to the spirit of ideological polarization that reigned in the decades after the Second World War. However, its inadequacy should be obvious when we turn to analyze the cases at its limits. This is typically true of perestroika, which marks the temporal end of the Cold War and which, as such, constitutes the pivotal moment when the Soviet experience becomes too similar to our own to be studied as an exceptional object, while remaining distinct enough that it cannot easily be subsumed within universal patterns. In scholarly works on late Soviet society, perestroika's ambiguous status results in an obvious methodological malaise. Some of the finest analyses cautiously stop at the dawn of perestroika, as if the era's beginnings suddenly put an end to Soviet exceptionalism.[24] Conversely, as we have seen, studies that approach perestroika from the perspective of ostensibly universal processes, such as modernization, the transition to democracy, or the creation of a multiparty system, tend to explain the behavior of its protagonists with reference to established ideological categories, which are then found to fit awkwardly with the reality of Russian politics.

A Study of Political Thought

The complexity of this teeming political and intellectual moment, which straddles eras and ideologies, invites a study of the Soviet liberal intelligentsia that proceeds from its own concepts and issues. To this end, I offer in the following chapters a nuanced interpretation of Soviet liberal political thought, elaborated as it was in the heat of the action and at the crossroads of ideals inherited from the past, through polemics of the moment, and according to the strategic considerations of the contemporary political struggle. In my interpretative and historical approach to the relevant texts, I have tried to maintain a sensitivity to the specific context in which they were expressed and received, for only then can we uncover the fault lines of the main debates between the liberals and their nationalist and conservative communist opponents, as well as those that divided the Soviet liberals among themselves, as so many milestones of a revolutionary process in which events followed one another at a speed that upset the expectations of all involved.

Such an approach highlights the contingency of thought rather than its structural determinations, but it also seeks to identify its normative foundations—that is, the implicit moral horizon that guided the various choices of political tactics. I seek, in other words, to reconstruct the hopes, disillusionments, and dilemmas of these intellectuals in order to elaborate a fine-grained understanding of the reasons for their political action, the consequences of which have proved so cruelly paradoxical. In doing so, my goal is not to advance yet another explanation of failure of democracy in post-Soviet Russia, which is due to a multitude of structural and conjunctural factors,[25] but more particularly to understand the role that the Soviet liberal intelligentsia played in this sad outcome. As we shall see, this is a historical episode rich in lessons for those who, in Russia and elsewhere, wish to enter the political arena in order to defend the ideals of truth, honesty, and democracy.

This book sheds light on the ideals with which the liberal intelligentsia confronted the imperatives of political struggle. It consists of two parts: first, a description of the moral perspective of these intellectuals as it crystallized from 1987 onward, a time when the Soviet public sphere experienced a partial opening and a relative drop in censorship, and second, an analysis of the trials faced by the liberal intelligentsia as a result of the emergence of political pluralism between 1989 and 1993.

I begin in chapter 1 by describing the moral and cultural conditions that set the stage for the spectacular rise of the liberal intelligentsia beginning in 1987. My approach to this question runs counter to that of most other scholars in this area. Rather than examining the factors that either facilitated or hindered the progress of liberal ideas—the desirability of which is too often taken for granted in most accounts—I seek to understand why these ideas were attractive to so many in the first place. In seeking to answer this question, I suggest that liberal ideas progressed during perestroika because they echoed widely shared concerns related to society's perceived moral decline.

One of the main arguments of this book, in fact, is that the spectacular popularity of Soviet liberal ideas cannot simply be considered a sort of default outcome of the bankruptcy of Marxism-Leninism, let alone of the erosion of ideology writ large; rather, these ideas were carried aloft by a powerful moral project that reflected the dominant sensibility of the period, marked as it was by the rejection of artificial structures that were seen to hinder society's natural development and the harmonious blossoming of individual expression. In presenting the elements of continuity between Soviet liberalism and the commonplace realities of late Soviet society, I do not seek to condemn this heritage as some burdensome ideological legacy, as the proponents of the inversion thesis tend to do, but rather to emphasize the correspondence between the ideas of the Soviet liberal intelligentsia and the moral concerns of the era more broadly, which in turn largely conditioned the expectations of the defenders of democracy.

This description of the rise of liberal ideas in the Soviet public sphere sets the stage for a more detailed characterization of perestroika-era liberalism. Once we set aside the presumed similarity with the canonical definitions of Western liberalism, the question remains: How was the so-called liberal intelligentsia liberal? Some readers may no doubt question the very applicability of this label, since most of these intellectuals abandoned socialism only in the final hours of the Soviet era, around 1990, and most preferred to call themselves democrats anyway.[26] But as I explain in chapter 2, my choice of the term "liberal" has merit insofar as that description corresponds to several of the most essential ideas espoused by the intellectuals in question, thereby opening the door to certain comparative reflections.[27]

But it is worth noting here that I define the content of this label inductively, starting from the particular thoughts and actions of Soviet intellectuals. Thus, I argue that late Soviet liberalism was mainly nourished by the legacy of socialist humanism, which combined Enlightenment ideals (rational control of society, linear and teleological progress, universal values like liberty and equality) and Romantic aspirations (the full and harmonious expression of the person and the organic development of society). This leads me to conclude that the main distinguishing feature of Soviet liberalism, in contrast to the currents of liberalism then dominant in the West, is its assumed moralism. This aspiration to make people better may seem outmoded in the twenty-first century, given our own relativistic sensibilities, but it should not be seen as a communist atavism fundamentally unsuited to today's world. Rather, I suggest that we view this assumed moralism as an attempt to respond to a well-known concern of political philosophy, especially in its republican tradition—namely, the need to base freedom on shared moral norms. Interestingly, this moral project was not exclusively Soviet but was widely shared throughout the Eastern Bloc, notably in Czechoslovakia, East Germany, and Poland. While this book does not claim to provide a comprehensive comparison of the political and intellectual developments in these diverse countries during that period, it consistently draws parallels in the hope of contributing to bridging the gap between two academic fields that are often studied in isolation from each other—the study of perestroika in the USSR and the study of the revolutions of 1989 in eastern Europe.

In chapter 3, I reconstruct the contradictory expectations of Soviet liberal intellectuals for the emancipated public sphere, torn as they were between a desire for a full and sincere expression of personal conscience, which implied the recognition of intellectual and ideological pluralism, and the promotion of a comprehensive conception of "universal values" as the sole basis for society's moral recovery, which implied the purification of public discourse according to a criterion of absolute truth, which undermined the desire for pluralism. The tension between these two desires gave the political discourse of Soviet liberals an ambiguous character: emancipatory in its refusal of any ideological orthodoxy and monopoly on truth yet simultaneously uncompromising in its propensity to reject as lies the principles defended by their communist and nationalist opponents, who, incidentally, did not hesitate to do the same. In 1987 and 1988, when intense debates broke out in the media—itself recently freed by the relaxation of censorship—few Soviet liberal intellectuals perceived this tension. They thought that democratization required the consolidation of power in the hands of reformers; only then could they overcome the resistance of the "opponents of perestroika" and implement the political and economic reforms by which the moral preconditions for freedom are created.

The second part of the book focuses on the dilemmas facing liberal intellectuals after 1989, when media debates began to give way to more overt forms of political struggle. Contrary to the expectations of many, the relaxation of censorship led not to society's consolidation around a specific set of universal values but rather to the increasing polarization of opinions and interests. Chapter 4 shows that after the government refused to listen to their advice and the possibility of a vast popular mobilization led by the liberal intelligentsia arose, those liberal intellectuals involved in the political arena became divided over their relationship with the reforming government.

Yet while the question of power, of who governs and how—so long neglected in favor of personal and universal demands deemed more important—took on a new salience, it gave rise to very different reactions. The increasingly radical moral opposition of liberal intellectuals to the communist system did not automatically entail, as is commonly assumed, their political opposition to Soviet power; on the contrary, a significant part of the liberal intelligentsia systematically resisted the idea of creating a formal opposition movement and unconditionally supported Gorbachev in order to protect his power against the corrosive effects of conflicts over values and interests. This argument invites us to reconsider the reputation for political extremism commonly associated with the liberal intellectuals of this era, in Russia and elsewhere, as it turns out that the majority of them constantly sought to consolidate the power of the executive in order to prevent any revolutionary outbursts, with the paradoxical result of preventing the institutionalization of conflict in a democratic framework.

Chapter 5 is devoted to the most extreme reaction to social polarization in this context—namely, the abandonment by some liberal intellectuals of their shared moralism in favor of an authoritarian and technocratic transition to democracy and a market economy. The chapter's analysis of the 1989 debate over the proposal to entrust democratization to a reforming "iron fist" illustrates the diversity of views that emerged on the question of power and its relation to morality among the Soviet liberal intelligentsia. The relative consensus on the purpose of reforms hid a deeper division over the best means of achieving them.

As early as 1990, the proponents of different political tactics came to a head within the democratic movement, as many liberal intellectuals finally abandoned socialism and shifted their allegiance to a new reformer whom they perceived to be more consistent, Boris Yeltsin. The examination of these debates in chapter 6 sheds new light on the motives for the concentration of power in contemporary Russia. In particular, we see that the concentration of power in the presidency was actively supported by many leading liberal intellectuals who were troubled by the growing chaos of political life and wanted to preserve the nascent democracy from the revenge of illiberal forces and from the moral corruption of the people. This interpretation echoes the arguments of those who trace the roots of Vladimir Putin's power back to the concentration of authority and the social isolation of the new political elite at the end of perestroika.

This renewed understanding of the sources of authoritarianism, however, does not imply an undifferentiated condemnation of the Soviet liberal intelligentsia and the role it played in the earliest stages of authoritarian consolidation. In my view, this role does not justify the contemptuous oblivion into which its most cherished ideals have fallen. The profound disillusionment of the 1990s, in fact, has not only discredited the excessive optimism of the triumphalist interpretations. In the name of "pragmatism," "realism," and more recently "conservatism," which have become the order of the day in contemporary Russia, many post-Soviet liberal intellectuals themselves tend to regard the aspirations associated with reforming socialism and building democracy as childishly naive. The moral and political dilemmas of perestroika are lost in many retrospective accounts, which are often told as narratives whose protagonists gradually overcome their previously held illusions.[28]

In a sense, then, the symbolic revolution of perestroika is a victim of its own success: it so thoroughly transformed our symbolic orientations as to preclude our ability to retroactively identify the intellectual foundations upon which it was originally built.[29] Hence the importance of recalling its initial moral aspirations. Likewise, liberal intellectuals' overwhelming support for the consolidation of power under Yeltsin should not cause us to forget the other proposals—certainly in the minority but nonetheless influential—put forward at the time in favor of an autonomous democratic opposition that could provide a check on the actions of the reformers. I present some of these (now largely forgotten) alternatives in the final chapter. If nothing else, this allows us to qualify the judgments now widely leveled against the liberal intelligentsia of perestroika and to recall that its moralism did not always translate into support for an authoritarian technocracy but could have served as the inspiration for a democracy based on shared values.

A Note on Sources

Writing in 1995, the liberal intellectual Dmitri Furman concluded that the democratic revolution in Russia was based "neither on great thinkers or ideologists nor on fully constituted ideologies or philosophies."[30] My selection of material in the following chapters is determined by this double constraint. On the one hand, I approach the political thought of the liberal intelligentsia via the writings of a number of authors who, although famous during perestroika, are very likely unknown to anyone who did not live in Russia at that time. This mode of selection, besides having the merit of broadening my study beyond a select list of "big names," stems from a circumstance peculiar to perestroika: the absence of an established body of canonical authors. If the intellectual historian of the French Revolution cannot ignore figures like Condorcet, Robespierre, and Saint-Just, or if the names Lenin and Trotsky come immediately to the mind for those who work on the ideological dimensions of the 1917 October Revolution, who are the great liberal intellectuals of perestroika?

The problem, of course, is not the absence of brilliant thinkers but the fact that no single name can reasonably be said to have eclipsed the others.[31] One solution would have been to deal with all of them at once, but this approach runs the risk of dispersion to the point of losing sight of the relationship of discourse to events, thereby giving a false impression of constancy and unanimity.[32] This is why I have chosen to focus on a small group of authors who were particularly active in the intellectual and political life of the period: the historians Yuri Afanasyev and Leonid Batkin, the literary critics Yuri Burtin and Yuri Karyakin, the journalist Len Karpinsky, and the physicist Andrei Sakharov. These intellectuals were linked by common experience, as each contributed to the famous volume *Inogo ne dano*, published in 1988, and to the foundation and development of the Moscow Tribune, the most prestigious political club in the capital. While these figures are not necessarily representative of the entire liberal intelligentsia committed to democratization, they were perhaps the most prominent representatives of its main current, embodied here by the so-called Sixtiers (*shestidesiatniki*), the generation that came to political maturity in the context of the de-Stalinization of the 1960s.

But rather than serving as the exclusive focus of this book, these six intellectuals are merely the starting point from which I approach the main lines of liberal debate between 1987 and 1991. Following the dynamics of these exchanges, my study gives voice to other representatives of the liberal intelligentsia, as well as to nationalist intellectuals and conservative communists, with the ultimate goal of reconstructing a mosaic of authors linked to different ideologies and generations.

The political thought examined in this book was not patiently elaborated by professional philosophers. Caught up in the frenzy of perestroika, very few intellectuals had the time or the will to synthesize their ideas in scholarly monographs. Their thinking was mainly expressed in a polemical genre that predominates among the intellectual output of the era: the *publicistika*, or committed essay. This literary genre, the preferred form of a generalist intelligentsia that did not limit its role to that of the specialized expert, was aimed at an educated public who were more likely to appreciate literary references—Pushkin, Gogol, Dostoevsky, Chekhov—than scientific or philosophical jargon. The *publicistika* appeared in newspapers, in the form of columns, editorials, and articles, and also in thick monthly intellectual journals, where it was found alongside fiction and literary essays, in a tradition dating back to the nineteenth century.

My selection of materials includes nearly two hundred documents from the period, mostly *publicistika* that I consulted in specialized libraries in Russia, France, and the United States. In order to avoid the trap of anachronism, I chose to focus on these contemporary sources rather than on retrospective testimonies, though I have collected a number of these as well in interviews with the intellectuals concerned and their relatives.[33] These interviews helped me to orient myself in the debates of the time, a contribution that, while it is not reflected in the formal references for each chapter, I hope is nonetheless palpable in a more general sense through my reconstruction of the historical texture of the intellectual and political life of perestroika.

CHAPTER 1

The Moral Challenge of Perestroika

> Today our main job is to lift the individual
> spiritually, respecting his inner world
> and giving him moral strength.
>
> —Mikhail Gorbachev, *Perestroika:
> New Thinking for Our Country and
> the World*, 1987

Morality was an omnipresent theme in the political discourse of early perestroika.[1] From leaders to dissidents, from communists to nationalists and liberals, all testified to the strong sense of moral decline in Soviet society, characterized in this case by the spread of hypocrisy, cynicism, and the moral disorientation of the youth. The relatively stable economic situation did not prevent many from experiencing a feeling of degradation, corruption, or decay. This feeling, in turn, inspired countless calls for a renewal, purification, or invigoration of morals. In this context, perestroika was widely welcomed by Soviet society as a salutary effort to remedy a moral decay many deemed increasingly unbearable. As one popular slogan from the period proclaimed, "We can no longer live like this."[2]

Viewed in retrospect, this sense of moral decline can sometimes appear to mean all things to all people. Indeed, it was equally associated with such contrasting positions on the political spectrum that one might be tempted to see it merely as a piece of rhetoric devoid of substantive content, concealing the "real" economic and political issues at stake during the period. But this would be a serious interpretative error insofar as it leads us to lose sight of one of the main characteristics of the cultural context in which perestroika first emerged. Never, since the birth of the USSR, had the topic of morality occupied such an important place in Soviet public life as it did during the Mikhail Gorbachev era, including in official party documents.[3]

We must therefore take seriously the moral discourse of the time, despite its sometimes nebulous character, if we are to understand the concerns and aspirations to which Soviet intellectuals hoped to respond in the 1980s. This is equally true of the Soviet liberal intelligentsia, whose rejection of Marxism-Leninism did not imply a break with all the ideas and beliefs commonly accepted in the USSR. Like their conservative and nationalist counterparts, liberal intellectuals active in the 1980s could not ignore the perception of a moral decline of Soviet society and the concomitant desire to clean it up.

By studying the moral dimensions of perestroika, this book seeks to address the broader intellectual transformation that accompanied the emergence of liberal ideas in the Soviet public sphere. In particular, I suggest that this transformation saw the culmination of what I define as political Romanticism. "Romanticism" here should not be confused with its more common (and politically trivial) usage, which normally describes an idealistic, superficial, and passive attitude.[4] At the same time, I wish to avoid simply repeating the commonplace assumptions of post-Soviet Russian elites who denigrate the "Romanticism" of perestroika in order to better emphasize the "pragmatism" and "professionalism" supposedly required for "serious" policy making and governance.[5]

Political Romanticism is understood here not as an attitude but rather as an ideological tradition—as a relatively coherent set of postulates, concepts, and ideals whose operation we can observe in the contemporary discourse. As the philosopher Michael Löwy and the sociologist Robert Sayre suggest, Romanticism is a current of thought that first developed in the nineteenth century, characterized by a revolt against the corrupting effects of modernity—the spirit of instrumental calculation, developed societies' disenchantment from religion, the quantification of existence, the dissolution of social bonds, bureaucratic domination—in the name of a lost or idealized past.[6] This melancholic revolt is based on two main positive values. The first is the expression of the richness of the individual personality. In this respect, it must be emphasized that Romanticism is a modern trend resulting from the dissolution of traditional communities and the elevation of the individual. The second is the integration of the individual into a social and universal totality. Against the fragmentation of modern life, Romantics seek to recover the harmony that is alleged to have once characterized relations between individuals and between humanity and nature. From this stems the typically Romantic critique of modern political systems as mechanical, artificial, lifeless, soulless.

If Romanticism was born of a reaction to the deleterious effects of the rationalist progressivism of the Enlightenment, it is not, however, wholly reducible to a conservative posture. Various political and intellectual currents throughout history have attempted to reconcile the aspirations of Romanticism with the modernism of the Enlightenment, and perhaps none more so than Marxism. Indeed, as the philosopher Charles Taylor observes, Marxism can be considered the most influential of these attempts at synthesis, since it combines the notion of rational scientific progress with the ideal of a humanity finally reconciled with itself and with nature, delivered from the alienation proper to capitalist modernity.[7] This duality is also at the heart of the moral outlook dictated by the official doctrine of the Soviet Union, Marxism-Leninism. But before we can understand the moral criticisms elaborated by Soviet liberals and their nationalist rivals, we must first understand the ideology that constituted their principal target.

The Moral Doctrine of Marxism-Leninism

As a materialist ideology, Marxism-Leninism might on the surface appear devoid of any moral considerations. A common prejudice, notably among Soviet liberal intellectuals, is that Marxism-Leninism offers a strictly instrumental conception of morality limited to the imperative to serve the state and the cause of the revolution, thus denying the notion of personal morality.[8] Viewed in this way, Soviet ideology is a sort of spiritual desert in which morality, if it survives at all, is present only in a few oases of subversive thought.

This view must be qualified in light of the many efforts over the decades to integrate personal morality into the doctrinal framework of Marxism-Leninism. This phenomenon was far from marginal: in the late 1960s, an American philosopher calculated that the volume of scientific literature devoted to morality produced in the USSR far exceeded the output of Western scholars and thinkers on the same subject.[9] In the same decade, the development of the personality became one of the key areas of research among Soviet social scientists, and it was elevated as the most important criterion in defining model behavior in Soviet mass printed biographies of heroic "revolutionaries."[10] In fact, the "ideologically correct" conception of morality in the post-Stalinist USSR was much more complex than the allegedly instrumental posture often caricatured by anti-Soviet writers. It is crucial that we attend to such nuance if we wish to understand how Soviet ideology was able to nourish a set of ideas that the regime's greatest critics were ultimately able to wield against it.

Two sources are especially useful when it comes to defining the official conception of morality at the dawn of perestroika: the last edition of the *Great Soviet Encyclopedia*, whose many volumes appeared between 1969 and

1978, and the 1983 edition (also the last) of the *Manual of Scientific Communism*, published by Politizdat.[11] The *Encyclopedia* sets out the official definition of morality, while the *Manual* explains its role in what was then called "developed socialist society."

Morality, according to the *Encyclopedia*, is "one of the means of normative regulation of the behavior of human society."[12] Contrary to law and customs—which the *Encyclopedia* identifies as the other means of normative regulation—morality is not based on institutions or habit but is exercised through the conscious internalization of norms by which man orients his behavior. Morality, in short, comes to man *from the outside in*. This reflects the essentially technocratic character of Marxist-Leninist doctrine, according to which morality is conceived first and foremost as a fabrication of the party-state. In accordance with the theses of historical materialism, morality is above all shaped by "objective factors"—that is, by the transformation of the relations of production that accompanies the construction of communism.

These objective factors, however, are not considered sufficient in and of themselves. Despite the "favorable conditions" created by socialism for "the full satisfaction of man's material and moral needs," official Soviet doctrine recognizes the necessity of "constantly raising the ideological-moral and cultural level of the people" in order to avoid "a relapse into philistine and petty-bourgeois psychology."[13] This is where the educational mission of the party comes in. Far from being limited to a formal school setting, this pedagogical task seeks to inculcate in all citizens "the Marxist-Leninist worldview," as well as the "fundamental principles and norms of Communist morality," as stated in the *Moral Codex of the Builder of Communism* attached to the party program.[14] Morality, in sum, refers to the cognitive faculty, often defined as *soznatel'nost'* or *soznanie* (consciousness), through which certain prescribed norms are internalized. These norms can then be broken down into different variants, such as socialist consciousness, social consciousness, and political consciousness. This cognitive faculty, moreover, can be quantified: scientific communism measures the morality of a society according to its "level of consciousness," the increase or decline of which can subsequently be observed and tallied.

The *Manual of Scientific Communism* insists on the dynamic character of the internalization of morality: "The elaboration of Communist morals is not a unilateral process in which man would be only the passive object of the transformation of the relations of production and education. This moral progress also depends on one's personality, on its aspiration to perfection."[15] This means that the teaching provided by the party must be put into *practice*: "Knowledge [alone] is not enough to form a worldview. It must become man's deep and inner convictions and be expressed in his practical and active relationship with his environment."[16]

The concept of "activity" (*aktivnost'*) commonly refers to the spirit of initiative that Soviets must show if they are to live out the principles of communist morality. To emphasize its importance, the *Manual* quotes the June 1983 Central Committee plenum, which adopted a resolution stating that "the perfection of socialism depends on the level of consciousness [*soznatel'nost'*] and activity [*aktivnost'*]."[17] This emphasis on the practical expression of deep-seated convictions is accompanied by a typically Romantic call for self-realization: "Communism is the regime in which the abilities and talents, the best moral qualities of the free man are most fully developed."[18] The party's objective is to guarantee the "complete development of the personality" so that "man harmoniously combines in himself richness of spirit, moral purity, and physical perfection."[19]

This Romantic aspiration is repeated in numerous publications intended for a wide audience. This is the case, for example, with Personality, Morality, and Education, the book series inaugurated by Politizdat in 1979. With its more than thirty titles, the explicit mission of the series was to guide the development of a "socialist personality," which is to say, a "rich personality, endowed with a generous and creative soul, that takes an active part in life and assumes responsibility for its actions."[20] Marxism-Leninism, in short, advocates both the internalization of prescribed norms and the realization of a set of deep convictions. In principle, these moral tasks are not in tension: control and the expression of one's convictions are two facets of the same vision, whereby morality is the cognitive faculty to internalize and realize the norms enacted and inculcated by the party-state. This complex definition, as formulated in official documents in the early 1980s, reflects the various aspirations at the heart of the project of Soviet modernity.

The Promises of Soviet Modernity

The philosopher Claude Lefort wrote that the logic of Soviet totalitarian power is based on two apparently contradictory principles: on one hand, society is conceived as an organism, "a great body whose organs and members function as a single unit"; on the other, it is conceived as an artifice, the result of the conscious work of the party-state following the directives of a scientific doctrine.[21] The duality observed by Lefort is linked to the Soviet regime's particular relationship with modernity, which presents communism as a technocratic utopia in which the rationalist ideals of the Enlightenment are radicalized, but it also has as its goal the advent of a harmonious community freed from the social division and alienation brought about by capitalist modernity. This duality is manifested in the official Soviet policy toward morality, which deploys the modern tools of control, education, quantification, and rationalization in order to promote the typically Romantic ideal of self-realization within an organic community. Throughout the history of the Soviet regime, however, the means employed by the Soviet state to fulfill its moral promises have varied greatly, as the emphasis shifted from discipline and external control to mobilization and self-expression.

The project of Soviet modernity was largely derived from the culture of the Russian intelligentsia, the emergence of which, in the middle of the nineteenth century, was marked by the failure of the Decembrists' putsch, an outcome that dealt a severe blow to the rationalist concepts inherited from the French Revolution.[22] By choice and by necessity—after 1830, in an attempt to counter the spread of subversive ideas, the tsarist government placed restrictions on Russian students hoping to study in France—the young Russian intelligentsia turned to Germany and greedily absorbed the ideas of Romantic thinkers like Friedrich von Schiller, Friedrich Schelling, Friedrich Schlegel, and Johann Gottfried von Herder, whose work embraced a cult of the hero, the influence of which exerted a substantial pull on young Russian intellectuals.

This profession of faith was followed by Westernists such as Vissarion Belinsky, who blamed the tsarist autocracy for suppressing the development of individual personality, but also by Belinsky's Slavophile opponents, who argued that this was the result of the artificial imposition of a Western way of life. In the ensuing debate, both camps shared the ideal of personality realization (*lichnost'*), which implies a typically Romantic form of "qualitative individualism" that defines the individual by his expressive abilities rather than by his intrinsic attributes.[23] These Romantic aspirations were popularized from the 1860s on by the agrarian socialist movement of the "populists" (*Narodniki*)[24] and by writers such as Lev Tolstoi, who denounced the traits associated with bourgeois "philistinism"—namely, a calculating mindset, opportunism, conformism, and a love of the mundane.

Among the left-wing intelligentsia, there was a relative weakening of Romantic aspirations with the rise of scientism and positivism at the end of the nineteenth century. The Bolsheviks, in particular, conceived of communist society as a machine, or, more precisely, as a giant factory. Thus, they followed the dominant tendency within Marxism at the turn of the nineteenth and into the early twentieth centuries, which treated the rational organization of society as a science. The Austrian Social Democrat Karl Kautsky, one of the leading figures of scientific socialism, wrote that "in the socialist society, which is after all just a single giant industrial enterprise, production and planning must be exactly and in a planned way organized, as they are organized in a modern large industrial enterprise."[25] Obviously, this is far from the Romantic ideal of an organic community based on human values alienated by modernity—a point emphasized by Lenin in a sharply worded pamphlet from 1897, in which he attacked the "economic romanticism" of the *Narodniki* and their idea of introducing modern technology while preserving the traditional organic community.[26]

After the October Revolution, the construction of the Soviet state took on a more technocratic and Promethean character: the regime sought above all to construct a vast modernizing utopia that, utilizing the tools of science and industrial progress, would lead to nothing less than the creation of a new society and a new man.[27] Certainly, this enterprise took on a moral valence, particularly with its criticism of bourgeois vices and, conversely, its promotion of the ascetic lifestyle adopted by professional Bolshevik revolutionaries. But as far as Soviet society itself was concerned, the Bolsheviks were faithful to the precepts of scientific socialism: they viewed morality as a matter of the superstructure and thus something determined by the relations of production. The idea of a universal morality that would have a value in and of itself was denounced as a bourgeois invention hiding the reality of class domination. By contrast, in 1920, Lenin defined communist morality in a strictly instrumental fashion, as precisely that which serves the cause of communism.[28] The result was a sort of tautology whereby the construction of communism would in turn create the material conditions that would then pave the way for the moral perfection of Soviet man. Moral deviance was subsequently attributed to environmental factors, such as class membership and the "vestiges" (*perezhitki*) of capitalism.

But as the historian David Hoffmann has shown, Soviet leaders' doctrinaire refusal to admit the existence of an autonomous morality independent of social determinants did not prevent them from taking a close interest in society's moral development, as was the case with most Western states during the interwar period.[29] In the 1920s and 1930s, the party conducted a series of large-scale campaigns aimed at inculcating in Soviet citizens the values of hygiene, politeness, discipline at work, and good manners, all of which were considered necessary for the functioning of a modern society. In the USSR, this task was considered all the more urgent with the influx of large numbers of people from the countryside to the cities as a result of forced industrialization, which had the effect of subjecting urban culture to the pressure of rural traditions deemed archaic by the Soviet regime.

The Soviet "civilizing" program differed from those of the capitalist countries in its emphasis on collectivism: through their devotion to this shared imperative, Soviet citizens were to free themselves from individual selfishness and learn to behave in an upright manner. Another peculiarity of the Soviet program was apparent in its careful avoidance of "morality" or other related terms—and its emphasis on "civility" (*kul'turnost'*).[30] To be sure, the situation was somewhat different among members of the party, who claimed for themselves the status of a moral elite; indeed, the party's membership cards bore an evocative phrase of Lenin's explaining that "the Party is the spirit, honour and personal conscience [*sovest'*] of our time."

In keeping with its civilizing mission, the party created control commissions in 1920 in order to fight against violations of proletarian morality among its members, yet it refused to produce a formal code of conduct, despite the repeated requests of some Bolsheviks. The director of the Central Control Commission, Yemelyan Yaroslavsky, preferred instead to evoke "our unwritten Communist morality."[31] The refusal to formalize such a code was perhaps rooted in the party leadership's desire to preserve its monopoly on the legitimate interpretation of communist morality and thus to avoid exposing the regime to criticism of its violations of the party's professed principles.

The historian Jochen Hellbeck has shown that the early 1930s saw "a momentous shift towards a Romantic sensibility" in the USSR, according to which the expression of personal consciousness was conceived as a motor for sociopolitical development, rather than merely an object to be shaped.[32] In other words, the technocratic impulse to inculcate communist morality *from the outside in* was accompanied during this period by an increasingly strong imperative to realize morality *from the inside out*. In a Soviet society now said to be "developed," environmental factors could no longer be considered the only influences on morality—to these were added personal initiative.

Official propaganda from this time sings the exploits of heroic individuals, who stand out from the mass by their initiative and strength of will. The Stakhanovist movement, which celebrated workers who went far beyond the required production quotas, is a case in point. The embrace of a Romantic sensibility was partly the result of a selective return to the thinking of the Russian intelligentsia of the nineteenth century, evidenced in the admiration of many Soviet intellectuals for Belinsky and, above all, the official reverence for the classics of Russian literature, as imposed by the Stalinist educational system. At the very moment when the last representatives of the old intelligentsia were decimated by the Stalinist purges of the late 1930s, many of their ideals were taken up by the regime and inculcated in the masses on an unprecedented scale, thus laying the cultural foundations for the generation of *shestidesiatniki* (Sixties), who grew up under Stalin, became politicized in the era of de-Stalinization, and later dominated the political life of perestroika, turning the very ideals championed by the Stalinist educational system against the last vestiges of Stalinism.

It was also under Stalin that the doctrinal framework of Marxism-Leninism was first established, including the notion that communist morality was to be realized by way of the internalization of party norms on the part of the individual, as was emphasized in 1954 in the second edition of the *Great Soviet Encyclopedia*.[33] "Stalinist neo-Romanticism," however, continued to be marked by several essential aspects of the Bolshevik technocratic project, starting with an unshakable faith in science and progress. Perhaps most importantly, the interpretation and dissemination of morality remained the exclusive prerogative of the party.

The novelty of the Nikita Khrushchev era, as far as morality as an object of politics was concerned, had less to do with a change of perspective than with the formalization of moral norms with a view to the universalization of self-realization through internalization. In February 1956, Khrushchev officially launched the policy of de-Stalinization with his infamous "Secret Speech" at the Twentieth Congress of the Communist Party of the Soviet Union. In the speech, the new general secretary mocked Stalin's propensity to see enemies in all who did not think like him, and he praised Lenin's ability to recognize the faults of honest communists as mistakes that could be corrected without resorting to repression. The following May, Khrushchev declared his belief that every individual, "including both political opponents and criminals," could be reeducated.[34]

This was the beginning of a new political strategy based on a significant reduction in repression—including a retroactive amnesty for thousands of prisoners of the gulag—but also on a wide extension of moral control. The new party program adopted in 1961 proclaimed with great pomp the moral mission of the party-state in the final phase of the construction of communism, the deadline for which was set for 1980. By that point—the dawn of the end of history, according to the party program—the exercise of coercion would be replaced by the regulating power of morality: "In the course of transition to communism, the moral principles of society become increasingly important; the sphere of action of the moral factor expands and the importance of the administrative control of human relation diminishes accordingly."[35]

In order to guide society along this path, the new party program included a document without precedent in the history of the USSR: the *Moral Codex of the Builder of Communism*, a sort of abbreviated catechism stipulating the twelve virtues expected of all Soviet citizens. The contents of this document were by no means revelatory. It reiterated the Leninist idea that morality must above all serve the cause of communism. Article 1, for example, calls for "devotion to the communist cause and love of the socialist fatherland." Subsequent articles concern typically Soviet values, such as collectivism (article 5), or traditional values already conveyed in the campaigns for discipline and civility, such as "conscientious work for the good of society" (article 2), "mutual respect" (article 6), "honesty" (article 8), and "respect for the family" (article 9).[36] However, the novelty of the *Moral Codex* was the very fact of its formalization, which allowed it to be used by the greatest possible number of people. Unlike the "unwritten code of communist morality" in force under Stalin, when the party's duly authorized bodies had an exclusive monopoly on its legitimate interpretation, the *Moral Codex* of 1961 was conceived as a way for Soviet society to exert moral control over itself.

To this end, the party sought to mobilize public opinion, as expressed in party newspapers and journals, the "trade unions" (*profsoiuzy*), the Komsomol (the communist youth organization), and the "creative unions" (*tvorcheskie soiuzy*) and their affiliated organizations. The party also mobilized the social sciences. Philosophers were given the task of developing and defending the *Moral Codex*, while sociologists, psychologists, and teachers were entrusted with perfecting the methods of moral correction. Even more ambitiously, the party-state sought to mobilize the entire population in the daily practice of communist morality. The sociologist Oleg Kharkhordin has shown that in the post-Stalin era, peer supervision was one of the state's primary methods of social control, used to encourage Soviet citizens to improve themselves at every stage of their lives.[37] Morality, which was supposed to gradually replace state coercion, thus acquired a much broader field of application than the narrower rules of conduct adopted by party members or the civility expected of a formerly rural population whose mores were considered fundamentally archaic. These were universal norms that all Soviet citizens were expected to practice in all aspects of their lives.

Khrushchev's ouster in 1964 put a stop to this ambitious program of moral rectification. The *Moral Codex* was retained, but its role was henceforth reduced in favor of the motto "Trust in cadres," which aimed to shield the party-state's bureaucratic elite from criticism. Many studies of this period have shown that the trivialization of ideological discourse on the part of Soviet citizens from the late 1960s onward led to disillusionment and withdrawal into the private sphere, barely concealed by a thin veneer of conformity to socialist principles. While this is certainly true of the generation that reached adulthood in the 1970s, it would be difficult to conclude that the moral promises of Soviet modernity, whether modernizing or Romantic, had been abandoned entirely. On the contrary, corruption and cynicism, which achieved endemic levels in the Leonid Brezhnev era, were experienced by many Soviet citizens as a painful betrayal of the fundamental principles of communist society. More than anything else, the sense of moral decline that took hold during this period was the impetus for the various attempts at moral rectification undertaken in the 1980s, which ultimately culminated in perestroika.

Perestroika and Moralization Campaigns

The first measures to address this sense of moral decline were introduced by Yuri Andropov, Brezhnev's successor as general secretary and Gorbachev's mentor. Andropov, who took office in 1982, was a puritanical communist largely devoid of Romantic sensibilities, but he was deeply disgusted by official corruption, the extent of which he was well aware as the former head of the KGB. Once installed as party leader, he duly set out to purge the bureaucracy of its corrupt elements and to restore productivity at the workplace, where slowdowns had been attributed to alcoholism and absenteeism. To do this, Andropov focused less on mobilizing society, as Khrushchev had done, than on disciplining it—for example, by launching police raids against restaurants, public baths, and cinemas to flush out those who had absconded from their official places of work.

After Andropov's early death and the even shorter tenure of his successor as general secretary, Konstantin Chernenko, the fight against moral corruption was taken up with considerable zeal by Mikhail Gorbachev and his first lieutenant at the time, Egor Ligachev, another former Andropov protégé. The campaigns for moral reform introduced during the first two years of perestroika (1985–86) were shaped by official Soviet doctrine, which made moral renewal dependent on the internalization of the norms of conduct laid down by the party.

The most famous of the measures taken by the Gorbachev-Ligachev tandem was the prohibition campaign launched in May 1985, which once again aimed to improve Soviet citizens' on-the-job productivity. The various restrictions—raising the legal drinking age to twenty-one and drastically reducing alcohol production, among others—were accompanied by a vast mobilization campaign that sought to involve the population in this revival of the norms of communist morality. That year, the party also celebrated the fiftieth anniversary of the Stakhanovist movement, one of the most striking illustrations of Stalinist neo-Romanticism, and one that, thanks to its legacy of "socialist emulation" and "moral stimuli,"[38] made for a potent symbol of moral rectification under Gorbachev.

The logic of self-realization through the internalization of party norms can also be seen in another major measure introduced in 1985: glasnost, which aimed at "transparency" in the public sphere. Lifting the leaden blanket of censorship, the party now invited the media to publicly denounce any deviations from socialist norms. Glasnost, it has often been pointed out, did not amount to genuine freedom of expression. The relaxation of censorship remained at best partial, and its application ultimately depended on the will of the party leadership. But from the perspective of Gorbachev and his collaborators, glasnost was in fact *much more* than freedom of expression, which they tended to denigrate as nothing more than an abstract and formal individual right: it was, rather, through the denunciation of deviance and the concomitant strengthening of communist morality, a powerful means of social transformation. Like Khrushchev before him, and unlike Andropov, Gorbachev sought to mobilize public opinion to exercise moral control over society. In a famous programmatic statement of perestroika—contained within his 1987 book of the same name—Gorbachev declared:

> People might be said to have developed a taste for glasnost. And not only because of their natural desire to know what is taking place, and who is working [and] how. People are becoming increasingly convinced that glasnost is an effective form of public control over the activities of all government bodies, without exception, and a powerful lever in correcting shortcomings. As a result, the moral potential of our society has been set in motion. . . . Naturally, it is not enough to know and tell the truth. Acting on the knowledge of the truth and of understanding it is the main thing.[39]

On the basis of the "knowledge and understanding" brought about by glasnost, Gorbachev instituted a vigorous suite of repressive measures against those deemed corrupt, starting with any "speculators" who were getting rich on the black market and bureaucrats accused of abusing their power. It was a question, Gorbachev said, of "liquidating the zones closed to criticism and the oases of hypocrisy and arbitrariness."[40] And while he claimed that Soviet society was generally healthy, it was above all Soviet youth who had suffered the most deleterious effects of this backward slide in morality. Against the "speculators," he therefore launched a campaign against illegal income in May 1986. Against the bureaucrats, he launched the same year a vast purge, cloaked with the term "cadre policy," the most important since the Stalinist period (with the important difference that this purge did not imply bloodshed).

True to the official Marxist-Leninist perspective, which viewed morality primarily as an object of control and activation, the moral sanitation campaigns undertaken at the beginning of perestroika aimed to mobilize the population in the denunciation of moral decay. Unsurprisingly, party leaders claimed that these lapses could only be corrected by way of a strengthening of party control. And yet this prognosis was not confined to the *nomenklatura*; indeed, it was also embraced by social scientists. Andrei Zdravomyslov, for example, a well-known researcher and one of the founders of Soviet sociology, explained in 1988 that "negative phenomena" within Soviet society—among which he counted insensitivity, formalism, bureaucratism, irresponsibility at work, alcoholism, crime, and corruption—were the result of a weakening of "the moral norms regulating individual behavior."[41] While "the most conscious people in society" had genuinely adopted these norms "in their daily behavior," a hypocritical minority had done so on a "strictly external" basis, as cover for their actual pursuit of "personal and immediate material interests."[42]

Zdravomyslov rejected as simplistic the idea, previously widespread, that this negative behavior was the result of "vestiges of the bourgeois past" and would therefore disappear with the advent of a genuinely socialist society. On the contrary, he argued, the resulting increase in the standard of living had in fact contributed to the diffusion of a "petty-bourgeois" mentality—namely, that of the "small proprietor," with his "love of material goods" and his veneration of "consumerism."[43] This attitude, Zdravomyslov argued, can be traced to the love of money, which he associated with the black market, and the enjoyment of power, which he claimed was characteristic of bureaucrats. This corrupt minority, in turn, gives rise to skepticism and cynicism in the minds of young people, who lose faith in the regulating principles and ideas of socialism and fall into alcoholism, prostitution, and drugs. Perestroika, then, is the moral renewal of socialism through the public denunciation—via glasnost—of corrupt pockets within Soviet society and their subsequent delivery before the disciplinary mechanisms of the party.

This view was widely shared throughout Soviet society, as illustrated by the fate of the Berezka stores during this period. Established in the late 1950s to finance the state's industrialization efforts, these stores offered highly sought-after products—notably Western ones—in exchange for foreign currency. Increasingly popular in the following decades among a large segment of the Soviet population—party elites as well as the growing middle class—owing to the rising standard of living and the constant demand for consumer goods, the stores nonetheless remained a sort of open secret. The Soviet media was prohibited from reporting on the stores' existence until glasnost, as they contradicted the egalitarian principles professed by the regime. When censorship was finally lifted, they were immediately condemned by the public, which saw them as a means to satisfy the selfish interests of a privileged minority. Popular pressure soon led the government to close the chain in 1988, regardless of the large profits it was bringing into state coffers.[44]

The public outcry against Berezka illustrates the prevalence of a moral discourse in Soviet society during perestroika and helps to qualify the thesis that support for reform was primarily motivated by a desire to emulate the consumerist lifestyles of the capitalist countries. If the wealth of the West exerted some pull on the Soviet citizenry, the egoism and social fragmentation said to result from individual consumerism still aroused a revulsion inspired by the Romantic ideals of Soviet modernity. These feelings were shared by communist reformers like Gorbachev and also, in an even more virulent form, by nationalist intellectuals who saw the influence of the West as one of the main sources of moral corruption.

Nationalist Criticism

While the party sought to inculcate communist morality, many intellectuals put forward what they considered a more genuine conception of morality, one rooted in personal conscience (*sovest'*) and guaranteed by the preservation of traditional values. Unlike communist morality, this perspective did not rely on the internalization of social norms; rather, morality was said to spring from the depths of the soul as an intrinsic attribute of the human spirit.

Moral fault, according to these thinkers, resulted not from a lack of control or education but from the failure of individuals to follow their conscience. This was often presented as a choice between truth and falsehood. Simply put, to follow one's conscience was to speak the truth of one's soul. For this reason, and unlike consciousness, conscience is not quantifiable: one cannot "raise the level" of it; one can only express (or not), at each given moment, the truth of one's conscience. Since the 1950s, this conception of morality was defended by Soviet intellectuals revolted by the disastrous consequences of forced communist modernization and the resulting moral degradation. These criticisms often took on a nationalistic tone marked by a nostalgia for the way of life and the traditional values of the Russian peasantry, sacrificed by Stalin on the altar of industrialization. This nostalgia for the rural world earned these writers and essayists the nickname of "village writers."[45]

Before perestroika, the most famous call for the awakening of personal conscience was Aleksandr Solzhenitsyn's manifesto "Live Not by Lies" (*Zhit' ne po lzhi*), published in samizdat the day after his arrest by the KGB in 1974.[46] In it, Solzhenitsyn denounces those of his fellow citizens who, condemning the Soviet regime in private, nonetheless willingly enter into compromises with it in order to preserve what little comfort and security they might enjoy, on the pretext that morality is a relative concept, determined solely by one's political environment and social conditions. For Solzhenitsyn, nothing could be further from the truth. Everyone, he argues, possesses the strength to resist evil: "But we can! We lie to ourselves to preserve our peace of mind. It is not they who should be blamed but ourselves."[47]

As a solution to these moral failures, Solzhenitsyn called for the preservation of "spiritual independence," which above all called for the refusal to participate in the regime's "lies." To this end, he urged his fellow citizens to avoid uttering any sentence that distorted the truth, even if that meant excluding themselves from Soviet society: "Though lies may conceal everything, though lies may control everything, we should be obstinate about this one small point: let them be in control but without any help from any of us."[48] According to Solzhenitsyn, all men possess the natural ability to distinguish lies from truth. It was therefore up to each individual to pick a side.

Unlike Solzhenitsyn, however, a majority of nationalist intellectuals did not advance a notion of personal conscience based on the radical subversion of the communist system. Indeed, those moral criticisms that appeared in the state-sanctioned press were rather conservative, with the so-called village writers expressing a resigned nostalgia for the lost values of the peasantry and calling for the preservation of this heritage. Insofar as they did not question the established order, these nationalist intellectuals were even encouraged by the party to intervene in the public life of perestroika. Their influence was particularly important in 1985 and 1986, before the liberal intelligentsia acquired the dominant position it would maintain until the early 1990s. And yet, for all their similarities, these writers did not form a homogeneous bloc, and their visions of perestroika sometimes sharply diverged.

Conservative Nationalists and Liberal Nationalists

From the mid-1960s on, the village writers were divided into two main camps, what political scientist Yitzhak Brudny has described as the "conservative nationalists" and the "liberal nationalists."[49]

The former were more critical of modernity. They denounced not only the brutality of collectivization but also the vagaries of urban life, the emancipation of women, and the influence of liberal intellectuals, Jews, and Freemasons, whom they accused of being responsible for the abandonment of traditional peasant values. In the 1970s, conservative nationalist writers were actively supported by the party, which guaranteed their works very large print runs and awarded them prestigious prizes. Although their worldview did not conform to the Marxist-Leninist doctrine, it had the advantage of reinforcing the patriotic legitimacy the party was trying to secure for itself as a bulwark against the corrupting influence of a decadent West.[50] Still enjoying a wide influence at the beginning of perestroika, writers Viktor Astafyev, Aleksandr Astrakhantsev, Vasily Belov, Yuri Bondarev, Petr Proskurin, Valentin Rasputin, and Vladimir Soloukhin spent the second half of the 1980s absorbed in their favorite themes: the moral corruption of Soviet society and the protection of the environment against the excesses of technology.

Liberal nationalists, for their part, deplored the degradation of nature and the erosion of traditional values without being fundamentally hostile to modernity and the West. Some of them were village writers, like Fedor Abramov, Boris Mozhaev, and Sergei Zalygin, or journalists who shared these writers' concern for the fate of the countryside, like Vasily Seliunin and Yuri Chernichenko. The most famous of the liberal nationalists was the academic and specialist in medieval Russian literature Dmitri Likhachev. In the era of perestroika, Likhachev established himself as one of the most respected moral figures in Soviet society, and he even enjoyed the explicit support of Gorbachev. He believed that Russia must preserve its culture in order to better participate in European affairs. For all that, however, he opposed the resolutely universalist, modernizing perspective of the liberal intellectuals (to which we will return in later chapters), claiming to detect in it a note of contempt toward the Russian people.[51]

In Likhachev's writings, morality is privileged as the main vehicle for the organic harmony within humanity and with nature; it is for Likhachev the foundation of culture, which he conceived in the broadest possible sense as the spiritual and aesthetic richness of a people. Here, he was of course referring to a "great culture" in the classical European sense, as opposed to the mass culture of superficial consumerism, which he classified as an "anti-culture."[52] Contrary to the materialist moral doctrine of Marxism-Leninism, however, which viewed morality above all as a fabrication of the party-state reflecting the relations of production, Likhachev located morality "in human nature. Its norms are fixed and eternal."[53] Arguing that morality and culture combine to form a sort of spiritual universe, he employed the concept of the "homosphere" to describe the universal totality in which man's creative spirituality is naturally registered.[54] Glasnost and the democratization advocated by Gorbachev are in his eyes the necessary preconditions for the realization of this typically Romantic ideal. And yet democracy, for Likhachev, is not simply an institutional arrangement or a formal procedure—rather, it is "the norm of life, the natural and permanent state of society, its breath."[55]

In order to secure this ideal democracy, Likhachev advocated above all for the awakening of personal conscience. This is the main argument of a widely discussed article published in 1987 under the title "The Pangs of Conscience."[56] In it, Likhachev describes conscience, "which comes from the depths of the soul," as the main focus of moral "purification," a force that can help Soviet citizens overcome their "moral color blindness."[57] The "pangs of conscience," he says, "teach us and help us not to violate moral norms, [and] to maintain our dignity, the dignity of a human being who lives morally."[58]

Echoing the sentiments contained within Solzhenitsyn's manifesto, but without ever quoting him, Likhachev also denounced the omnipresence of lies in Soviet society and called on his fellow citizens to act morally, regardless of the circumstances: "What is important for any human being? How should one live his life? First and foremost, never act in a way that would harm one's dignity. One can do many things in life, but he can bring the greatest good by not breaking with his conscience, even in the slightest way."[59] And while Likhachev recognized that following one's conscience can have disastrous consequences for the individual living in a morally degraded society, he nevertheless maintained that "one must know how to sacrifice oneself."[60] In short, the moral program consists of purifying society by awakening the conscience of each citizen,. a program summed up by a popular slogan from the period, "Start with yourself!" (*Nachni s sebia!*)[61]

Nationalist Intellectuals and Perestroika

The moral discourse of most nationalist intellectuals, with its emphasis on conscience, tended to attribute responsibility for the "negative phenomena" of Soviet society to the subjective moral faults of individuals, without questioning the larger social and political system in which these individuals were embedded. These criticisms struck party reformers as constructive to the extent that they shook the conservative apparatchiks who resisted the reforms of perestroika.

In 1985 and 1986, the mobilization of several nationalist intellectuals for the defense of the environment and Russia's architectural heritage received strong support from the government. The most important of these efforts, which brought together conservative and liberal nationalists, was launched in 1985 in the nationalist journal *Nash sovremennik* against a project to divert several Siberian rivers for the irrigation of agricultural areas in central Asia. Although the project had initially been set in motion by a minor ministry, the order to cancel it, given in August 1986, came from the highest levels of the party—a clear signal of the leadership's support for the nationalist writers. This victory was followed by the appointment of writer Sergei Zalygin as director of the journal *Novyi Mir* and the award of a prestigious prize to writer Valentin Rasputin.

This development dovetailed with another pet concern of the nationalist intellectuals: the defense and promotion of culture. To this end, nationalist intellectuals agitated for more direct state support for cultural production. Under the direct patronage of Gorbachev and his wife, the Soviet Cultural Foundation was duly created in November 1987, with Dmitri Likhachev appointed as its head. And in keeping with Likhachev's concern for morality, the foundation did not limit its efforts to the mere protection of cultural heritage but also concerned itself with the country's moral recovery.

As Likhachev explained in July 1987, "It seems to us that the objective of the foundation is to fight for the purification of morality and for the heightening of spirituality in the deeds and thoughts of the people, in their interests. It is to promote the values of man's inner self, to which too little attention has been devoted lately, that is, the concepts of good, justice, honesty, honor, active love for nature and pride for the fatherland. Spirituality must be central in the work of the foundation, in its ideas and programs."[62]

In Likhachev's view, the Soviet Cultural Foundation would take up the torch of the party's ongoing effort to offer moral instruction to the Soviet populace. But rather than seeking to inculcate moral norms derived from political doctrine, Likhachev envisioned a moral education capable of awakening the eternal, natural norms within each person, without having to resort to a reinforcement of state control.

This last point was in direct opposition to that of many conservative nationalists, led by Bondarev and Rasputin, for whom moral rectification required exactly that—an increased vigilance against deviant behavior. For these intellectuals, it was not enough to promote traditional values; the state also had to defend them against corrupting foreign influences. Invoking a striking image from the Soviet past, Bondarev compared the situation of the USSR in 1987, facing an ascendant West, to that of the Red Army in July 1941, when the country seemed to be on the verge of collapse in the face of Nazi barbarism, and he asserted that the country could only be saved by fighting a "cultural Stalingrad."[63]

The Soviet Union's relationship to the Western capitalist countries was indeed a crucial point of divergence between conservative and liberal nationalists during this period, and from the end of 1986, the two camps would follow very different political paths. Conservative nationalists would ultimately move closer to the radical Slavophiles[64] and adopt an increasingly critical stance toward perestroika, while liberal nationalists would stop associating with *Nash sovremennik* and attending meetings of the Union of Writers of Russia, dominated as it was by conservative nationalists, and would instead form closer ties with the liberal intelligentsia. This last group would henceforth emerge as the most influential branch of the intelligentsia in the late Soviet era.

As we will see in the following chapter, these liberal intellectuals proposed their own interpretation of the causes of moral decline, and they had their own remedies too, based on a new synthesis of the modernist and Romantic ideals contained within Soviet modernity.

Chapter 2

Liberal Moralism in the USSR

> Another aspect . . . is the moral degradation of society. . . . Corrupting lies, dissimulation and hypocrisy must leave our lives forever. Only the man internally free can show the initiative that society demands.
>
> —Andrei Sakharov, "Neizbezhnost' perestroiki"

The liberal intelligentsia's rise to public prominence in the era of perestroika was made possible by the support of influential figures within Gorbachev's immediate entourage.[1] From 1986 onward, these government reformers appointed liberals to head important media outlets, and they repeatedly intervened against the decisions of the censor, thereby allowing the publication of essays by contemporary thinkers as well as literary works that had long been banned by the regime. From 1987 onward, thanks to the flowering of this liberal press, these works became the subject of a tremendous craze among the Soviet public. From 1985 to 1989, for example, the circulation of the weekly *Ogonek* climbed from 1,500,000 to 3,350,000; that of the monthly *Znamia* from 1,750,000 to 1,980,000; and that of the monthly *Novyi Mir* from 425,000 to 1,573,000.[2] And yet even these spectacular increases in circulation were not enough to satisfy the demands of readers, who were ready to line up at newsstands to ensure that they got their hands on the latest issues. Liberal intellectuals quickly established themselves as some of the most popular political thinkers in the country.[3] In the following years, they set the tone for the debates that would come to occupy center stage in Soviet public life—namely, the struggle against the Stalinist legacy, the return to "world civilization" (i.e., an embrace of Western standards), democratization, and the introduction of a market economy, among others.

Morality occupied an important place in the political discourse of these liberal intellectuals. Like many public intellectuals of the time, they were not averse to assuming the role of moralists: they sought to convince their contemporaries to live up to their principles, and they made moral rectification both a condition and an end of political and economic reform. However, they did not advocate the mobilization of communist morality or the return to Russian traditions. Rather, they proclaimed their commitment to "universal values," which they associated with liberal ideas such as parliamentary democracy, human rights, constitutionalism, and the rule of law. To this end, they rejected the Soviet state's official Marxist-Leninist doctrine while maintaining a nominal adherence to socialism. In fact, most Soviet liberals claimed to be socialists until at least 1990.[4] While the sincerity of this commitment is often difficult to assess, given the widespread practice of self-censorship, many of the ideals and arguments invoked by these writers did indeed align with the socialist humanism many of them had advocated during the de-Stalinization of the 1950s and 1960s. These included the modernist belief in the progress of humanity through reason and science, as well as the Romantic ideal of the harmonious realization of the individual and of the organic development of society more broadly. This perspective was not distinctly Soviet: the sociologists Gil Eyal, Ivan Szelenyi, and Eleanor R. Townsley observed that the ideology cultivated by eastern European dissidents at the time aspired to a society that "reconciled the fundamental antinomies of modernity," combining rationality with the renewed promise of enchantment of the world.[5] Furthermore, similar to their eastern European counterparts, Soviet liberals criticized Stalinism using some of the very same terms by which Stalinism had once impugned Western capitalist society, invoking, for instance, the alienation of the individual at the hands of an artificial bureaucratic system or the structural generalization of hypocrisy and cynicism.

The idea of "universal values" was not new, of course—indeed, the universality of moral norms had long ago been recognized within Marxism-Leninism. *The Great Soviet Encyclopedia* itself posits that "socialist and communist morality concentrates in itself the most complete expression of the norms of universal morality."[6] Soviet liberals, however, adopted a perspective that Marxism-Leninism had rejected as an abstract and bourgeois humanism because it implied the existence of certain "universal values" that are common to all humanity, independent of the relations of production in which they are embedded. By virtue of this abstract universalism, the Cold War binary between communism and capitalism lost its importance in the eyes of Soviet liberals; in its place, they proclaimed a worldwide rapprochement around shared values: honesty, sincerity, and social justice, as well as certain forms of social and political organization, such as parliamentary democracy and a market economy. This defense of "universal values" in turn gave rise to a particular sense of moral decline that—in a further sign of the times—also had an important Romantic dimension in its call for the emancipation of society from the artificial yoke of Stalinism and a return to the course of natural progress.

The Melancholy of Natural Progress

Liberal intellectuals were modernists. For them, perestroika was above all an effort to set the USSR on the road to progress by enabling it to catch up with the "civilized world" (i.e., the West). The historian Yuri Afanasyev called for an end to the "demonization of capitalism," even a mobilization of its legacy. The physicist Andrei Sakharov, for his part, envisaged a future "convergence" of socialism and capitalism, with the former subordinated and adapted to the latter, while the historian Leonid Batkin wanted Soviet society to assume its European character.[7] Each of them wanted to pursue the type of modernization that the Soviet model had failed to deliver and whose path seemed to them to be marked out by reason and science. The transition to democracy and the market, in their eyes, would meet the objective requirements of a modern, rational, and efficient society. However, these intellectuals also showed a strong Romantic melancholy at the deviation from what they viewed as society's natural developmental path, which was interrupted by the USSR's adherence to an artificial and soulless social experiment. The recurrent use of natural metaphors is a striking feature of the literary output from this period.

Afanasyev, for example, compares Soviet citizens' loss of historical consciousness to an ecological catastrophe: "From this point of view, we can and must see that the historical, sociological, and psychological ecology of a significant portion of Soviet society is now substantially distorted, and that the alarm about this must be sounded as forcefully as the warning over the diversion of the northern rivers. The only difference is that in this case the rivers are almost completely diverted already, and therefore we cannot be satisfied with prevention and warnings but must call for a restoration of the living environment."[8]

Leonid Batkin defended a similar vision of progress by opposing society's artificial construction to a process of natural growth. In August 1989, for example, he concluded an article in which he inveighed against the Communist Party's monopoly over Soviet society by affirming that "now, we are not going to 'live according to [official] instructions,' but simply to live: to work, to think, to confront each other in the Parliament and to fight in the elections. Society will not be built but will grow and mature as a forest grows and the harvest matures according to partially secret laws."[9]

According to this view, genuinely rational progress and scientific truth aim not to *create* a new world but rather to *return* to the natural-historical development of society by following its intrinsic moral dispositions, here exemplified by the West. Liberal intellectuals were hardly the only ones to think in this way, as the historian Timur Atnashev shows in his extensive study of the public discourse of perestroika.[10] Atnashev argues that the vast majority of Soviet intellectuals in this period, regardless of their ideological orientation, shared a teleological assumption concerning the inherently wholistic nature of historical progress. Many of those who took part in the pitched intellectual debates of this time were looking, in one way or another, for the fateful moment when Soviet society could be said to have deviated from its natural developmental path. Liberals, nationalists, and conservative communists, of course, did not agree on the moment of this deviation—Was it the Stalinist Terror? The abolition of Lenin's New Economic Policy? The October Revolution, or even earlier?—but they shared the conviction that society could not progress without first returning to the moment before this bifurcation. Progress, according to these thinkers, was not a question of man's detachment from nature, as in the rationalist and mechanistic Enlightenment worldview espoused by Marxism-Leninism; rather, the goal was the Romantic reconciliation between society and the course of "natural-historical development," as it was then called.[11] Liberal intellectuals, for their part, tended not to grieve society's supposed deviation from a past grounded in long-standing traditions, as was the case among conservative nationalists. They wanted to reconnect with progress, which they saw as a natural process leading to a harmonious and civilized life based on universal values, one that had been interrupted by an artificial project. Within the liberal intelligentsia, this tension between faith in progress and the Romantic ideal of natural development operated in different ways, according to specific intellectual trajectories. By way of illustration, the following section offers a brief overview of the views of the literary critics Yuri Burtin and Yuri Karyakin, the journalist Len Karpinsky, and the writer Ales Adamovich.

The Naturalization of Socialist Ideals

For Burtin and Karpinsky, the melancholic notion of a natural progress toward a harmonious society was inspired by a typically *narodnik* perspective,[12] one that shared the revolutionary and egalitarian ethos of Marxism-

Leninism while deferring its ideal of social harmony to a natural condition predating state intervention: a society based on the horizontal cooperation of autonomous owners and self-managed cooperatives. A characteristic feature of the *narodnik* vision is the opposition between the autonomous activity of the people and the artificial domination of the bureaucracy. In the post-Stalinist USSR, this perspective was famously embodied in the *"nomenklatura* theory" elaborated by the Yugoslav Milovan Djilas and the Soviet Mikhail Voslensky, which posits that socialist societies are ruled by a new exploiting class: the *nomenklatura*, or bureaucratic elite, of the party-state. This theory blamed socialist society for the very same tendencies that Marxist thinkers normally ascribed to capitalism, particularly class division, exploitation, alienation, and bureaucratic domination. This is undoubtedly what made it so attractive to socialist humanists disenchanted with Marxism-Leninism, who found in it the condemnation of the "petit bourgeois" vices that their Stalinist educations, nourished by the classics of Russian literature, taught them to despise and whose omnipresence they observed in their own society.

Yuri Burtin, by his own admission, was a fervent Stalinist in his youth.[13] The grandson of an educated peasant, and himself raised in the countryside, he took a passionate interest in the tragic fate of the Russian peasantry. This preoccupation was expressed in his literary tastes and public statements, which earned him the condemnation of his superiors while at university and ultimately ruined his chances of entering the party. After a series of further disappointments undermined his faith in Marxism-Leninism, he finally rejected socialism in the early 1960s under the influence of Solzhenitsyn, whose uncompromising criticism of Soviet power he took up as his own. Burtin, however, did not share Solzhenitsyn's condemnation of Western capitalism. Projecting onto that system the ideals of the *Narodniki*, Burtin instead saw in it the flowering of an organic community devoid of class division, while socialism appeared to him as the preeminent example of the arbitrary domination of a privileged minority over the masses, as affirmed by the *"nomenklatura* theory" mentioned above, which circulated in samizdat at the time.

The Romantic character of Burtin's revolt against the artificiality of the Soviet system is perhaps most apparent in his main theoretical article, which he began in secret in 1975 before finally publishing it in 1989.[14] In this long essay, Burtin denounces what he considers to be Marx's main mistake—namely, his failure to see that capitalism contained certain universal elements, especially the market and democracy, that allow it to evolve in a natural way. The socialist revolution, in Burtin's view, "did not so much eliminate what was outdated . . . as *cut through the living*, 'dynamiting' and trampling everything that was alive and viable, and which retained historical perspective. It was a violent rupture of the natural and historical evolution of capitalist society, which pushed aside all the viable social structure that was developing upwards."¹⁵ Burtin insisted on the artificial character of this act, which broke with the dynamic natural forces of capitalist society. Unlike the bourgeois revolution, which, he says, was the "midwife" of a whole being—capitalism— "with its head, arms, legs and everything it needs to live," the socialist revolution "created a social structure that had never existed in nature."¹⁶ Perestroika, according to Burtin, must therefore reconnect with the universal values of democracy and the market, which correspond to the very path of natural development from which the communist system had long ago deviated.

Like Burtin, the journalist Len Karpinsky saw Soviet society as marked by a class division between the great majority of people and a privileged few whose domination rested on the power of the bureaucratic state. But unlike that of many of his contemporaries, Karpinsky's criticism of the *nomenklatura* was informed by his own experience since he himself came from this elite environment. His father, Viacheslav Karpinsky, was an early Bolshevik who had served as Lenin's personal secretary during his years of exile in Switzerland. Len—whose first name was in fact chosen in honor of Lenin—was raised in the famous House on the Embankment, a large apartment building in Moscow where the cream of the Soviet elite resided. Destined for the highest positions in the party, he made a brilliant career in the Komsomol as a student, but the persecution of a Jewish friend, and his discovery of the difficulties of life in the rural hinterland, where he was sent as a propagandist as a young man, made him doubt Marxism-Leninism. He was a supporter of socialist humanism by the time he joined the ranks of the Moscow intelligentsia, where he met Karyakin and Burtin.

Unlike Burtin, however, Karpinsky remained faithful to socialism, which he conceived, in a close echo of the *narodnik* ideal, as a society of small independent landowners who govern themselves democratically and regulate production horizontally according to the laws of the market. For Karpinsky, the market was a "universal achievement of human civilization" that was "discovered" long before capitalism's formal development, which is why he thought it only natural that it could be better realized under socialism.¹⁷ In contrast to capitalism, which in his view was characterized above all by the concentration of property in the hands of a small minority, Karpinsky saw socialism as the type of social formation that allows "each person to realize his or her strengths and possibilities, to realize his or her full moral potential."¹⁸ For him, this Romantic ideal of self-realization did not require state intervention, because it corresponded to the natural state of society. Socialism, moreover, allows "everyone to live as he wishes, socialism corresponds to a fully human and normal life, a life with others and not at the expense of others."[19] For Karpinsky as for Burtin, then, the Romantic ideals of self-realization and a socially organic form of human organization could not be achieved by way of the party and the state, as Marxist-Leninist doctrine posited, but rather must be achieved *in opposition to* the party and the state.

Yuri Karyakin and Ales Adamovich's shared melancholy at the loss of natural progress stemmed from the internalization of the notion of moral purity advocated by the Communist Party, which they interpreted as intrinsically a matter of personal conscience, but one that takes on a universalist dimension in the context of the struggle for peace and nuclear disarmament. Raised according to the socialist ideal of moral intransigence and the refusal to compromise on matters of principle, Karyakin was increasingly troubled in the 1960s by what he saw as the immoral behavior of the Soviet leadership.[20] Renouncing Marxism-Leninism—but not yet socialism—he found in the likes of Fedor Dostoevsky and Aleksandr Solzhenitsyn his intellectual masters: these were the writers who would teach him to judge the world according to the criterion of personal conscience, to maintain an absolute fidelity to honesty, truth, and sincerity.

For Karyakin, however, this particular moral outlook was based not on traditional Russian values but rather on the idea of a common humanity united by the threat of nuclear annihilation. Together with his friend, the writer Ales Adamovich, he became involved in the movement for peace and nuclear disarmament in the early 1980s.[21] In an article published at the very beginning of perestroika,[22] Karyakin asserted that the possibility of nuclear war places humanity in a situation in which it has no choice but to overcome its divisions in order to forge a politics based on morality. The nuclear threat, for him, demonstrated the mortal danger represented by any transgression of the "objective moral norms," which, in his eyes, were comparable in their absolute necessity to the laws of physics.

Karyakin was strongly influenced by the writings of Likhachev, whom he quoted with approval when he described the moral sphere as an ecosystem that must be restored in order to "gather all the living forces and sources of life in the fight against death." Like Adamovich at the same time,[23] he indignantly denounced the "bunker mentality" leading many people to worry about their personal survival rather than the shared fate of humanity. In so doing, Karyakin and Adamovich condemned selfish individualism just as forcefully as they had in their Stalinist youth; only now, they asserted that morality depends on personal conscience, not the dictates of any worldly party or doctrine, and that it is an intrinsic attribute of humanity, one to which the threat of nuclear annihilation gives particularly urgent relevance.

Both writers believed that the course of human progress could bring about a restoration of the universal values that guarantee the proper functioning of the moral ecosystem.

These brief thumbnail sketches of four members of the liberal intelligentsia serve merely to hint at the origins of the Romantic sensibility underlying their cohort's output during the era of perestroika. But in considering their intellectual trajectories, we might observe a general tendency among this group of thinkers to *naturalize* the ideals originally associated with socialism. I borrow the concept of naturalization from the historian Sheila Fitzpatrick, who uses it to designate the process—which she believes was already well underway by the mid-1960s—whereby Soviet identity ceased to be projected into an as yet unrealized future and instead appeared as an established fact to be reckoned with.[24] With the fading over time of the Promethean image of the new man, the features of Soviet society were more frequently presented as universal attributes whose validity transcended the historical context of the class struggle. As early as the 1950s, for example, communist morality was designated in official documents as the best incarnation of *universal* morality.

This claim found a sympathetic audience among Soviet intellectuals in favor of de-Stalinization, who tended to insist on socialism's universal dimensions and who were later at the forefront of the group of liberal intellectuals who committed themselves to perestroika. Their growing disillusionment with reformist socialism, especially since the crushing of the Prague Spring in 1968 and its promise of a "Socialism with a human face," coupled with the influence of deeply Romantic nationalist intellectuals like Solzhenitsyn and Likhachev, saw these liberal intellectuals move further away from the earlier tendency to associate morality with the building of communism. Instead, they came to embrace the liberal ideas of parliamentary democracy and the market economy, which seemed to them to better embody the natural development of society. The moral promises of Soviet modernity were exhausted, as far as they were concerned, and while the ideals of individual realization and integration into an organic society were preserved, the Romantic dimension of their thought was enhanced, such that it became an object of melancholy: these ideals seem to have been lost on the way to communism. This melancholy, in turn, inspired a typically Romantic revolt against the artificial system under whose influence these values were discarded.

A Sense of the System

According to Marxist-Leninist doctrine, as we have seen, moral decline is explained in the narrowest of terms, and above all by the deviance of corrupt individuals. Moral criticism, in this sense, is essentially reformist, since it is based on the mobilization of the fundamental values of society, the norms of communist morality. By contrast, the moral perspective of the liberal intelligentsia, based as it was on a melancholic view of universal values, put Soviet society on trial from the point of a higher absolute: humanity, civilization, nature, life. This moral criticism was fundamentally *revolutionary*, since it aimed to dismantle the very system that had created the conditions for individual moral deviance. In the vocabulary of the time, this approach to social reality was "systemic"—today we might describe it as "structural"—and, as such, was judged by liberal intellectuals to be more profound and more consequential than the reformist approaches that sought merely to denounce the "negative phenomena" of Soviet society.

In order to understand this systemic approach, let us return to the work of Yuri Burtin, whose articles provide valuable insight into the role of social criticism and its conditions of possibility under perestroika. For most intellectuals engaged in public debates, this kind of question is self-evident and therefore implicit: their criticism is virulent, but it is rarely reflexive. Burtin, for his part, was concerned with making his mode of reflection explicit out of a desire to transmit the heritage of his generation, which reached political maturity in the context of Khrushchev's efforts at de-Stalinization, to the Soviet youth of the 1980s, who knew only Brezhnevian stagnation. "What," Burtin asked, "do most contemporary readers, who are now 30–35 years old, and especially those who are 20, know about that time, about our 1960s? We venture to say: almost nothing."[25] In an attempt to remedy this, he published, starting in 1987, a series of articles in which he not only formulated a systemic critique of the Soviet reality—many of his colleagues and friends were already doing that—but also explained *how* this critique should be expressed.[26] In doing so, his goal was not to propose a new method of his own but simply to teach young Soviets what his own generation understood a true critique to mean.

Burtin recognized from the outset that the Soviet press did not lack critical voices. On the contrary, many newspapers and journals of the period readily denounced all sorts of social problems, whether the attitude of the local party leader, a worker's alcoholism, or the deplorable state of the environment. And yet, as far as Burtin was concerned, most of these criticisms were incomplete insofar as they insisted on highlighting only discrete, isolated problems without seeing the more subtle and insidious connections that united many of the issues then facing Soviet society. Worthwhile criticism, according to Burtin, must therefore be "systemic"—that is, it must reveal the structural causes of the generalized rot that lies behind any one problem. To this end, Burtin called on his readers to cultivate a "sense of the system," and he pointed to Nikolai Dobroliubov, the initiator of the genre of "real criticism" in the nineteenth century, as an exemplar of this outlook:

> Dobroliubov's decisive superiority lay, in a word, in the systematic nature of his understanding of reality. Where others saw only a mass of small and large cases gathered by chance, a disparate conglomerate of separate phenomena, processes, groups, and social forces, he saw something internally homogeneous answering to common regularities. In other words, he saw a system.... Thanks to this "sense of the system," Dobroliubov interprets the apparent singularity of almost any single literary theme as a characteristic and significant phenomenon of the social totality, and, in so doing, "elevates" them to this level of totality and conceives of them in all their social-moral significance.[27]

Burtin is dealing specifically with literary criticism in the passage just quoted, but his reference to the "sense of the system" corresponds more generally to the criticisms he and his liberal colleagues leveled at Soviet society. The "systemic" character of their approach is particularly evident in their reflections on Stalin and his legacy. Seeking to go beyond the Khrushchevian critique of the "cult of personality," they insisted on denouncing not just Stalin but Stalin*ism*, the system he created. Once again, Burtin made explicit the epistemological and ethical stakes of this application of systemic criticism. In an article from 1989, he asserted that this kind of critique is indispensable for the establishment of a definitive and objective judgment.[28] He recalled that, beginning with the Twentieth Congress, the reflection on Stalin had been devoted primarily to the man's personality, a tendency that gave rise to endless debates between those, like Anatoly Rybakov, who depicted Stalin as a vile and Machiavellian being and those, like Konstantin Simonov, who presented Stalin as a wise and subtle strategist.[29] Burtin denounced the weakness of these psychologizing arguments: "How to reconcile these two truths, how to lead them to a common denominator? The task is obviously impossible within the framework of a personality-driven approach."[30]

Cultivating a "sense of the system" would allow one to overcome this dual image of Stalin, thanks to the retrospective lessons that could be drawn from the timid reforms of the Khrushchev and Brezhnev eras, which showed that "the essential is not in the individuals or even in the concrete forms taken by the system of bureaucratic dictatorship forged by Stalin; the essential is in the system itself."[31] The knowledge of this fact, according to Burtin, brought to the criticism of Stalin the objectivity that previously had been lacking: "Thus becomes possible a completely different view of the object of this endless debate: the judgment of the historical role played by Stalin according to a decisive and fully objective criterion like the type of social system created under his leadership. . . . And if we look at Stalin from *this* point of view, then objectively there is no room for any dualistic judgments."[32] For Burtin and many others, the criticism of Stalin was not only a historical question. A "sense of the system" also helped these critics focus their revolt against contemporary Soviet institutions, which constituted, in their eyes, a continuation of the Stalinist system. For Len Karpinsky, for example, this is self-evident: it takes only a "a quick glance," he says, to see that all the obstacles to perestroika have "a single branching root that is embodied in Stalinism."[33]

Liberal intellectuals' systemic approach allowed them to distance themselves from a type of reformism that was particularly common among nationalist intellectuals—namely, the idea that society's moral degradation is the result of the individual cowardice of those who refuse to follow their conscience. While liberal intellectuals tended to agree with their nationalist counterparts on the paramount importance of following one's conscience (*sovest'*)—a concept they used extensively—they nonetheless argued that its sincere expression implies not the activation of an inherently Russian tradition but rather the instrumentalization of certain universal values that are common to the whole of humanity. Moreover, they claimed that individual cowardice is not the primary explanation for moral decline but that it is itself conditioned by an artificial and oppressive system. It was therefore not necessarily true, in their eyes, that one must first "start with oneself."

In a 1987 article, Burtin therefore sought to correct the image of moral corruption depicted in *The Fire*, a novel published a short time previously by the conservative nationalist writer Valentin Rasputin. In this book, the titular fire that devastates a Siberian village is fueled by the indifference, selfishness, and venality of its inhabitants, who have forgotten the ancient traditions of mutual aid. The book is a cry of alarm at the decay of the Russian countryside and its perversion by modern individualistic values. The book was widely celebrated by literary critics, and even by Soviet leaders, for its critique of Soviet reality. For Burtin, however, Rasputin's and his champions' lamentations over moral decline failed to get to the heart of the matter:

> The most common idea among critics, however, seems to be one-sided in that they posit that we should "ask only of ourselves" and that "we ask too much of society, forgetting our personal responsibility." It is obvious that we must proceed "from ourselves," otherwise any discussion of contemporary problems would lose its moral sense. But why proceed only from oneself . . . when what is at stake is "the people,"

profound upheavals in the moral aspect of the human masses? . . . The writer [Rasputin]—and he is not the only one—seems to imagine things as if the demands of one's individual personality on oneself and on society were mutually exclusive.³⁴

This opposition between social norms and the demands of conscience, according to Burtin, is an illusion. First, because each person is not only a reflection of what they choose to be but also a sum of their social relations. Second, and more importantly, because the moral quality of one's personal conscience is measured, among other things, by one's interest in the wider social good. In contrast to the "Stoic" position of Solzhenitsyn and Likhachev, who called on their readers to lead a virtuous life even in a society deprived of freedom, Burtin expressed doubts about the capacity for self-improvement of someone who can accommodate themselves to any and all social situations. The purification of one's personal conscience is certainly necessary, but by itself it is insufficient since it does not challenge the harmful system that encourages individual compromises. It is necessary to extend one's moral outlook from the denunciation of individual faults to include a structural analysis as well.

Leonid Batkin described a similar outlook: "Whatever one says, the main problem is not 'the inertia within us,' it is not the fact that everyone must start perestroika 'from themselves.' There are, of course, accurate psychological observations in these clichés, but we are not so stupid as to replace politics with psychology and hope to win the battle against the powerful bureaucratic machine by working on ourselves."³⁵

For Burtin and Batkin, then, as for most of the liberal intellectuals committed to democratization, the recovery of morality requires first and foremost the reversal of the structural source of discrete perversions. This idea of an artificial system distorting the consciousness of its subjects was perhaps best expressed by a concept that became extremely popular at that time, that of the "administrative system of command."³⁶

Against the "Administrative System of Command"

The concept of the "administrative system of command" was first coined by the economist Gavriil Popov in the spring of 1987. It was an immediate success and quickly became the most widespread designation for—and thus interpretation of—the artificial system that perestroika was intended to dismantle. Popov used Aleksandr Bek's portrait of the typical Stalinist administrator, which appeared in his novel *A New Assignment*, to analyze the contemporary Soviet administrative system.³⁷

This system, Popov argued, was the source of society's moral decline: "Many people think that all we have to do is to return to Stalinist methods of command to get rid of such problems as indiscipline at work, failure to fulfill the plan, shortsighted bookkeeping, avarice, and drug addiction. . . . But some [including Popov himself] consider that the real roots of all these phenomena lie precisely in the Administrative System, and that they developed precisely during the years of installation and consolidation of this System."[38]

According to Popov, this system was based on the centralization of decisions and their blind application by those at the lower echelons of state authority, who were reduced to the rank of mere submissive and cynical executors. In so doing, the economist rejected the criticism of the bureaucrat corrupted by the enjoyment of power, which, as we have seen, was typical of the official moral doctrine. For Popov, the bureaucrat was in fact a *victim* of the larger system in which he was a cog. The demand for blind obedience caused "a dissonance between thought and action, between feelings and their expression."[39] It produced, in short, systemic duplicity.

This dissociation of thought, speech, and gesture has been noted many times by Western observers of Soviet society, most often to celebrate the ability of its citizens to adapt to and resist the most severe social and political constraints.[40] This heroic vision of duplicity is based more or less implicitly on a conception of the individual that is widespread in the social sciences, which assumes that the integrity of the individual precedes his or her relations with society and power, with which he or she maintains relations of either resistance or obedience. Winston, the hero of George Orwell's novel *1984*, with his ability to preserve his individual integrity through rational strategies of resistance to totalitarian domination, is perhaps the paradigmatic example of this tendency. But unlike Winston, whose tragic fate betrays Orwell's pessimism at the apogee of Stalinism, Soviet citizens, it seemed, had been victorious in the defense of their individual integrity. Perestroika, indeed, is often interpreted as the moment when Soviet citizens' individualism, long hidden under the guise of conformist collectivism and ritual demonstrations of loyalty, finally came to light.[41]

This is not, however, the meaning of Popov's influential critique of systemic duplicity. Far from celebrating the adaptive capacities of bureaucrats who seek only to preserve their own consciences in a context of extreme constraint, he denounced the deleterious effects of this duplicity on the development of these bureaucrats' personalities and, consequently, on the whole of society. Employing a scientific vocabulary borrowed from the famous biologist Ivan Pavlov, Popov described the "shocks" provoked by this duplicity as a sort of cognitive dysfunction that causes acute suffering in those who experience it—in this case, the first generation of Soviet administrators to be raised as devoted communists. Popov recognized that the administrators of the subsequent generation had become so accustomed to duplicity that they took it for granted. But this lack of psychological suffering did not make their cynicism more legitimate in Popov's eyes, because it constituted a threat to society. On this point, the economist echoed a fear that was widespread at the time, that of the moral contagion stemming from corrupt minorities. According to Popov, bureaucrats' structural cynicism was harmful precisely because it had a demoralizing effect on all of society, thereby causing such calamities as "the slowing down of economic and technical progress, innumerable moral losses, and the nihilism of youth."[42]

This criticism of the administrative system of command, far from illustrating the prevalence in the USSR of a heroic individualism, in fact painted an image of a Soviet regime that provoked one's alienation from oneself—something that socialists had always denounced as a structural product of capitalism. Popov, however, while he did not abandon socialism—at least not openly, for the time being—nonetheless criticized it for having failed to keep its moral promises. In his famous 1987 article, he was careful to point out that the duplicity of the system's administrators "contradicts the socialist idea itself, at the center of which is the person, his spiritual world and his moral aspect."[43]

The conclusion drawn from this radical critique implied a complete shift in the reform strategy of perestroika: Popov was calling not for more discipline and new restrictive measures—on alcohol consumption, for example—but for the dismantling of the administrative system and the introduction of "democratic and economic methods."[44] In doing so, he invoked the dichotomy, widely recognized among Soviet reformist economists of the 1960s and 1970s, between the inefficiency of the "administrative mechanisms" deployed by the bureaucracy and the efficiency of the "economic mechanisms" intrinsic to exchange relations—namely, material and moral motivations. But unlike those earlier economists, who sought largely to rationalize the planning system by relying on cybernetics and mathematical economics, Popov presented the embrace of scientific objectivity as a return to the laws of nature, in contrast to the mechanical artificiality of the bureaucratic state. He described the administrative system as a "perfectly exact machine" that turns people into "small cogs in the immense mechanism of the state," thus contravening the "truth of life."[45]

The notion of an "administrative system of command" was a resounding success among the liberal intelligentsia, who adopted it as a general descriptor for Stalinism, the overcoming of which, in turn, was necessary for the establishment of democracy and the market. Several authors, including

Burtin and Afanasyev, explicitly quoted Popov approvingly, but, in a sign of the wide currency the concept had acquired by the end of the 1980s, most used it in more of a general sense and without specific reference to Popov.[46] Indeed, a journalist remarked in 1991 that "the concept of an 'administrative system' has become so established and widespread that we use it without even remembering that it was created by Gavriil Kh. Popov."[47] The concept's exceptionally wide application is explained by the fact that it reflects and supports the liberal intelligentsia's widely shared belief that Soviet society suffers—especially in the moral sphere—from *too much* state control, not too little. The purpose of perestroika, therefore, is not so much to build a better system as to dismantle the existing one in order to return society to the course of "natural-historical" development, based on universal values such as democracy and the market.

The Specificity of Soviet Liberalism

The three moral perspectives presented here and in the previous chapter illustrate some of the various meanings conveyed by the political discourse on morality during perestroika. For some it was reformist, for others it was conservative, and for others still it was revolutionary. In the perspective of Marxist-Leninist moral doctrine as it was instrumentalized by party leaders during the first two years of perestroika, this moral criticism was essentially *reformist* insofar as it spoke of accelerating social development by mobilizing the fundamental tenets of communist morality, whose internalization was seen as an essential condition for self-realization. The pathways to moral rectification—education, control, and mobilization—were utilized in the promotion of this internalization.

A *conservative* conception of morality under perestroika, by contrast, aimed at the restitution or preservation of traditional Russian values that had been alienated in the course of the USSR's push toward modernization. Nationalist intellectuals expressed a deeply Romantic melancholy toward an idealized vision of Russia's past, according to which man was assumed to have been spiritually integrated into the social totality.

Beyond the call to spiritual awakening—"Start with yourself!"—the nationalists offered divergent political proposals: conservative nationalists demanded the banishment of Western influences through the strengthening of party control, while liberal nationalists emphasized the promotion and preservation of national culture.

Finally, there was also a conception of morality that we can call *revolutionary* since it aimed at the dismantling of the communist system, as it then existed, in the name of the universal values of humanity, which, before 1990, were still generally associated with socialism. The liberal intellectuals who promoted this conception of morality firmly believed in progress and modernity, whose exemplar they saw in the Western capitalist countries. At the same time, they, too, showed a strong Romantic melancholy toward a "normal" society whose "natural-historical" development they claimed had been interrupted by an artificial project of social engineering. The defense of democracy and the market, according to this perspective, was inspired by a revolt against the perversions—cynicism, egoism, careerism—provoked by a mechanical system that, in their eyes, hindered full self-realization.

From 1987 onward, with the official launching of democratization as a key aspect of perestroika, liberal intellectuals' revolutionary moral critique achieved a predominant status in the public discourse at the expense of the reformist and conservative perspectives. The main effect of this change in public opinion was to channel *against* the communist system the powerful and diffuse feeling of moral crisis. This phenomenon reinforced a vision of politics that was focused not on building new structures and developing a new ideology but on dismantling structures and abandoning all ideology in order to facilitate the expression of the natural moral dispositions of both the individual and the wider society. As mentioned in the introduction, this emancipatory project led many analysts of Russian politics to conclude that the democratic mobilization led by the liberal intelligentsia was essentially *negative*, insofar as it did not propose a substantial vision of the future beyond the overthrow of the established system.

This interpretation must be qualified. The negative character of the Soviet liberal project derived from the fact that its main substantive objectives were related to morality and, in a typically Romantic way, were formulated against institutional and ideological constructions that were considered artificial. These aspirations, moreover, were resistant to doctrinal formalization since they were assumed to express the requirements of a "normal life." They were not, however, negative in the sense that they were devoid of substantial content. On the contrary, they carried some of the most powerful modern aspirations—both rationalist and Romantic—to animate Soviet society for decades.

The study of this moral perspective also allows us to understand the particular character of Soviet liberalism under perestroika within the broader context of twentieth-century political thought. In particular, it invites us to qualify the notion that the ideas of Soviet liberals derived from some putative break with "Soviet ideology," followed by a more or less successful conversion to Western liberalism. Even the historian Igor Timofeyev, whose analysis follows this triumphalist interpretation, acknowledges that there is "a certain illiberal quality in the thought [of Soviet liberals], for they consider that the individual and society must pursue a certain goal of which they consider themselves the interpreters."[48] Similarly, the intellectual historian Andrzej Walicki, after positing that the ideal of freedom that motivated Gorbachev amounted to a piece of "liberal common sense," asserts that this notion was not fully understood by the intelligentsia, which was still marked by a "moral fundamentalism" in which individual freedom was confused with a socially just moral order that would provide each person with unlimited opportunities for self-fulfillment.[49] This particular trait corresponds to what contemporary Anglo-American political philosophy calls political perfectionism—that is, the idea that the state must undertake reforms in order to create the conditions for the moral development of its citizens.[50] What led Timofeyev and Walicki to label this an illiberal idea is the tendency, which they shared with most Western liberal theorists since the 1970s, to reject perfectionism and to defend the neutrality of the state with respect to any substantive definition of the good.[51] Soviet liberals, therefore, differed from their Western counterparts in one essential respect: they were perfectionists, a label that implies a greater sensitivity to the question of which moral norms are necessary for the functioning of institutions.

The particularity of Soviet liberalism can largely be explained, as has been suggested, by the naturalization of the moral promises of socialist humanism. It would be simplistic, however, to see in this intellectual heritage an atavistic mentality preventing the development of a true liberalism in Russia. From a broader historical perspective, it becomes apparent that this perfectionism was prevalent among liberal thinkers in the nineteenth and early twentieth centuries but underwent varied trajectories in the second half of the twentieth century. While it remained influential among Russian and eastern European intellectuals, it declined in the West, becoming a minority trend within liberal political theory.[52] We would therefore be guilty of presentism and ethnocentrism if we regarded the moral project of Soviet liberal intellectuals as a naive or immature form of Western liberalism. It would be more fruitful, I suggest, to see it as a particular branch of the liberal tradition that developed in response to the widespread sense of moral decline in late communist societies, associated with the spread of hypocrisy, cynicism, a calculating spirit, and more. The particularity of liberalism harbored by Soviet liberals—and no doubt one of the reasons for its success—was therefore to link the model of Western liberalism to the aspirations of its time, marked by the apogee of political Romanticism in the USSR.

An alternative interpretation would be to consider liberal intellectuals' use of the ideas and beliefs of their time as nothing more than a rhetorical technique, a conscious tactic of discursive mimicry aimed at undermining the regime from within (as was said, for example, of Soviet dissidents' revival of socialist legalism).[53] This strategic dimension, while it cannot be excluded, is by itself insufficient to explain the unprecedented political commitment of liberal intellectuals and the powerful social resonance of their moral critique. An indication of the sincerity of their moral convictions can be found a posteriori in the bitter disappointment to which many of them later confessed in response to the moral failures of capitalist Russia in the 1990s, marked by the flowering of an uninhibited cynicism. In any case, whether this criticism was a matter of calculation or conviction, the result remains the same: the liberal intelligentsia managed to popularize liberal ideas by associating them with the moral promises of Soviet modernity at the very moment when Gorbachev's reforms were gathering steam.

Chapter 3

Opinion and Truth

> The devil is born from the foam on the lips of an angel who fights for the good, truth, and justice.
>
> —Grigory Pomerants, "Son o spravedlivom vozmezdii"

At the beginning of 1987, Gorbachev, inspired by the ideas of the liberal intelligentsia, embarked upon a major political shift. This timing can be explained by a number of factors, including the rapprochement between the USSR and the United States and the subsequent negotiation of disarmament agreements between the two countries. It also stemmed from the observation, based on the first two years of perestroika, that the party-state had been unable to raise productivity levels by strengthening control—a result of the fact that coercion often proved ineffective, even counterproductive, as the prohibition campaign demonstrated, but also of the fact that much of the resistance to reform came from within the party-state's own ranks. Having recognized this failure, Gorbachev could have chosen to back down and compromise with the bureaucratic apparatus, as Khrushchev and Brezhnev had done before him.[1] But, guided by his convictions and those of his entourage, he instead opted to forge ahead by committing to even deeper reforms whose ambition was nothing short of revolutionary—in this case, the very transformation of the regime. From that moment on, Gorbachev referred to perestroika itself as a revolution, a sort of corollary of the great transformation originally set in motion in 1917. To this end, he elaborated a new program that he said represented a return to the path on which Lenin had originally set the Soviet Union, but which was also full of ideas from the liberal intelligentsia: representative democracy, a market economy, the rule of law, the separation of powers, and the guarantee of individual rights, among others.

Of course, it would be a gross exaggeration of liberal intellectuals' power to say that they were the authors of this new policy direction. At that time, most of them lacked the sort of political leverage that would allow them to push the leadership in their preferred direction. Instead, what influence they could bring to bear was exerted indirectly, through public opinion, and especially through the dissemination of new concepts that could then be taken up by the party's reform team. This claim is echoed by the political scientist Archie Brown, who insists on Gorbachev's predominant role in the passage of these reforms yet recognizes that "many reformist concepts are to be encountered first in the writings of scholarly specialists, and only later in the speeches of Party leaders."[2]

For example, we can observe a qualitative shift in Gorbachev's use during this period of the concept of "universal values," which originally referred to that which unites humanity in the face of global threats—first and foremost nuclear war—before gradually coming to include economic and political principles embodied by the West, such as economic competition, private property, and democracy.[3] Perestroika underwent a similar transformation in Gorbachev's statements: from a program aimed at accelerating the development of Soviet society by strengthening state control and mobilizing the norms of communist morality to a more general dismantling of the "administrative system of command" by way of democratization and the introduction of "economic mechanisms" (read: some form of market economy). First enunciated at the January 1987 Central Committee plenum, the new strategy was then confirmed at the June 1987 plenum before being expressed more fully in the book *Perestroika*, prepared that summer. And it assumed its ultimate form in the decisions of the Nineteenth Party Conference in June 1988, which provided for the democratization of the political system.

For Gorbachev, democratization, like glasnost, was about overcoming the resistance to reform embodied by conservative elements within the party by mobilizing the force of public opinion and citizen activism; only then would a truly united front in support of perestroika be achieved. From the very beginning, Soviet intellectuals were called on to play a leading role in this vast mobilization campaign. Gorbachev regularly invited important figures of the intelligentsia—writers, scientists, editors—to the meetings of the party's Central Committee, during which he implored them to take up the cause of perestroika and get involved in glasnost in order to help reverse the problems then plaguing the regime.

However, it soon became clear that glasnost had had an unforeseen effect: the expression of polarized opinions. Initially enthusiastic about the reforms adopted in 1985 and 1986, communists and conservative nationalists became increasingly hostile to the Gorbachevian strategy when it moved toward rapprochement with the West. From 1987 onward, various intellectual camps waged an ideological battle with one another via the media, resurrecting in a new form the old nineteenth-century opposition between Westernizers and Slavophiles, with some advocating reforms inspired by Western models and others defending the idea of a historical path specific to Russia. This split was particularly evident in the Soviet Writers' Union, which was supposed to embody the conscience of artists and intellectuals but which became a bastion of communist and nationalist conservatism, thereby encouraging the desertion of its liberal members. Far from producing a united front in support of perestroika, glasnost brought to the surface a conflict over values that had thus far remained more or less latent.

Gorbachev, in his role as general secretary of the party, did not hide his concern over this increase in polarization. During his regular meetings with leading figures from the intelligentsia, he insisted on the need for a consolidation of society. But while he recognized the problem, he seemed to minimize its importance. In his book *Perestroika*, for example, he dismissed these tensions as a transitory phenomenon: "Group prejudices and intolerance have indeed surfaced among writers in view of the new openness (*glasnost'*). There was a moment when passions were running high in the literary community." Although he claimed to defend pluralism of opinion, he insisted that such division is unacceptable: "We brought home to them the view of the Central Committee, namely that it would be very sad if the creative and artistic intelligentsia squabbled instead of consolidating."[4] The Central Committee's sermons, however, no longer had the same effect, since glasnost had brought critical opinions to the fore. This conflict of values would only increase in the coming years.

For the liberal intelligentsia, the Gorbachevian turn in 1987 represented a long-awaited chance to complete the de-Stalinization begun by Khrushchev some thirty years earlier but interrupted by Brezhnev. The trauma of this first, unfortunate attempt weighed heavily on the minds of liberal intellectuals, who consequently sought to guarantee perestroika's "irreversibility," a term that appears often in their writings. Seizing Gorbachev's outstretched hand, many of them took it upon themselves to support him unconditionally so as to help him remove all obstacles to perestroika, commonly referred to as its "brake mechanisms." This initial support for the reformer was reflected in the oft-repeated claim that "there is no other option than Gorbachev" or that "there is no other way [than perestroika]," this last comment serving as the title of the famous collection of liberal reformist texts edited by Yuri Afanasyev in the summer of 1988, *Inogo ne dano*.[5] This tactic earned these committed intellectuals the epithet "perestroika foremen" (*prorabi perestroiki*), a term that initially had a pejorative meaning but which was later adopted as a sort of badge of honor by those against whom it was leveled.

For a small number of high-ranking intellectuals, such as the sociologist Tatyana Zaslavskaya and the economists Oleg Bogomolov and Leonid Abalkin, the commitment to perestroika took the form of an advisory role on Gorbachev's team. But for the vast majority, who did not have the privilege of having the ear of senior party leaders, the commitment to perestroika was expressed through the media, in a struggle for the hearts and minds of millions of their fellow Soviet citizens. This battle for public opinion was seen as a decisive aspect of perestroika because, as journalist Len Karpinsky put it in an article from 1988, its most important "braking forces" were to be found precisely in the moral field.[6] For Karpinsky and many of his colleagues, the most important task was not to dismantle the Stalinist institutions of the administrative command system but rather to combat the opinions, ideas, and beliefs inherited from the Stalinist era—namely, egoism, cynicism, dogmatism, a preference for authoritarian leadership, and a distrust of personal initiative. In short, it was a matter of creating, through criticism and persuasion, the proper moral conditions for Gorbachev's reforms. This implied nothing less than a "cultural and psychological transformation of society, which would touch the root of the mental structures of millions of people and help them recover a capacity for judgment."[7]

Political Pluralism and Moral Monism

This civilizing mission, suffused as it was with the spirit of the Enlightenment and its confidence in human perfectibility and in the persuasive power of the rational word, was also riven by an internal tension in the context of glasnost. On the one hand, the ideal of a full and sincere expression of conscience implies the public recognition of a plurality of valid opinions. For most liberal intellectuals, this ideal translated into a categorical rejection of censorship and of the party's claim to hold a monopoly on truth, in favor of a revaluation of personal convictions as legitimate objects of public discourse and debate. On the other hand, these intellectuals tended to feel that perestroika should be based on a unique and coherent set of ostensibly universal values that would enable society's natural development.

To put this in the terms of contemporary political philosophy, one could say that this perfectionist project was based on moral monism—not in the sense of a single, supreme good but rather in the sense that "universal values" form a wholesome and coherent vision of the world that is the foundation of any sound political principle. To be sure, the values defended by Soviet liberals included things like honesty and sincerity, about which almost everyone can agree. But some of the other values they defended implied a substantial definition of the good, as well as the sociopolitical order that makes it possible: in this case, the free expression of individual conscience and initiative through representative democracy and a market economy.

These substantial values, however, were highly controversial in Soviet society, where they conflicted with the values of patriotism, class membership, loyalty to the party, and doctrinal conformity with the tenets of Marxism-Leninism. In such a context, "universal values" were far from universal; in fact, they were only one of the various sets of values that clashed in the public sphere. Soviet liberals, however, tended to regard their "universal values" as the only principles by which society should function, and for this reason, they intended for these values to supplant those held by their communist and conservative nationalist opponents. These latter intellectuals, for their part, tended to think in a similar fashion—namely, that perestroika should be based exclusively on communist morality or Russian national traditions. Soviet public life therefore assumed a fundamentally antagonistic character once critical opinions that diverged from the official doctrine were expressed more widely. This explains why the democratization and liberalization of society, despite Gorbachev's hopes, led not to society's consolidation but to its fragmentation along fault lines that had long been hidden by censorship.

If moral monism was a relatively common feature of political discourse in this period, it played a more problematic role among liberal intellectuals, insofar as it came into direct conflict with their ideal of a free and full expression of one's conscience. This was manifested in the liberals' ambiguous attitude toward the opinions of their opponents, torn as they were between the competing desires to recognize the value of pluralism and preserve an intransigent moral monism. In a society accustomed to ritual expressions of unanimity, where differences of opinion were usually expressed only in private conversation, the public clash of values was a cause for concern, and not only for Gorbachev. Many intellectuals wondered whether these social divisions would ruin perestroika, since it needed broad popular support in order to succeed. A pressing question of this period, then, concerned the extent to which the heated debates occasioned by the burgeoning of civic life could play a constructive role in perestroika. Should those opinions that are contrary to the ideas of the Soviet liberals be considered, to use Karpinsky's words once again, debatable "variants of perestroika" or inacceptable "variants outside perestroika"?[8] This raised the related question of the extent of legitimate pluralism in glasnost: Was it merely a matter of confronting a plurality of opinions *within* the general framework of universal values that had guided perestroika since 1987, or could a plurality of values be confronted, even if it meant potentially challenging the new principles of perestroika?

In 1987 and 1988, these concerns were still quite amorphous since there was not yet any open political struggle to speak of, and there was a general assumption that glasnost was simply about telling the truth and fighting lies, which seemed to provide an obvious criterion for separating legitimate and illegitimate speech. But this presumption was based on the superimposition of two aspects of glasnost's civilizing mission: its epistemological aim, by which it sought to combat dogma and restore *factual truth* according to a scientific method, and its moral aim, which was to combat egoism and cynicism by restoring *moral truth* through the sincere expression of conscience. For many liberal intellectuals, these two forms of truth went hand in hand—indeed, they constituted as it were two sides of the same coin. It therefore seemed natural to them to reject the opinions of their opponents not only as errors of judgment or the result of some moral or intellectual deficiency that could be corrected but as deliberate, and thus intolerable, lies.

On an epistemological level, glasnost aimed to replace dogmatic beliefs with true knowledge predicated on the scientific study of society. This implied not only correcting the knowledge of the past, ridding it of the many mystifications and omissions of official history, but also proposing an accurate analysis of Soviet society in the present and enumerating the reforms that would be necessary for its rectification. This last ambition often gave rise to an illusion of objectivity, something to which Aleksandr Yakovlev, Gorbachev's right-hand man during perestroika, testified a few years later: "An illusion was created that what needs to be done is to gather as full and reliable information as possible, analyse it strictly scientifically and [then] act in a corresponding way—in that case everything will go in the necessary direction, an honest and reasonable policy will be found. This is an illusion which I also shared."[9] By virtue of this illusion, many thought it possible to engage in a discourse on human affairs as objective as that which science had brought to bear on nature—provided, of course, that one rids oneself of myths, stereotypes, and other "ideological" distortions.[10]

Within the liberal intelligentsia, this positivist outlook manifested itself above all in the work of certain influential Soviet economists, with their unanimous confidence in the "objective laws of the economy." The most famous of these was Nikolai Shmelev, whose 1987 article "Advances and Debts" had a huge impact on the contemporary discourse.[11] In it, Shmelev presents the market as the objective and natural mode of economic organization. The "objective laws" of economic life, he asserts, include "motivations for work that have been formed over several centuries and that correspond to human nature."[12] The validity of these laws, for him, is as self-evident as the laws of physics: "Who will make all our economic executives, from the top to the bottom, understand that the time of administrative methods of managing economic life is over, that the economy has laws the transgression of which is just as inadmissible and frightening as that of the laws of the Chernobyl nuclear reactor, that modern leaders must know these laws and base their decisions in accordance with them and not in spite of them?"[13] As this passage illustrates, Shmelev fully shared the Romantic sensibility of the liberal intelligentsia discussed in the previous chapter, which held that the development of society follows organic laws that have been perverted by an artificial system. Shmelev associated the "objective laws of the market" with "normality and health" and "common sense," qualities that he contrasted with the artificiality of any ideology of economic organization. He denounced "a system of economic management that was merely invented in offices," where prices are "established . . . according to concepts still detached from life."[14] A telling sign of this emphasis on organic spontaneity is Shmelev's use of the word "life," which appears no less than twenty-six times in his seventeen-page article.

Soviet liberals' tendency to see the economy as shrouded in an aura of objectivity helps explain why they so eagerly adopted the idea that the market corresponds to the laws of life, thereby transforming a highly polemical notion in the USSR into a perceived scientific truth. Thus, the historian Leonid Batkin, who readily admitted that he was incompetent in the field of economics, did not hesitate to assert that "entrepreneurial spirit and the market system appear on the natural basis of human nature and in accordance with the contemporary technical and economic level of development, and not in spite of them, like barracks socialism. Creating a new economy is difficult, but it is easier than some people think, because it is a matter less of 'creating' it as simply allowing it to happen."[15] This idea seemed so obvious at the time that it even found ardent supporters among nominal Leninists, as was the case with Len Karpinsky, who declared that "to oppose the market to socialism is to oppose socialism in a nihilistic way to the whole of history, to the fundamental human forms of relations and life in common."[16]

Certainly, the idea that the market is somehow natural, the result of so-called objective economic laws, is not a specifically Soviet belief. But in contrast to the situation in Western capitalist countries, where these notions acquired a certain validity as a result of a long process whereby the economy was "disembedded" from social relations,[17] they were very quickly and almost unanimously adopted during perestroika by Soviet economists, and by liberal intellectuals more broadly,[18] even though these ideas remained highly controversial in Soviet society at large. This was a reflection of liberal intellectuals' peculiar tendency to consider certain political and economic propositions as absolute truths when they seem to directly correspond to the truth of life, without the need of an ideological or doctrinal intermediary—indeed, they deemed such propositions all the truer precisely because they were unmediated by any extraneous intellectual construction. In Shmelev's terms, the scientific validity of the market was based on "common sense" and "life," not on "concepts." The objective character of this scientific truth, moreover, was supported by another form of truth that was said to stem naturally from the human mind and whose validity was deemed superior to any social or political doctrine: the moral truth dictated by conscience.

Indeed, liberal intellectuals often observed that factual truth about the Soviet past and present was by itself insufficient to guide society away from Stalinism. It must be supplemented by morality, as Karpinsky bluntly put it: "But if all this [Stalinist] mythology is torn away, swept from human souls thanks to glasnost, what will these souls be able to lean on, to hold on to? The answer is clear: to the truth and to what is called the inner moral law or conscience, that is, the tacit judgment of each personality by ancestors, contemporaries, descendants. Such a tribunal is already underway on the gigantic scale of the whole country."[19] Karpinsky expressed confidence that the moral law stemming from individual conscience would be able to guide the judgments of each citizen in conformity with both justice and science. But is the voice of conscience always compatible with the conclusions of science? And how does one know that the voice of conscience is indeed the truth rather than a mere opinion? For Karpinsky these questions were not worth asking, because the connection between truth and conscience to him seemed self-evident and did not require justification—a presumption that he believed his readers shared.

In this, he was right. Indeed, his remarks were based on a commonplace, one that the academic Dmitri Likhachev had done much to popularize (as we saw in chapter 1)—namely, that conscience is a source of truth. In a famous article from 1987, Likhachev wrote that "conscience always comes from the depths of the soul, and through it one purifies oneself in one way or another. . . . Conscience cannot be deceptive."[20] Many liberal intellectuals shared this view of conscience as a source of truth that can help to relieve Soviet society of its moral corruption and thereby pave the way for a healthy and democratic collective life. Here the imperative to follow one's conscience implied the rehabilitation of personal opinion, which had long been discredited in Soviet public discourse as a form of "subjectivism." Hence the virulent calls of liberal intellectuals for pluralism of opinion and dialogue and against the monopolization of truth by any individual or specific group. This rehabilitation of opinion, however, was not aimed at celebrating diversity for its own sake; rather, it carried the hope—which Karpinsky expresses in the passage quoted above—that conscience shall guide opinion toward justice once the soul is freed from dogma by factual truth. Moral truth was thus seen as the essential complement of factual truth. This presumption of complementarity, in turn, gave rise to the conflation of these two forms of truth, which were often indistinctly designated by the same word, "truth" (*pravda*), and carried out by the same act, truth telling (*govorit' pravdu*).[21]

The Tyranny of Truth Telling

It is worth evoking here Hannah Arendt's reflections on truth and politics.[22] Factual truth, she argues, is a necessary condition for the existence of the political realm since genuine discussion is impossible without the initial premise that there is an immutable, factual world about and on which we can expound and ultimately act. "Conceptually," she says, "we may call truth what we cannot change; metaphorically, it is the ground on which we stand and the sky that stretches above us."[23] Arendt, for this reason, is deeply concerned about the threat represented by what she calls "organized lying." Totalitarian regimes, in particular, are so effective at spreading lies that they blur the categorical distinction between truth and falsehood. In this way, organized lying "pulls the ground from under our feet and provides no other ground on which to stand."[24] In this desperate situation, the one who persists in telling the truth is really performing a political gesture.

Indeed, truth telling had been the political weapon of choice for Soviet dissidents in the face of the regime's systemic lies. With the adoption of glasnost and the relaxation of censorship, it became possible in the USSR to speak the truth publicly on an increasing number of issues. But for this truth to serve as a basis for transformative action, it first had to overcome the cynicism engendered by decades of lies. For Sakharov and many other reformers, democratic change necessarily required the restoration of people's confidence in the truthfulness of public discourse: "Everyone must have a moral and material stake in the success of perestroika!" he insisted. "The people must be able to believe that they are being told the truth, and for that to happen, they must be told only the truth and the whole truth, and always act accordingly."[25] The liberal intelligentsia's truth telling, in this context, was part of a larger effort to restore the distinction between truth and falsity and ultimately to create the basic conditions for a healthy political life.

Despite the importance of preserving factual truth, truth and politics, according to Arendt, do not fit well together. When transposed directly into the political domain, truth is apolitical, potentially even antipolitical.[26] For truth, unlike opinion, does not aim at persuasion and does not sustain debate. Insofar as it draws its source of validity from outside the political domain, it is "as independent of the wishes and desires of the citizens as is the will of the worst tyrant."[27] Truth, in this sense, has "a despotic character" that manifests in the "frequently tyrannical tendencies" of "professional truthtellers."[28]

It was not rare in the era of perestroika for truth telling to assume somewhat of a despotic character. Writing in 1987, Daniil Granin, who otherwise approved of the impulse to live according to the truth, in the debates in the Soviet press from this period saw that "possessed fanatics of truth" can be cruel in their "demand for absolute truth."[29] Liberal intellectuals were not immune to this phenomenon. Their elevation of scientific and moral truth to the status of a precondition for public discourse, although motivated by the desire to restore the fundamental distinction between truth and falsehood, often led them to make uncompromising judgments about complex social realities and to disqualify from the outset the positions of their opponents as lies unworthy of public debate. In other words, liberal intellectuals encouraged debate and discussion—but only up to a point. They were quite willing to engage a range of opinions about the best ways to achieve perestroika, but they were inclined to dismiss as fundamentally unacceptable any positions that differed from their own in terms of *values*, or, to use the word of the time, *principles*. The arguments of communists and nationalists were the object of a particularly vigorous denunciation, as they were seen not just as erroneous—disagreement being the hallmark of any debate—but as contrary to the requirements of truth and thus unworthy of public expression. The extension of intellectual pluralism was thus accompanied by a quest for the *purification of social conscience* guided by factual truth and the moral law dictated by personal conscience. This phenomenon was a particularly striking feature of debates about Stalinism, a topic of burning relevance at the time, because, as Afanasyev said, "We are talking about the past, but what is being decided is the future of socialism."[30]

Never Compromise on Principles: The Andreeva Case

Perestroika's liberal turn, as initiated by Gorbachev in 1987, was strongly resisted in intellectual circles, in the bureaucratic apparatus, and among the general population, where many denounced what they saw as an excessive criticism of the past. The most famous public defense of conservative communist principles was a letter published in March 1988 in the newspaper *Sovetskaia Rossiia* by a previously unknown Leningrad chemistry professor by the name of Nina Andreeva. Thanks to the support of Politburo members hostile to Gorbachev's new strategy for perestroika, the letter was immediately picked up by local newspapers throughout the country. Knowing that such letters periodically serve as harbingers of radical political change, those who experienced the overthrow of Khrushchev in 1964 expected that Gorbachev would soon suffer a similar fate.

The effect was indeed explosive. In essence, Andreeva's letter constituted a defense of the communist principles of the Brezhnev era against the values emerging in the context of glasnost. Titled "I Cannot Give Up My Principles," it expressed a typical communist concern about excessive criticism (*razoblachenie*) of Soviet society and relayed the fear that it would sow confusion and nihilism in the minds of youth.[31] The letter is particularly harsh on those whom Andreeva calls "left-liberal socialists" or "neoliberals," who claim to express a "humanism that is very true and 'clean' from class incrustations," and who reject proletarian collectivism in the name of "the intrinsic worth of the individual."[32] Claiming to have access to a "complete historical truth," they "replace the socio-political criteria of the development of society with the scholasticism of ethical categories."[33] And so doing, they in fact falsify the history of socialism: "They try to persuade us that the only things about our country's past that are real are the errors and crimes, thus hiding the great achievements" of Soviet society.[34] She concludes, "Under the aegis of a moral and spiritual 'cleansing' [the liberals] are eroding the boundaries and criteria of scientific ideology, manipulating openness and propagating an extra-socialist pluralism, which objectively impedes a restructuring of social consciousness."[35]

After more than three weeks of suspense during which almost no one dared to reply to Andreeva, assuming that her letter was a harbinger of some new wave of state repression, an official denial finally appeared in *Pravda*.[36] Written in part by Aleksandr Yakovlev—Gorbachev's right-hand man and a figure close to the liberal intelligentsia—it clearly delineated the limits of glasnost, in this case the threshold between "real discussion" and an unproductive desire "to turn democratization and glasnost . . . against perestroika."[37] Despite Andreeva's stated support for perestroika—the title of her letter is taken from a speech by Gorbachev—the *Pravda* rebuttal argued that the chemistry professor had overstepped the acceptable boundaries of public debate by giving voice to positions that are "entirely incompatible and opposed" to the "fundamental directions of perestroika." This is because they deviated from the "path dictated by life and necessary for perestroika," based on the "Leninist principles" of democracy, social justice, financial autonomy, and respect for honor, life, and personal dignity. Regarding the interpretation of the past, the article accused Andreeva of trying to "separate socialism from morality" and for failing to contribute to the effort to "restore the Truth." Finally, it also reproached her for creating what it described as an "artificial division" among the Soviet people "at the very moment when unity of creative efforts—despite all the nuances of opinion—is more necessary than ever."

Having denounced Andreeva, Yakovlev and his coauthors then took the opportunity to reaffirm the core principles of perestroika and extend congratulations to those members of the intelligentsia who supported them: "Our intelligentsia has done much to prepare the social conscience necessary for an understanding of the need for certain profound, cardinal changes. It has committed itself to perestroika. It arms itself with the best traditions forged by our predecessors, invokes conscience, morality, honesty, defends humanistic principles and socialist standards of life."[38] The argument presented in the *Pravda* article can be summarized as follows: the boundaries of "constructive" discussion within the context of glasnost are dictated by the prevailing party line, and Andreeva's departure from it is condemned. The historian Timur Atnashev characterizes this forceful rejection of Andreeva's position as an unexpected resurgence of traditional Soviet rules governing public discourse, now for the sake of glasnost: "At the peak of perestroika, the freedom of speech triumph manifested itself through the sudden enforcement of the party unity and hierarchy norms, which at that time were aimed against more conservative defenders of 'socialist achievements.'"[39] In taking this stance, Gorbachev sent a clear signal that any principles that contradict the official understanding of perestroika were not only wrong but unworthy of public debate.

In the wake of these events, Andreeva was duly punished for her affront to the regime's official message: she and her husband lost their jobs at the institute where they taught. In many ways, this was a typical reaction from a party that claimed to want to enlighten society for its own good. Even more disturbing, however, was the response of liberal intellectuals to Andreeva's positions. Having been reassured by the *Pravda* article, liberals also forcefully stated that this challenge to perestroika's values went beyond the acceptable framework of glasnost, and, in so doing, they defended the new principles promoted by the party.

As if in a hall of mirrors, the liberals treated any criticism of their values in much the same way as Andreeva had reacted to the assault on an earlier orthodoxy—as an unacceptable attack on the only true "principles." This similarity of attitude, despite the two camps' ideological opposition, can be seen in a famous article by the literary critic Yuri Karyakin.[40] Inspired by the Andreeva case, Karyakin indicted all those who wanted to prevent the publication of critical works under the pretext that they denigrated reality. Archetypical in this regard is the Stalinist apparatchik Andrei Zhdanov, who was responsible for the persecution of several great artists, including the poet Anna Akhmatova and the writer Mikhail Zoshchenko.

Karyakin's argument consisted in turning the accusation of denigration against those who professed it. It was the Stalinists, he asserted, who were denigrating socialism and culture, while their victims expressed the truth, which by definition could not be a denigration: "Denigration is a lie. Truth cannot be denigration. It can only be a purification."[41] For Karyakin, the debate against Andreeva and Zhdanov was not a matter of opinion but rather a binary struggle between Stalinism, based on "fear of the people, fear of truth and conscience," and the principles dictated by conscience and embodied by perestroika. He concluded: "But without such pure, noble, elevated values, without the values of the new way of thinking, it will simply be impossible for us to survive. As for the hateful and vile, nasty, envious, and vindictive values of Zhdanovism-Stalinism, they are literally suicidal today."[42] It is hard to imagine what kind of discussion such a dichotomy would enable in the context of glasnost.

A view widely held by liberals during this period was that Andreeva's principles were not in fact worthy of that name—the implied meaning being that they were not a reflection of her true conscience but merely a regurgitation of party dogmas. And dogmas, the argument went, were not worthy of inclusion in the grand intellectual debate over the course of reforms since they ultimately call into question the very foundations of perestroika, as Len Karpinsky stated in 1988:

> Any point of view, of course, can be expressed. . . . The diversity of views and proposals is precisely one of the achievements of the renewal of our society. . . . The problem lies elsewhere: the article [by Andreeva] in *Sovetskaia Rossiia*, pretentious and intolerant in spirit and language, reflected the position of dogmatic thought as a whole and thus had a general and programmatic character that served as a kind of platform for the gathering of people with conservative orientations. . . . The question of whether or not perestroika should take place is no longer a matter of discussion—the people said yes! Perestroika has no alternative; it cannot be reversed. And it is precisely this that was attacked.

Nina Andreeva's "letter" did not simply criticize perestroika, it questioned the new image of socialism to which we aspire and called for a return to Stalinism.[43]

However, in spite of Karpinsky's claims to the contrary, this new vision of socialism based on representative democracy and the market was by no means an object of unanimous enthusiasm. It should also be noted that as Karpinsky was writing these lines, no election had yet taken place that would allow one to assert with such assurance that perestroika had the support of the majority of the population.

Everything That Is Not White Is Black: The Rejection of Half-Truths

A few months later, in an article published in the 1988 collection *Inogo ne dano*, Yuri Afanasyev also denounced Andreeva's letter, which he described as "a true political manifesto against perestroika, based on both the falsification and the dogmatization of history."[44] The opponents of perestroika, he added, had another, less "crude" and more "slender" weapon: the practice of half-truth (*polupravda*). The year before, Dmitri Likhachev had claimed that "we have lost the habit of telling the truth—the whole truth—but half-truth is the worst form of lying: in the half-truth, the lie takes on the appearance of truth, it hides under the cover of a partial truth."[45]

The idea that half-truths are the worst form of lie became a commonplace in the discourse of the liberal intelligentsia. According to this logic, the closer a lie comes to the truth, the more condemnable it is because it resembles the truth without actually corresponding to it. This conclusion followed from the assumption that the political domain, like the moral domain, constitutes a positive and coherent entity about which it is possible to hold a properly truthful discourse, as the literary critic Igor Vinogradov clearly stated in his own contribution to *Inogo ne dano*: "Truth is as indivisible and integral as reality itself. And a 'partial' or 'gradual' truth about this reality is at best only a half-truth, a quarter or a tenth of a truth—that is, the truth united with a lie. Now, excuse me, but the truth *seasoned with a lie* is anything but the truth."[46] Like moral truth, the truth about society cannot be boiled down to a certain proportion of truth and falsehood. Either it is whole, and therefore true, or it is partial, and therefore false. In Likhachev's words, the expression of truth consists in "distinguishing black from white."[47] Again, this assumption was deeply rooted in Soviet intellectual history. One is reminded, for instance, of a 1966 poem from the gulag survivor Anatoly Zhigulin, whose memoir of life in the camps stirred much debate when it was published in 1988. The poem is titled "Truth" (*Pravda*):

> Who thought that truth
> Could be cut in pieces
> And in the name of truth
> Create non-truth?
>
> It is a living body
> Not a sweet cake
> From which one could cut and take
> A fitting piece
>
> Only the full truth
> Is alive and *prava* [true/right]
> An incomplete truth
> Is only empty words[48]

In the political sphere, however, it is often difficult, if not impossible, to establish an unequivocal truth. The denunciation by many Soviet liberals of any "half-truth" testifies to their categorical refusal to compromise with their own conception of truth, however controversial it may be.

In the article quoted earlier, Afanasyev condemned two types of half-truths. The first relates to omission, which Afanasyev illustrates by way of some articles published a short time previously that he says give a more accurate picture of the past while continuing to conceal some important facts, thereby painting a "false picture."[49] Such is the case, he claims, in works on historical figures like Lev Trotsky, Grigory Zinoviev, and Lev Kamenev, who by the 1980s were acknowledged to have played leading roles in the October Revolution and Civil War but whose achievements were downplayed and who were still portrayed as enemies of the people. The second type of half-truth, according to Afanasyev, consists in creating "a kind of hybrid image" of social consciousness by trying to balance its positive and negative aspects. The paradigmatic case here is the different interpretations of the Stalinist era: "On the one hand, repression and mass crimes, on the other hand, daily joy and [the breaking of] records."[50] However, according to Afanasyev, this kind of hybridity is necessarily sterile:

> The almost arithmetical nature of the "on the one hand, on the other hand" formula will obviously never contribute to a synthetic apprehension of the past. Much more is needed to achieve this. Overcoming the past means understanding it, making it one's own, letting it

pass through oneself, engaging in a dialogue of equals with all our ancestors without exception, whether they are "good" or "bad." This means accomplishing a kind of collective moral cleansing. Of course, we will not be able to move forward if, in place of creeping, gradual, and secret attempts—in the Brezhnevian manner—to rehabilitate Stalin, and thereby reanimate Stalinism, we instead try, as some people have, to place sole responsibility for the misfortune that has befallen our people on Stalin alone.[51]

For Afanasyev, "balanced" judgments about the Stalinist era serve no other purpose than to save Stalinism by sacrificing Stalin. It is of course worth noting that the reasons that Afanasyev gives in this passage for condemning this approach illustrate the assumed complementarity between scientific truth and moral truth. In fact, Afanasyev condemns this approach above all for epistemological reasons—namely, the impossibility of synthesizing its positive and negative aspects into a coherent totality. But how to achieve the assimilation of contradictory facts, where the "good" and the "bad" are opposed? For Afanasyev, the apprehension of the totality is guaranteed by the intervention of conscience. He does not say how this can be achieved, but his reference to a "moral purification" suggests that the synthesis is based not on the reconciliation of opposing facts and judgments but on the eradication of elements that contaminate the understanding of the past.

Such criticism of half-truths was common among liberal intellectuals at the time, especially in discussions of the role of Stalin, a very sensitive subject on which the Soviet population often made ambiguous judgments.[52] For Yuri Burtin, as for Afanasyev, this hybrid image of Stalin was the result of a long-running attempt at moral rehabilitation that began under Brezhnev. Rather than seeking to completely reverse the achievements of de-Stalinization, this rehabilitation consisted, as Burtin put it, "in a combination of half-truths and omissions. The half-truths concerned Stalin's role in the Great Patriotic War, the only time in his biography when he could appear to be morally successful in the eyes of society. The omission concerned everything else."[53] Unlike Afanasyev, Burtin distinguished between omissions and half-truths, which he associated exclusively with the creation of a hybrid image. For him, half-truths appeared in the search for a "balance" between positive and negative aspects.

Burtin liked to mock the kind of writing to which this measured approach gave rise: "For a novel, play, or story, a happy ending (or at least indication of the possibility of such an ending); a finely calibrated 'balance' between light and shadow; little words like 'sometimes,' 'here and there,' etc., when we are talking about massive and generalized phenomena; the search for quotations from authority figures that can be used as a cover if necessary; other manifestations of fearful circumspection toward ideological stereotypes and other concessions to the inner reviewer, to the half-truth, to the lie."[54]

In a documentary presented the following year, Burtin referred to the need to stop telling half-truths and express oneself with sincerity and honesty as the "moral imperative of the moment."[55] For him, this meant going beyond partial criticism in order to condemn the whole system according to a true and objective judgment.[56]

In the debates around glasnost, liberals were often accused by their opponents of making one-sided judgments about the past and present. In her famous letter, Nina Andreeva protested against the Soviet press's "monochromatic colouring" of contradictory historical events.[57] However, Andreeva did not defend a more "balanced" approach. She also thought it essential to establish an "objective and unambiguous" assessment:

> Needless to say, it will be unambiguous not in the sense of being one-sided, of whitewashing or eclectically summing up contradictory phenomena, of an assessment that makes it possible, with qualifications, to create any kind of subjectivism, to "forgive or not forgive," to "discard or keep" certain elements of history. An unambiguous assessment means above all a historically concrete, non-opportunistic assessment that manifests—in term of historical result!—the dialectics of the conformity of a given individual's activity according to the basic laws of social development. . . . If we are to follow the Marxist-Leninist methodology of historical research, then we must first of all, in M. S. Gorbachev's words, vividly show how millions of people lived, how they worked and what they believed in, and how their victories and setbacks, discoveries and mistakes, their radiant and their tragic aspects, their revolutionary enthusiasm and their violations of socialist legality, and sometimes even their crimes, were combined.[58]

If the communist Andreeva shared with liberals like Afanasyev and Burtin a desire for absolute truth that made her reject "eclectic" judgments, she conceived this truth in a very different way: for Andreeva, the truth must be based on the Marxist-Leninist method, while for liberals, it must be based on the objective observation of life and on personal conscience. Between the "principles" espoused by the two sides, what was at stake was above all a conflict of values, and yet it was not recognized as such: each side was absolutely convinced that it was telling the truth and that its opponents, being unable to ignore this truth, not only were mistaken but were in fact lying.

For each of the parties, truth telling, then, aimed not to persuade or to take into account the opposing position in order to get closer to the truth but to achieve its categorical denial, with the ultimate aim of purifying social consciousness. Everyone recognized the importance of discussion, but they refused to include in it those who, in any case, did not say what they thought. Hence the constant suspicion that one's opponents were in the final analysis hypocrites.

The collection *Inogo ne dano*, edited by Yuri Afanasyev, was prepared in a record four months in the spring of 1988 and published just in time for the Nineteenth Party Congress. In a review of the collection, one critic emphasized the diversity of the texts gathered there: thirty-four authors covering a wide variety of subjects.[59] This critic pointed out, however, that this diversity had a limit: all the authors belonged to the same political camp. For the sake of objectivity, he asks, should not Nina Andreeva or an author from the conservative nationalist journal *Molodaia gvardiia* have been included?[60] Nevertheless, he concludes that it is perfectly legitimate for a polemical collection to choose to express a clear and univocal political position. That said, the reasons Afanasyev gives in his preface to the collection to justify the selection of texts are very revealing of his conception of public debate:

> We have invited to the debate, for understandable reasons, those who *really* consider the politics of perestroika a great historical opportunity that we are obliged to seize. Not included in this book, in the first place, are the opponents of perestroika. We would have liked to get their participation in the collection, but we were convinced in advance that they would not respond, that they would refuse to expose their ideas frankly. Secondly, this book does not reflect the opinions of the many intellectuals for whom perestroika is a welcome thaw, but one that is destined to be short-lived and will inevitably be followed by new cold spells. In other words, this book does not collect negative, frankly retrograde or outright skeptical views on the changes taking place in our country.[61]

As we can see, from the very outset, two types of positions were excluded from the debate: the hypocrites and the skeptics. The second category refers to those who, in keeping with the legacy of Soviet dissidence, are deeply suspicious of any policy established by the party, however virtuous its principles. An example of such a skeptical stance appeared in the spring of 1987 in the weekly *Moskovskie novosti*, which published an open letter signed by ten dissident émigrés, including Aleksandr Zinoviev and Vladimir Bukovsky, demanding that Gorbachev provide concrete evidence of his commitments.

The editorial staff of the newspaper—one of the flagships of the liberal intelligentsia—published a reply depicting these skeptics as completely out of touch with Soviet reality.[62] Among the Soviet public, however, these skeptics were much less influential than all those whom Afanasyev included in the first category, the "opponents of perestroika." These were communists like Nina Andreeva and conservative nationalists like Yuri Bondarev, Valentin Rasputin, and Vasily Belov (mentioned in chapter 1). However, if there was a public debate in the USSR at that time, it was precisely between the conservative nationalists and the liberals. In the context of these heated debates, it is significant that Afanasyev dismissed the positions of his main opponents not only because he disapproved of them but because he assumed that they were basically hypocrites. This was a typical attitude of the time. While nationalists and communists often suggested that liberals were merely following orders from the CIA or some Judeo-Masonic conspiracy, liberals tended to see their opponents as pawns manipulated by members of the *nomenklatura* who wished to preserve their selfish privileges. In both cases, the polemic was structured around a moral principle that targeted not opponents' ideas but rather the secret forces they were said to represent. The least one could say was that this attitude was not conducive to discussion or the formation of the compromises necessary for the practice of democracy.

Hopes for Self-Censorship

In general, liberal intellectuals remained evasive regarding the precise method for achieving the purification of social consciousness—how to abolish, or at least marginalize, falsehood in the public sphere. One thing was clear: by virtue of their reverence for the expression of personal conscience, they ruled out any recourse to state censorship from the outset. It seems that this hope for moral purification rested largely on the moral authority of truth, with its holder thereby exercising a form of power that sociologist Gil Eyal, drawing on a notion by Michel Foucault, identifies among Czechoslovak intellectuals as "pastoral power":[63] moral exemplarity, truthful speech, and the exposure of lies would shame the hypocrites and, over time, prompt them toward self-censorship. At least that was the hope formulated by Dmitri Likhachev:

> Now [social consciousness] has changed and it favors honest people, which means that bad people are forced to hide, to mask themselves, to conceal their discontent, their vices and their bad deeds. They now have to pretend to be good, benevolent, well-behaved, etc. Let them pretend! Let them pretend! In time they will be replaced by good

people, for I am convinced that the change in social consciousness brings about a change in the character of people. . . . In a healthy and open society, in accordance with our current demands for transparency [glasnost] and social judgment, it will be much more difficult to deceive society, to make arbitrary decisions, to write anonymous letters of denunciation.[64]

Similarly, Yuri Karyakin expressed the hope that his polemical articles would contribute to a broad movement of self-censorship on the part of all those who cast aspersions on their fellow man.[65] Karpinsky, too, argued that censorship should not be handled by the state but should be left, rather, to the moral conscience of each individual, which dictates the limits of what is acceptable to say in public:

> Glasnost does not fall under administrative control except in cases specified by law, and that is why the role of moral regulators is all the more important. In the end, it is precisely the moral imperative that has the supreme power within freedom. Thus, each of us must act in the sphere of glasnost according to the famous dictum "measure twice, cut once."[66]

We should bear in mind here that this idea was not unanimous among liberal intellectuals. Consider the position, for our purposes quite heterodox, of Leonid Batkin. Stressing the potential danger of judging the legitimacy of public discourse according to a criterion of truth, he concluded that "it is better for everyone to be able to lie and for everyone to be able to denounce lies."[67]

Those who hoped that social consciousness would be purified through the dissemination of truth and the struggle against falsehood would be bitterly disappointed in the following years, as the opening of the political scene allowed for the enunciation of an even wider range of contradictory ideas. The intransigence of liberals toward this sort of pluralism of opinion in the debates around glasnost foreshadowed their ambiguous relationship to political pluralism more broadly.

Chapter 4

A Reluctant Opposition (1989)

> It is now readily acknowledged that each of our ills and misfortunes, which are growing week by week, take their root in the "question of power." That is to say, how *in practice* to carry out the *selection of leaders* at all levels, *who* will make the decisions and, consequently, *what* those decisions will be. This is the most important problem, if not the only one.
>
> —Leonid Batkin, "Ostanetsia li vlast' u partii?," August 1989

Political pluralism is based on the institutionalization of conflict. But in a one-party state like the USSR, where ritual declarations of unanimity were a perennial feature of public life after the banning of factions in the early 1920s, it was by no means obvious that political conflict would be treated as a legitimate form of popular expression. In such a context, it was not easy to accept the fact that the relaxation of censorship, rather than leading to the unfettered expression of an emancipated, unified popular will, had instead unleashed an open confrontation between various competing visions of Soviet society.

How, then, should be considered the often-acrimonious conflicts that engulfed the USSR at a time when it seemed most in need of unity? For Soviet liberals, typically, political conflict did not result from a confrontation between groups with divergent interests, nor was the solution to such conflict to be found in institutional mediation; it was, rather, a binary moral struggle between those who defended "universal values," on the one hand, and those who selfishly defended their privileges or who were too morally corrupt to break free of Stalinist dogma, on the other. In the context of the debates unleashed by glasnost between 1987 and 1989—the subject of the previous chapters—we saw that this binary struggle took the form of a dichotomy between the "defenders" and "opponents" of perestroika. In concrete terms, this meant that all those, like Nina Andreeva, who expressed a clearly divergent opinion about the direction of perestroika were excluded from public debate on the pretext that they were contaminating the discourse with their lies. Simply put, anyone who did not support Gorbachev and his program was against perestroika. The political strategy of the liberals was therefore to support Gorbachev and defend him from serious criticism while also seeking to influence him, either by conferring advice or by criticizing certain elements of his program.

Of course, this strategy was also conditioned by the Soviet political system, characterized as it was by the Communist Party's monopoly on power. Whatever disagreements Soviet liberals might have had with the reformist leader, the latter nonetheless appeared to most of them to be the only political force capable of achieving the desired reforms. This is precisely what changed in 1989, when Gorbachev unwittingly introduced de facto political pluralism by allowing competitive elections for a new parliament.[1] Henceforth, the binary opposition between the "defenders" and "opponents" of perestroika was steadily eroded by the fact that elected deputies could, for the first time in decades, defend programs that differed from those championed by the party. It was now possible to envisage several variants of perestroika, among which Gorbachev's was not necessarily considered the best. In this respect, 1989 is the pivotal year of perestroika—and not only because the Communist Bloc in eastern Europe collapsed, severely undermining the hope for socialist reform but also because that year marked the emergence in Soviet Russia of the proponents of radical reform, who thereby broke Gorbachev's monopoly on perestroika. By the same token, the *question of power* moved to the very heart of the debate. No longer was it merely a question of being either for or against perestroika; at issue was *who* should lead perestroika, and just as importantly, *how*.

Soviet liberals played a leading role in the emergence of these radical forces and the resulting pluralization of the political scene. But it is important to note that they were not alone. Liberal reformers relied to a large extent on the informal organizations that had multiplied since 1987 and that had done the lion's share of the work to mobilize popular opinion, as well as on the miners who launched a vast wave of strikes in the country's coal regions in the summer of 1989. But it was the elite liberal intellectuals in Moscow who emerged as the symbols of the radical reformers. Through organizations like the Interregional Group of Deputies, these intellectuals shaped a new political program and a new strategy for making their claims heard. The founders of the Moscow Tribune—the thinkers who most concern us here—were among the main actors steering this political movement.

Thus, 1989 was also the year when a large part of the liberal intelligentsia assumed a more overtly oppositional stance vis-à-vis Gorbachev, overtaking him from his "left," to use the parlance of the time. In the specific context of perestroika, the left was represented by the reformists and the right by the conservatives, which had the curious effect of inverting the standard categories of the Western political spectrum, placing the proponents of a market economy on the left and the communists on the right. But what did "opposition" mean to liberal intellectuals? This concept is so overused today that it can sometimes be difficult to excavate its various layers of historical meaning. It is usually taken for granted that the shift to an oppositional stance reflects a transition from a partial or nuanced critique to a more fundamental and coherent—and therefore contentious—denunciation of one's ideological opponents as soon as circumstances allowed. And indeed, the Soviet liberal intelligentsia did take advantage of the new political opening engendered by the 1989 elections to express in more forthright terms its rejection of the communist system, and it eventually also began to distance itself from Gorbachev.

However, this idea of an increasingly radical expression of an ingrained opposition deserves to be qualified because it reinforces a certain confusion about the nature and scope of the opposition in question. It is useful, in fact, to ask a rather straightforward but no less important question: *At what or whom was this opposition directed?* From this point of view, 1989 saw the liberal intelligentsia embark on a highly paradoxical political evolution: despite an increasingly resolute rejection of the communist system and its ideological underpinnings, the majority of Soviet liberals refused to openly oppose Gorbachev and instead pursued a strategy of cooperation aimed at consolidating his power against "conservative" forces. The intransigence of the liberals toward the nationalists and conservative communists contrasted with their often-desperate search for collaborators among the reformers in the Soviet government, which led them to accept many compromises. Opposition to the communist system, in short, did not necessarily lead to opposition to Soviet power as such. While the idea of distancing oneself from Gorbachev did make considerable headway among Soviet liberals that year, we will see in this chapter that it was a stumbling, tentative process that constantly came up against the imperative of consolidating progressive forces in a binary moral struggle against the "opponents" of reform. The turbulent events of 1989 shook the radical deputies from the liberal intelligentsia and pushed them to adopt an oppositional strategy vis-à-vis the Soviet government—a stance they had in fact been reluctant to take up to that point.

This chapter examines this paradoxical phenomenon from the point of view of the Moscow liberal intelligentsia as it debated its political strategy toward the Soviet regime in the course of 1989, taking the intellectual and political trajectory of Andrei Sakharov as its main thread. The choice to focus on the famous physicist is a rather obvious one, for two reasons. First, Sakharov was indisputably the figurehead of the liberal intelligentsia in that pivotal year, as well as the main architect of its radicalization. Second, the fact that a dissident like him, who had long opposed the Soviet regime and who could not be suspected of secretly harboring any sympathies for the communist system, had resisted for so long the idea of forming an opposition to Gorbachev demonstrates that this reluctance cannot be simply attributed to softness of mind or self-serving compromises with the establishment. The liberal intelligentsia during this period was characterized by a marked aversion to opposition as such, which in itself was very revealing of the presumptions on which their political thinking rested—namely, a moral perspective that put the dismantling of an artificial system and the expression of personal conscience far ahead of the question of how to institutionalize democratic power. As this chapter aims to show, a careful analysis of the events of 1989 highlights the reactive, hesitant, and precarious character of the radicalization that led Sakharov and several other liberal deputies to gradually move away from their initial support for the consolidation of the reforming power to a strategy of outright opposition. We will see that this gradual radicalization reflected the liberals' perennial resistance to the idea of an opposition to Soviet power, in spite of the regime's obstinate refusal to collaborate with its allies and in spite of the growing discontent of the population—a citizenry that, to the great astonishment of the liberals, proved to be politically active.

Sakharov and the Question of Power

From the authorization of his return to Moscow in December 1986, after seven years under house arrest in the closed city of Gorky,[2] Andrei Sakharov threw himself body and soul into the political effervescence of perestroika. In this way he was to resume his long-running fight for two great political causes, the first of which was the defense of human rights. During perestroika, he was particularly concerned with defending the rights of political prisoners as well as the Crimean Tatars and the Armenians of Nagorno-Karabakh. He also advocated for a reform of the Criminal Code, to put an end to the arbitrary manipulation of the law. The second cause assumed nothing short of a global scale: the struggle for the survival of humanity through a commitment to the ecological cause, to nuclear disarmament, and, more broadly, to a new international policy based on trust and cooperation.

Each of these claims was presented in the first of his political articles published during perestroika, which appeared in the 1988 collection *Inogo ne dano*, compiled under the direction of his friend Yuri Afanasyev.[3] Sakharov's contribution stood out for its brevity, its clarity, and its impressive number of concrete claims. Yet, while he extensively addresses fundamental issues like human rights and human survival, he says very little about power. As for the organization of the political system, he expresses a preference for democracy, but without going into much detail.

To understand his views on this issue, we must examine two central concepts in his political thought, those of "open society" and "pluralism." Sakharov used these two concepts long before perestroika. Already in 1980, for example, he was describing his "ideal" society as an "open and pluralist" one.[4] However, a closer look at these two concepts shows that the question of power occupied but a secondary place in Sakharov's thinking during this period, especially when compared to the pride of place he gave to the defense of individual rights and the destiny of humanity.

Sakharov's notion of an "open society" should not be confused with the classical definition given by the philosopher Karl Popper.[5] In both cases, certainly, the open society is presented as the opposite of the Soviet model, which is said to be totalitarian and closed; and yet the particular meaning of this opening is not the same. For Popper, this implies democratic procedures. For Sakharov, by contrast, its implications are more modest—namely, the free circulation of ideas and persons. Sakharov, who does not mention Popper in his writings, probably adapted the "open society" concept from the term "open world," which he borrowed from thinkers like Albert Einstein, Bertrand Russell, Niels Bohr, and René Cassin.[6] These scholars, Sakharov wrote in 1975, "called for the defense of human rights throughout the world, for national altruism and for the realization of an 'open world.'"[7] This last concept, Sakharov pointed out, was most explicit in the thought of Niels Bohr, who "stressed that no one should stand in the way of the exchange of information and the free movement of people."[8] For Sakharov, this parallel between the "open world" and the "open society" is quite natural since he considered the general state of the world to be closely related to that of each individual society.

And yet, for all his emphasis on the need for "openness," Sakharov had little to say about power. In his contribution to *Inogo ne dano*, he added an element to the definition of the open society—namely, a certain form of social control: "Perestroika is to allow for the 'openness of society' as one of the conditions for the country's moral and economic health, international trust, and security. The notion of openness includes the control of society over the making of key decisions (the mistake of the invasion of Afghanistan must not be repeated), freedom of belief, freedom of consultation and dissemination of information, freedom of choice of country of residence and place of residence within the country."⁹ However, this idea of social control remained vague. First of all, Sakharov did not specify its political modalities. Second, he suggested that it would only apply to "key decisions." One was left to wonder whether, in an open society, the population would intervene in political decision-making only when it came to questions of war and peace or also when individual liberties were violated.

But then how should ordinary political decisions be made? On this point, Sakharov's views reflected a long-standing elitism, which his biographer Jay Bergman described as "a fundamental aspect of his political thinking."¹⁰ While Sakharov always favored democratization—by which he meant the participation of the people in political life—he was nevertheless reluctant to embrace democracy. In his essays of the 1960s and 1970s, for example, he warned of the dangers of introducing this regime to the USSR, claiming that the people could succumb to the lure of "demagogues" and "iron-fisted supporters," thus tipping society into anarchy or a new tyranny.¹¹ And even on those occasions when he mounted an explicit defense of democracy, as was the case during his debate against Solzhenitsyn in 1973, the example he normally gave was the reforms of Tsar Alexander II in the nineteenth century: in other words, progressive reforms imposed in an authoritarian way.¹²

Sakharov was in fact convinced that political decisions must be guided by reason. It thus seemed to him essential that the ruler be advised by experts. Indeed, this idea appears several times in his political writings, including in his electoral program of 1989.¹³ As for "social control" on the part of the population, Sakharov associated this with elections and above all with glasnost, which he rightly defined as a measure that "promotes social control of legality and justice and the coherence of the measures adopted."¹⁴ The open society championed by Sakharov, in short, did not necessarily imply democracy but rather indicated a more or less institutionalized form of social control and, above all, the free circulation of ideas and people.

We must also distinguish the concept of "pluralism," on which Sakharov regularly insisted, from the meaning commonly given to it in Western political theory. The liberal theorist Isaiah Berlin, for example, argued that individual freedom is guaranteed by pluralism—that is, by the expression of a diversity of interests, beliefs, and ways of life.¹⁵ For Sakharov, however, pluralism primarily meant challenging the Marxist-Leninist pretense of defining the one and only valid socioeconomic model, which he denounced as "ideological monism."¹⁶ Sakharov defended a binary vision of world politics in which the two large socioeconomic models of the Cold War could coexist peacefully, eventually converging in what he referred to as "the convergence," a concept popular in the late 1950s and 1960s symbolizing a gradual but inevitable rapprochement.[17] The pluralism advocated by Sakharov had nothing to do with the institutional recognition of a diversity of particular interests and worldviews: not only is the plurality that he recognized summarized in the socialist-capitalist duality but the ultimate goal of this dual pluralism is *to be overcome* in the convergence according to a more fundamental monism, the one embodying universal values, which must prevail over all other particular values or interests.

Sakharov expressed this clearly in an article published in January 1989, titled, tellingly, "Pluralism Is Convergence": "Convergence is closely related to economic, cultural, political, and ideological pluralism. If we recognize that this pluralism is necessary and possible, we recognize by the same token the necessity and possibility of convergence. Convergence implies the refusal of capitalist or socialist dogmatism in the economic and political spheres. The idea of convergence is based on the foundations of a new way of thinking, the principle of which is the priority of the objective of the survival of humanity over all state, national, class, ideological, departmental, group, or personal interests."[18]

In the light of this apologia for the supreme interests of humanity, Sakharov's condemnation of the "ideological monism" of Marxism-Leninism takes on a new color. In his eyes, the official Soviet doctrine had erred by committing to a narrow particularism—one that ignores the achievements of capitalism—and not by its imperial universalism. That is why Sakharov's preferred solution is not the recognition of an irreducible plurality but rather its replacement by a superior universalism that would rest not on an "ideological," and therefore doctrinal, foundation but on universal values. As we have seen, this was a conviction common to many Soviet liberals, who championed what they saw as universally valid principles that any sincere and sane person could reach through the exercise of reason and conscience. The pluralism that Sakharov defended, in short, was based on and realized through a moral monism.

What were the concrete implications, for political reform, of the perceived global convergence of Socialism and capitalism? In the passage quoted above, we see that Sakharov distinguishes the political aspect of pluralism from its economic, cultural, and ideological aspects; it is clear that he does not give equal weight to each of these. Prior to the 1989 election campaign, he tended to emphasize the economic dimension in his writings, to the point of sometimes overshadowing other aspects. Thus, in an article published the previous year, Sakharov treats the "basis of the pluralist development of society" in strictly economic terms. Similarly, his electoral program began with the demand for "pluralistic competition," and yet political pluralism was conspicuously absent.[19] What are we to make of this silence, given that Sakharov had spoken in favor of the introduction of a multiparty system in the past and had reiterated his preference for this system in an interview at the end of 1988?[20] It seems likely that this was a strategic choice. From the time he returned from exile until the 1989 election campaign, Sakharov chose not to call for political pluralism because he did not want to challenge Gorbachev's rule. In his memoirs, written in the summer of 1989, he underlined the consistency of his position in this respect since the beginning of perestroika:

> I thought (and I still think) that there is no other choice than Gorbachev as the leader of the country in this important period of its history. It is precisely Gorbachev who is behind many of the decisions that have completely changed the situation in the country and in the psychology of the people in the last four years. Having said that, I do not idealize the personality of Mr. Gorbachev at all. I don't think he does everything that is necessary. . . . I think it is very dangerous to concentrate unlimited power in the hands of one person. But this does not prevent the fact that there is no other choice than Gorbachev.[21]

There is another reason why he chose not to emphasize political pluralism at this time: the question of power simply did not seem to him to be a priority in relation to the issues he really cared about—namely, the defense of human rights and the survival of humanity. But the main effect of Sakharov's radicalization during 1989 was to change his views on the relative priority of the question of power, as events led him to conclude that it was impossible to achieve his primary goals without first reforming the political system. From the summer of 1989, his main struggle related directly to an issue that just months earlier had been entirely absent from his campaign program: the abolition of the Communist Party's monopoly on political representation and the adoption of a new constitution.

Gorbachev's Political Reform

While Sakharov had chosen to leave the question of power to the side, Gorbachev himself confronted this issue head-on. His goal, however, was not to introduce political pluralism to the USSR—at least not in the form it would eventually take—but rather to consolidate his own power at the expense of the Communist Party so as to facilitate the adoption and the implementation of his chosen reforms. At the plenum of the party's Central Committee in January 1987, Gorbachev promoted democratization as one of the main slogans of perestroika. In lieu of the principle of reinforced discipline that had inspired the reforms of previous years, he committed himself to transforming society through the participation of the masses and the dismantling of the "administrative system of command."

Among the promises he made at the plenum, Gorbachev pledged to introduce competitive elections (i.e., those with more than one candidate) for all positions of power. After some hesitation, this new strategy was formalized a year and a half later, in June 1988, at the Nineteenth Party Congress, which adopted with great fanfare a program of reforms of the Soviet political system. This program included several new proposals, such as the introduction of the concept of the "rule of law" and an overhaul of the relationship between the "nationalities" in favor of more autonomy for the republics. In terms of the organization of central power, this reform provided for the reappraisal of the soviets, which were henceforth called on to become the instruments of popular sovereignty.[22] In his opening speech to the Congress, Gorbachev stated that the "cardinal reform of the political system" was aimed at "doing everything possible to ensure that millions and millions of workers are truly included in the leadership of the country," as well as "opening up as much space as possible for the processes of self-regulation and self-management of society, creating conditions for the full realization of the initiatives of citizens, representatives of power, Party organizations, social organizations and working communities."[23] In addition to the local soviets, which were henceforth to play a more important role in cities and regions, this "cardinal reform" provided for the creation of a gigantic, pan-union soviet with no less than 2,250 deputies: the Congress of People's Deputies of the USSR (hereafter referred to as the "USSR Congress"),[24] the "new supreme representative body of state power," which would be responsible for "resolving the most important constitutional, political, and socioeconomic issues in the life of the country."[25] Most importantly, elections to the USSR Congress were to be held on a competitive basis. These elections were scheduled for March 1989, and the Congress was to meet for its first session the following May.

His call for competitive elections notwithstanding, Gorbachev's aim was not the end of the Communist Party's monopoly on power, let alone the abdication of his own position as the architect of perestroika. He intended, rather, to introduce a new principle of legitimacy, that of popular sovereignty, so as to counterbalance the principle of *partiinost'* (loyalty to the Communist Party) in order to give to himself, as the reforming power, the room to maneuver against the party's conservative members. The elections were seen as a popular plebiscite on perestroika and thus a tool to rally society behind the reformer and his program. In practice, the election of the USSR Congress was meant to weaken or co-opt radical elements for the benefit of the centrist reformer. It also aimed to strengthen Gorbachev's personal power by creating for him a new position as head of state, that of chair of the Supreme Soviet. This granted Gorbachev extensive powers: the appointment and direction of the executive branch—the Council of Ministers of the USSR—and the direction of the legislative branch between sessions of Congress.

This position at the head of the Soviet state was supposed to allow Gorbachev to distance himself from the Communist Party; while he remained its leader, his decisions were subjected to collegial bodies such as the Politburo and the Central Committee. The reform did not provide for the direct election of the new head of state by popular vote, which would have made the USSR a plebiscitary democracy in the Weberian sense. Instead, the president of the Supreme Soviet was to be elected by an indirect vote of the deputies of the USSR Congress, of which only two-thirds were elected directly by the people, while the remaining third were elected by a corporatist vote.[26] This complex procedure was designed to ensure the loyalty of the Congress, thus securing Gorbachev's election. Gorbachevian democratization, in short, advanced the principle of popular legitimacy without abandoning that of party loyalty, in order to ensure that the elections did indeed rally society behind the reformer's program.

Despite its limitations, Gorbachev's proposed political reform brought to the Soviet political landscape several decidedly new elements, including multicandidate elections that, for the first time, offered citizens the opportunity to express their discontent at the ballot box. Gorbachev assumed that this protest vote would be directed against the privileges of the *nomenklatura* and thus in favor of the reform program. What he failed to foresee, however, was that the people would instead use this as an opportunity to lodge a protest vote against his own inability to fulfill the promises of perestroika. This is precisely what happened in the wake of the congressional elections of March 1989, which led not to a rallying of society but to the public expression of its divisions.

The Moscow Tribune: A Consultative Opposition

The political reform adopted at the Nineteenth Party Congress was received with great enthusiasm in the USSR. Gorbachev's popularity, which in recent months had been undermined by the failure of the state's initial economic reforms, experienced a powerful—if ultimately short-lived—revival. Andrei Sakharov was among those who supported Gorbachev, albeit with some reservations. On the initiative of his friend, the historian Yuri Afanasyev, he signed a collective letter denouncing the undemocratic methods by which the delegates who were authorized to participate in the party conference were selected. A similar concern led the historian Leonid Batkin to propose the creation of a political discussion club; the idea was to gather the most important figures of the Moscow liberal intelligentsia. With Afanasyev as intermediary, Batkin invited Sakharov to participate in the creation of this club. Sakharov accepted and even came up with the name: the Moscow Tribune (MT).[27] In addition to Batkin, Afanasyev, and Sakharov, the founding group included the essayists Len Karpinsky, Yuri Karyakin, and Yuri Burtin; the writer Ales Adamovich; and the historian Mikhail Gefter, as well as the physicists Arkady Migdal and Roald Sagdeev. With the exception of the two physicists, who joined at Sakharov's behest, all of them had contributed to the collection *Inogo ne dano*, published a few months earlier. Until the end of perestroika, the MT was the most prestigious and the most important political club of the liberal intelligentsia.

It is worth pausing for a moment to look at the political strategy the members of this club adopted vis-à-vis Soviet power, as this serves as something of a window into the general attitude of the Soviet liberal elite during the period. Before the 1989 elections, this strategy consisted mainly of supporting and aspiring to advise the regime.

In their respective memoirs, written more than twenty years apart, both Sakharov and Batkin justify the creation of the MT by invoking their desire to create the "seeds of an opposition." Published in 1989, Sakharov's includes the claim that "the appreciation of the highly contradictory nature of the political situation at that time, marked by dangerous symptoms of pushes to the 'right,' was the main argument in favor of the need to organize such a club as one of the seeds of a legal opposition."[28] Writing in 2014, Batkin used a similar formula: the idea of founding the MT, he asserts, was inspired by his thinking, "Isn't it time . . . to create an independent and influential civic discussion club as the *first seed of a political opposition?*"[29]

But while the MT did become the intellectual incubator of the radical reformist opposition in the course of 1989 and 1990, its initial vocation was not that of an oppositional movement. To see this, it is enough to compare the position adopted by the MT at its origins with those of the other political clubs already active at the time. These clubs had multiplied in number since the autumn of 1986, especially in Moscow, within the framework of what was called the "informal movement." One of the most important among these was the Perestroika Club, created in March 1987. In the words of one of its founders, this club took the form of "a kind of think tank of economists and lawyers for the use of the reformers in power."[30] It organized scientific debates at two of Moscow's most prestigious scientific institutes, the Central Institute of Economics and Mathematics and the Institute of Economics of the World Socialist System, in addition to regularly publishing a newsletter to disseminate its ideas and actively seeking to influence the authorities. On the occasion of the Nineteenth Party Congress in the summer of 1988, the club produced a political program for the delegates whose title—*Society's Mandate*—spoke volumes about the role the club attributed to itself as an intermediary between the people and the regime.

This kind of political strategy, however, based as it was on the act of advising and thereby collaborating with the authorities, was not unanimously accepted. Members of an informal seminar called "Democracy and Humanism," led by the dissident Valeriya Novodvorskaya, caused a scandal in May 1988 when they formed a self-proclaimed "opposition party" under the name of the Democratic Union, even though at the time there was no institutional structure for political competition, let alone a multiparty system. In the eyes of many liberals, the members of the Democratic Union were radicals who repeated the simplistic and unproductive methods of other, less successful dissidents. Their "party" certainly did not find favor with the government. Unlike the demonstrations organized by other clubs, those of the Democratic Union were severely repressed by the police. In explicit contrast, the MT officially declared to operate on the ground of "political realism," a notion Batkin defined as the ability to bring change by seriously taking into account all the constraints of the situation.[31] Not the least among these constraints was a challenge typical of oppositions in communist countries: "to establish its credibility as a loyal, non-insurrectionary group working to improve the existing body politic [in a society where] public opposition violates one of the most important mores of the political culture."[32] Taking this situation into account, the MT designed its initial strategies with great caution.

Between the opposition model embodied by the Democratic Union and the think tank model of the Perestroika Club, the founders of the MT clearly opted for the latter and scrupulously avoided any mention of the term "opposition." In their founding declaration, drafted by Batkin and adopted at the group's first meeting, they claimed their autonomy from Soviet power in order to make "independent, lucid and critical" judgments, even while declaring their intention to establish with the authorities a relationship "of mutual respect and reasonable dialogue."³³ In the same statement, they also offered the following declaration of their intentions:

> A free public opinion is reborn in the country. We are creating the Moscow Tribune primarily to contribute fully to this process and to express the conscience of the intelligentsia. We consider that a mature spiritual and political consciousness is not only the instrument, but also the cultural and political outcome of the social reforms that are finally being launched. . . . The direct aim of these discussions is the full revelation and confrontation of different approaches, as well as the elaboration of common judgments, diagnoses, and especially positive recommendations in the fields of the economy, politics, and culture.³⁴

In practice, the MT sought to make the results of its discussions known to both the government and the general public. Thus, the club's first session, which took place on October 12, 1988, was marked by the adoption of three open letters addressed to the highest state authorities, one calling for the release of political prisoners, another for the amendment of the law relating to the control of demonstrations, and the last for the resolution of the crisis that had just broken out in Nagorno-Karabakh between Armenia and Azerbaijan. The next session, held a month later, was devoted to the planned amendments to the constitution and electoral laws in the framework of the political reforms adopted at the Nineteenth Party Congress. The conclusions drawn from this discussion were the subject of an "Open Appeal of the Moscow Tribune Club," which the MT addressed to both the Presidium of the Supreme Soviet and to the media.³⁵

How to understand, in this context, the unanimity between Sakharov and Batkin in their retrospective accounts of the creation of the MT as an expression of the will to create the "seed of an opposition"? Should we see in it a subtle effort to undermine the reforming power under the cover of supposedly constructive proposals? Whatever the deep-seated reasons of its chief protagonists, the actions undertaken by the MT demonstrate that its main priority at the time was to advise the reforming power, not to challenge it, as confirmed by the disillusioned testimony of Yakov Berger, a regular participant in the MT, in an interview many years later:

> We hoped that this Moscow discussion club of the intelligentsia would provide material for decision-making. Then we realized that they didn't give a damn about what we were saying, that it was just intellectual talk and nothing more. These people in power, they governed according to considerations that were very different from the logic and argumentation of these intellectuals who offered their knowledge,

their visions, etc. It didn't work. But in the beginning, there was this idea, yes. We invited them, every time we invited them, but as far as I remember nobody of high rank came to listen to us. They were busy with other tasks. No, the dialogue with the authorities did not work.[36]

In this respect, the MT had adopted a position toward the reformist government that was quite typical of the liberal intelligentsia before the election campaign in the spring of 1989. That is, they criticized Gorbachev's policies, but only in order to support him, because they believed that he alone could overcome the resistance of the bureaucratic apparatus and carry out the reforms that they hoped would lead to the transition to democracy and a market economy.

This delicate balance between criticism and loyalty was in many respects an ambiguous and blurred one, but it should not be discarded ex post facto as a contradiction symptomatic of pathological doublethink.[37] In late communist regimes prior to 1989, as a rule, most of those denouncing the abuses of communism considered it reasonable to attempt to change the system from within, while illegal forms of pressure on the regime were deemed both unreasonable and dangerous.[38] This was also true in Poland and Hungary, where informal groups could operate somewhat more freely than in the USSR prior to perestroika. Batkin's "political realism," in this sense, closely echoed Adam Michnik's "new evolutionism" and Janos Kis's "radical reformism," which meant openly recognizing and working within the boundaries of established realities, including the leading role of the party.[39] In documents from the MT, this balanced strategy was called "constructive opposition," thus anticipating a common expression in post-Soviet Russia to designate an opposition that is relatively autonomous yet loyal to the Kremlin.[40]

It was in the context of this support for Gorbachev that they expressed their disagreement with several aspects of his political program that they considered counterproductive. In the abovementioned collective letter, whose contents were adopted at the November 12, 1988, session of the MT devoted to constitutional reforms, the club's members denounced the future Congress of People's Deputies as "a facade, not a working body," that meets only a few days a year for the sole purpose of legitimizing the decisions of the party leadership. In its place, they proposed direct, competitive elections for the deputies to the Supreme Soviet as well as its chair. This reform, they finally suggested, should be approved by the people through a "constitutional referendum."[41] But for all their rhetorical flare, these criticisms were presented as amendments to the Gorbachevian program, not as parts of an alternative political system in their own right.

This was noticed by an American political scientist during a roundtable discussion with Sakharov and several other liberal intellectuals the same month: "What kind of relationship between the state and society do you, the advocates of radical perestroika, want to create . . . ? What is your ideal, what is your model, what are its institutions and mechanisms? I cannot find a satisfactory discussion of this question either in the Soviet press or at this table. Discussions about cuts in the budget of state ministries, about elections and legal reforms, all touch on this question, but do not answer it directly."[42] For the coordinators of the MT, as for Sakharov, the more fundamental question of power did not yet appear as a central stake of democratization.

The Election Campaign and the First Session of the Congress

The political strategy of the liberal intelligentsia, and in particular of the Moscow elites who gathered under the banner of the MT, changed greatly over the course of 1989. From a strategy of support and advice for the reforming ruler, several of the most famous Soviet liberals shifted to a strategy of opposition, a change that implied the formation of an independent organization that had a distinct program and was supported by popular mobilization. Andrei Sakharov was undoubtedly the main figure behind this radicalization and the attendant prioritization of the question of power: having once served as a mere accessory to reform, this question would henceforth move to the very center of political debate, insofar as it appeared as the underlying condition for all the other demands. Yet the move toward opposition was a reactive, hesitant, and precarious process, mostly inspired by the sense that the MT had not been heard by the Soviet reformists in power as well as the growing discontent of the population. For many liberals, entering the opposition implied a dangerous division of progressive forces, which in turn threatened the implementation of reforms.

Several liberal intellectuals in the MT ran for office in the hope that they would be able to participate in the elaboration and adoption of reforms; most of them were elected.[43] In this way, they engaged in a political struggle that, at the end of the electoral campaign and the first session of the USSR Congress, would lead to a radicalization of their positions toward Gorbachev. This was notably the case with Sakharov. When the electoral campaign began, in early 1989, the veteran dissident presented the first goal of his program in a typically Gorbachevian vocabulary: "the deepening and widening of perestroika."[44] As has been indicated, the notions of "pluralism" and the "opening of society" did not imply a genuine transformation of the political system. And there was no mention of a multiparty system. Six months later, however, the whole country witnessed, live on television, the confrontation between Gorbachev and Sakharov at the USSR Congress, when the physicist launched a resounding "Decree on Power," calling for, among other things, the abolition of the Communist Party's monopoly and the transfer of all legislative power to the soviets as essential conditions for any real perestroika.

In just six months, then, much of the liberal intelligentsia, led by Andrei Sakharov and other Moscow deputies, came to accept that Gorbachev did not have a legitimate monopoly on perestroika. The binary logic of the political scene was cracking. Revising one of the most popular slogans of the previous years, Burtin wrote in the summer of 1989, "They say there is no other option than perestroika. This is true, but there are other options than perestroika 'à la Gorbachev.' And more than one."[45] This rapid radicalization was a direct consequence of the political struggle that emerged in the spring of 1989, and more specifically of two decisive phenomena: the perceived failure to be heard by Gorbachev and the increase in popular mobilization.

The most obvious cause of the drift toward opposition in 1989 was the liberal intelligentsia's failure to influence the course of reforms by its intellectual and moral authority alone. Like Yakov Berger, quoted earlier on this subject, Sakharov directed his disappointment primarily at Gorbachev, who seemed to him to be more willing to rely on conservative forces. In the summer of 1989, he drew up an assessment of the evolution of his feelings since the Nineteenth Party Congress: "My concern about Gorbachev's domestic policy has increased in the course of the last year. . . . In the political sphere, I am concerned about Gorbachev's obvious ambition to obtain unlimited personal power. I am concerned about Gorbachev's permanent orientation not toward progressive and pro-perestroika forces, but toward 'obedient' and manageable forces, even if reactionary."[46] Indeed, Gorbachev had increasingly shown signs of annoyance with the diverging "advice" he was receiving from all parts of the political spectrum. At a January 1989 meeting with representatives of the intelligentsia—a meeting to which Sakharov was for the first time invited—Gorbachev said, "Today, when we have a mass of new tasks, we need as never before a consolidation of our forces, their maximum concentration on solving the problems of perestroika and, I would say once again, on constructive work."[47]

Moving from words to deeds, on April 8, 1989, Gorbachev passed a decree to ensure the stability of the social order, stipulating, among other things, that "public offense" to the organs of state power and social organizations—including the Communist Party—would be punishable by up to three years of imprisonment or a fine of as much as 2,000 rubles. This decree provoked a wave of indignation. On May 3, 1989, at a meeting between newly elected Moscow deputies and representatives of the party, Sakharov demanded—in Gorbachev's presence—the abrogation of the April 8 decree, arguing that it was unacceptable to condemn the peaceful expression of citizens' individual convictions. In response, Gorbachev justified the measure, arguing that democracy must be able to defend itself, to which Sakharov retorted, "Including by violating democracy?" The exchange elicited obvious displeasure from the general secretary.[48]

Sakharov's disillusionment vis-à-vis Gorbachev only increased as the USSR Congress undertook its work. It is worth recalling here that Gorbachev had described this body as the principal venue through which popular sovereignty would be exercised. The deputies' debates, moreover, were broadcast live on television, which fostered an unprecedented—and never again repeated—enthusiasm for parliamentary activity. When he entered the huge Kremlin hall where the Congress met, Sakharov's first objective was to propose a draft agenda that he had prepared during the previous months with a group of deputies from Moscow, including the reformist apparatchik Boris Yeltsin and the economists Gavriil Popov and Nikolai Shmelev.[49] But it soon became clear that the Congress was to function in a way that would preclude the discussion of projects beyond those proposed by Communist Party leaders.

Indeed, from the rostrum, Gorbachev presided over the debates at his own pleasure, without regard to protocol. The Congress duly adopted the general secretary's proposed agenda without discussion and then proceeded to elect the Supreme Soviet, the permanent legislative body, from a single list prepared by the party, with Gorbachev as the sole candidate for the post of chair of the Supreme Soviet—in practice, the head of state. Sakharov's proposal to include in the agenda the discussion of a "Decree on Power" was flatly ignored. The majority of the deputies systematically approved Gorbachev's decisions and scorned the criticisms formulated by the deputies of the Moscow delegation. Outraged, the deputy and rising liberal intellectual Yuri Afanasyev immortalized this general attitude by calling the deputies an "aggressively obedient majority." Without legislative power or the possibility of real discussion, the Congress left sorely disappointed those who believed that it would provide a space for constructive collaboration with the authorities.

One month later, Sakharov offered the following account of this missed opportunity: "For all the people of our country, the Congress has completely destroyed all the illusions with which we were lulled and put to sleep, along with the whole world. . . . The psychological and political consequences are enormous and will have long-term effects. The Congress has cut off any way back. Now it is clear to everyone that there is only one way forward and one way to ruin."[50]

And as he explained in the same account, this disillusionment was to necessitate a change in political strategy: "The Congress has shifted the engine of change into a higher gear," wrote Sakharov. "Only the radicalization of perestroika can overcome the crisis and avoid a catastrophic backlash."[51]

In addition to this disillusionment with the reformers in the government, the shift toward opposition of Sakharov and some of his liberal colleagues was also inspired by the vast popular mobilization that unfolded during the spring 1989 election campaign. The people's readiness to support reforms and democracy impressed Soviet liberals, who often did not hold ordinary Soviet citizens in high esteem.

Indeed, Sakharov, in a moment of surprising candor, said as much in the summer of 1989: "For the first time in our country for many years, a lively electoral political struggle began. And then we discovered what we had not dared to hope for, we who in the past had waged a lonely and seemingly hopeless struggle with very limited objectives. The population, who have been deceived many times and who live in conditions of generalized hypocrisy and degrading corruption, revealed itself to be alive."[52]

This was of course a pleasant surprise for Sakharov, who had repeatedly confessed his discouragement at the apparent apathy and cynicism of the Soviet population. Only a year before, he had expressed doubts about his fellow citizens' moral capacity to realize perestroika. However, during the 1989 election campaign, while the demonstrations were going on, he became much more optimistic: "The recovery of society is only possible on a moral basis. Our people have been severely deformed by terror and many years of lies and hypocrisy. But I believe that the population has always retained moral strength."[53]

However, this interpretation was by no means universally shared, with many liberal intellectuals expressing skepticism on this count. This concern was expressed even before the election was called. At the November 12, 1988, session of the MT, which was devoted to constitutional reform, Batkin's proposal to introduce the direct and universal election of the head of state was greeted with considerable suspicion by the sociologists Vladimir Shubkin and Leonid Gordon, who warned their colleagues that the population was simply unfit for democracy. The two speakers had their own interpretations; Gordon claimed that the people had been undermined by widespread alcoholism, while Shubkin denounced their ignorance of all things political:

> I have heard here several speakers who say that if we had direct, secret, universal elections, then Gorbachev would probably be the elected candidate. But I have great doubts about this, because generations have been formed in the absence of democracy and any form of honest competition in this field. They have never even felt what a real democracy can be.... It seems to me that if one considers not the intellectual elite of Moscow, who have been reading samizdats for twenty years already..., but the great mass of the people, who were busy earning their daily bread and who had no access to samizdats, one will discover that they [the majority of Soviet citizens] are now in a state of great anxiety and do not know what to do or where to go.[54]

The intelligentsia's feelings of isolation from ordinary Soviet citizens explains Sakharov's wonder at coming face-to-face with the diversity on display in the political mobilizations of spring 1989:

> They were mostly faces of a familiar type—those who also line up at Chagall exhibitions or film festivals: honest, intelligent people who understand everything and are proletarians of intellectual labor [i.e., intellectuals] with limited material means. But there were also, without a doubt, new faces on the historical scene.... They were people who had been awakened from the dream of passivity by the hopes of perestroika, workers and white collars, [in sum] the largest mass of the intelligentsia.[55]

The discovery of a well of popular support for reform from outside the usual circles of the intelligentsia, as well as Gorbachev's apparent refusal to listen to the advice proffered by Sakharov and his colleagues, led the members of the MT to adopt what in the Soviet context were considered more radical modes of political action—namely, demonstrations and political meetings. The MT organized its first demonstration—with rather lackluster results, it must be said—in front of the Georgian Cultural Center in Moscow to protest against the Soviet Army's violent repression of a peaceful demonstration on April 9, 1989, in Tbilisi. Despite their public profiles, these intellectuals were not charismatic crowd leaders; the event attracted barely a few hundred people and was quickly dispersed by the police. Commenting on this event, one of the leaders of the informal movement remarked sarcastically: "The decision of members of Moscow Tribune to hold a demonstration was proof of their complete indignation at the actions of the authorities—members of this respectable organisation preferred to meet in the comfortable hall of the House of Scholars. However, even now, the streets were still an alien and comfortless place."⁵⁶

By contrast, the assemblies that were organized in support of the independent deputies of Moscow and held at the Luzhniki Stadium on the eve of the opening of the Congress assumed a completely different scale. These were a result of the collaboration between the MT and several informal organizations, including the Moscow Popular Front. The first, which took place on May 21, 1989, attracted more than 150,000 people. According to a journalist covering the event, the most popular speakers were Telman Gdlyan and Boris Yeltsin, two men from the Soviet establishment who had earned a reputation as critics of corruption and of the privileges of the *nomenklatura*, followed by the liberal intellectuals Andrei Sakharov and Yuri Karyakin.⁵⁷ This was a striking turn of events, to say the least: less than a year after creating the MT in order to advise the government, intellectuals like Sakharov, Batkin, Afanasyev, and Karyakin found themselves at the microphone of a completely different kind of platform, haranguing a huge crowd alongside more "radical" political actors who openly demanded the abolition of the Communist Party's monopoly on power.

The radicalization of the liberal intelligentsia—which as we have seen was provoked by the regime's perceived disinterest in its advice and by the discovery of the politicization of the people—was further encouraged by groundbreaking developments abroad. With the unexpected electoral triumph of Solidarność in the elections in Poland on June 4, 1989, the Soviet liberals could begin to consider open contestation of the regime as something other than political suicide. In an article published at the time, Batkin explicitly called on the democratic forces to follow the "Polish model" in creating an opposition that would enter in dialogue with the government with the support of a powerful mass movement.⁵⁸

The Soviet liberals' growing assertiveness expressed itself most strikingly on the last day of the Congress, June 9, 1989, when millions of Soviet television viewers witnessed the notorious confrontation between Gorbachev and Sakharov. Authorized to take the floor as the curtain was about to fall on the Congress, Sakharov launched into an impassioned reading of the "Decree on Power," which he had thus far failed to add to the Congress's agenda. The atmosphere quickly became tense. Gorbachev, tired of the length of the speech—to say nothing of its contents—interrupted Sakharov many times to ask him to return to his seat; the deputies, meanwhile, were growing noisier and noisier. Finally, Gorbachev asked that the microphones be turned off. That order fulfilled, Sakharov was no longer audible to the deputies in the room, who now looked, alternately dumbfounded and mocking, at the old man gesticulating at the tribune. The television cameras kept rolling, however, and in this way Sakharov's speech reached a sizable portion of Soviet society. Indeed, even today, many Russians remember it as one of the most significant episodes of perestroika.

Sakharov's "Decree on Power" speech was more than anything else a call for a much more far-reaching reform of the political system than that envisaged by Gorbachev. Its revolutionary character was perhaps most clearly expressed in the slogan "All power to the soviets!" and in its invocation of the term "decree," both of which hark back to language used by the Bolsheviks at the time of the October Revolution. The "Decree on Power" called, in the name of the principle of popular sovereignty, for the transformation of the USSR into a parliamentary regime. To this end, it demanded, first, that article 6 of the Soviet Constitution, which established the party's "leading role" in Soviet society, be abolished, thus ending the party's monopoly on political life and leading to the adoption of a multiparty system. The decree also called for the "future consideration" of the direct and competitive election of the chair and vice-chair of the Supreme Soviet, as well as the amendment of the electoral law to abolish the corporatist vote of "social organizations."[59]

The importance of the "Decree on Power" obviously does not lie in its legislative effectiveness. Under the conditions under which it was articulated, it could only be ignored by Congress. Moreover, as Sakharov acknowledged in his memoirs, its proposals were not particularly original. The idea of making the Congress the main legislative body and giving it responsibility for passing reforms, as well as the idea of the direct and competitive election of the president and changes in the electoral law, had been put forward by the MT some six months earlier. As for the abolition of the monopoly of the Communist Party, which Sakharov claimed to have added to his speech on the eve of the Congress without discussing it with anyone, it was, as we have seen, among the demands of some informal organizations at the assembly in which he had participated a few days earlier in the Luzhniki Stadium. The cardinal virtue of the "Decree on Power," according to Sakharov, lies in fact in its "psychological and political significance," which succeeded in bringing the Congress to an end on a note "more radical and more constructive."[60] The declamation of the "Decree on Power," in fact, led to the public questioning of the alliance established in 1987 between the reformist power and the Moscow liberal intelligentsia, with the latter now considering, for the first time, taking the lead as an autonomous political force.

This strategic shift implied a reappraisal of the question of power, long neglected by the liberal intelligentsia in favor of issues considered more pressing, such as those related to the guarantee of individual expression and the reform of the economic system. For the first time, concerns about *who* should carry out reforms seemed as important as concerns about their direction and pace. The evolution of Sakharov's political thought between the summer of 1988 and the summer of 1989 illustrates this new priority given to the question of power. We have seen that this question was previously addressed only in passing in his writings, where it was overshadowed by issues that held more priority for him, such as the protection of human rights and the survival of humanity in the nuclear age. The concepts of democracy, an open society, and pluralism that he was putting forward were actually compatible with a variety of political models, including the one envisioned in Gorbachev's program. However, Sakharov's views on this subject changed in the context of the election campaign, leading to his confrontation with Gorbachev precisely on the question of power.

A revealing sign of Sakharov's new emphasis on this question is the trouble he took to justify his interest in it; it was as if he felt he had to excuse himself from neglecting the truly important issues: "Congress cannot immediately feed the country. It cannot immediately solve the national problems. It cannot immediately liquidate the budget deficit. It cannot immediately give us back clean air, water, and forests. But what we do have an obligation to do is to create the political guarantees that these problems will be solved. This is precisely what the country expects from us! All power to the soviets!"[61]

To address the issue of power here is to question that which was previously taken for granted—namely, the assumption that perestroika must be led by its initiator, Gorbachev, and that support for reform necessarily implies support for his policies. What was in reality a plurality of opinions was then commonly reduced to a binary opposition between the defenders and opponents of perestroika: a dichotomy often presented in moral terms, as a conflict between those who sincerely expressed their conscience and those who, under the guise of "false principles," selfishly defended their privileges. This binary view did not imply that perestroika's defenders all agreed with one another or held the same views; the point, rather, was that the different opinions in favor of perestroika could and should be harmonized in a sincere and constructive dialogue. In this respect, the Congress proved to be a great disappointment for many Soviet liberals, whose proposals were flatly ignored by the majority of deputies, who then adopted without discussion the proposals prepared by the party. In this context, the confrontation between Sakharov and Gorbachev, witnessed by millions of Soviet television viewers, served to publicly consecrate the new configuration of the Soviet political scene, marked as it was by a de facto pluralism between groups that defended different visions of perestroika.

Indeed, in the space of just a few months, the editors of the liberal newspaper *Moskovskie novosti* were already able to present this new reality as something of a fait accompli: "It is universally accepted that there is no other option than perestroika, but there are of course variants to its movement. What are they?"[62] To be sure, this openness to the existence of a plurality of perspectives on reform remained limited, as it often presupposed that it was acceptable only within the (rather ill-defined) framework of perestroika, which led to the exclusion from the outset of the opinions expressed by nationalists and conservative communists. As was the case in the debate initiated by Nina Andreeva in March 1988 (discussed in the previous chapter), the recognition of a plurality of opinions was based on the prior affirmation of a moral monism: that one cannot compromise with principles. Even if limited, the recognition of a plurality of "perestroika variants" in the summer of 1989 implied a change in Soviet liberals' interpretation of political life, whereby open conflict came to be gradually accepted as a normal phenomenon rather than as a symptom of the breakdown of society and the failure of perestroika.

This new vision of politics, however, did not come without strong resistance, not only from the party elite, who denounced what they claimed was an attempt at factionalism (a point to which we shall return), but also from the liberal deputies themselves. Despite their many disagreements with Soviet power, these deputies sought above all to overcome conflict and support the reforming power, which they still hoped to enlighten with their advice. The categorical opposition of the Soviet liberals to the nationalist and conservative communist organizations emerging at the same time, as well as the fear of instability caused by the popular mobilization, encouraged them to seek to support the "enlightened ruler." They thus strongly resisted the idea of designating their growing divergence from Gorbachev as an example of opposition, since this would imply that they had abandoned their hopes of collaboration in favor of open confrontation. This resistance to the notion of opposition was at the very heart of the debates on political strategy of the first parliamentary faction to be organized in the summer of 1989 by the liberal deputies of the USSR Congress: the Interregional Group of Deputies.

The Interregional Group of Deputies

In the wake of the first session of Congress, the splintering of the supporters of perestroika gave birth to a parliamentary faction devoted to the promotion of a competing reformist program. The initiative for its creation came from the deputy Gavriil Popov, who, on May 27, 1989, surprised the Congress by calling for the formation of an "interregional and independent group of deputies."⁶³ Thus was born the Interregional Group of Deputies (Mezhregional'naia deputatskaia gruppa, or MDG), which brought together nearly four hundred deputies around the most famous figures of the Moscow delegation: Boris Yeltsin, Gavriil Popov, Yuri Afanasyev, and Andrei Sakharov.⁶⁴ During the turbulent summer and autumn of 1989, the MDG quickly became the standard-bearer of the liberal reformist forces of the USSR, before being abandoned by its founders in early 1990. Despite its brief existence, the MDG played a decisive role in Soviet political life, notably through the elaboration of a political platform that competed with that of the party and Gorbachev. Not only were most of the group's proposals contained in this platform— starting with the call for the abolition of Article 6 of the Constitution— eventually endorsed by the Soviet government, but the very fact of its existence already implied that the party had lost its monopoly on the leadership and initiative of reforms.

The MDG, for all these reasons, is generally considered the first legal opposition in the USSR. This conclusion is correct if one considers the political stance taken by several of its leaders in the late autumn of 1989 and the legacy it bequeathed to the democratic movement that took shape the following year, but this should not distract us from the fact that the MDG's leaders came to form an opposition only belatedly and, in the end, *in spite of themselves*, as a result of the failure of their strategy of collaboration with and support for the reformist government. Their constant reluctance to use the concept of "opposition," even though precedents existed at the same time in eastern Europe and on a smaller scale in the USSR, was a clear sign of their desire to prevent any open conflict within society and among reformist forces. Sakharov, once again, was the main protagonist of the radicalization that finally pushed the MDG to adopt, in mid-autumn 1989, a program that explicitly challenged that of the party and to begin seriously considering its role in the formation of a democratic opposition.

The MDG's original purpose was to voice the ideas of independent deputies who were outvoted in the USSR Congress by the majority, which was aligned with the Communist Party. It should be remembered that in the absence of a multiparty system, the goal of Gorbachev's democratization program was to rally the entire country around his vision of perestroika, specifically through a plebiscite in Congress. However, as the deputy Gavriil Popov pointed out on the first day of the session, May 25, 1989, the geographical principle by which Congress was organized had led to the censorship of minority positions in each of the regional delegations. Therefore, the more radical-minded deputies had to gather on an "interregional" basis, a principle that gave the MDG its name.

At the Congress, Popov carefully *avoided* presenting such a group as a formal opposition movement, or even as a faction. Instead, he presented his initiative as a reasonable way to channel popular discontent and thus prevent the formation of just such an oppositional movement. At the same time, he purposefully formulated his statement in a way that would be worrying for the authorities: "We can wait. We have waited for decades, being ignored. We can do without an opposition. But what worries me is this: how long will our people wait?"[65] Initially, the threat to create an independent group of deputies seemed like mere bravado, an attempt to frighten the regime in order to obtain its ear. Indeed, it was not even clear that Popov seriously considered organizing such a group, at least at first. Like Yeltsin, he did not even deign to attend the meeting organized the next day by informal activists to take steps toward the group's founding. Among the most famous Moscow deputies, only Sakharov demonstrated a real interest in this initiative and attended the meeting until the end.

In the Congress, however, the "aggressively obedient majority" of deputies took the announcement of the creation of an independent parliamentary group very seriously. Not only did this completely contradict the idea of a "consolidation" of society behind the regime but the term "faction" itself carried extremely negative connotations for anyone educated in the Communist Party tradition, in which factions had been banned since 1921. Factions were commonly associated with "schism" (*raskol*), the fracturing of an entity that should by rights be unified. For Gorbachev, Popov's proposal "leads to the schism of the Congress, to fractions," and, consequently, Gorbachev said, "I would consider my mission useless if today this Congress, this first Congress convened after such an election campaign, was torn into pieces and lost the opportunity to work fruitfully on behalf of what makes perestroika and the whole country move forward, solving the accumulated problems."[66] Several deputies agreed. One of them declared, outraged, "You proposed to the Congress to create a faction, this is madness. Come to your senses and realize what you are about to do. . . . You are creating disagreements in the work of the Congress and distracting it from the essential problems."[67] Another warned of the social consequences of the creation of a parliamentary faction: "I see in this series of speeches attempts to simply divide Congress. Which in practice means dividing our society."[68]

In fact, the opposite was happening: the division of society was leading to the creation of the MDG and, thereby, the breakup of the reformist camp. Popov's threat, in fact, would probably have remained unheeded had the events of the following weeks not suddenly reinforced the need for an independent reformist group. First, the confrontation between Sakharov and the general secretary on the last day of the Congress, mentioned earlier, destroyed whatever illusions remained about society's unanimous support for Gorbachev. Then, more importantly, the outbreak in July 1989 of a wave of strikes among coal miners, especially in the Kuzbass region, demonstrated that Sakharov's demands enjoyed wider support, outside the circles of the intelligentsia and even beyond the big cities.[69] The miners' strike, which initially focused on working conditions, quickly took a more overtly political turn. On national television, the miner and deputy Vladimir Lushnikov supported the main demand of Sakharov's "Decree on Power"—namely, the abolition of Article 6 of the Constitution. The miners' mobilization caused a real shock in the country of the dictatorship of the proletariat, especially since the Solidarność movement in Poland had just forced that country's Communist Party to share power after several strike waves. Democratic deputies from Moscow invited Adam Michnik, one of the leading figures in the Polish trade union, to share his political experience at one of the preparatory meetings for the founding of the MDG, yet it seems they were not fully prepared to follow the Polish example. On learning of the miners' strikes, Michnik was astonished to learn that Russia's democrats were not yet on the scene.[70]

Spontaneous popular mobilizations were greeted with ambivalence by liberal intellectuals. While they were pleased to see their proposals supported by the wider population, they were also concerned about what they saw as the irrational and disorderly character of mass politics. Accustomed to decades of relative social passivity, these intellectuals were deeply troubled by the chaotic nature of this new form of political life, punctuated as it was by demonstrations, meetings, and strikes. The literary scholar Marietta Chudakova testified, a year later, to the shock felt in 1989: "Faces, voices, shouts, expansive speeches—the Russian reality was so profoundly new for many of us that it gave an impression of times of trouble [*smuta*] and confusion."[71] A common trope of liberal discourse at this time was a famous phrase of Pushkin's about the "absurd and merciless" (*bessmyslennyi i besposhchadnyi*) character of the "Russian riot," which was invoked as a warning against the imminent danger of tipping over into senseless violence and civil war.

This concern about spontaneous popular mobilization was felt among the deputies who attended the founding meeting of the MDG on July 29-30, 1989. Popov and Afanasyev, whose speeches set the tone of the ensuing debate, were quick to emphasize the "constructive" character of the group being created, in contrast to the chaotic and irrational popular forces that, they warned, threatened the social order and the course of reforms. For Popov, the failure of the Congress and the miners' strikes definitively broke the binary opposition that was said to divide the supporters and opponents of perestroika. However, he hastened to add that the situation did not correspond to a choice between a "revolutionary-democratic" version of perestroika and the version put forward by the regime, since the latter had been thoroughly discredited by recent events. The question, he concluded, was whether "revolutionary-democratic" perestroika would follow a legal or more disorderly course. He then used Pushkin's famous phrase about the dangers of the "Russian riot" to present the MDG, by contrast, as a reasonable partner for the reformist power in those uncertain times.[72] In the most radical intervention of the meeting, Afanasyev also warned against "the irrational and horrible riot" and the destructive forces unfolding in the political vacuum caused by the regime's hesitation: "In fact, we do not have a political crisis. We are not even there yet. We have a political vacuum. Any destructive force will immediately fill it, unless we have something organized, independent, and creative."[73] Afanasyev argued that the MDG must play a "constructive" role, or more precisely, must provide an intellectual complement to the policy of the reformist power, thus taking up the dashed hopes of the MT: "The interregional group is not only an extraterritorial gathering of deputies ... it is also an attempt to create, not a parallel Supreme Soviet, but an additional and more precise intellectual and conceptual supply that is absolutely necessary for the Supreme Soviet and the Congress of People's Deputies."[74] The notion of opposition, in other words, was categorically rejected. As for the general proposals of the group, they were not very different from those put forward by Gorbachev: democratization and the introduction of the market in the name of the return to civilization and the triumph of "universal values."

A year later, the political analyst Igor Kliamkin summarized the situation at the end of the summer of 1989: "The majority of liberal-democratic intellectuals ... thought that the reason why market relations and democracy were being established so slowly was because of the hesitations of the initiators of perestroika, and not because of some complex problem requiring further theoretical reflection. That is why the oppositionally oriented part of society ... assumed that their disagreement with Gorbachev's group was only about the pace of reforms. This idea persisted for a long time."[75]

Afanasyev's speeches at the time of his involvement in the MDG confirms this observation. He mentioned many times that his disagreements with the reforming power amounted to a difference over pace, not principles: in diagnosing the situation, he spoke of an "incompatibility of tempo," a "delay on the tempo," an "arrhythmia of reforms," a "political arrhythmia." The reformer, he affirmed, was "standing still." The government, he said, was "stalling," seeking to maintain the "status quo," and for this reason it was being outpaced by events.[76] Sakharov saw things in a similar way: he spoke of a "scissor effect" between "the social conscience that is developing rapidly" and the "political, economic, social, and national reality that is stalling."[77]

Once again, the example of eastern Europe played a decisive role in fueling a sense of urgency among Soviet liberals. Many became convinced that, after leading the way with perestroika, the Soviet Union was now falling behind its Western neighbors and urgently needed to catch up. In Poland, by the end of the summer, Tadeusz Mazowiecki from Solidarność became prime minister and oversaw a series of reforms aimed at transitioning to liberal democracy and a market economy. In Hungary, the reformist wing of the party, led by Imre Pozsgay, did not wait for the emergence of a powerful democratic movement before transforming the Hungarian Socialist Workers' Party. This gave them control over the roundtable discussions held in the summer of 1989 with opposition forces. In October, the Hungarian Party changed its name, renounced one-party rule, and embraced a package of reforms ensuring political pluralism and economic liberalization.

The immense interest shown by Soviet democrats in the Polish and Hungarian negotiated transitions stemmed from the fact that they fulfilled promises that seemed attainable in the USSR. Both achieved rapid and substantial democratization from a situation similar to that of Russia's democrats: a Communist Party led by a reformist. The thinking among Soviet liberals was that if only Gorbachev would stop hesitating, similar results could be achieved in the socialist homeland. A Soviet liberal deputy, after traveling to Poland at the invitation of Solidarność and witnessing the course of reforms, declared, "What Poland has already managed to accomplish is precisely what we [in the USSR] would like to achieve in the near future."[78]

This "revolution envy" directed toward eastern Europe was a relatively new sentiment for Soviet liberals.[79] This phenomenon occurred within the broader context of the reversal in the "spillover" effect between the USSR and eastern Europe, triggered by the monumental events in Poland and Hungary. Before 1989, the influence largely flowed in one direction: while Gorbachev aimed to export perestroika to the Socialist Bloc, Russia's leading democratic figures sought inspiration from their own country's past for models of political reform.[80] This was evident, for instance, in the famous 1988 collection of texts *Inogo ne dano*, where references to eastern Europe were virtually absent, overshadowed by numerous references to previous Soviet reform experiments such as Lenin, the New Economic Policy, and Khrushchev. At best, Poland and Hungary were considered model pupils of perestroika.[81]

The revolutions of 1989 thus came as a massive surprise to Soviet liberals, albeit a pleasant one. They were celebrated as remarkable democratic breakthroughs, affirming the righteousness of the path opened by perestroika. Typically, events in Poland and Hungary were interpreted in the same moral terms as reforms in the USSR—a binary struggle between defenders of reactionary monolithic thinking and reformers advocating new pluralist thinking. This perspective was shared, for example, by Marina Pavlova-Silvanskaya, a historian and special correspondent in Poland for the weekly *Literaturnaia gazeta*.

Seeking to challenge the biases perpetuated by mainstream Soviet media regarding Solidarność's alleged extremism, Pavlova-Silvanskaya emphasized the moderation of its intellectual leaders, who sought national accord through compromise with the Communist Party. She contrasted the political culture of "new thought" shared by roundtable participants with the "old political culture" found in both the conservative wing of the party and what she termed "fundamentalists" among Solidarność members, who she argued played dangerous populist games with people's crisis-induced illusions.[82] According to her, Solidarność's progressive character lay precisely in its refusal to adopt an oppositional stance against the Communist Party and its commitment to preserving social concord in the face of the violent disruption threatened by various extremist forces. Throughout the summer, she defended Solidarność and urged Gorbachev to accept its electoral victory, presenting the Polish opposition as the "last dam" against the potential violent radicalization of the masses.[83]

This veiled threat echoed the views of many Soviet liberals regarding their own role as the sole reasonable partners of the Communist Party in the face of an impending "Russian riot, irrational and horrible." Torn between the desire to rely on popular mobilization and the fear of social unrest, MDG members remained uncertain about whether—and how—they should take advantage of growing popular discontent with Gorbachev. Consequently, MDG members tended to celebrate the examples of Poland and Hungary indiscriminately, despite the differing roles that popular mobilization played in each revolution.[84] At a conference of democratic movements on September 16, 1989, Afanasyev declared, "Poland and Hungary are the standard-bearers, the initiators of more radical changes, who need our support as we need theirs."[85] Twelve days later, in an interview with the French newspaper *Le Monde*, Sakharov asserted, "What is happening in Poland and Hungary, as well as in the Baltic republics, is very positive and a magnificent example for us."[86]

Despite all his criticism of Soviet reforms "stalling" and lagging behind eastern Europe, Sakharov consistently declared that "perestroika is an objective necessity" and that he still supported Gorbachev as "the only real candidate."[87] Yet he nonetheless reproached Gorbachev for what he saw as Gorbachev's "passivity," his lack of eagerness to realize his program, which Sakharov described as a "gap between words and gestures." Sakharov did not consider himself to be in opposition to Gorbachev, but the firmness of his position on political reform nevertheless made him one of the most radical figures among the MDG members—indeed, only half of his fellow deputies present at the founding meeting in late July fully supported his proposal to abolish Article 6 of the Constitution. Of the five cochairs of the MDG elected on this occasion, Sakharov was also the one who obtained the least votes: 69 against Yeltsin's 144 and Afanasyev's 143.[88] At the end of a series of long debates, this meeting concluded with the adoption of a certain number of "theses for a program" that the members of the MDG wished to add to the agenda of the next session of the Congress. These included the proposals prepared by the Moscow delegation in the spring. The abolition of article 6—and thus the beginning of multipartyism—was not among them.

As had already happened with the MT, those MDG members who had hoped for collaboration with the reforming power were soon disappointed. Once again, the Soviet leadership refused to cooperate with an autonomous political group, even though it claimed to pursue the same goals as the regime and had made no claim to power. Unsurprisingly, the most hostile reaction came from the upper echelons of the Communist Party, where the *nomenklatura* took a rather dim view of what it saw as a challenge to its monopoly on the course of perestroika. The Central Committee and the Politburo harshly condemned the MDG, and this was echoed in a campaign in *Pravda* against the group's most popular leaders, Yeltsin and Afanasyev. If the hostility of the conservative wing of the party was predictable, much more disappointing for the MDG was the reaction of the reformist wing, with which it wanted to form an alliance. Gorbachev, relying on information from the KGB concerning the MDG's alleged extremism, refused to allow Aleksandr Yakovlev, his right-hand man, to attend the group's meetings. Evgeny Primakov, who was sent in his place, told the MDG that the activity of the deputies could be useful only in the congressional commissions, and he accused them of forming a "closed group" opposed to the Supreme Soviet.[89]

The autumn of 1989 brought another worrying turn of events for the liberal intelligentsia. Nationalist and conservative communist groups began to organize themselves into a new political force, the United Workers' Front, and they opposed Gorbachev with radical criticism from the other side of the political spectrum. The deputies of the MDG, worried that their opponents would resort to mass mobilization and bruised by the refusal of the reformist authorities to accept their demands, met for their second general meeting on September 23 and 24, 1989. They adopted a more clear-cut position, particularly with regard to the demand for the abolition of Article 6 of the Constitution. Afanasyev once again pronounced the most radical demand and called on the group to consider itself a proper opposition. To justify this position, he mobilized an argument typical of the moral perspective of the liberal intelligentsia, describing the imperative of a sincere expression of moral truth, dictated by conscience: "What should you do when you hear in your conscience a reproach coming from the depths of the soul that for the second time (first under Brezhnev and now under Gorbachev) you could be an accomplice and responsible for the burial of the nascent democracy . . . ? There is no doubt about it: we must speak out!"[90]

By virtue of the implicit moral monism discussed in chapter 3, the imperative of expressing one's conscience was not seen as the source of an irreducible divergence of opinions but rather as the way to their rapprochement. Thus, Afanasyev insisted that the oppositional stance dictated by his conscience was inherently "constructive." Rather than simply supporting Gorbachev, a radicalized MDG would form an "alliance" with him under certain conditions. While seemingly conciliatory, this insistence on conditions was a step toward the MDG's transition to political opposition. However, Afanasyev insisted that the aim of this opposition was the consolidation of political forces and society in a multilateral manner, allowing for the consideration of a range of proposals different from those of the authorities, rather than by a unilateral consensus imposed by the Politburo. To overcome the division of society, which he variously called "social polarization," "spiritual schism," and "political division," Afanasyev called for an extraordinary session of the Congress to discuss the "unifying" ideas proposed by the MDG. In the meantime, he even proposed "a general armistice, a national moratorium on strikes and on all forms of conflict, confrontation, and discord." Opposition, in short, was deemed "constructive" when it consolidated society rather than mobilized it.[91]

Even in this consensual form, the idea of making the MDG a formal opposition group was hardly an object of unanimous acceptance among the members. The deputy Yuri Boldyrev observed at the same meeting in September 1989 that "there are . . . two different visions of the MDG's tactics in Congress: a rigid confrontation or the search for ways to influence decision-making."[92] The failure to work with the government, he said, was a result of the MDG's excessively oppositional character: "We push the undecided into the conservative camp with our sharp statements. The discussion with the government does not work because of excessive and partly unthinking pressure."[93]

The division between "moderates" and "radicals" at the MDG was also evident in the debates at the MT. It is important to note that these labels, used in the club's working documents and by journalists reporting on the club's sessions,[94] did not reflect the members' respective stances toward the communist system. All members, in fact, aligned themselves with the camp supporting democracy, westernization, and a market economy. While some members aspired to reform Socialism and admired Scandinavian social democracy, others advocated a clear shift toward capitalism. However, this distinction was not considered politically relevant at the time. The moderate-radical divide within the MT focused on a more immediate concern: whether the Soviet liberals should act as an opposition or not. In the session of November 18, 1989, the deputy Viktor Sheinis, a member of the MDG, said that the most serious problem for democratization was not Gorbachev's excessive passivity but rather the emergence of certain "right-wing populist" movements, such as the United Workers' Front. In order to ensure that the reforming power would not prefer to rely on these latter groups, he urged his fellow democratic deputies to abandon their excessive criticism in favor of constructive proposals. In this way, he hoped, "the dividing line [would] shift to the right of Gorbachev."[95] This was not the opinion of Yakov Berger and Leonid Batkin, however, who countered that Gorbachev and the state apparatus were obviously incapable of making the necessary decisions on their own—hence the need for a democratic movement strong enough to force Gorbachev's hand. The philosopher Vladimir Bibler even proposed that the MT should take the lead in this democratic opposition since the MDG seemed incapable of playing such a role.

Sakharov, for his part, belonged to the most radical camp within the MDG. At a meeting with workers in the Urals in September 1989, he had already expressed his hope that pressure from the working class, especially through strikes, would lead the government to pursue a more "energetic and real" policy of reform.[96] But since he was counting on Gorbachev to carry out these reforms, he still refused to consider himself a member of the opposition: "The Interregional Group of Deputies is neither an opposition to perestroika nor a faction, although one should not be afraid of these words. It is a group of active supporters of perestroika, which, as we know, enjoys broad support in the country."[97] Sakharov still believed that the best strategy was to support and advise the regime. The project that was closest to his heart at the time was the drafting of a new constitution, which he planned to submit to a dedicated commission of the Supreme Soviet. Sakharov, indeed, rejoiced at having been appointed by Gorbachev to this commission, and he took his work on it very seriously. His hope was that it would submit a new draft constitution to the next session of the Congress.

The Opposition as Political Testament

However, the events of October and November 1989 were to shake Sakharov's confidence in the possibilities of collaboration with Gorbachev. As the second session of the USSR Congress—planned for December 1989—approached, it became clear that the work of the commission was going nowhere. During its first session, which took place only at the end of November, Sakharov was the sole committee member to present a proposal. More crucially, the Supreme Soviet did not include on the agenda of the Congress the MDG's proposals, starting with the abolition of article 6 and several laws considered decisive for economic reform, such as that governing the transfer of land ownership to those who cultivate it and the legalization of private ownership for enterprises.

The impending deadlock in the USSR Congress, where the radical deputies were still in the minority, was all the more desperate for MDG members because in recent weeks the USSR had suddenly found itself lagging even further behind the wider movement of democratic reform, following the revolutions that swept away communist rule in East Germany, Czechoslovakia, and Romania. The Velvet Revolution in Czechoslovakia made the strongest impression on Soviet liberals because of the moral character infused in the mobilization and the analogous strategies previously adopted by Czechoslovak dissidents. Until the fall of 1989, they tended to consider themselves "apolitical" or even "antipolitical" out of a commitment to a sense of authenticity.

However, on November 17, the brutal suppression of a student demonstration triggered a shift toward more contentious actions. Prague's students, followed by actors, declared an indefinite strike. Initially caught off guard, dissidents seized the initiative two days later, establishing Civic Forum in Prague and Public against Violence in Bratislava to coordinate popular mobilization and demands. Similar to events in East Germany a few weeks earlier, mass mobilization unfolded in Czechoslovakia throughout the rest of November and into December, attracting ever larger crowds. A two-hour general strike on November 27 led to a cascade of resignations at the head of the Communist Party and, a month later, to the election of Vaclav Havel as Czechoslovakia's new president.[98]

In the Soviet liberal press, these events were greeted as warmly as the Polish and Hungarian revolutions earlier that year. A distinctive political phenomenon of the autumn 1989 revolutions that struck many democratic observers in Russia, however, was the peaceful and disciplined nature of the large-scale demonstrations in Czechoslovakia. This observation contrasted with common concerns about the destabilizing potential of Solidarność's "fundamentalist" wing.

In the prodemocratic weekly *Moskovskie novosti*, a Soviet journalist marveled at the order prevailing in Prague: "Meetings are held every day on Václav Square. They are many thousands strong and well organized. There are no broken shopwindows, no overturned urns, no crashed cars and, most importantly, no victims. Football fans act much more aggressively. And here is big politics and big passions. But the passions, so to speak, are civilized."[99]

A week later, Oleg Bogomolov, one of Gorbachev's advisers as director of the Institute of Economics of the World Socialist System, made a similar observation, noting that in recent weeks the peoples of eastern Europe have moved ahead of the USSR: "The considerable discipline of popular movements, their orderly, and non-confrontational nature give the reform in these countries perhaps a greater chance of success than the Soviet reforms have."[100] Soviet perestroika, he concluded, should take heed of that example.

This is precisely what the "radical" faction of the MDG did. Sakharov, angered by what he perceived as a conservative shift in the USSR, proposed organizing a two-hour nationwide political strike on December 11, 1989, following the Czechoslovak example two weeks earlier. The call for the strike, endorsed by five prominent MDG figures, including Gavriil Popov, Yuri Afanasyev, and the essayist Yuri Chernichenko, was broadcast multiple times a day from December 3 on Radio Svoboda and Voice of America.

The prospect of an open opposition based on popular mobilization brought forth a deluge of criticism from all parts of the political spectrum, from the conservative press and the Central Committee, predictably enough, but also from the liberal press, leading Chernichenko to withdraw his signature a few days later. Evgeny Ambartsumov, a longtime supporter of reform communism and a member of the MT who warmly welcomed the 1989 revolutions in eastern Europe, wrote in *Literaturnaia gazeta* about the imperative need to support Gorbachev, contrary to the excessive proposals of certain "left-wing radicals." The latter's "unfounded and pointless attacks" on the perestroika leader, he argued, undermined the authority of all parties and disorientated the people at a time when they were already in a very radical mood. "Any call for a strike," he warned, would be "absolutely imprudent." The mission of the "progressive intelligentsia," he concluded, was to stop the populist backlash and unite the people's aspirations with the leader of perestroika.[101]

Even the members of the MDG, who had not been consulted prior to the call to strike, harshly attacked Sakharov during the group's next meeting, held December 9–10. They accused him of having acted irresponsibly and of failing to see the harmful consequences of the strike for the country. Of the hundreds of deputies present, only thirty added their signatures to the initial call.[102] The strike itself, which took place on December 11, obtained mixed but nevertheless substantial results, given the improvised nature of the initiative.[103] At the very moment it was taking place, Sakharov delivered a speech at the Institute of Physics in which he denounced the "slowdown" of reforms and called for the defense of perestroika against those who had first initiated it. Although he expressed hope for "peaceful and progressive" developments, he stated bluntly that "the apparatus must understand that it must follow the course of perestroika, or it will be replaced." The strike, he continued, was not only a means of pressuring the regime; it was also "a psychological factor of colossal importance" since it would lead the workers to understand that they were taking control of their destiny and exerting their rightful influence over the country's future course.[104]

Sakharov continued this idea in his speech to the December 14 meeting of the MDG, delivered just a few hours before his death. He was responding to the criticism of deputy Vitaly Goldansky, a member of the MDG, who put forward a rather typical argument in support of Gorbachev—namely, that oppositional actions such as strikes were nothing more than "gifts" to the opponents of reform. Sakharov answered that "the only gift we can give to right-wing forces is the passivity of our criticism. They don't need anything more than that."[105] Pronouncing, inadvertently no doubt, what would stand as his political will and testament, Sakharov finally broke with his long reluctance to consider himself a figure of opposition:

> I wish to give a formulation of the opposition. What is an opposition? We cannot take all the responsibility for what the leaders are doing now. They are leading the country to disaster by dragging out the process of perestroika over many years. They are leaving the country in a state where everything will collapse, and collapse violently. All the plans for the transition to an intensive market economy will be unrealizable and the disenchantment will increase further. And this disenchantment will make it impossible for the country to embark on an evolutionary path of development. The only way, the only possible evolutionary way, is the radicalization of perestroika.[106]

In this, his last speech, Sakharov put forward an important argument against the strategy of supporting the "enlightened ruler": the democrats could not be satisfied with expressing their disagreement with Gorbachev while supporting him politically, because they would then become liable for measures of which they disapproved and thus compromise their cause with the population. He observed, moreover, that, unless it was subjected to an opposite popular pressure, the reforming power would tend—fatally—to yield to the pressure of the *nomenklatura*. For Sakharov, then, conflict in the political sphere was henceforth not only a source of division and instability—it was the only guarantee of peaceful evolution. It was for this reason that he chose the way of opposition. His goal in doing so was not to trigger a violent revolution—an option he categorically rejected in the name of an "evolutionary" vision of political change—but to negotiate with the reforming power according to a new balance of power, as Polish liberal intellectuals had just done by allying themselves with the workers within the Solidarność coalition.

That same evening, Sakharov died of heart failure in his apartment. After his death, he was unanimously celebrated by the liberal intelligentsia as a model of conscience and morality, but his political testament tended to arouse less enthusiasm. The general strike was largely forgotten. Threatened with expulsion from the USSR Congress, the signatories of the appeal agreed to renounce the action in order to keep their status as deputies. Shortly afterward, the MDG split over the question of whether to form an opposition and subsequently fell into disarray. Its leaders largely abandoned it in favor of two new political strategies: the conquest of power through the institutions of the Russian Republic, and the creation of a democratic faction—the "Democratic Platform"—within the Communist Party.[107]

Although the "Polish way" defended by Sakharov at the end of his life remained without immediate follow-up, his own radicalization and that of the MDG left an indelible mark on the political scene. From then on, it was possible to advance versions of perestroika that differed from Gorbachev's and to organize nonviolent mass protests without being seen solely within one's own camp as a "provocateur" in the service of perestroika's opponents. This idea led to the establishment in early 1990 of the short-lived Civic Action movement, initiated by Afanasyev despite the opposing views of several democrats. Explicitly inspired by the Estonian Popular Front and reflecting developments in eastern Europe, the movement aimed to organize a roundtable with reform-oriented authorities from the Communist Party.[108] As large-scale prodemocratization demonstrations unfolded in Soviet cities on February 24 and 25, 1990, leaders of the Civic Action movement, alongside their democratic counterparts in the party's Democratic Platform, cautioned that widespread unrest—similar to events in East Germany, Czechoslovakia, and Romania—could ensue if authorities did not agree to engage in negotiations at a roundtable.

Political pluralism, in short, had been internalized as an effective road to reform—to such an extent, in fact, that in the spring of 1990 when Gorbachev formalized this pluralism by annulling Article 6 of the Soviet Constitution, while rejecting formal negotiations similar to a roundtable, this major constitutional change ultimately provoked very little emotion. For many political actors, the existence of pluralism was no longer an issue: the question was what to do with it.

Opposition to the System and Opposition to the Government

Despite the deepening political crisis in the country and the drop in Gorbachev's popularity, most liberal intellectuals continued to resist the idea of forming a formal opposition to the Soviet government. According to their moral perspective on politics, the conflict over the organization of power was overshadowed by a higher struggle between the honest supporters of "universal values" and the hypocritical or dogmatic defenders of the "administrative command system." Any division in the reformist camp tended to be interpreted as a factor of disorder, a "gift" to the opponents of perestroika. Although several liberal deputies did gradually join the opposition to Gorbachev in the course of 1989, this process was far from self-evident: mostly provoked by events, it was reactive and hesitant. It was also highly precarious. As we will see in chapter 6, debates on the relevance of the opposition would again divide the democratic movement in 1990 and 1991—this time over the question of its relationship to the new reformist leader, Yeltsin—and once again, the majority of the liberal intelligentsia would prefer to stand in support of the "enlightened leader," even if that meant compromising its cause in the eyes of the population by accepting responsibility for authoritarian measures.

Given this stubborn resistance to the idea of forming an opposition to the regime, how are we to understand the many accounts by liberal intellectuals stating that their political commitment was always driven by the desire to create an opposition? As mentioned earlier, this is both Sakharov's and Batkin's version of the motives for the creation of the MT in the summer of 1988. This is also what Popov argued about the creation of the MDG in the summer of 1989: "All democratically oriented deputies, not only deputies from Moscow, quickly realized after the Congress that it was necessary to create an opposition group. . . . The Interregional Group worked out the strategy and tactics of its struggle. We assumed that the [party] apparatus would be in power for a long time to come. And that we would have to learn to struggle while remaining in the minority: petitions, amendments, criticism, etc. In a word, to create a normal opposition, even if everyone was afraid of this word at the time."[109]

And yet not only did the MT and the MDG forgo the "opposition" label; they also refused to act as such. With the exception of the general strike of December 1989, which, tellingly, was condemned by the majority of MDG members, both organizations opted for a strategy of supporting and advising the government, even when the opportunity arose to capitalize on popular discontent in order to change the balance of power and demand power sharing, as was done at the same time in several eastern European communist countries. In their retrospective testimonies, Sakharov, Batkin, and Popov suggest that their conciliatory strategy was in fact hiding secret oppositional motives. In other words, the MT and the MDG were actually quasi-clandestine undertakings aimed at enfeebling the Soviet regime. This view is espoused by the political scientist Michael Urban in his remarkable book on the renaissance of politics in Russia during this period: the MDG was in fact "an association embodying the apogee of the democratic movement in the USSR, disguised as a legislative faction."[110] According to Urban, opposition constituted the fundamental vocation of the MDG, whatever its members may have said at the time, and this echoed the political attitude of Soviet liberals in general: "Concepts of opposition were central to the liberal worldview: first opposition to stagnation, bureaucrats and conservatives; then when perestroika proved disappointing, opposition to everything connected with the communist system, including perestroika and its main promoter."[111]

The paradoxical character of this embrace of opposition on the part of Soviet liberals, as shown throughout this chapter, invites us to qualify this interpretation by unpacking the meaning of opposition in the perestroika era. On the one hand, there was *opposition to the communist system*, which meant the rejection of official Soviet ideology, totalitarian politics, and the rule of the bureaucratized *nomenklatura*—in short, of the "administrative command system" writ large. By this standard, the liberal intelligentsia was indeed in opposition before 1989 and, arguably, long before the beginning of perestroika. But then, one could also say that Gorbachev himself shared this "basic orientation" toward opposition, as Urban would say. His political program in 1989, indeed, aimed to reduce the power of the Communist Party, to abandon the dogmatic adherence to Marxism-Leninism, to dismantle the "administrative system of command," and to embrace a vision of Socialism that was largely inspired by Western social democracy.

Yet it is important to differentiate such *opposition to the system* from *opposition to the Soviet government*, which implied the redistribution of power and thus the questioning of Gorbachev's status as the chief architect of perestroika. Contrary to what is usually assumed, opposition to the communist system did *not* necessarily lead to opposition to the Soviet government as soon as circumstances allowed. As a matter of fact, most liberal intellectuals, to say nothing of Gorbachev himself, thought that support for the reformist leader was the best way to achieve the reforms that would put an end to the communist system. This explains, for example, why Batkin and Sakharov referred to the MT as a seed of opposition—to the communist system, that is—even though the entirety of its actions were initially aimed at supporting and advising the Soviet government. In line with this distinction, the emergence of political pluralism in 1989 was not the natural outcome of the liberated expression of deep-seated recriminations against communism but rather the unintended and reactive result of the perceived failure of the Soviet government to incorporate a plurality of views when reforming the system.

The distinction between these two types of opposition may seem counterintuitive: Could one really count on the Soviet government to dismantle the communist system? Upon closer examination of the context, however, there is no contradiction: it was a perfectly coherent and, moreover, quite common political strategy to rely on the extensive powers of an "enlightened reformer" in order to radically transform the inherited system. Before the 1989 elections, this was probably the only plausible reformist strategy as long the Communist Party maintained its monopoly on power. But the emergence of de facto pluralism in 1989 profoundly changed the situation. Henceforth, the question of power could and indeed was openly raised: *Who* should carry out perestroika, and *how*? For the liberal deputies, in the autumn of 1989 a new possibility arose, of taking advantage of Gorbachev's faltering popularity and the example of the protest movements in eastern Europe to enter into an organized opposition to the Soviet government and to attempt to radically alter the balance of power. Most liberal deputies, however, resisted adopting the path of confrontation and generally preferred to stick to the old strategy of supporting and advising the government.

This decision was highly indicative of the liberals' appreciation of the legitimacy of conflict in politics: on the one hand, liberal intellectuals displayed an absolute intransigence toward nationalists and conservative communists, despite sharing with them a common criticism of the inadequacy of Gorbachev's perestroika; on the other, they desperately sought to collaborate with the Soviet government and to avoid any open conflict with it. If confrontation over values and principles came to seem necessary, even inevitable, then *political* conflict seemed merely destructive when it came to the question of power. According to the moral perspective of the liberal intelligentsia, the question of power was therefore less of a priority than the struggle of truth against lies and the dismantling of the artificial system that alienated the full expression of personal conscience. This did not mean that democracy was not important but rather that democracy was to be achieved primarily through personal emancipation and only secondarily through its embodiment in institutions and laws. The subsidiary nature of the issue of the design of political institutions explains the attraction, in the years that followed, of theories of authoritarian transition that promised a faster path to reforms, at the cost of certain temporary departures from democratic procedures. This is the subject of the next two chapters.

Chapter 5

Modernization and the Iron Fist

> Sakharov's position seems extremely attractive. But it is only a certain moral benchmark for the society, its ideal. While we are talking about transition paths.
>
> —Igor' Kliamkin, "Nuzhna li zheleznaia ruka?," August 1989

In November 1988, Andrei Sakharov took part in a roundtable jointly organized by the American academic journal *Soviet Economy* and the Soviet weekly *Ogonek*. Invited to comment on the political situation of the moment, he distinguished three "political paths" for perestroika: "The first is Stalinism; the second, enlightened monarchy, if you will; and the third is democracy, coming from below. I think the only real way of carrying out *perestroyka* is the third method. The second path, which is very popular among the Soviet intelligentsia and our friends in the West, boils down to the slogan 'Don't interfere with Gorbachev.' . . . One must simply understand that *perestroyka* is now experiencing a very difficult, pivotal period, when a choice must be made between the second and third alternatives."[1]

The events of 1989 were to prove him right. The ensuing waves of popular mobilization received very different welcomes from the various sectors of the liberal intelligentsia. While Sakharov applauded these actions, seeing them as a way to exert democratic pressure on Gorbachev, others were worried and insisted on supporting the general secretary in order to consolidate his power and help him carry out his planned reforms. Others still went even further, suggesting that political freedoms be restricted in order to stabilize the situation and to impose the desired reforms on society. These voices did not advocate "enlightened monarchy," to use Sakharov's phrase, but they did call for a "democratic dictator."

The most famous advocates of this strategy were the liberal intellectuals Andranik Migranian and Igor Kliamkin. Both men caused a stir when, in a joint interview published in August 1989 in the mass-circulation weekly *Literaturnaia gazeta*, they declared that perestroika should be entrusted to an "iron fist."[2]

Migranian and Kliamkin nevertheless differed in terms of their interpretations of the political situation. We can see this, for example, in their diverging views on the role of the new USSR Congress and the radical deputies who were elected to that body. For Kliamkin, it was important that these deputies put pressure on Gorbachev, so as to give the general secretary more room to maneuver and thus strengthen his hand vis-à-vis the conservatives. According to Migranian, on the contrary, the radical deputies should voluntarily relinquish their power to Gorbachev. But these differences aside, both authors agreed on an essential point: the transition to democracy must be led by an authoritarian reformer—indeed, they insisted that various examples from world history demonstrate exactly this point. Furthermore, contrary to the prevailing belief at the time, Migranian and Kliamkin insisted that the lessons drawn from the 1989 revolutions did not directly apply to the USSR. They argued that the Soviet Union had not yet progressed beyond the preliminary stage of the emergence of civil society within an authoritarian context, a stage that Poland and Hungary had experienced over thirty years. While they acknowledged, along with other democrats, that the revolutions in these two countries indicated a general direction of reform, they remained convinced that drawing inspiration from them to address the issue of power in the USSR could be perilous, as they feared it might lead to "upheavals, victims, and disappointments" akin to what they observed happening in Poland in the aftermath of radical reforms.[3]

The journalist conducting the interview with the two men knew, of course, that this was an explosive thesis, as evidenced by his final words: "I'm sure you will find opponents."[4] And sure enough, the interview did indeed provoke a lively debate among the liberal intelligentsia, first in the pages of *Literaturnaia gazeta*[5] and then beyond.[6]

The idea of using authoritarian rule to carry out a program of broad reform was certainly not original. Those who are primarily concerned with the preservation of social order have always warned of the instability that results from mass politics. In Russia, where the state has often been seen as the preeminent modernizing instrument in the face of a supposedly backward society, the idea of the iron fist has over time assumed many forms and ideological colors. And as we shall see in this chapter, the figure of the enlightened despot was still alive and well in the era of perestroika; some indication of this fact was reflected in the vogue for works by the notoriously antidemocratic philosopher José Ortega y Gasset or the popularity of contemporary political figures known for their autocratic proclivities, including Margaret Thatcher, the so-called Iron Lady.

Less common, however, was the idea that authoritarian rule was the most suitable foundation for democracy. This idea required a strict distinction between the order of legitimacy of the means—authoritarian—and the ends—democratic. By contrast, the vision of perestroika promoted by Gorbachev since January 1987, to which the liberal intelligentsia still largely adhered in 1989, was based precisely on the harmony of means and ends. This reform was meant to be "systemic" in the sense that all its aspects—political, economic, and moral—were supposed to feed one another and must therefore be carried out in concert, unlike, for example, the reform carried out by the Chinese government at the same time. Of course, there was ample room for debate about how democratic principles should be implemented. We saw in the previous chapter that Sakharov's "Decree on Power" in the summer of 1989 diverged from Gorbachev's own interpretation of the principle of popular sovereignty: Sakharov interpreted it as the exercise of power by the representatives of the people, while Gorbachev saw it as a plebiscite on the progressive program carried out by an enlightened reformer. This debate between the "radicals" and those who would prioritize the consolidation of the reformist power did not, however, call into question the very principle of democracy as both the means and the end of reform. It was precisely this consensus that Migranian and Kliamkin sought to challenge with their proposal for an authoritarian transition to democracy.

From a theoretical perspective, Migranian's and Kliamkin's proposals dismissed out of hand one of the most widespread ideas among the liberal intelligentsia during this period—namely, the interdependence of politics and morality. As we saw in earlier chapters, perestroika was indeed a perfectionist project,[7] one aimed at creating the conditions for the harmonious realization of the individual and the triumph of truth over falsehood. For many Soviet liberals, this project was to ensure nothing less than the march of progress and a return to civilization. For Migranian and Kliamkin, on the contrary, the modernization of society implied the dissociation of politics from lofty ideals. In contrast to the moralism that predominated at the time, they proposed a method of "objective" and "realistic" political analysis, aimed at defining the "models" and "laws" governing the transformation and functioning of political systems. In this way they helped lay the foundations for political science as an academic field in post-Soviet Russia.

However, we will see that Kliamkin and Migranian sought to detach politics from morality for very different reasons. While Kliamkin, like many other Soviet liberals, believed that reform must serve to emancipate the individual from the artificial structure that oppresses them, he felt that this emancipation is only possible through the flourishing of self-interest in the market, rather than through the dissemination of moral ideals and democratization. Migranian, on the other hand, almost entirely ignored contemporary moral discourse and instead imported the technocratic logic of a certain branch of Western political science. Both positions represented a direct challenge to the perfectionist project of perestroika and democratization as a means of transitioning to modernity. Moreover, because it clashed so forcefully with the moral valence of the time, their call for an iron fist was rejected categorically by Soviet liberals in 1989, despite the support that many of them had expressed for a consolidation of power.

Kliamkin: Life against Ideals

A discreet, quiet man, Igor Moiseevich Kliamkin was totally unknown to the Soviet public before perestroika. Thanks to a few remarkable articles, glasnost propelled him to the center of the Soviet intellectual firmament. Born in 1941, he belonged to the youngest fringe of the "Sixties," those intellectuals who had been politicized in the context of de-Stalinization. From the beginning of his career, he devoted himself to *publicistika*, or committed essay. In 1968, he completed a correspondence course with Moscow University's Faculty of Journalism, and thereafter, he worked for several years in the press, in particular as an editor of the newspaper *Molodoi Kommunist* (Young Communist). At that time, he regularly attended the gatherings of critically minded people who put their hopes in a democratized socialism, and there he met other intellectuals who were to become famous during perestroika, such as Len Karpinsky, Otto Latsis, Aleksandr Tsipko, Grigory Vodolazov, Yuri Burtin, and Yuri Karyakin. After the crushing of the Prague Spring and the tightening of censorship in the USSR, some of these writers and thinkers created a samizdat newspaper called *Soliaris* to circulate their (now banned) ideas. However, the paper ran only one issue; its small network of collaborators was quickly dismantled by the KGB.

This episode ultimately led to Kliamkin's dismissal from his position as a journalist.[8] After being removed from public life, he immersed himself in research on Russian social and political thought, taking advantage of the access that his status as a researcher gave him to the special reserves of the Lenin State Library in Moscow, where the works that had been banned by the state were housed. In July 1987, he presented the results of his reflections in a lengthy article published in the journal *Novyi Mir* under the title "Which Way Leads to the Church?"[9]

The article caused a great stir, its publication undoubtedly one of the main intellectual events of perestroika. In it, Kliamkin discussed the political views of many Russian thinkers, including some who had long been blacklisted by the regime, among them the liberal conservative Mikhail Katkov[10] and the émigré authors of the volumes *Vekhi* and *Smena vekh*.[11] But Kliamkin's article is perhaps best known for its provocative historical argument that Stalinism was inevitable because it corresponded to the collectivist and utopian mentality that prevailed in the Soviet Union after the Civil War. This thesis caused a scandal among the liberal intelligentsia, as it directly contradicted the dominant teleological interpretation that treated Stalinism as a historical accident, a mere diversion in socialism's otherwise "normal" evolution toward more democratic forms.

After publishing his article, Kliamkin was invited to numerous debates in the press and in liberal intellectual clubs, where he acquired a reputation as a formidable polemicist. Together with the other members of the editorial team of *Novyi Mir*, he gave lectures throughout the country.[12] While maintaining successive affiliations with two different research institutes,[13] he kept up a very active career as a public commentator as perestroika progressed: he wrote another lengthy article that appeared in 1989, also in *Novyi Mir*, and then, beginning in the summer of 1989, many shorter articles in which he analyzed contemporary political life. In 1990, he, together with Yuri Burtin, was appointed codirector of the weekly newspaper *Demokraticheskaia Rossiia* (Democratic Russia).

From the publication of his 1987 article on the historical inevitability of Stalinism and his defense of the "iron fist" in 1989 to his political analyses of the 1990s, Kliamkin's writings were marked by his desire to distinguish between "ideals" and "life," in contrast to the widespread postulate favored by many liberal intellectuals that saw "universal values" as the natural expression of personal conscience, void of any distortions caused by an artificial system. This distinction had an *epistemological* dimension, based on an analysis of reality that sought to identify objective laws independent of moral judgments, as well as a *political* dimension, which translated into the promotion of an authoritarian power charged with dissociating the political, economic, and spiritual spheres.

Positivism and Determinism

In his first articles during perestroika, Kliamkin seemed to enjoy taking up what he saw as the moralistic clichés of the liberal intelligentsia, all the better to subvert them. The title of his famous 1987 article "Which Way Leads to the Church?" refers to a film that had caused a stir at the time, *Repentance*, a mystical parable about the moral weight of the Stalinist legacy. The film's final scene depicts an elderly woman searching in vain for the road to a church; in a dejected tone, she exclaims, "What good is a road if it doesn't lead to the church?" Kliamkin opened his article with this very question, but in an attempt to criticize the kinds of reflections it usually elicited in the Soviet press.

For Kliamkin, this question should lead not to a normative reflection on the nature of the right historical path so much as to a study of the objective reasons that led the country to follow one path instead of another. The correct "way to the church," despite the phrase's religious character, was not in his view a moral judgment but rather an effort at rational understanding. He thus attacked the binary judgments offered by those who conceived of Soviet history as an "uninterrupted struggle between truth and error, between the law and those who break it."[14] If the truth was already known and did indeed correspond to the logic of history, why, he asked, did it fail so miserably? Why had "errors" and "accidents of history" occurred again and again? Kliamkin denounced the "monological reasoning" of this perspective in favor of a type of "dialogical thinking" that would be sensitive to the constant conflict of ideas and the plurality of available historical paths. Such an approach would "restore the history of spiritual culture as a highly dramatic dialogue of different traditions and orientations."

At the same time, however, Kliamkin sought to defend himself from any charges of relativism. His approach did not aim to place perpetrators and victims on a similar footing but rather intended to base moral judgment on a "lucid" understanding of past phenomena. For him, a "serious relationship to history" entailed examining the roles and interests of the social forces involved in the light of the "laws of social development." His epistemology of history and politics, in fact, was positivist and technocratic; he believed that reality obeys certain social laws and that it is essential to know them in order to carry out perestroika: "To speak in a scholarly way, reality has laws of development that trace their path independently of my preferences and yours. . . . Forgetting the notion of social laws is perhaps our greatest spiritual loss, and it will be difficult to conceive a new thought without correcting this." He added, "All the 'whys?' are based on objective laws of social development. . . . This means that the study of the laws of real socialism is not an incidental, secondary, or speculative task that takes us away from the real business of perestroika; it is the very task of perestroika."[15] Objective social laws, for Kliamkin, have an explanatory, not a normative, vocation. In his eyes, this is what distinguishes them from the social laws taught to Soviets in the textbooks of "scientific communism," which dealt "not with why things are the way they are and not otherwise, but rather how they should be."

In "Which Way Leads to the Church?" Kliamkin applied this positivist method to the analysis of Stalinism. In contrast to his liberal colleagues and friends, who tended to blame Stalin for interrupting the march of socialism toward democracy and the market, Kliamkin explained Stalinism in terms of the configuration of power relations between social groups and the evolution of their respective mentalities. In this perspective, Stalinism appears to him not as a historical anomaly but as the inevitable result of the predominance in the USSR at the end of the 1920s of an egalitarian and consensualistic mentality, one that was willing to make any individual sacrifice in the name of a collective good. While formulating this conclusion, which he knew to be provocative, he defended himself against critics who claimed he was *excusing* Stalinism:

> It was the strong ones who won out in the end, and only them who could win, for there was no other "construction project" of our path that could then compete with that of collectivization. Recognizing this does not mean condemning those who thought otherwise. In fact, the position of many of them seems more attractive today than that of the victorious. But our point is that the historical balance of power was in favor of the latter and not the former. And nothing more. When one knows the fate that awaited our peasantry and our agriculture, it is difficult to resign oneself to it. That is why, while the hand follows reason and traces a positive answer, the soul suffers again and again by wondering: Could it have been otherwise? The lucid reasoning is inflexible: No, it was not possible. But how one would like to be wrong!

The distinction Kliamkin draws here between the "soul," associated with moral judgment, and "reason," which includes objective social laws, is typical of his approach to politics, and he used this trope regularly in subsequent years in his analysis of the power relations that characterized the contemporary Soviet political scene.

In 1987, Kliamkin was already skeptical of Gorbachev's program of consolidating society through democratization: "Perestroika will not overcome the contradictions, on the contrary, it will accentuate them." But, he added reassuringly, "There is nothing to fear: contradictions, it is well known, do not slow down but accelerate social development. But so that contradictions do not catch us off guard, we must be prepared for them, and we cannot be prepared for them without understanding the laws that govern our lives." As far as the accentuation of contradictions is concerned, Kliamkin's prediction was proved right: Soviet political life became more and more fragmented and complex from the summer of 1989 onward as several emerging forces began to challenge Gorbachev's monopoly on the elaboration and direction of perestroika.

Leaving aside his scholarly research on Russian intellectual and political history, Kliamkin then wrote a series of political analyses following a common pattern: exposing the forces at play, analyzing their roles in the present circumstances, evaluating their respective chances of success according to the balance of power, and then making predictions and proposals for action. The first of these articles, published in July 1989, can be considered a model of its kind. Titled "What Lies Ahead?,"[16] it is accompanied by a subtitle that clearly sums up its object: "Reflections on the Way the Different Political Forces Accomplished Their Tasks in the Congress." In this article, Kliamkin outlines the "tasks" of the three main forces in the political arena: the "reformer" must gain more power to carry out democratic and market-oriented reforms without losing the support of the state apparatus; the "apparatus" must seek to share power with society while retaining control over the main levers of authority; and the "radicals" must put pressure on the reformer to give him room to maneuver in relation to the apparatus. Ultimately, Kliamkin expressed the hope that Gorbachev would rely on popular mobilization, including extraparliamentary mobilization, to strengthen his power and thus overcome "conservative" resistance.

While Kliamkin insisted on distinguishing his analytical arguments from his personal preferences, this distinction was often difficult for his readers to grasp; at least that is how Kliamkin himself seemed to feel, since he complained of being misunderstood. In his December 1989 reply to the debate on the "iron fist" in *Literaturnaia gazeta*, he claimed that no one gave any real importance to the fact that, unlike Migranian, he did not call for the establishment of an authoritarian regime but only noted its inevitability. Exasperated, he said that his contemporaries seemed incapable of distinguishing between objective findings and value judgments: "Could it be . . . that one does not suspect that historical necessity is neither good nor bad and that one is not obliged to love it?"[17]

The fact that Kliamkin was largely misunderstood by his contemporaries can be explained in part by the ambiguity of his own position on historical necessity. On the one hand, as we have seen, he advocated "dialogical thinking" in order to explain events by taking into account a multiplicity of factors. Serious analysis, according to him, cannot take the form of a study of the past with reference to the ideals of the present, in search of remarkable examples, fatal mistakes, or missed opportunities; rather, it must explain events by taking into account the complex mechanisms that determined their unfolding. In identifying these mechanisms, Kliamkin adopted a minor form of determinism, whereby every event is shaped by causes that must be studied without resort to value judgments—a view that distanced him from the sententious history found in Soviet textbooks and brought him closer to the Weberian principle of axiological neutrality. On the other hand, Kliamkin's analyses often displayed a stronger, more demanding determinism, which held that *events could not have happened otherwise*, a rejection of the possibility of any meaningful against historical necessity.

Both forms of determinism coexist in Kliamkin's work, but he generally opted for "strong" determinism in his analyses of particular events. Thus, in dealing with the phenomenon of Stalinism, he did not only indicate the set of factors that determine its advent but categorically stated that the phenomenon was inevitable. He applied the same reasoning to current events, which he did not see as the result of a choice between different development paths but rather as the historically necessary achievement of modernization. For him, to admit that this modernization included other historical possibilities would imply that Russia had pursued an exceptional path, which, like most liberal intellectuals, he rejected out of hand. If one accepts the idea that Russia participates in universal history, then it follows, according to Kliamkin, that the country is subject to the same historical necessities as other countries—in this case the passage to democracy through an authoritarian transition.[18] His public statements to this effect, although devoid of value judgments, still have a strong normative dimension, aiming to restrict the spectrum of possible paths. This is what Yuri Burtin reproached him for in a discussion between the two codirectors of the weekly newspaper *Demokraticheskaia Rossiia*: "I note in your reasoning a tinge of historical fatalism: there is only what is and one cannot go beyond it. In times like ours, this is hardly appropriate. I would still distinguish between the inevitable facts that must be explained and what depends on people, their internal disposition and the extent of their activity."[19] In sum, there is a tension in Kliamkin's epistemology: while insisting on the dissociation of scientific explanation from moral judgments, he remained committed to a strong determinism, whereby modernization is said to obey a historical necessity that permits no genuine alternative. In wanting to see things as they *are* rather than as they *should be*, Kliamkin came to ignore what *could be*.

Lying to Oneself

In his 1989 draft for a new Soviet constitution, Andrei Sakharov made the realization of a "happy and meaningful life" one of the primary goals of the state.[20] Kliamkin, for his part, argued that perestroika should *not* pursue moral ends, because it is based precisely on the separation of the moral, political, and economic spheres—spheres he claimed had been artificially merged under the Soviet regime. This argument was to be the subject of his second major article in *Novyi Mir*, published in February 1989 and titled "Why It Is Difficult to Tell the Truth." Here, Kliamkin once again took up one of the main tropes of contemporary moral discourse—in this case *pravda*, or truth—in order to better subvert it. From the outset, he indicated his wish not to "swell the ranks of moralists" by writing a sermon on the fact that politics must be in accordance with "the principles of the good and the indications of conscience."[21] Nor did he want to give credence to the cliché that all politics is based on lies. What interested him were the conditions that enabled the institutionalization of lies in the USSR on such a catastrophic scale—and this under the leadership of a regime that claimed to serve the truth and abolish the "bourgeois lie."

The key to this puzzle, according to Kliamkin, is to be found in the "disease" of "lying to oneself" (*samoobman*). Lying to oneself, for Kliamkin, involves the naive belief in the "way to the enchanted kingdom of freedom, equality and fraternity." It is the willingness to sacrifice present interests for the sake of an ideal that can only be realized in the future. In itself, Kliamkin acknowledged, this is a perfectly normal human inclination since it stems from dissatisfaction with life and the desire to transform it. Many people in the twentieth century succumbed to the sirens of these high ideals, but they quickly "sobered up." According to Kliamkin, however, the USSR was unique in that it was fully committed to the realization of an ideal—a society without money or market—that could advance only through discipline and enthusiasm: "No one before us has tried to build life, forgetting one's salary, personal ease and independence, for the lights that shine at the end of the tunnel, which make us dream of a world where all will be comfortable, but for which it is necessary to sacrifice everything first and demand nothing immediately." In accordance with the argument that he advanced in his previous article, Kliamkin explained this particularity with reference to the balance of power between the various social groups in the USSR at the end of the 1920s. The most decisive factor, in his view, was the collectivist and utopian mentality of the uprooted peasant masses who migrated to the cities in the context of accelerated industrialization: "Stalin won because the ideology of wartime communism was more familiar to the millions of industrialization recruits than the ideology of the market and monetary relations." For Kliamkin, Stalinism was based on the institutionalization of a culture of self-delusion, which it elevated to the level of state doctrine: "The practice of lying to oneself . . . became the ideological norm, the highest form of consciousness. Its triumph was described in political documents and textbooks as the triumph of the 'socialist cultural revolution.'" The Stalinist party, in Kliamkin's words, thus played the role of a "church of the economy," a "monopoly on the interpretation of daily work and life as a whole," an "ambassador of the future in the present," a "plenipotentiary of ideals and goals," an intermediary "between the base and the superstructure, between the economy and man's consciousness, between his work and his soul, between reality and the ideal."

Yet, according to Kliamkin, the elevation of these lofty ideals to the status of state doctrine was to be the ruin of morality because the latter can only stem from one's present conscience and actions. The sacrifice of this "present" in the name of the future opens the door to all manner of moral compromises:

> If everything that happens with me today is devoid of autonomous moral value, if everything is only a means to higher ends, then this justifies not only the daily discomforts of the present, but also the betrayal of family and friends, and the crimes, and the generalized fear, and the suspicion (also generalized) that presents itself as vigilance, and the lying, and the tears of children who are guilty of having parents who did not please someone.

Kliamkin thus gave to morality a much narrower meaning than was standard in the political discourse of the time. Rather than a set of shared values, he saw it as an immanent and strictly personal disposition of one's individual conscience. Transposed into the political realm, it would be perverted into a dangerous utopia: "Life without the present"—by which he meant a life entirely devoted to the pursuit of a higher ideal—"is a life in a spiritual desert. It is the transformation of the ideal into an abstraction, into a myth."

This defense of the "present" did not imply the renunciation of all ideals for the exclusive sake of pragmatic matters; rather, it called for the pursuit of another kind of ideal: "the modern ideal—the ideal of the autonomous development of the individual." The motor of this ideal, for Kliamkin, was another natural disposition of the individual: self-interest. The objective of reform, in this perspective, is to free individuals from their collectivist and egalitarian illusions. Commenting on Khrushchev's first reforms, he writes, "We began to give people back their present, we valued their personal lives and their individual interests. Timidly, cautiously, in the shadows, material interest was legalized." To pursue this initiative, he called for perestroika to abandon the ideal of equality and "replace the impersonal 'must' with a personal 'I want.'" Kliamkin did not hesitate to call this a "moral revolution."[22]

A little more than a year later, in the summer of 1990, a roundtable discussion titled "Perestroika and Morality" gave Kliamkin the opportunity to clarify his thoughts on the relationship between morality, politics, and the economy. To restore morality, he said, it was necessary to separate it from other spheres of human activity. Only then, he added, could the error of the Soviet regime, which made morality the measure of everything, be corrected: "Nowhere is the paradoxical character of our development after the revolution more evident than in the annihilation of morality by the very original way of elevating it above the other spheres and measures of human life."[23] Kliamkin was, then, categorically opposed to the idea, advanced by many liberal intellectuals, that the market economy is morally superior to the planned economy—a position held, for example, by the economist Nikolai Shmelev, who had stated two years earlier, in a sentence that subsequently became famous, "What is economically inefficient is immoral and, conversely, what is efficient is moral."[24] For Kliamkin, this idea betrayed a typically totalitarian propensity to link economics and morality:

> It seems that the "new thought" is once again the same totalitarian consciousness, but with reversed signs. If before it was assumed that an economy could not be morally based on commodity and money relations, on market relations, that morality was something higher than money, then now we have to hear more and more often that humanity has never invented anything more moral than money. We have before us the same type of totalitarian reasoning, which seeks to identify the eternal and the absolute with the transitory and the relative, or to put it more concretely, to identify again, but in a new mode, the economy with morality.[25]

The task of perestroika, for Kliamkin, is to "dismember" the social totality. It is therefore necessary to leave morality to individual consciousness and the realm of art, as morality is concerned with the "eternal and the absolute," and to accept the "temporary and contingent" character of economics and politics. Yet, as contingent as they are, Kliamkin believed that these domains obey certain social laws and therefore must be organized according to very precise models: the market and, during a first, transitional phase, an authoritarian power. Like his epistemology, Kliamkin's political thought proceeded from a double movement by which politics and economics were to be detached from morality; he then sought to link them to the historical imperatives of modernization.

The Role of the Democratic Opposition in the Authoritarian Transition

We saw in chapter 2 that the vast majority of liberal intellectuals saw the market as nothing less than the natural mode of economic regulation. Kliamkin shared this conviction, which he expressed in a particularly lapidary manner when he affirmed that outside the market, "there is only famine, cold, with the upheavals and blood that accompany them."[26] As far as socioeconomic organization is concerned, the choice for Kliamkin is a very simple one: "Unfortunately, or perhaps fortunately, the choice offered to contemporary man is not very rich. He can either prefer a well-organized and economically efficient society, which we call capitalist, or a poor and chaotic society, which until recently we called socialist."[27] However, the passage to a market economy was not, according to him, reducible to the same stage of social development as the passage to the democracy: it would first be necessary to impose the market—only then could the state introduce democracy.

Kliamkin supported this conclusion with an analysis of the contemporary political situation in the USSR, where he anticipated strong popular resistance to such a turn to the market: "Democratization . . . does not promote reforms at all. Let us suppose that the reformer proposes the introduction of the market. Will he be able to do this by relying on the masses? No, of course not! Eighty percent of the population will not accept it. Because the market means stratification, differentiation according to income levels. You have to work a lot to live well."[28]

At the same time, Kliamkin drew on the global history of democratic transition in order to demonstrate that such transformations have always depended on the prior creation of a national market, regardless of popular resistance. "There is no example in the history of any people," he wrote, "of a transition to a market economy that parallels democratization."[29] That is why an enlightened despot is needed to free economic life from the dictates of the state, to create the legal regulators of economic relations, and to ensure the legal guarantees of individual property. He cited the example of Napoleon, who built a national market and introduced the Civil Code by force.

Kliamkin nevertheless insisted on preserving some aspects of democracy under the rule of the "iron fist." As we saw in chapter 2, one of the most important ideals for Soviet liberals was the expression of personal conscience. Kliamkin was no exception: "What would I do in these circumstances, I who hold democratic convictions? . . . I do not want to associate myself with any dictator, even if he becomes one for the sake of democracy. I want to be able to express my 'democratic opinion.'"[30] This concern was the source of his disagreement with Migranian over the role of the democratic opposition.

Unlike Migranian, who, as we shall see, believed that civil society should not constitute itself as a "legal" or "serious" opposition during the period of authoritarian transition, Kliamkin argued that the democratic minority that formed at the USSR Congress in the summer of 1989 should not hesitate to place itself in opposition to Gorbachev and to adopt an alternative program. But contrary to the wishes of Sakharov and some of his collaborators at the MDG, Kliamkin held that the job of this democratic opposition was not to accelerate the passage to full democracy but rather to strengthen the hand of the enlightened reformer. This strategy, according to Kliamkin, was dictated by the current balance of forces: insofar as the democratic opposition was too weak to maintain any plausible pretense to power, its usefulness was limited to acting as a counterbalance to the pressure that the conservative bureaucratic apparatus would exert on the reformer, thus carving out for the latter a greater margin of maneuverability: "Only the experience of a constant pressure from the left, only the constant confrontation with demands of the 'impossible' allows [the reformer] to grasp the real measure of his own possibilities."[31]

The historian Leonid Batkin, in an article responding to Kliamkin's call for an "iron fist," was dubious: "To what kind of opposition is Igor Moiseevich prepared to take part? An illegal opposition? A light opposition? Does he have any idea of the limits that will be imposed on his thoughts in these circumstances? Shall we not have to conclude this discussion in exile in case of the victory of yet another progressive dictatorship?"[32] But Kliamkin did not see the problem in the same way. His main goal was to free life—both moral and economic life—from the totalitarian grip. A year later, he summarized his specific stance from this time:

> In this situation, everything objectively pushes [the reformer] to try to gain a certain independence from the existing apparatus and also to begin to form new institutions of power. This is only possible through the activation and participation of society, that is, through democratization. On this point, I disagree with those who feel that perestroika took the wrong path and that it was necessary to form a market economy following the Hungarian or Chinese model. But I also disagree on this point with a great number of liberal intellectuals, who do not see that democratization was from the beginning a way to strengthen the personal power of the reformer and to detach him from the old structures of the state apparatus.[33]

In referring to liberal intellectuals who favor democratization for its own sake, Kliamkin probably had in mind Sakharov and his MDG allies. When he spoke of those who prefer the Chinese or Hungarian model of authoritarian reform, he was obviously referring to Migranian.

Migranian and Western-Style Technocracy

Andranik Movsesovich Migranian was a post-Soviet "expert" before his time. In a context in which Soviet intellectuals were generally perceived as a moral elite, he intervened in the public arena by way of a technocratic claim to highly specialized knowledge. At a time when political science did not yet exist as a discipline in the Soviet Union, he declared himself a political scientist.[34] In an era characterized by a pronounced moralism, he defended a soulless technocracy. Long before many of his colleagues, he sought to address a host of questions that he borrowed from Western social science, such as that of "state building." His main interest during perestroika was how to reform the political system in the context of the transition to democracy. On the eve of the first session of the USSR Congress in 1989, he described this pursuit as follows: "It seems to me that the main task of our political science at this time is the analysis of potential difficulties that may arise in the realization of reforms, as well as contradictions that are already immanent in the political system and that, under the influence of objective and subjective factors, may develop in undesirable directions for perestroika."[35]

Like Kliamkin, Migranian prided himself on his "lucid" and "serious" approach to perestroika. But unlike Kliamkin, who devoted long articles to arguing for the epistemological dissociation of politics and morality, Migranian analyzed the various political mechanisms as if the question of values and principles did not even deserve to be raised. For this reason, he has been described as a "Soviet Machiavelli."[36] But it is worth noting that Migranian shared this "Machiavellian" approach with a large current of Western political science, which based its objectivity on the principle of axiological neutrality. Migranian openly claimed this filiation, quoting extensively from such authors as Max Weber and Karl Popper, as well as several contemporary American political scientists who had not been translated into Russian and whose work he studied in the course of his research.[37] Migranian, as a matter of fact, was trained as a specialist of the United States. Unlike the Sixties, who reached political maturity during the Khrushchev Thaw, Migranian, born in 1949, came of age in the politically supine but ideologically flexible context of Brezhnevian "real socialism." Numerous opportunities were offered to those who, like him, had a diploma from the prestigious Moscow State Institute of International Relations and who showed the marks of loyalty demanded by the authorities. He obtained permission to travel abroad several times and was granted access to works confined to the special reserves of Soviet libraries. These were formative experiences for the budding political scientist.

Against Perfectionism

In the six theoretical articles he published during perestroika, as well as in his many press appearances, Migranian was sparing in his comments about morality. For him, this was simply not a priority issue. It is therefore curious, to say the least, that the only monograph he published during this entire period was the 1989 work *Democracy and Morality*.[38] When asked about this in retrospect, Migranian said that he wanted to conform to both the demands of his editor, a philosopher specializing in ethics, and the mood of the time.[39] In fact, the book is only partly about morality; its first half is largely based on an article published two years earlier detailing the relationship between the individual, society, and the state.[40] In that article, Migranian criticized the idea of an organic harmony of interests based on the common good between these three realms. In his subsequent monograph, he continued this argument and proposed a broad historical overview demonstrating that the perfectionist project of human improvement within a harmonious society implies the bankruptcy of democracy as well as of morality. From antiquity to the Middle Ages, he explained, philosophers were concerned with organizing societies in such a way that would "cultivate the best individuals and the best in each individual," a task for which they gave the state the "honorable function of educating citizens in virtue."[41] He gave as an example the Roman Republic, where he claimed a "spirit of true civility" had flourished.[42] While Migranian recognized the nobility of the perfectionist enterprise, he condemned it as a source of despotism.

In contrast, he celebrated as "a colossal feat of human genius" the idea of individual independence from society and the state, which he attributed to the "bourgeois political philosophy" of the eighteenth and nineteenth centuries.[43] According to this political theory, which he described as "liberal-democratic," the state must be the protector of the inalienable rights of individuals and the guarantor of the conditions for the realization of their egoistic interests, their potentialities, their desires, and their passions.[44] This guarantee is based on the distinction between the state and civil society, whose interactions are regulated by a system of checks and balances. This system, Migranian pointed out, is not intended to overcome the conflict between individual and collective passions but to place it within a legitimate and institutional framework so as to guarantee the stability of the state and the well-being of its citizens. The founding of the American republic, in this respect, served as an inspiring model. Quoting approvingly from the comments of the American journalist George Will[45] on the political thought of John Madison, he wrote, "The political problem was approached [at the founding of the United States] exclusively from the standpoint of the control of the passions given by nature, and not from the education of a type of character that the political system might require."[46] Democracy, in this view, is based not on the principle of popular sovereignty but on the "legitimization (legalization) of conflict and [on] the ability of everyone to fight for the conquest of power"—an idea he attributed to Popper and, more generously, to "all the theorists of democracy in the modern age."[47] The main advantage of this political system, argued Migranian, is that it avoids tyranny. On the other hand, he recognized that this system pays little attention to virtue and gives free rein to individual egoism. This is precisely what Marxism sought to correct, an effort that, according to Migranian, amounts to a revival of the ancient and medieval ideal of the organic unity between the individual, society, and the state.

But Migranian also had a warning: socialist states produce results that are in fact contrary to their noble ambitions. First, the abolition of the separation of powers in the name of a direct expression of the people's will by the soviets had meant that both society and the individual had been completely engulfed by the state; in Migranian's view, this was the very negation of democracy. The result was "a barracks in which man's life does not consist in realizing his own potentialities and abilities, but in slavishly obeying orders from above."[48] Second, the regulation of human activity implies the negation of individual responsibility and thus the exhaustion of morality. Without openly rejecting Marxism—Migranian was careful to spare the ideological sensitivities of his readers—he called on his fellow citizens to combat egoism by a method that was clearly far from Marxist: "the protection and enlargement of the individual sphere, independent from the regulation of society and the state, so that each individual has the possibility of making voluntary choices in accordance with his natural capacities and inclinations."[49] He concluded his book by reaffirming the principle of the interdependence of politics and morality—a common view in the discourse of the time. And yet, in doing so, he actually subverted it: the moral health of society, he argued, stems from the *inaction* of the state in the moral sphere.

Like Kliamkin, Migranian argued that morality is only possible if accompanied by individual freedom, which itself consists, as the liberal philosopher Benjamin Constant wrote at the beginning of the nineteenth century, of "peaceful enjoyment and private independence."[50] As for the state, its actions are guided by a set of considerations that are specific to the political domain, which, according to Migranian, aims above all for stability. This priority left him extremely skeptical of the possibility of an immediate democratization of the political system.

The Long Road to Democracy

Migranian's ideal political system was based on the American model: a strong, popularly elected president and a clear separation of powers.[51] However, he was categorically opposed to the idea that Western democracy could be "imported" into the USSR—a position expressed most clearly in a debate with the historian Leonid Batkin in 1988. In the spring of that year, Batkin had published a short article in the intellectual journal *Vek XX i mir* titled "Becoming Europe," in which he expressed a resolutely Western-oriented position and called on the USSR to catch up with "contemporary civilization."[52] Batkin referred to the example of Japan, "which was also a completely backward and closed country" but which "imported world history and replanted it in its Japanese soil and . . . made a local variety of the universal grow there."[53] Of course, Migranian agreed entirely with Batkin that modernization has only one historical path and that this path was traced by the West. In his writings, he is tireless in his insistence on the fact that the political mechanisms he presents are "universal" and that, although they are elaborated by "bourgeois philosophy," they apply as well to the USSR as anywhere else in the world. On the other hand, he resolutely opposed the idea that the return to the "civilized world" could be accomplished by direct imitation of Western political models.

A few months after Batkin's article appeared, Migranian published in the same journal a piece titled "Is It Easy to Become Europe?" In it he attacked "the prejudice that democracy can be exported."[54] He also repeated an argument that often appeared in his articles from this time—namely, that no country has ever advanced directly from a traditional, absolutist society (a totalitarian one, in his case) to "democratic values and institutions." Britain, Holland, and the countries of northern Europe, he asserted, "were lucky" because this transition took place "organically" over several centuries.[55] In contrast, France seemed to him to illustrate the harmful consequences of a "rushed" transition toward democracy. Citing Tocqueville, he denounced the "attempt to achieve freedom immediately as the surest way to slavery."[56] He pointed to the fact that for two hundred years France had to go through "countless revolutions, dictatorships, ochlocracies, overthrows of the monarchy by the republic, and vice versa." Only then could it finally establish a stable political system, when the alliance of socialists and communists came to power in 1980 and subsequently gave rise to an American-style two-party system.[57]

In the USSR, as elsewhere, according to Migranian, the transition to democracy faced two great dangers: the resistance of the bureaucracy and social polarization. To the first of these dangers, he dedicated a long article, published in 1988 in the collection *Inogo ne dano*, titled "The Braking Mechanism of the Political System and the Ways to Overcome It."[58] This "braking mechanism," he explained, is the "uncontrolled, all-powerful, and invasive bureaucracy" that opposes democracy.[59]

On the surface, Migranian's thesis was not very original. Several of his concepts were already commonplace among the liberal *publicistika* of the time: notably, the dichotomy between acceleration and braking and between bureaucracy and democracy, as well as the references to the classics of Marxism-Leninism to defend a very un-Marxist perspective. But behind this conventional vocabulary, the author proposed an original analysis. The establishment of bureaucratic "totalitarianism," for him, was not the result of the seizure of power by a new dominant class—the *nomenklatura*—that would seek to jealously preserve its privileges; it stemmed, rather, from a dysfunction of the political system itself: specifically, the lack of separation of powers.[60] The failure of Soviet democracy, he argued, was the result of the attempt to imitate the model of the Paris Commune through soviets made up of nonprofessional representatives who embodied both executive and legislative power. Lacking the political and financial autonomy necessary for the exercise of counterpower, the soviets were transformed by the 1930s into mere instruments for the ritual approval of the bureaucracy's decisions.

Migranian painted a political portrait of Stalin that is surprising, to say the least, coming from a liberal intellectual of that time: rather than depicting a criminal responsible for the perversion of universal values, he portrayed Stalin as a charismatic leader who, in the absence of democratic political institutions, was the only one able to contain the bureaucracy's omnipotence. The state's totalitarian domination, according to Migranian, was consolidated *after* the Twentieth Party Congress, owing to the absence of democracy *or* a charismatic leader. This is how the "brake mechanism" of the political system became institutionalized, and its harmful effects could also be felt in the economic and moral spheres.

Migranian saw in this system the origin of the moral decay of Soviet society: "The harmful consequences of the braking mechanism go beyond the political system and affect all spheres of societal activity. They distort the economic system, paralyze the normal functioning of economic mechanisms, and poison the moral sphere of our society. Unlimited power in the hands of public officials leads to intoxication of power, servility, corruption, squandering of state funds. It leads to the dissolution of morality, to the alienation of the broad masses from the political system, and it causes irreparable damage to our socialist ideals."[61] Like most other liberal intellectuals, Migranian therefore called for the overthrow of the "administrative system of command" in order to liberate the autonomous expression of values and market mechanisms. He insisted, however, that this could not be done in a democratic way.

The second danger Migranian saw in the transition to democracy was "social polarization" resulting from the hasty political emancipation of the masses. In the absence of legal mechanisms for conflict resolution, this would threaten the stability of the political system. In his articles, Migranian resorted to natural imagery to describe the masses, likening them to an "impetuous torrent" that had been unleashed in a chaotic manner, without regard to the "rational" and "serious" measures that circumstances required.[62]

Their direct involvement in politics, according to Migranian, would bring disastrous consequences: "The direct appeal to the people can be harmful to the fate of perestroika. The experience of the French and Russian Revolutions shows that when the necessary conditions are not met, when a revolution from above is interrupted by a massive engagement from below and by the adoption of radical measures of social transformation, it ends in a bloodbath for the people itself and by the establishment of a regime even harsher and more tyrannical than the one that had preceded these revolutionary actions from below."[63]

Migranian was so worried about the consequences of social polarization that he declared it worse than a conservative power grab and a return to Brezhnevian stagnation. This anxiety at the prospect of mass mobilization was fed above all by the spectacle of the 1989 electoral campaign and the first session of the USSR Congress, which, according to him, led to the emergence of "populist" and "neo-Bolshevik" leaders like Yeltsin.[64] These leaders, according to Migranian, took advantage of the disarray of the people to incite their rejection of the *nomenklatura* and to propose solutions deemed "simple, fast, and effective": that is, to put an end to privileges and achieve equality and social justice. Such leaders, Migranian claimed, "[could not] modernize the system, only destroy it."[65] For him, these radical voices reflected the "socioeconomic and cultural unpreparedness of society," as they expressed radical positions that could not be institutionalized within the political system and which therefore fueled polarization.[66]

It may seem paradoxical that Migranian would be so critical of the Congress deputies and the new legislative activity that emerged in 1989 while at the same time stressing the importance of an autonomous legislative power and the need for free expression of conflicting interests. In fact, Migranian's political model was not so different from the one described by Sakharov in his draft constitution. Sakharov had also been inspired by the American political system, proposing in his draft the establishment of a representative democracy with a strict division of powers. Indeed, the disagreement between Migranian and Sakharov had little to do with the *direction* of the proposed political reforms and everything to do with the *means* of their implementation. In contrast to rapid democratization supported by mass mobilization, Migranian called for a gradual democratization based on the party-state apparatus, a democratization from above, as it were, inspired by the examples of Hungary and China. Democratization, he never tired of arguing, must be carried out under the guidance of a strong, stable, centralized reforming power informed by a comprehensive concept of reform. For Migranian, this could only be carried out by a reformer with the attributes of "enlightened authoritarianism," by a "charismatic leader"—in a word, by a "dictator."[67] He cited numerous examples—Spain, Greece, Portugal, South Korea, Brazil, Argentina, the Philippines, "and perhaps soon Chile"— illustrating the need for such power to achieve the transition to democracy despite the resistance of the bureaucracy and the risk of social polarization.[68]

Authoritarianism as a Guarantor of Civil Society

For Migranian, democratization was not the same as democracy. To a journalist who objected to this claim by repeating the official credo that democracy is both the means and the end of perestroika, Migranian replied that the "experience of world civilization" had shown that these two moments are not in fact synchronous: on the passage from totalitarianism to democracy, society must first pass through an intermediate authoritarian phase. The journalist pressed Migranian on this point: Aren't totalitarianism and authoritarianism synonymous? Not at all, he retorted, because authoritarianism admits the conflicting expression of forces and interests within society and the state, thereby creating the institutions and values necessary for a transition to democracy.[69] Migranian returned to this distinction between totalitarianism and authoritarianism several times in his articles from this period.

The transition from totalitarianism to authoritarianism, Migranian explained, is guaranteed by the creation of institutional barriers against the omnipotence of bureaucracy. The first of these is the separation of powers. Migranian suggested creating permanent, politically and financially independent legislative bodies at all levels of government, to be formed through direct, multicandidate elections. Their purpose, however, would not be the expression of popular sovereignty; they would serve, rather, as professional, nonpartisan checks and balances that give voice to the "nation's elite" and aim to represent "interest groups." The model Migranian had in mind was that of the West European and United States parliaments of the early nineteenth century, as they operated before the rise of mass political parties.[70] This is why he did not consider these parliaments to be incompatible with the maintenance of a one-party system.[71] Indeed, he called for other typically "democratic" institutional safeguards, including the adoption of a constitution and a constitutional court.[72] These provisions were intended to prevent authoritarian rule from descending into the sort of "despotism" and "arbitrariness" that characterizes regimes wherever politics is governed by the will of the ruler rather than by laws. What matters, in short, is not the democratic legitimacy of power but its legality—that is, its institutional framework. The latter would not be complete, however, if it did not also rely on one last essential barrier to the power of the bureaucracy: the institutionalization of civil society.

Migranian was both the most famous defender of the iron fist and one of the pioneering theorists of civil society in the USSR. The coincidence of these qualities in a single intellectual just so happened to call into question the widely held view that civil society and democracy necessarily go hand in hand. While the legal guarantee that autonomous organizations would enjoy freedom of activity is undoubtedly a necessary condition for the functioning of a parliamentary democracy—a fact that many Soviet dissidents had emphasized since the 1970s—it is not in itself sufficient because freedom from state coercion does not necessarily imply participation in political decision-making. Migranian was very clear on this point, explicitly distinguishing "democratic values and principles" from "liberal values and principles" that underlie civil society. He associated democracy with the value of equality and the principle of broad popular participation in the exercise of power, and civil society with the values of individualism and the inalienable individual rights and freedoms that form the basis of negative liberty—that is, the freedom of the individual from interference by the state and society. Drawing on examples from Western political history, he showed that these two sets of values and principles have not always been linked. Britain, for example, first "built the democratic political mechanism" on an aristocratic basis that kept the popular masses out of politics.[73] For Migranian, this is a universal lesson: the first step in founding a democracy is to ensure "negative liberty, clearly prioritizing liberal values over democratic ones, and in particular liberty over equality."[74]

This is, in his view, a historical necessity: "Based on the experience of many countries that have gone through the transition to a democratic political system, I think we can deduce the following law [*zakonomernost'*]. The democratic mechanism is very fragile in the first stage of its foundation and can easily be destroyed by a broad involvement of the masses in political action, while they do not have enough general culture, and especially political culture. The guarantee of freedom and independence of the individual, which derives from the doctrine of liberalism, makes it necessary to create a mechanism."[75]

The mechanism in question includes, in addition to the separation of powers and constitutional control mentioned above, the "institutionalization of civil society"—that is, the legal guarantee of the organization and autonomous expression of individual and collective interests. Like many of his contemporaries, Migranian saw the proliferation of informal groups as a sign of the emergence of a civil society. Their role, he observed, is to express the important problems experienced by certain categories of citizens or by society as a whole, as well as to encourage the authorities to adopt appropriate solutions to these problems. To this end, he saw acts of civil disobedience as an effective means of exerting pressure on the bureaucracy, especially when they are widely reported in the media. As early as 1988, Migranian went so far as to propose legislation to authorize acts of civil disobedience, which he defined—invoking "the vast majority of political scientists"—as "public, nonviolent, consciously prepared but illegal acts, usually aimed at changing the law or the actions of the various powers."[76] As an example, he referred to the mobilization that began in 1987 in Leningrad, which sought to protect the city's architectural heritage and forced municipal authorities to explain their plans for the destruction of the Angleterre Hotel. Migranian, however, did not share the eagerness of many these informal activists, especially their desire to have their activity emancipated from existing constraints in the political sphere. The institutionalization of civil society, he argued, necessarily translates into the public expression of social conflicts that, if exacerbated, pose a real threat to the stability of the political system. For this reason, he believed it essential that the reformer retain an authoritarian power of "correction and arbitration" to oversee the gradual transfer of power to civil society.[77]

In practical terms, of course, the reformer's authoritarianism would imply serious restrictions on political participation: "Certainly, the political rights of citizens and sociopolitical organizations will be curtailed, serious legal opposition will be prohibited, and the political behavior of citizens and political organizations will be severely regulated. Unlike totalitarianism, however, which prohibits all heterodox thought and political opposition, authoritarianism allows and determines the limits of permissible heterodoxy and legal opposition."[78] In the summer of 1989, during the miners' strike, Migranian proposed that Congress vote to give full powers to Gorbachev to form a National Salvation Committee and dissolve all legislative bodies, including the Congress and local soviets.[79]

Moral Freedom and Paternalism

For Migranian, the plurality of interests and ideas expressed in civil society is compatible with the existence of absolute rule because pluralization takes place at a different pace in each sphere of human activity. The spiritual sphere is the first to emancipate itself from the absolute control of the state. In the USSR, this process, which began with de-Stalinization, was already complete: "In the moral sphere, we have already moved to a managed democracy, and even almost to a complete democracy, as shown by the publication of *Inogo ne dano*: every institution, every phenomenon of our society can present itself before the critical mind of the researcher, independently of the opinion or decisions of the powerful state forces."[80] In the economic sphere, however, the pluralization of property forms had only just begun, and its implementation was unpopular—all the more reason, in Migranian's mind, to establish a strong, centralized power.

We saw earlier that Migranian conceived of morality as a private disposition that relies on individuals taking responsibility for their actions; as well, it was in the name of this principle of individual autonomy that Migranian condemned the claim of socialist states to instill moral qualities in their citizens (indeed, he condemned any attempt in this direction, claiming that it led to tyranny). It may seem surprising, in this context, that he also stated that the authoritarian reformer must act in an "enlightened" and "paternalistic" manner to create the mechanisms for the acquisition of a "political culture."[81] Migranian did not give a clear definition of political culture. Most often, he described it as a set of practices geared at moderation and respect for the law. At other times, however, he gave it a substantive moral content, treating it as a set of shared values that would ensure social cohesion beyond individual interests. He thus justified the preservation of a one-party system with reference to a political culture that he claimed was incapable of expressing a clear consensus on the fundamental values and goals of society beyond divergent interests.

Migranian described the task of the reformer as a *pedagogical* enterprise whose principal goal ought to be leading society to maturity: "[At the end of the authoritarian transition] will come to an end the period of infantilism of our society, when its thoughts, its goals, and its tasks were imposed from above. This will be followed by a period of maturity, when society becomes sufficiently competent and developed, when its civil institutions can effectively formulate goals and tasks and carry them out themselves for the good of the whole society, through established autonomous mechanisms."[82]

The paternalism that Migranian is here advocating is not perfectionism. Whatever content he gives to political culture, he does not claim that it makes people better, only that it is necessary for the functioning of the political system. Its value, in short, is strictly instrumental to the stability of the system. This paternalism, moreover, does not interfere with the principle of individual autonomy as understood by Migranian—that is, with the freedom of the individual against the encroachment of the state into the private sphere. In this perspective, Migranian saw the individual as no less autonomous because an authoritarian state prohibits him from participating in the exercise of power and imposes mechanisms deemed useful for the stability of the political system. On the contrary, the exclusion—nominally on a temporary basis—of the majority of the population from the political domain constitutes, according to Migranian, the best guarantee of the preservation of individual freedom against the tyranny of the masses and totalitarianism.

Democracy as Fabrication, Democracy as Liberation

The political reform proposed by Migranian was a technocratic program amounting to the state-enforced establishment of a legal framework of democracy—namely, civil society and the separation of powers. It was, in short, a work of *fabrication*. Like a craftsperson, the reformer must "construct" the "mechanisms" of the relationship between the individual, society, and the state in such a way that they correspond to the "model" dictated to him by specialized knowledge, in this case the global experience of both a market and a democratic transition. The authoritarian dimension is intrinsic to this technocratic perspective: by possessing specialized knowledge, the role of the craftsperson is reserved for an enlightened elite that, furthermore, must exert a certain degree of force on the given material to shape it into the desired form.[83]

Kliamkin, on the other hand, saw the aim of political reform as the liberation of individuals' natural dispositions—what he calls simply "life" and "the present"—from the grip of artificial and abstract schemes. He presented this liberation as an antitechnocratic enterprise: "The normal society we seek to achieve must not be projected and constructed, just as the organism and soul of each of us cannot be projected and constructed."[84] From this point of view, it is "life" that must orient politics: "Here I would like to be particularly precise: as long as we dance not from life, but from language, to which life must always correspond . . . , then on our earth there will be neither ease nor moral health and we will be governed by specialists in ideological linguistics."[85] In this, Kliamkin shared the anti-artificialist and anti-ideological moral perspective common to most Soviet liberals in the perestroika era. Yet he endorsed the main conclusions of Migranian's technocratic program: the establishment of an enlightened despot, the restriction of political freedoms, and the imposition of a market economy as a prerequisite for future democratization. This program, by Kliamkin's own admission, did not correspond to his "democratic convictions," but it nevertheless seemed inevitable to him given the historical experience of democratic transitions and the disposition of contemporary power relations in the USSR. By such reasoning, Kliamkin *anticipated* the change of attitude that was to sweep most of the liberal intelligentsia in favor of the "iron fist" in the following years.

In the summer of 1989, when the joint interview with Kliamkin and Migranian appeared in the press, their position caused a scandal. Readers inundated the editorial office of *Literaturnaia gazeta* with hundreds of indignant letters: "I was reading and I couldn't believe my eyes," wrote one of them. "At first I thought it was an April Fools' joke," wrote another.[86] For many, the idea of the "iron fist" would mean moving *away* from any sense of genuine reform. One reader called Migranian and Kliamkin "dinosaurs" and "pterodactyls," while another accused them of returning to the darkest days of the Soviet past: "I don't want an 'iron fist' to lead me into a bright future. We have already been there and paid dearly enough. For that is precisely where Stalin's 'super iron fist' took us."

The journalist who compiled excerpts of these reader letters into an article observed, moreover, that the criticism of the "iron fist" often reflected a moral indignation that left little room for discussion: "He who passionately defends democracy may have, without suspecting it, a conscience contaminated by the virus of authoritarianism. I write this because there are, unfortunately, far too many swear words in the letters against those authors who have dared to express an unusual and unpopular point of view. There is far too much distrust and willingness to accuse those who think differently of all deadly sins. I doubt that these attitudes are compatible with a true democratic conscience."

As was often the case in those days, disagreement led to the suspicion that one's opponent was guilty of concealing certain selfish motives. Many readers, for example, declared that Migranian and Kliamkin had been "bought" or that they were puppets in a political "campaign" to prepare society for the establishment of a dictatorship. For most of the readers of *Literaturnaia gazeta*, as for most of the intellectuals who published their own retorts to Migranian and Kliamkin, the idea of the "iron fist" was fundamentally contrary to perestroika.

And yet, while they considered the "iron fist" to be an unacceptable idea, a considerable number of Soviet liberals were not fundamentally hostile to many of the arguments voiced by Migranian and Kliamkin. Liberal intellectuals who supported the consolidation of democratic forces in support of the reformer shared a desire to strengthen executive power and a concern about the potential instability brought on by mass mobilization. Gavriil Popov, for example, an influential liberal deputy and soon to be the leader of the Moscow city soviet, was one of those who supported the creation of the post of president of the USSR in the spring of 1990, a move that further expanded Gorbachev's authority, despite the fact that he had once again been elected on an indirect basis—in this case, by congressional deputies rather than at the ballot box. Popov justified his support for this measure by arguing that "it is impossible to create an effective political system without a strong and independent executive."[87] Other radical deputies, for their part, denounced the introduction of the presidency as a step toward authoritarianism. Afanasyev asked, "What has [the presidency] brought, if not an unusual leap toward the authoritarian rule of a certain oligarchy, a certain anonymous junta?"[88]

It is in this context that a curious article titled "By the Strong Method..." appeared in the journal *Vek XX i mir*, where it was described as an "analytical note prepared by the specialists of the Leningrad Association of Socioeconomic Sciences."[89] This association was composed of a group of neoliberal economists led by Anatoly Chubais who expressed the necessity of an accelerated transition to a market economy—what they called the "great leap"—aimed at achieving fiscal balance and the immediate establishment of private property. Their article can be seen as the quintessential expression of a technocratic approach to perestroika. Without even attempting to justify their position with arguments, the authors declare from the outset that their conception of economic reform is "rational and timely"; they then devote the entire article to outlining the political measures that must be taken to ensure its success.

The implementation of these economic reforms, the anonymous authors predicted, would stir resistance from the majority of the population because of the sharp decline in living standards, the increase in income inequality, and the emergence of mass unemployment. To maintain control over the country and ensure the progress of reforms, the authors argue, the government must adopt authoritarian measures, such as censorship of its critics and the adoption of exceptional laws against strikes. The institution of the

Soviet presidency, in their view, was a good step toward the concentration of power. Like Migranian, the Leningrad economists also considered that civil society, insofar as it was not contentious, was perfectly compatible with authoritarian power. In their eyes, it allowed "the preservation of political outlets: pluralism and glasnost for everything that does not concern political reform." But unlike the bluntness of Kliamkin and Migranian, Chubais and his colleagues advised a more subtle approach to public opinion, by which the government would not openly break with democratization but would claim to pursue democratic reforms while breaking in practice with its "programs and promises."

At the time of its publication, in a journal with a small circulation, this article went largely unnoticed. Within a year, however, the program described by Chubais and his colleagues would inspire the official policy of the Russian government. Behind-the-scenes games led these Leningrad economists, in collaboration with neoliberal economists from Moscow led by Egor Gaidar, to form the team charged by Yeltsin with the elaboration and implementation of economic reforms in Russia.[90] Without being elected, Gaidar was appointed prime minister of the Russian government in November 1991, and Chubais, deputy prime minister and chair of the Committee on State Property in June 1992. Yeltsin did not hesitate to use authoritarian measures to carry out unpopular economic reforms, but he was careful to declare his allegiance to democratic principles. Only by strengthening his personal power, he argued, could he guarantee the victory of democracy over his nationalist and communist opponents.

Cast in this "democratic" light, the authoritarian policy of the Russian government attracted the support of most liberal intellectuals. Like Kliamkin a few years earlier, they recognized that this policy did not respect all the moral principles dictated by their conscience, but they nevertheless considered it *inevitable*. The reasons for this reversal in favor of the "iron fist" are discussed in the next chapter.

Chapter 6

The Dilemma of the Democratic Movement (1990–93)

> My collaborators and I are currently in a complex situation. We criticize Yeltsin's policy, because we cannot do otherwise, but—
> —But you cannot criticize it either, at least in Congress, because it brings water to the mill of the national-communist opposition?
> —That's about it.
>
> Yuri Afanasyev, "Molchanie demokraticheskih 'iagniat,'" being interviewed in 1993

A few hours before his death in December 1989, Andrei Sakharov had expressed his wish to see the country's democratic forces unite in a broad-based, popular opposition movement, following the example of Poland and Czechoslovakia. In a little less than a year, such a movement had indeed taken shape in the Soviet Union. On October 20–21, 1990, 1,273 delegates from local democratic committees, representatives of ten political parties and thirty-one organizations, and delegates from seventy regions of Russia met in Moscow to create the coalition known as Democratic Russia (Demokraticheskaia Rossiia, hereafter DR). Like the broad social movements that had recently had such an impact across eastern Europe, DR was not a formal political party designed for parliamentary activity but a nimbler organization whose aim was the broadest possible mobilization of society. DR's leaders—those who sat on its two governing councils—came mainly from the Moscow liberal intelligentsia. Some of them, like Yuri Afanasyev and Gavriil Popov and other members of the MDG, had been active in politics since the spring of 1989. For others, such as Leonid Batkin and Yuri Burtin, election to the head of DR was a first step into politics. The social profile of DR's leaders was, however, less exclusive than those of the MDG or the MT.

As we shall see below, the prestigious intellectuals who formed the membership of the MDG and the MT would henceforth collaborate with a new generation of liberal political actors who distinguished themselves by their organizational skills in the 1989 and 1990 election campaigns. All came together to assume a common task: opposition to the communist system. This clear negative vocation was the key to the coalition's success. Thanks to its impressive mobilization capacities, it quickly established itself as the main vehicle for the "democratic movement," which is to say the wide array of political forces fighting under the banner of democracy against the Communist Party.[1] In 1990 and 1991, DR organized the largest demonstrations in Russian history. These mobilizations played a decisive role in the successful conquest of power of the rising radical deputies, starting with Boris Yeltsin, who was elected head of the Russian government in March 1990 and then president of Russia in June 1991. DR's successful mobilization of an incipient democratic electorate also made possible the election of Gavriil Popov and Anatoly Sobchak to the top executive positions in Moscow and Leningrad, respectively. Moreover, the popular legitimacy behind DR's support for these new leaders proved decisive in their struggle against Gorbachev and the Communist Party, which ended in the defeat of the conservative putsch of August 1991 and the subsequent collapse of the institutions of Soviet power.

The statutes of DR made clear that its purpose was "to coordinate democratic forces in opposition to the Communist Party's monopoly on the state and politics, to conduct joint electoral campaigns, [and] to coordinate parliamentary activity and other actions aimed at the creation of a civil society."[2] However, there was no consensus as to the best strategy for achieving these goals. As was the case in the MDG in 1989, the liberal intelligentsia within DR was divided between the "moderates" who favored the consolidation of the reformist power and the "radicals" who favored the creation of an autonomous political force that could potentially oppose Gorbachev. For the former, civil society had to collaborate with the reformer in the struggle against the communist system and for democracy, while for the latter, democracy lay in the autonomy of civil society from any government, whether reformist or not. The outcome of this debate was decisive for the fate of democracy in Russia. The victory of the supporters of consolidation within DR in 1992, along with the downfall of the proponents of an autonomous democratic opposition, led to the depletion of the pluralism that had emerged in 1989, encompassing multiple versions of perestroika. This resulted in the contraction of the political arena into a seemingly existential clash between two incompatible factions: those in favor of reforms and those opposed to them. A year later, this polarization was finally overcome by the consolidation, with the support of many liberal intellectuals, of a superpresidential regime that succeeded in definitively marginalizing the democratic movement and the liberal intellectuals who had committed themselves to perestroika.

The Two Ideological Shifts of 1990

Throughout 1990 and 1991, the liberal intellectuals who joined the DR coalition experienced a two-speed radicalization that followed a similar dynamic to that of the MDG in the autumn of 1989.

On the one hand, they became more and more opposed to the communist system and, in the process, made two impressive ideological shifts that confirmed their break with Marxism-Leninism: the adoption of the discourse of national liberation and their abandonment of socialism. On the other hand, the DR leadership continued to struggle with the same strategic dilemma between opposition and consolidation of power when it came to determining its relationship with the new reformist leader in Russia, Boris Yeltsin. And as in 1989, the majority of DR leaders favored a strategy of support vis-à-vis the "enlightened reformer," even when creating an opposition became both thinkable and feasible.

Andrei Sakharov would probably have rejoiced to see the democratic movement coalesce into the sort of coalition that DR became in the course of 1990 before placing itself in direct opposition to Gorbachev some months later. He nevertheless would have been very surprised by the two major ideological shifts that the liberal intelligentsia underwent at the time. The first was the valorization of concepts previously championed by the nationalist opposition, such as Russian sovereignty and national liberation. It should be remembered that the liberal intelligentsia had since 1987 maintained a position of open hostility toward the nationalist intelligentsia and that these two ideological camps had been vigorously inveighing against each other via their respective media outlets. From the beginning of 1990, however, this ideological distinction became less rigid, mainly for reasons related to the contemporary political situation. The MDG's inability to impose its demands on the agenda of the USSR Congress in the autumn of 1989 led several of its members to abandon Soviet parliamentary institutions entirely and focus their attention specifically on Russia,[3] which they hoped to use as a stronghold from which to counterbalance the power of the central Soviet government. They were inspired by the example of the Baltic states, which were granted financial autonomy in July 1989, raising the prospect of using the political institutions of the constituent Soviet republics as real institutions of power. Many deputies of the MDG expressed similar ideas as they ran in the elections of March 1990 for deputies at all legislative levels—local, municipal, regional, national—in Russia. Borrowing the rhetoric employed by the Baltic Popular Fronts, they presented their struggle against the central

THE DILEMMA OF THE DEMOCRATIC MOVEMENT (1990-93)   143

Soviet power as a struggle against imperialism and for the affirmation of national sovereignty.

The use of this nationalist discourse in Russia was also facilitated by the important role that a new generation of liberal political actors played in the 1990 election campaign.[4] These young academics and professionals did not share the traditional distrust of the Soviet liberal Sixties toward the Russian national question.[5] While they did not enjoy the same prestige as the more prominent liberal intellectuals who gathered under the banner of the MT, these new activists were very effective at organizing and mobilizing the masses. In addition to contributing to DR's electoral successes, they brought a more patriotic color to it—an emphasis that is apparent from its choice of the name Democratic Russia. However, it must be stressed that this ideological change did not translate into a rapprochement with the political forces of Russian nationalism. Despite a certain thematic overlap, DR was systematically opposed to the full gamut of Russian nationalist organizations, who defended the idea of a particular path for Russia and the restoration of traditional values against the deleterious influence of the West or national minorities. Here as well, the DR deputies who defended Russia's "national sovereignty" gave this concept a completely different meaning from the one put forward by the nationalist movements of several Soviet republics since the spring of 1989, among other ways by refusing to take up the project of national cultural affirmation. In Russia, where Russians can hardly claim the status of an oppressed minority, DR activists used the concept of national sovereignty above all to justify the devolution of power to the republics in order to carry out the democratic and market reforms that the central Soviet power was accused of slowing down.

The second ideological shift that characterized the democratic movement in the course of 1990 was the shift from reform communism to outright anti-communism. Here again, the members of DR were sensitive to the example of the Baltic Popular Fronts and also to that of the eastern European revolutions, which demonstrated the potential of a mobilization based on the pure and simple rejection of the communist system and its underlying ideology rather than on the promise of its renewal. Thus, the agenda of reform communism was severely shaken by the landslide victories of anti-communist forces in eastern Europe, including in countries with a traditionally left-leaning intelligentsia, such as East Germany.[6] Another circumstance encouraging this shift to anti-communism was the failed attempt by many MDG deputies, including Yeltsin and Afanasyev, to collaborate with Gorbachev's team in reforming the Communist Party from the inside, following the Hungarian example. In January 1990, these deputies had created a "Democratic Platform" within the Communist Party with the aim of transforming it into a democratic parliamentary party after provoking a split with its more conservative elements. In early July 1990, at the Twenty-Eighth Party Congress, Yeltsin proposed renaming the Communist Party of the Soviet Union the Party of Democratic Socialism, as well as authorizing factions and carrying out the reforms advocated by the Democratic Platform. This initiative proved a failure: the conservative forces within the party managed to prevent such a schism by blocking Yeltsin's proposal and obtaining the expulsion from the party of several members of the Democratic Platform. In a dramatic move, more than fifty other members of the Democratic Platform left the party in one fell swoop. Sensing such an outcome, Afanasyev had already turned in his membership card in April. Now without any hope of transforming the communist system from within, these deputies adopted a resolutely anticommunist discourse. The Polish mobilizational model, from that moment onward, began to take on a self-evident significance it had lacked just a year earlier, when it was still invoked indiscriminately alongside the Hungarian Party–led revolution. At an international conference of Social Democratic organizations discussing the eastern European revolutions in Vienna in the autumn of 1990, Afanasyev asserted that Solidarność "had definitively convinced many—though regrettably not all—that reforming regimes originating from the October matrix was impossible, and that only by departing from communism could these regimes be overcome."[7]

Although momentous in its own right, this ideological shift was not as sudden or as profound as it might at first seem. For the members of the liberal intelligentsia who had already committed themselves to perestroika for several years, the abandonment of socialism in 1990 was the culmination of a long-running reinterpretation of this concept, whereby its sociopolitical content was gradually eroded and given a universalist moral scope that, in the end, had nothing particularly socialist about it.[8]

The evolution of the political discourse of Yuri Afanasyev is quite typical of socialism's dissolution via universalization. A virulent critic of official Marxism-Leninism since 1985, Afanasyev nonetheless continued to defend a conception of socialism that he claimed was faithful to the "true" Leninist principles from which the USSR departed in favor of Stalinism during collectivization. This position, let us recall, was typical of the time: it was defended by none other than Gorbachev himself. But Afanasyev went even further. For him, it was a question not of reforming the existing Soviet system but rather of renewing it by moving beyond the opposition with the capitalist world and establishing a dialogue with Western social sciences.[9] In the fall of

1989, when he was one of the most radical figures in the MDG, his political program included three points: the transition to the market, the dismantling of the Soviet empire, and the transition to democracy. At that time, however, he maintained that this program was still compatible with socialism. The meaning he gave to this notion, however, stripped it of all its socioeconomic content. He asserted that the market "is not a capitalist concept" and that, for this reason, it is entirely compatible with socialism. Indeed, the very opposition between capitalism and socialism was an "ideological division," and hence something that should be overcome. Moreover, he specified that the socialism he called for had little to do with what was built in the USSR and everything to do with universal humanist ideals: "The socialist idea must continue to guide us. Not in its Russian and Bolshevik, plebeian-revolutionary version, but in a broader perspective, that of Jesus Christ, of late Lenin and of contemporary social democracy."[10]

In this kaleidoscope of ideological references, the mention of "late Lenin" certainly does not carry as much weight as social democracy, since Afanasyev presents in the same breath the Swedish and Danish models as "the paradise" toward which the USSR must advance, while Lenin himself ever only had harsh words for social democracy. In this perspective, Afanasyev's abandonment of Lenin and socialism in the spring of 1990, in reaction to the impending failure of the Democratic platform, was far from a major break in his political thinking. In fact, Afanasyev's program had not changed at all: he still defended the market, called for the end of imperialism, and embraced democracy. But Lenin and socialism no longer had a place in his worldview. When he left the Communist Party, he cut all the ideological ties that linked him to it: he openly blamed Lenin for the Soviet state's reliance on terror and referred to socialism as a "delusional idea."[11] He still declared himself in favor of the Social Democratic model, but he now insisted on contrasting it with Soviet socialism. More precisely, he claimed to be in the tradition of the "socio-democrats and constitutional democrats that Lenin and his successor had mercilessly crushed." The Scandinavian model became for him the embodiment par excellence of "socialism with a human face," one in which he claimed that he "can hardly identify features of Marx's communism, but where Christian and universal-humanist ideals are clearly at work," and which thus corresponds to the notion of a "capitalism with a human face" founded on "liberal individualism."[12] A year later, Afanasyev associated his Social Democratic program with "political and economic liberalism" and defined his convictions as "radical-liberal."[13]

The transition from socialism to liberalism in the final days of the USSR has been described by some analysts as a "dramatic transformation," a "cognitive revolution."[14] This was undoubtedly true for a significant portion of the population, who had not questioned the fundamental principles of socialism and who now struggled to absorb the radical criticism found in the Soviet press. Similarly, there has been extensive discussion about the late communist intelligentsia's striking ideological shift, marked by the definitive discrediting of Marxism-Leninism and the decline of reform communism.[15] However momentous, this ideological shift does not suffice to explain the Soviet liberals' main lines of action during perestroika. As a matter of fact, the debates during this period were not driven by ideology in the sense of a confrontation of clear-cut social and political worldviews. This lack of ideological clarity can be lamented, as it resulted in many misunderstandings regarding the real objectives of the reforms. Yet it is crucial not to impose a misleading ideological clarity on the fluid landscape of ideas that prevailed at the time. For many Soviet liberal intellectuals, the rejection of communism and its symbols did not substantially alter their political views. In 1990, they aspired—just as they had in 1989—to "join the world civilization" and to create the conditions for the realization of "universal values" through the transition to democracy and the embrace of the market. Only this project was now considered liberal and no longer socialist. This rapid swapping of ideological labels and the great fluidity of their meaning demonstrated that these labels, in the context of perestroika, had served above all as a way of marking one's relative distance from the Communist Party and hence could not be considered faithful indicators of one's true political beliefs. Indeed, when one looks at the positions of the liberal intelligentsia on a concrete issue such as the question of power, it appears that the stance of DR in 1990 and 1991, despite these ideological upheavals, was in fact very similar to that of the MDG in 1989. And as in those days, the democratic movement remained divided as to whether to prioritize the consolidation of reformist power or the formation of an autonomous opposition.

The Democratic Movement and the Reformist Leader in 1991

In the course of 1989, the failed attempts to collaborate with Soviet power, combined with Sakharov's moral weight, convinced a part of the liberal intelligentsia that the best way to push through their desired reforms was to pressure Gorbachev by forming an autonomous opposition with its own program, supported by large-scale popular mobilizations, as had recently happened in Poland. Sakharov's sudden death, however, cooled this oppositional ardor, and several democratic deputies who had called for a political strike in December 1989 subsequently resumed their efforts in the spring of 1990 to consolidate democratic forces around the reformer, this time within the Democratic Platform. As mentioned, it was precisely the failure of this umpteenth attempt at consolidation that led to the creation of the DR coalition in October 1990 in explicit opposition to the Communist Party. Revealingly, DR's oppositional vocation was not initially aimed at Gorbachev, for whom many liberal intellectuals still maintained a deep respect, albeit one mixed with a nagging hope that he would eventually position himself squarely on the side of the democratic movement, despite his increasingly obvious propensity to rely on conservative elements in the party.[16] The Soviet Army's bloody intervention in Vilnius on January 11, 1991, however, shattered this hope—including among the most loyal Gorbachevians, such as Karpinsky and Adamovich. On January 20, DR organized a demonstration that brought together nearly two hundred thousand people on Manege Square in Moscow to protest against the events in Lithuania. The coalition now gave all its support to Yeltsin, who in turn called for Gorbachev's resignation. This oppositional strategy brought DR into something of a golden age, with its popularity increasing tenfold.[17] On March 10, 1991, the coalition set an all-time record in Russia by organizing a demonstration of half a million people in Moscow, with several others taking place in major cities throughout the country. The goal was to bring about the resignation of Gorbachev and his entire government. At the end of March, several hundred thousand miners in Donbass and Kuzbass went on strike with the same demands, raising the possibility of an overthrow of the government through a general political strike.

The opposition to Gorbachev and the Communist Party, now nearly unanimous within DR, concealed a latent conflict regarding the coalition's strategy toward its new reformist "champion," Boris Yeltsin. Although Yeltsin owed his political survival to the coalition's support,[18] his own strategy favored backroom deals over popular mobilization, even if it meant undermining the work of DR when it no longer seemed useful. The examples of this attitude are numerous, but the most striking was undoubtedly the signing by Yeltsin and Gorbachev, on April 23, 1991, of the so-called Novo-Ogarevo agreement, which aimed to stabilize the Soviet Union through the conclusion of a new treaty between Moscow and the republics.[19] The signing, which occurred just as the March demonstrations seemed on the verge of bringing about the overthrow of Soviet power, caused a shock wave within DR. Not only was the text of the agreement judged a wholly insufficient response to the coalition's demands; even more importantly, it threatened to undercut the coalition's attempts to mobilize the masses in opposition to Gorbachev. The protocol of the agreement provided for a moratorium on strikes and condemned the activists as "instigators of illegal strikes." Yeltsin, as a token of goodwill toward his new partner, personally asked the miners to call off the strike, thus putting an end to any prospect of a political transformation through popular pressure, "Polish style." Within DR, a debate began over the coalition's position toward Yeltsin: Would it not be better to adopt an autonomous position, even if it meant entering into opposition to both Gorbachev and Yeltsin? Once again, the strategy of consolidation prevailed. It was decided that DR should support the democratic reformer in order to ensure his victory over the "conservatives," especially in the elections for the new position of president of Russia, scheduled for June. With DR's support, Yeltsin won 57.31 percent of the vote, beating his competitors by a wide margin. After the elections, however, a group of DR leaders led by Yuri Afanasyev, Leonid Batkin, and Yuri Burtin proposed the adoption of an autonomous position that would put pressure on the Russian president to ensure that he acted democratically and carried out the promised reforms.[20]

While this issue threatened to split the coalition, an unforeseen event caused the democratic forces to rally once again behind Yeltsin. On August 19, 1991, a group of senior Soviet leaders took advantage of the fact that Gorbachev was on vacation in Crimea to seize power and declare a state of emergency in order to "save" the USSR from the reforms they claimed threatened its integrity. It would later be discovered that the KGB had prepared a special list of seventy people to be arrested in the putsch; this included Boris Yeltsin and his main advisers, and also several of the leaders of DR, including Afanasyev and Batkin. But the army hesitated to follow these orders, allowing Yeltsin to avoid arrest and take back the initiative. His legitimacy strengthened as the newly elected president of Russia, Yeltsin then rallied important figures in the army, as well as several democratic deputies, and with the backing of tens of thousands of supporters, mostly from the educated urban elite, he and his entourage barricaded themselves in the parliament building. Faced with this resolute opposition, which it was assumed could only be swept away in a bloodbath, the attempted putsch collapsed miserably after three days. Crowned as the hero of democracy, Yeltsin emerged as the great winner of these events against a discredited Gorbachev, who appeared at best a victim and at worst an accomplice of the putschists.[21] Aware of his newfound strength, Yeltsin then obtained the dissolution of the Communist Party. With this move, all Soviet political institutions collapsed: the USSR Congress, the Supreme Soviet, the Council of Ministers. Until the dissolution of the USSR in December, Gorbachev was little more than a president without a country.

For the activists of DR, this was the long-awaited victory they had been working for. In the euphoric atmosphere that followed the events of August, even those liberals who were most critical of Yeltsin recognized him as their hero. A year later, Burtin would offer the following recollection: "I remember the days of August last year, at first painfully disturbing, then full of happy enthusiasm. For the first time in our lives, we felt a full unity with the top leaders of Russia. We did not want to remember what we had previously reproached them for. We admired them, we were proud of them. They were our comrades in arms, they were—could we doubt it?—our popular and democratic power! No government in Russia has ever enjoyed such confidence of the society!"[22]

But the honeymoon was short-lived. In the autumn of 1991, debates about the political role of DR and its relation to Yeltsin's government resumed. What was the appropriate vocation of the democratic movement once its main adversary, the Communist Party of the USSR, had been defeated? The question was the subject of bitter debate. In fact, during its Second Congress in November 1991, DR underwent an initial split as several parties withdrew in protest against the coalition's support for the dissolution of the Soviet Union and its refusal to transform itself into a professional political party.[23] For the majority of its members, DR should continue to act as a broad coalition based on popular mobilization, in order to support reforms, create a civil society, and deal with the "red-brown" threat—a pejorative term for the alliance of Communists and nationalists at the time.

The principal question, though, was how to achieve these goals. As in the autumn of 1989, the liberal intelligentsia was divided between those who favored a strategy of consolidation of society and unconditional support for Yeltsin and those who favored a more autonomous position, even if it meant entering into opposition against the reformer in order to force him to respect his commitments. To be sure, the issue went beyond conjunctural tactical considerations: the debates of autumn 1991 expressed two visions of political conflict in a democratic society. And typically for the time, these were presented in moral terms. The subsequent debate saw liberals reproach one another for succumbing to two opposite forms of "depravities" (*blud*): the depravity of struggle and the depravity of conformism.

Two Forms of Depravity

On October 26, 1991, the literary scholar Marietta Chudakova delivered a polemical speech at the rostrum of the MT; four days later it occupied a full page in the mass-circulation newspaper *Literaturnaia gazeta*, where it was published under the title "The Depravity of Struggle."[24] The subtitle left little doubt as to the speech's main argument: "The struggle of democrats among themselves is destructive, it undermines the confidence of the people." In essence, the author was arguing that the country's democratic forces should rally behind Yeltsin and his government so as to help them overcome the resistance of the conservative forces and achieve the desired economic reforms. In order to do this, Chudakova argued, democrats must overcome their bad taste for opposition—"the depravity of struggle"—and refrain from publicly criticizing Yeltsin, even when they disagreed with his actions. Chudakova explained that she was inspired by her indignation at an article by Leonid Batkin, which had appeared a few days earlier in *Literaturnaia gazeta*, in which he raised the hypothesis that Gorbachev had given tacit support to the putschists.[25] Why heap such criticism on a man who had the "personal will and personal courage" to choose to oppose the coup plotters? she asked.[26] This unfair suspicion of great men and great deeds was clearly a remnant of the "quibbling method" adopted by the intelligentsia under Stalin, which consisted of expressing only "negative emotion." This attitude was obviously justified against the Soviet regime, she conceded, but "the situation after August [i.e., after the failed coup] is new and requires a new tone." Now that democratic forces had taken power in Russia, intellectuals should abandon their penchant for opposition. While "Bolshevik structures seek to consolidate . . . with nationalist forces"—a reference to the coalescing conservative forces at the time—"democratic forces must rally behind President Yeltsin and, to begin with, help him carry out the first radical—and therefore unpopular—reforms." It was the "personal responsibility" of democrats, Chudakova insisted, to preserve the people's trust in democracy, as this was "the most important achievement of the last six years." In her speech to the MT, she invited the premier political club of Moscow's liberal intellectual elite to rally the country's democratic forces behind Yeltsin.

For Chudakova, these democratic forces must consolidate around a common goal, of which she claimed certain overly critical spirits were losing sight: "We have become insensitive to the fact that totalitarian power and democratic power (whatever its mistakes) differ in their *essence*."[27] Thus, she called on democrats to "unite with the Russian leadership on any platform, even if it [was] not the best of the best," if for no other reason than that they shared a precious affinity: "Unforgivably, we are missing a rare and happy opportunity: for the first time in six years, let alone in the 'Soviet' era, we are seeing a real affinity between the democratic forces and the Russian leadership, which strengthens the latter's power. These leaders, the vast majority of whom have passed through the crucible of the Bolshevik Party, harbor a sincere disgust with that party and its methods. Honesty and personal courage are also valuable qualities in our country!"

This apparent affinity between democrats and Russian leaders was essentially moral; it was based on the personal qualities of the latter—honesty and courage—and their opposition to the hated communist system. For Chudakova, this affinity implied that the Russian leaders embodied, if not fully implemented, the cause defended by the liberal intelligentsia. She writes, "These are our people, this is our power [*nasha vlast'*], we walk on the same ground and the cold autumn rain falls on us from the same sky." As far as the essayist Yuri Karyakin, who sided with Chudakova in the debate at the MT, was concerned, the issue of the relationship to power had already been resolved: "I dare say that there is currently no problem of democracy and power. You, the democrats, are the power. You, us—it is the power. [Addressing Leonid Batkin:] Dear Lenia, you are the power now and on you depend Yeltsin and the current power; it is useless to attribute blame—future or present—to anyone."[28]

Unconditional support for the Russian leadership, in addition to being motivated by an essential "affinity," was also justified by tactical considerations—namely, the need to preserve a united front against the "red-brown" menace. This tactic, in turn, was itself based on a certain interpretation of the political struggle, which was perceived not as the confrontation of a plurality of interests and worldviews but rather as the irreconcilable confrontation of the democratic forces of progress against those who supposedly sought to restore totalitarianism.[29] For the writer Ales Adamovich, who supported Chudakova in the MT, there was no reason for democrats to seek an independent position "when democracy [was] the only chance to save the country and save us," implying that democracy was first and foremost a result of the political victory of democratic leaders.[30] Considering the greater necessity of winning this binary struggle, Chudakova asked the democratic press to abandon its critical position toward the government: "I dream of a moratorium on all impertinent emotions for all those who write and speak about the present and future of Russia."[31] Of course, she recognized that this limitation on freedom of expression did not correspond "to the standards of Western journalism," but she believed this to be justified in light of the substantial differences between the two contexts: in the West, this kind of criticism is "almost neutral," while in Russia it is dangerous because it could disturb the "exhausted people," who would then lose confidence in the democratic forces. "Democrats," she concluded, "cannot afford to proudly maintain a distance from the government. Russia would not understand."

At the MT, Chudakova's speech was greeted with enthusiastic applause. However, her position was by no means met with general agreement. She was the object of a sharp retort from Leonid Batkin and other liberal intellectuals. Against the criticism of the "depravity of struggle," they denounced another sin, that of conformism. The sinologist Yakov Berger added, "If we want to talk about sin and depravity, then there is indeed sin and depravity. It is depravity in conformism, the sin of seeking coupling [*soitie*] with any power. It is a very old sin which, unfortunately, still exists today."[32] The liberals who supported the DR's autonomy also put forward tactical arguments. They recalled what many of them had been denouncing since the spring of 1991 and the signing of the Novo-Ogarevo agreement behind their backs—namely, that Russia's "democratic" leaders did not in fact act democratically. Deputy Yuri Boldyrev said, "As soon as our people came to power, we realized that their methods of action were very similar to the methods of those they replaced.... The positions taken by politicians, unfortunately, are often linked to their basic personal interests." For this reason, it seemed essential to exert pressure on the government from below so that it would not succumb to its selfish inclinations or to the opposite pressures of the old *nomenklatura*.[33] Batkin said, "We will support the present leaders if they pursue a good policy. But they won't do it without a strong opposition. Nothing will be achieved without strong support from below, especially because these measures should be achieved by a revolution from below." Chudakova's opponents also made principled arguments in favor of DR's autonomy. For Batkin, unconditional support for power was simply incompatible with the vocation of the intelligentsia: "I'm sorry, but the intelligentsia is like that ..., it cannot fail to be intelligent, critical, reflective." For the philosopher Vladimir Bibler, society's autonomy is a precondition of democracy: "If democracy is equated with the government, then there is no democracy. For democracy is a democratic government, a democratic opposition, a democratic press, and a civil society that, by definition, does not correspond to the state."

The arguments put forward by the protagonists of this debate were based on different conceptions of the role of political conflict in a democracy. Chudakova and the proponents of the consolidation of reformist power presented this conflict as a binary confrontation between the "red-browns" and those who embodied democracy because the latter shared, despite their differences of opinion and their varying attachments to democratic practices, a common *essence* expressed through certain personal dispositions such as honesty, courage, and the categorical rejection of the communist system. In accordance with the moral perspective of the liberal intelligentsia (discussed at length in earlier chapters), they considered the question of power to be secondary to the struggle of honest people against hypocrites and dogmatists. Leonid Batkin and the advocates of DR autonomy were equally uncompromising about the communist system and their nationalist and communist opponents, but they saw political conflict and popular mobilization as essential conditions for the institutionalization of democracy, not as dangers to its survival. For them, democracy was based on society's autonomy vis-à-vis power, not on the power of those who would embody the democratic "essence." This debate was not unique to the Soviet context; it resonates with the fundamental struggle over the nature of democracy, as highlighted by the historian James Krapfl in his analysis of the 1989 revolution in Czechoslovakia: a struggle "between the deontological imperative of democracy and pragmatic concerns to achieve results efficiently."[34]

In contrast to Chudakova's proposal, several DR leaders, including Leonid Batkin, Yuri Burtin, and Yuri Afanasyev, sought in the autumn of 1991 to transform DR into an autonomous democratic movement and to institutionalize the sources of its popular mobilization. Burtin proposed in particular the creation, under the aegis of DR, of a network of "citizens' committees" whose job would be to supervise the progress of the reforms at the local level and to make sure in particular that privatization would not redound to the sole benefit of the *nomenklatura*.[35] At the Second DR Congress, held November 11–12, 1991, in Moscow, these supporters of autonomy won a majority of votes on a number of questions. But other DR leaders from the new generation of political entrepreneurs, in particular Lev Ponomarev and Gleb Yakunin, sought to commit the coalition to a strategy of unconditional support for the Russian government. To this end, they managed to postpone the election of the DR Coordination Council by two months—until January 1992. In the meantime, they took up the idea of the citizens' committees, except that, with the financial and logistical support of the Russian government, they implemented it in a completely different form. In December 1991, the Public Committees for Russian Reforms were created under the aegis of DR to serve as the government's emissaries at the local level, tasked with promoting the government's preferred policy and keeping it informed about the progress of reforms. Lev Ponomarev was elected to head this network of committees, whose coordination with the state was entrusted to high-ranking Russian government figures.

When DR's Council of Representatives finally met on January 18–19, 1992, after the government had embarked on its policy of economic shock therapy, the advocates of autonomy within DR suffered an unexpected and crushing defeat. While their proposals had attracted a majority of votes just two months earlier, they were now effectively pushed out of the coalition's leadership. Yuri Afanasyev was reelected, but several well-known liberal figures, including Leonid Batkin and Yuri Burtin, lost their places on the Coordinating Council, and political organizers little known to the public were elected in their place. Ponomarev, in particular, was elected cochair. Now an apparent minority within the coalition, supporters of the autonomy strategy chose to suspend their participation in the coalition and publicly question the legitimacy of its new leadership, which they accused of lacking the moral qualities necessary to practice "serious politics" and thus compromising "the name and idea of democracy" in the eyes of the population.[36] The departure of these famous figures, followed by the members of the Social Democratic bloc of the coalition, produced the second split in a few months in the DR coalition. The supporters of autonomy then sought to create a new democratic coalition, but in vain. At DR's Third Congress, held in December 1992, their position was formally rejected, and they were subsequently expelled from the coalition. Afanasyev, Batkin, and Burtin continued their democratic activism through other channels. Along with Vladimir Bibler, Elena Bonner, and Lev Timofeev, they had formed the previous year the group Independent Civic Initiative, which published statements on the course of political life in the newspapers. But by 1993, the voice of this group, like those of its once famous members, had grown inaudible. The strategy of autonomy, still influential at the time of the debate on the two forms of "depravity" in the autumn of 1991, gradually disappeared from public discourse. DR and most of the liberal intellectuals who remained active in the media, for their part, engaged in a campaign of unconditional support for Yeltsin, thus helping to maintain in the post-Soviet Russian political scene the binary moral vision inherited from the early time of perestroika, in which two camps confronted each other in an irreconcilable struggle, each convinced that they were the only bearer of truth and honesty in the face of lying, rigidly dogmatic opponents.

The Victory of the "Moderates"

In June 1990, Anatoly Chubais and other liberal economists in Leningrad published an anonymous "analytical note" in the journal *Vek XX i mir*, in which they explained that Gorbachev should use authoritarian measures to carry out unpopular neoliberal reforms.[37] As explained in the previous chapter, these economists completely ignored the moralistic paradigm dominant among Soviet liberals; indeed, they did not even bother to argue for the legitimacy of the proposed reforms. Yet they wrote candidly about the difficulties that awaited the democratic movement:

> The most painful problem for the democrats, which will also be one of their main lines of division, will be their attitude toward the undemocratic measures of the government that will inevitably accompany the reforms (the ban on strikes, control over information, etc.). On the

whole, the democrats' position on the reforms will be seen by the popular masses as inconsistent, which will be used to the full against them by their political opponents. The weakening and loss of influence of the democratic movement in the course of the reforms will undermine its social base, which will not be without consequences.

To deal with this inevitable weakening of the democratic movement, the authors suggested an "accelerated institutionalization of neoliberal economic and political ideology, based on the democratic forces that most strongly support economic reforms." Such a "movement," they argued, would have much less influence on public opinion. They proposed, in short, to get rid of the mass movement and create a smaller, more coherent "party of power" fully loyal to the government.

The Russian government, probably following the advice of its team of economists, had been working since 1991 to undermine the autonomy of the DR coalition, which, while it had certainly done the government a great service, proved difficult to control. For this purpose, Yeltsin postponed indefinitely the parliamentary elections that were expected to be held in the autumn of 1991 (by contrast, elections had happened in most eastern European countries after the collapse of communism). This decision may seem surprising at first glance, since DR's polling indicated that the coalition would have won a majority of seats in the Russian Congress, thus potentially giving Yeltsin much greater parliamentary support than he currently enjoyed among sitting deputies. But such a success in the parliamentary elections would have likely left DR in the unavoidable position of serving as a partner to the reformist camp, which would have implied some form of power sharing with the government. Yeltsin and his advisers preferred making occasional agreements with the government's numerous but weak opponents in the Russian Congress rather than sharing power with a strong and autonomous ally. This strategy of marginalizing DR also allowed the Russian government to present itself to the media and Western funding agencies as the only bulwark against the "red-brown" threat, without any strong dissenting voices within its own camp challenging its way of practicing democracy.

Faced with the refusal of DR members to dissolve their movement, the Russian government tried to subjugate it. In December 1991, as mentioned above, the introduction of the Public Committees for Russian Reforms sought to mobilize DR's local networks in the service of the Russian government. In effect, DR joined shortly thereafter a loose coalition called Democratic Choice, initiated by the government and led by Prime Minister Gaidar; its task was to provide unconditional support for the Russian government.

Such an outcome was not inevitable. Two years earlier, in the summer of 1990, the new liberal government in Poland had also tried to incorporate the local committees of the democratic movement Solidarność into a party of power, but its efforts were thwarted by a group of intellectuals and trade union activists, led by Lech Wałęsa, who were prepared to defend the autonomy of the mass movement from the government. In Russia, by contrast, the advocates of DR's autonomy strategy failed to gain ground, as most liberals chose to support the reformer's consolidation of power amid the growing tensions between the government and the Parliament over economic reforms.

This development raises questions about the established narrative regarding the conclusion of perestroika, which supposedly heralded the victory of the "radicals" over more cautious democrats. Initially, this perspective was articulated by supporters of Gorbachev within the liberal camp who were infuriated to witness their leader challenged by unruly popular elements under the guidance of DR. Aleksandr Tsipko, an early open critic of Marxism and a longtime admirer of Solidarność, exemplifies this shift. Despite the creation of DR on the Polish model in late 1990, Tsipko began denouncing the "radicals, with their irritated intolerance and lack of constructive ideas," who opposed Gorbachev. According to Tsipko, this attitude stemmed from "the egotism of the intelligentsia" and was directly inspired by Bolshevik methods, which consisted in aligning "not with [Russia's] best minority, but with the illiterate and excited crowd." Anticipating Chudakova's declaration the following year, Tsipko called for a "moratorium on political struggle" so that all democrats would unite in support of the enlightened leader, notwithstanding his shortcomings. "I prefer Gorbachev's so-called 'monarchist tendencies,'" he declared, "to the terrorist tendencies of a mob mad with permissiveness."[38] This harsh criticism of Soviet liberals from within their own ranks gained even more prominence in the 1990s against the backdrop of growing disappointment with the purported transition to democracy.[39] In academic literature, this polemical stance found more complete expression in what I have referred to in this book's introduction as the "inversion thesis"—a trend in the historiography of perestroika that criticizes the excessive radicalism of democrats, drawing on *Vekhi*'s classical argument about the inherent radicalism of the Russian intelligentsia and drawing parallels with Bolshevik practices. A recent example of this perspective is evident in the work of the historian Vladislav Zubok, who, in his book on the collapse of the Soviet Union, depicts DR liberals as "rational minds swelled with revolutionary hubris," "radicalizing 'democrats' . . . who fomented political anarchy" and whose objective was "to destroy the state by any means possible."[40]

However, as argued in chapter 4, the shift of Soviet liberals toward opposition to Gorbachev did not naturally emanate from an ingrained revolutionary mindset. On the contrary, it was a reactive, reluctant, and precarious process, consistently contested by a significant faction within their own ranks. Many were apprehensive about the potential chaos resulting from opposing the reformer and resorting to mass mobilization. Even the most radical figures among Soviet liberals, such as Sakharov, insisted that an autonomous opposition movement was crucial precisely to ensure peaceful reforms and the preservation of statehood. In this chapter, I have demonstrated that this enduring dilemma resurfaced in 1991 concerning DR's stance toward Yeltsin. The outcome was the decisive victory of the "moderates," who assumed leadership of DR in subsequent years and championed its strategy of support of the reformer. Meanwhile, "radicals" like Afanasyev and Batkin were marginalized and eventually retreated to academia.

To avoid misunderstanding, it is essential to address a key question: Were not Soviet liberals who unconditionally supported Yeltsin, like Chudakova or Karyakin, also "radicals" in their own right, given their categorical rejection of the entire Soviet legacy and refusal to compromise with their opponents? The argument here does not hinge on retrospective labeling. In chapter 4, I propose drawing a distinction between opposition to the communist system and opposition to Soviet power. The crucial point is that the shared growing opposition to the communist system among Soviet liberals did not translate into a unified oppositionist stance toward the government. Instead, it resulted in at least two diverging views on the necessity of opposition.[41] According to the MT's working documents and contemporary observers, these perspectives were termed "radical" when advocating autonomous opposition and "moderate" when calling for unconditional support of the reformist leader. In the context of this specific debate on the strategic positioning and repertoire of actions of Soviet liberals, the majority's definitive pro-government stance at the end of perestroika marked the victory of none other than the "moderates." This victory implied the rejection of oppositional politics by most Soviet liberals to avoid hindering the course of reforms—an underappreciated consequence that had far-reaching implications afterward.[42]

The rationale behind this strategic decision had little to do with the emerging ideologies within the intelligentsia at the time. Both "radicals" and "moderates" were vehement opponents of communism, yet very few among them endorsed the neoliberal ideology promoted by Russian government economists or the theory of authoritarian transition notably championed by Andranik Migranian and Igor Kliamkin. Instead, the choice to support an "enlightened reformer" was rooted in a political vision deeply influenced by the ideals, concepts, and moral assumptions long articulated by the liberal intelligentsia.

Gil Eyal, in his study of analogous developments in Czechoslovakia, highlighted how the alliance between morally driven liberal intellectuals and neoliberal economists, personified by Vaclav Havel and Vaclav Klaus respectively, initially seemed counterintuitive. These two groups had previously developed in distinct milieus with markedly different values.[43] A similar social gap was evident in Soviet Russia between Soviet liberal intellectuals, on one hand, and apparatchiks like Yeltsin (looked upon with suspicion) and technocratic figures like Egor Gaidar and Anatoly Chubais (largely unknown to the majority), on the other hand. In fact, Igor Chubais, a philosopher and sociologist, was more widely recognized by fellow intellectuals during the perestroika era than his younger economist brother.

So, how did many Soviet liberals come to staunchly support longtime apparatchiks who had undergone a transformation into believers of capitalism and their neoliberal advisers, instead of, for instance, advocates of gradual reform communism seated in the Congress? As observed in Czechoslovakia, the alliance between moralist liberals and the "shock therapy" government materialized, despite glaring sociological and ideological disparities, because both groups shared an "elective affinity" in an anti-ideological vision of democracy—as liberation from artificial schemes and as an essence of morality or progress—rather than as a set of practices.[44] It is remarkable, in this respect, to note the persistence, even after the collapse of the Communist Party and of the Soviet state itself, of a certain strain of thought that saw the transition to democracy and the embrace of the market primarily as the dismantling of an artificial communist system that had prevented society's natural development based on universal values. Insofar as this ideal was supposed to correspond to scientific and moral truth, the political conflict was generally perceived as a struggle between those who were honest and those who, out of self-interest or dogmatism, sought to preserve or restore the communist system. The moral essence of democracy was thought to be embodied in a leader, who was thereby defined as a "democrat."

Conversely, many liberal intellectuals understood dictatorship not as the concentration of power in the hands of a single person or faction but as the rule of the opponents of democracy. This was already explicit in the declarations of Marietta Chudakova and several others during the "depravity debate" in the autumn of 1991, and it was reiterated during a roundtable discussion convened by Yuri Burtin in May 1992, which brought together supporters of both the strategies of consolidation and of autonomy.[45] At this event, the essayist Vasily Seliunin accused those who left DR to create a democratic opposition of being "deserters," claiming that their departure divided the democratic forces. He asked "the first and most famous tribunes" of DR to "forget their pride" and to rally behind the president and the government. According to Seliunin, the only possible counterweight to dictatorship was a strong executive power supported by a new legislative power that "would not slow down the reforms but would accelerate them."[46] To achieve this, he supported a referendum on whether to hold early elections to the Russian Congress. In short, he saw the concentration of power in the hands of democrats as the best remedy against dictatorship. The sociologist Leonid Gordon held a similar view, criticizing those who feared the "Bonapartism" of the Russian president of being preoccupied with "details such as the forms of privatization and the organization of executive power," when the real issue, in his mind, was the struggle between supporters and opponents of the restoration of state socialism.[47] The sinologist Yakov Berger summarized the binary character of the current situation: "Either one declares oneself in opposition and obtains—by legal means—the ousting of the current power . . . and thus favors the establishment of a red-brown dictatorship, or one takes sides all the same, but with reservations, by supporting [the current power]. If one is fully consistent, there is no third way."[48]

Unlike economists like Gaidar and Chubais, or political scientists like Migranian, most liberal intellectuals who supported Yeltsin did not advocate the use of the iron fist as such. They favored democratic, if not wholly constitutional, means. However, their binary moral prism for analyzing political life, coupled with their apprehension of the chaos brought about by political opposition, led them to support Yeltsin unconditionally despite his evident democratic shortcomings. This was because he alone at the time seemed capable of embodying an "emergency reformism," which they believed would be executed on their behalf but without direct institutional oversight.[49] This sense of urgency was not new to the Soviet liberals who, since the reversal of Khrushchev's de-Stalinization, had been preoccupied with the "irreversibility" of reforms. However, this urgency gripped them even more painfully in 1992, paradoxically at the very moment when they were witnessing their long-awaited triumph over communism and ushering in an era of bold reforms.

Denouement: The Liberal Iron Fist

The launch of "shock therapy" in early 1992 caused the political scene to quickly polarize around a clash between the executive and legislative branches of the young Russian democracy. The same deputies who in the fall of 1991 had voted to grant extraordinary powers to Yeltsin to carry out economic reforms became increasingly critical of the government and the president in the course of 1992 and 1993, as they witnessed the catastrophic social consequences of these reforms. In March 1993, 617 deputies of the Russian Congress voted to remove Yeltsin from office—seventy-two short of the required two-thirds for the impeachment procedure. As many nationalist and communist groups participated in this protest movement, it was condemned by liberals as the embodiment of the infamous "red-brown plague." In Lithuania and Poland, where the early reforms also produced widespread social discontent, the liberals lost power to a coalition of ex-communists in 1992 and 1993, thus initiating a tradition of democratic alternation between different political forces that continued in subsequent decades. In Russia, however, the rise of opposition to the government was widely perceived by the liberal intelligentsia as an existential threat, nothing less than a death struggle between the supporters of democracy and those who wished to see the restoration of totalitarianism, or a shift to fascism. This demonization of the parliamentary opposition did not do justice to the complexity of the relationship between the forces involved, as many opposition leaders were former Yeltsin allies or DR activists who disagreed with the *path* chosen for reforms, not with the conduct of reforms per se.[50]

The escalating polarization of the Russian post-Soviet political landscape in 1992 and 1993 reinforced the conviction among many liberal intellectuals that, to safeguard their nascent democracy, they had to support Yeltsin unequivocally, even if it meant resorting to strong-arm measures. The conflict-ridden nature of the newly formed Russian democratic arena began to be widely perceived as an intolerable curse, reminiscent of the dire situation of "dual power" that, according to established knowledge, had sealed the fate of the short-lived Russian liberal regime after the February revolution some seventy-five years earlier. This perception prompted the belief that the president must be granted emergency powers to prevent society from descending into civil war.[51]

However, to challenge the myth of retrospective inevitability, it is crucial to explore, by considering alternative possibilities, how this portrayal of politics as an existential struggle became self-evident at the time. In this case, polarization was, at least in part, the outcome of the prior failure to transform DR into an autonomous organization. A successful transformation would have resulted in a form of political pluralism where the Russian government would face criticism not only from the "opponents" of reform but also from a robust pro-reform political faction in a tripartite configuration. In this sense, the decision of DR members to align with Yeltsin in 1992 and to quash any opposition to his reforms became a self-fulfilling prophecy. By denying the democratic coalition an autonomous position, they unwittingly ensured that post-Soviet political life adopted a binary logic, leaving them with no alternative but to support the reformist government against the mounting discontent.[52]

The possibility of supporting illegal repressive measures was finally realized when the question arose of what to do with the results of the April 1993 referendum, in which the population was asked to express its confidence or lack thereof in the presidency and the Parliament.[53] Despite the ambiguity of the results, which did not reach the threshold required to trigger early elections, a group of liberal intellectuals, including Marietta Chudakova, urged Yeltsin to take the opportunity to dissolve the Parliament.[54] The president, after securing the support of Western governments and international financial institutions, effectively dissolved the Supreme Soviet on September 21, 1993, which led a large group of deputies to barricade themselves in the White House, the seat of parliament. A few days later, after several confusing events, including violent clashes that left more than a hundred people dead, the conflict between the executive and legislative branches of government ended in explosions and the smell of half-burned parliamentary papers as the White House came under fire from government tanks.

The next day, forty-two eminent representatives of the liberal intelligentsia, among them Marietta Chudakova and also early members of the MT such as Ales Adamovich, Vasily Seliunin, and Yuri Chernichenko, wrote an open letter of support to Yeltsin in which they demanded, in defiance of the law, an end once and for all to what they qualified as an "anti-people" opposition.[55] In this document, known as the "Letter of 42," these intellectuals and artists asked the president to ban all communist or nationalist parties, to close down all "hateful" newspapers, and to dissolve all local soviets that had supported the Parliament. It is worth quoting at length from their famous letter because it is typical of the reasoning employed by Soviet liberals to justify the use of force:

> Thank God the army and security forces remained on the side of the people, did not divide themselves and did not allow this bloody adventure to give rise to a fatal civil war. But what if it had been otherwise? We would have had no one to blame but ourselves. After the putsch of August 1991, we "felt compassion" and begged the authorities not to "take revenge," not to "punish," not to "ban," not to "close," not to launch a "witch hunt." We wanted to be good, generous, tolerant. To be good . . . to whom? To murderers? Tolerant of what? To fascism?

And the witches, or more exactly, the red-brown vampires, who had become impudent through impunity, covered the walls with poisonous leaflets before the eyes of the militia, leaflets in which they grossly offended the people, the state, its legal leaders, and in which they explained with delight how they would hang us. What to say? It is no longer time to talk. It is time to learn to act. These scoundrels only hear force. . . . We do not call for revenge or cruelty, although grief for the new innocent victims and anger at their cold-blooded executioners fill our hearts (and, probably, yours). But . . . enough is enough! We cannot allow the fate of the people, the fate of democracy to depend on a handful of ideological crooks and political adventurers. This time we must firmly demand that the government and the president do what they should have done long ago, but have not done. . . . [There follows here a list of repressive measures.] History has given us another chance to take a big step toward democracy and civilization. Let us not lose this opportunity, as we have already done once![56]

In this open letter, the rejection of the values of "tolerance," "goodness," and "generosity" does not mark an abandonment of moral principles. On the contrary, it is justified by the overriding imperative to fight evil, which in the eyes of the signatories is embodied in the deputies of the Parliament, whom they call "murderers," "fascists," "witches," and "vampires." A week later, a second letter appeared in the newspaper *Nezavisimaia gazeta*, this time lacking signatures but emanating from a certain "assembly of the society of Moscow democrats."[57] Within its first few lines, the letter painted Yeltsin as nothing less than the embodiment of democracy, describing him as "the undisputed leader of democratic changes, authorized by the people to express their will and their higher interests." According to the letter's anonymous authors, this status would give Yeltsin the legitimacy to exercise power above the law. They insisted that the banning of all "parties, fronts, organizations, and their propaganda organs that have been and remain on the side of the opponents of the reforms" should not be entrusted to the judicial organs but should be imposed by presidential decree, in defiance of the constitutional order. They also demanded that not only the "organizers" and "executors" of the "criminal uprising" but also its "ideologues" be repressed. The desire to censor so-called immoral positions, which had long been a latent feature of the liberal intelligentsia, was now given explicit formulation: "Bearing in mind the lessons of the past, we consider it necessary to bring criminal proceedings against the theorists and ideologists of communo-fascism, those who in recent years have cultivated the ideas of national-patriotism, implanted them in the consciousness of the people, and used for this purpose the platforms of all possible congresses and the pages of numerous national-patriotic publications." In practical terms, this would mean sending to prison the very authors with whom the members of the liberal intelligentsia had been debating for years. To recall the terms laid out in chapter 3, this letter basically called for the restriction of pluralism of opinion in order to purify social consciousness.

After the events of October 1993, President Yeltsin effectively concentrated all power in his hands. He took advantage of the situation to have the existing Constitution annulled and the Constitutional Court dissolved, though he did not go so far as to crack down systematically on nationalist and communist forces, as the authors of the two open letters had so forcefully recommended. In the spirit of Chubais's anonymous programmatic article of 1990, Yeltsin was careful to claim his respect for democratic and moral ideals, even while exercising an iron fist. This was illustrated by an exchange on television with the film director Eldar Ryazanov, a star of the liberal intelligentsia, in November 1993. Ryazanov mildly criticized the president for not explaining his decisions to the population during the October crisis, suggesting that the most important quality in this period of absolute power was "openness" (*otkrytost'*), by which he meant regular—but one-sided—contact between the leader and the people. Yeltsin frowned at this reproach and offered a response that demonstrated his perfect command of the codes of moral discourse of the time:

> As far as checks and balances are concerned, I can now tell you with precision and firmness that I have no other check and balance than my conscience [*sovest'*]—that's a check and balance. Even if one speaks every day on television, one can in any case inwardly disagree with what one says. But you can't escape your own conscience! It will always be behind you, in the back of your head. . . . Thus, it is my own conscience that incites me during this period [in the absence of institutional checks and balances] not to take any decision that would be serious enough to influence the fate of Russia.[58]

Yeltsin was appealing here to the idea that politics should be guided by personal conscience. As we saw in chapter 2, this was one of the main animating principles behind the liberal intelligentsia's commitment to politics. However, Yeltsin took the detachment of this moral issue from the question of power to its logical conclusion: if conscience is to reign unchallenged, it does not need political counterpowers. Democracy is the democratic conscience *in power.* The most obvious corollary of this maxim is that those who do not support Yeltsin must themselves lack conscience, whether through selfishness, dogmatism, or mere stupidity.

Some liberal intellectuals protested strongly against the president's policies, which they denounced as a betrayal of democratic ideals, but the majority of the liberal intelligentsia remained loyal to Yeltsin after the events of October 1993, if only because they thought he represented a necessary evil to combat the "red-brown" threat.[59] Indeed, interviews conducted the following year by French sociologists Alexis Berelowitch and Michel Wieviorka with democratic intellectuals indicate that most of them supported Yeltsin even if they disapproved of his despotic attitude.[60] This also aligns with the findings of the political scientist Steven Fish, who conducted interviews at the same time with about a hundred politicians, all self-described democrats, who to a person said they had voted in December 1993 in favor of the new Constitution enshrining the concentration of power in the hands of the president.[61]

The Constitution was adopted in a referendum—with little regard for the fact that turnout was too small to validate the result—and it is still in force as of this writing. As for the parliamentary elections that were held at the same time, they resulted in a large protest vote against Yeltsin, mostly in favor of the nationalist party of Vladimir Zhirinovsky. For a liberal intellectual like Yuri Karyakin, these results confirmed the long-held suspicions about the irrationality of the people. In comments made on live television the night of the election, he declared his disgust with the results with a sentence that would become famous: "Russia, come to your senses, you've become stupid!" (*Rossiia, odumaisia, ty odurela!*). In a similar vein, the writer Fazil Iskander, who was committed to democracy from the very beginning of perestroika, described his own feelings about the parliamentary elections in the following words:

> I would risk saying that such a people do not need a parliament, do not need elections. Such a people and its elected representatives (because we know whom such a people can elect) are not capable of elaborating new laws, of making them more human, more civilized, more reasonable. . . . It would be a hundred times more useful and cheaper to gather an assembly of the best of Russian society, of its moral and intellectual elites, who would choose from their midst the men capable of leading the country for several years, while waiting for the arrival of the younger generation.[62]

At this same time, a new party called Yabloko was formed around a liberal and democratic program in opposition to Yeltsin. However, the new rules of the superpresidential constitutional game consigned Yabloko, along with all other parties, to a position of eternal criticism, leaving no other option, in the end, than collaboration or insignificance. Despite some initial electoral successes, this party was unable to break the symbolic legacy of the path taken by DR in 1992, which assumed that Yeltsin had come to embody democracy and liberalism and that these concepts should therefore be judged according to his actions.[63]

On the surface, Yeltsin's victory in the autumn of 1993 was a victory for the liberals: the "red-brown" threat was defeated for years to come, and the power of the country's "democratic" leaders was consolidated under the new Constitution. But the aftermath was bitter for those who had supported Yeltsin. By placing themselves at the service of the Russian leadership, a large number of Soviet liberal intellectuals—including several DR leaders and some of the most famous figures in the intelligentsia—helped to convince the population that Yeltsin and his government were the true embodiment of democratic ideals, if not democrats in practice. In this way, they created the institutional and symbolic conditions—the concentration of power and the association of their ideals with the rule of a corrupt and predatory elite—for their own political marginalization and the exhaustion of their political project.

The liberal intelligentsia greeted with dismay its vertiginous fall from the heights of public adulation it had enjoyed during perestroika. Hated by the majority of the population, who called them *der'mokraty* (a play on *demokraty*—democrats—and *der'mo*—shit), and despised by the new business elite, who had no use for their moral ideals, the liberal intellectuals who had once led the democratic movement were ultimately relegated to the margins of post-Soviet political life, mostly in the fields of human rights activism or academia—if not to unemployment and poverty. In 1994, the mobilization of several of them against the war in Chechnya was all but ignored by the government as well as the general population. The liberal intelligentsia's predominance in the public sphere was now over.

In 1994, the DR leaders had to dissolve their coalition, undermined as it was by demobilization and abandoned by the Russian government, which completely lost interest in it following its poor performance in the December 1993 elections. Several attempts were made in the following years to create a new, DR-like organization, but the new constitutional order made this task almost impossible, as the extremely broad powers granted to the president insulated him from the pressure of the legislature and reduced the influence of mass mobilization.

In the new constitutional order founded in December 1993, the dilemma between consolidation and opposition would henceforth take the form of an alternative between collaboration and irrelevance. Hence, the main distinction between the Russian liberal parties of the 1990s was to be found in their relationship with the executive: while Yabloko chose the path of opposition out of principle and gradually sank into insignificance, its importance entirely dependent on the degree of attention it received from the government, the liberal parties created at the initiative of the Russian government (i.e., Choice of Russia, Democratic Choice of Russia, and the Union of Right Forces) followed a "moderate" strategy of support and collaboration with the government, which ensured their (short-lived) existence despite little popular support. This duality among liberal parties ended after the Kremlin, in 2000, created a single large "party of power," United Russia, aimed at gathering supporters of the government across the ideological spectrum. All liberal parties were then definitively wiped off the national electoral map following their crushing defeat in the 2003 parliamentary elections. They never recovered.

Beyond marginalizing liberal intellectuals and activists, the concentration of power in the hands of an "enlightened" reformer had more damaging and lasting consequences for the fledgling Russian democracy by significantly undermining citizens' sense of political efficacy. By legitimizing the notion that democratic alternation should be prevented because opposition poses an existential threat to reform, Soviet liberals unintentionally signaled to the population that, for its own sake, it should be deprived of the ability it had enjoyed during late perestroika to pursue its claims through contentious forms of political participation such as demonstrations, party organization, and strikes. This is evident in the comparative study conducted by political scientist Danielle Lussier on post-Soviet Russia and postdictatorship Indonesia. The study reveals that citizens who do not experience political alternation through elections lose faith in their ability to influence political outcomes and consequently tend to favor patriarchal forms of participation, such as writing complaints and supplications to the authorities, leaving the elites unconstrained.[64] In this sense, Russians' acquiescence to democratic erosion in subsequent years need not be traced back to an alleged atavistic legacy of apathy inherited from Soviet times—an assumption spectacularly contradicted during perestroika. Instead, it is closely tied to the sense of political efficacy experienced in the first years of the new regime. "By prioritizing outcomes over procedure," Lussier writes, "Russians have allowed

THE DILEMMA OF THE DEMOCRATIC MOVEMENT (1990-93)

political elites to hollow out potentially democratic political institutions."[65] In doing so, Russians were dutifully following the example set by their former moral elite, the late Soviet intelligentsia.

The moral perspective of the Soviet liberals conditioned their strategic choices, but it did not guide them in the manner of a clear and univocal doctrine. An understanding of the dilemmas faced by Soviet liberals in their relationship to reformist power would not be complete without an examination of the reasons that led some of them to support—in vain, it would turn out—an alternative strategy, that of the autonomy of the democratic movement. These arguments, which we touched on briefly in this chapter, are all the more deserving of greater attention because they have largely been forgotten and thus constitute one of the lost intellectual legacies of perestroika. This is the subject of the next chapter.

CHAPTER 7

Forgotten Democratic Opposition Projects

> Democrats, be democrats in the end!
> —Yuri Burtin, "Gorbachev prodolzhaetsia," 1992

At the end of perestroika, different tendencies coexisted within the Democratic Russia (Demokraticheskaia Rossiia, hereafter DR) coalition. On the one hand, DR's pro-government leaders, including Gleb Yakunin and Lev Ponomarev, claimed to be following a pragmatic course when they justified their support for the consolidation of executive power, which they deemed necessary for the victory over the "red-brown" threat. Pragmatism, in this sense, would be the mark of a professional and mature political actor, one shorn of the naive illusions of idealists. On the other hand, Yuri Burtin and other influential figures of DR eschewed such pragmatism in favor of what they presented as a renewed idealism, thereby affirming that politics is above all a question of principles. Idealism, according to this view, implied the submission of politics to a set of lofty ideals. Following this distinction between pragmatism and idealism, the support of a large number of liberal intellectuals for the concentration of power in the hands of an "enlightened" reformer in 1991–93 would seem to mark a departure from their moralist attitude during the perestroika era. This viewpoint on moving beyond past idealism, proudly embraced in late perestroika by self-styled "serious experts" like Migranian, became commonplace among democratic leaders in the 1990s. Figures such as Anatoly Sobchak, the mayor of St. Petersburg, and Gavriil Popov, the mayor of Moscow, emphasized their own "pragmatism," contrasting themselves with former colleagues in the democratic movement who, out of fidelity to outdated ideals, maintained a skeptical view of the emerging regime.[1]

In academic literature, this polemical stance found elaborate expression in what I have referred to in this book's introduction as the "negativity thesis"—a trend in the historiography of perestroika that highlights the Soviet liberals' lack of a constructive program, thereby explaining why they were promptly sidelined after 1991 and replaced by technocrats. A recent example of this perspective is presented by the political scientist Vladimir Gel'man, who argues that 1990s Russia, in contrast to its eastern European counterparts, witnessed a "divorce" between old moralist democrats and young cynic liberals.[2] Gel'man suggests that while the "democrats without liberalism" were intellectual *shestidesiatniki* (Sixties) pursuing humanistic ideals who were at best naive and at worse incompetent in solving real problems, the "liberals without illusions" were technocrat *semidesiatniki* (Seventiers) who envisioned concrete paths for transformation without indulging in "castles in the air." According to Gel'man, this generational and intellectual divide explains diverging political trajectories: pragmatic liberals supported Yeltsin, while idealist democrats distanced themselves from him and, on principle, accompanied Yabloko's slow but inexorable descent into political marginality. Upon closer scrutiny, the distinction between pragmatism and idealism falls short of capturing the complexity of the situation. First, the debate surrounding the democratic movement's relationship with power and the crucial decision between supporting reformers and maintaining autonomous opposition does not simply boil down to a clash of generations. While it holds true that most advocates of autonomous opposition belonged to the *shestidesiatniki*, such as Afanasyev, Batkin, and Burtin, they found significant allies among *semidesiatniki* democrats like Boldyrev. More importantly, a very substantial number of *shestidesiatniki*, such as Adamovich, Chernichenko, Chudakova, Karyakin, Granin, Likhachev, and Seliunin, advocated rallying behind Yeltsin. Therefore, this attitude was evidently not the prerogative of the *semidesiatniki*; it was pervasive among the broader Soviet liberal intelligentsia.

Moreover, the distinction between pragmatism and idealism suggests that proponents of consolidation discounted moral considerations in their political commitment, while proponents of autonomy promoted a moral agenda. Yet we saw in the previous chapter how the Soviet liberals' unconditional support for Yeltsin was based on a binary moral vision of political life and on a conception of democratic power embodying a certain moral essence. Their arguments, in fact, had little to do with the technocratic theories of the economists who ran the government they supported. Conversely, not all proponents of a democratic opposition were idealists willing to sacrifice political efficiency for moral principles. While some called for the creation of a "moral opposition," others saw democratic opposition to Yeltsin as a strictly pragmatic strategy.

In this chapter, we turn to these different proposals, which, it must be admitted, have been largely forgotten. In 1992, the supporters of democratic autonomy bowed to those who advocated support for Yeltsin within DR and, subsequently, the former no longer played an important political role. Among the most famous of them, Afanasyev and Batkin eventually left active politics to devote themselves to academia, while Burtin continued to comment on politics as a journalist, without succeeding in rebuilding DR on a new basis. Today, few people remember the dissident wing of DR that sought to create an autonomous democratic opposition. As far as we know, the arguments of these authors have not been the subject of any retrospective study, either in Russia or elsewhere. It seems important here to engage fully with their reflections, especially since such a work of historical excavation serves a double purpose in the present discussion. First, it allows us to challenge the idea, now widely held in Russia, that support for "enlightened" authoritarianism and compromise of the democratic cause necessarily stemmed from the political perspective shared by the liberal intelligentsia. This perspective was not monolithic; it had several contradictory tendencies, of which the one that ultimately won was neither necessarily the best argued nor necessarily the most popular. It should be remembered that Afanasyev, Batkin, and Burtin, before being removed from the political struggle in 1992 under the circumstances described above, were very influential intellectuals within the democratic movement and that the movement constituted the main political organization in the country in the autumn of 1991, with nearly seven million supporters and three hundred thousand active members. The ideas these intellectuals were espousing, then, were in no way marginal, of interest only to historians of obscure intellectual tendencies. They were real political options that, even if they did not prevail, are capable of inspiring contemporary political thought—or at least imparting some lessons. Second, the study of these challenging ideas allows us to better understand, by comparison, the relative singularity of the path chosen by DR and many liberal intellectuals after 1991, especially with regard to the role of morality in justifying authoritarianism. The ideas of Yuri Burtin and Leonid Batkin illustrate different visions of the democratic opposition in their relationship to morality: the former placed his hopes in the creation of a moral opposition and criticized the pragmatism of the Russian leadership, while the latter claimed pragmatism and warned democrats against a policy guided solely by moral imperatives. The exemplary nature of this distinction justifies our focusing on these two authors, leaving aside the thought of Afanasyev, who borrows from both perspectives.

Burtin and the Moral Opposition

Yuri Burtin shared the dominant view of the liberal intelligentsia regarding the ultimate goals of Soviet reforms—namely, the establishment of democracy and the market. The differences arose when it came to determining the concrete actions that should lead to these ends: "The question is who will accomplish this transformation, how and in whose interest. The question is: will we become the masters of our destiny or will we simply change masters for an indefinite period of time?"[3] To the question of power—*who* should govern and *how*—as it was generally raised by Soviet liberals from 1989 onward,[4] Burtin added two other issues: the interests served by the reforms and the ability of the people to control their own destiny. These concerns were inspired by Burtin's vision of Soviet society, which he saw as divided into two classes with contradictory interests: the people, who seek to live freely, on the one hand, and the *nomenklatura*, who seek to dominate the people, on the other.

He analyzed Soviet society in the following terms: "Unlike contemporary capitalism, where social distinctions tend to fade more and more, 'real socialism' remained a class society until the end of its days. Not in the sense that it would have two classes and an intermediate class, as our comrade Stalin taught us. A much more important dividing line is that between the leaders of the Party bureaucracy, the 'nomenklatura,' the 'new class' (according to M. Djilas), and the rest of the people."[5]

Like many other liberal intellectuals who came of age politically in the 1960s, and were marked by the theses on the bureaucratic "new class" in socialist societies, Burtin believed that the *nomenklatura* would consciously seek to hinder democratic and market reforms for fear that they would undermine its power and privileges. This antibureaucratic perspective was accompanied by a particular sensitivity to the cause of "the people," which Burtin spoke of in terms reminiscent of his models of the past, the *Narodniki*. For him, perestroika was democratic only insofar as it helped realize a "revolution from below"—that is, for the people and *by* the people. Democracy and the market are, in his view, mechanisms of the political and economic self-regulation of society; therefore, they cannot be established from above, and especially not by the *nomenklatura*. For this reason, Burtin was one of the first to oppose the Gorbachevian project of democratic consolidation under the leadership of an enlightened reformer, denouncing as early as 1989 "the new bureaucratic dictatorship of the Party headed by the initiator of perestroika."[6] For him, the consolidation of democratic forces around the reformer was nonsensical because it would mean reconciling the irreconcilable: "the interests of the people" and "the interests of a corrupt and parasitic bureaucracy."[7]

The dichotomy that Burtin envisaged between the people and the *nomenklatura* was not, however, merely a matter of intellectual speculation. When it came to judging political actors and the forces they embodied, "objective" criteria about their "social nature" merged closely with "subjective" criteria about their moral qualities. On this point, Burtin shared with the majority of the liberal intelligentsia a conception of morality as a sincere expression of personal conscience. In chapter 3, we saw that this conception motivated the rejection of the values and arguments of the liberals' opponents as marks of hypocrisy. Taking the moral refusal to compromise with the "enemies of democracy," Burtin made the heterodox choice to transfer this otherwise common judgment against the one most liberals considered as their champion: Gorbachev. If the latter was not loved by the people, he affirmed in January 1991, it was mainly for his "personal traits," which he identified as "the love of power, self-satisfaction, finality, insincerity, the absence of a lively interest in the people in his endless speeches, moral dryness."[8] Like Stalin and Hitler, he says, Gorbachev distinguished himself by his "total absence of moral criteria in politics."[9]

A year later, even as the liberal press was paying fulsome tribute to Gorbachev for peacefully resigning from the presidency of the USSR, Burtin was still denouncing "his absence of moral rules, his hypocrisy, his cunning, his lies, his indifference to the life and fate of ordinary people."[10] Conversely, Yeltsin appeared to him as "much more human than Gorbachev."[11] A few months later, Burtin would be fully disillusioned by Yeltsin's policies, conceding that what he had initially assumed were "errors" on the part of the Russian president were in fact a conscious governing program. This was, in Burtin's terms, the continuation of the "revolution from above" by way of a transition "from partocracy to plutocracy."[12] It was, in short, the betrayal of the people and the installation of a new *nomenklatura* in alliance with the old: "If it were necessary to describe in one sentence the character and the results of our revolution of August, it would be the following: the democratic revolution dissolved, its fruits were monopolized by the new and the old nomenklatura, and the hopes of the people were again deceived."[13]

To Start (Again) from Oneself

It was not enough, according to Burtin, to denounce the plutocratic character of the new power in Russia: one must also see that it was made possible by a deeper and more serious phenomenon—namely, the moral bankruptcy of the democrats themselves. It is we, he told his readers belonging mainly to the liberal intelligentsia, who are primarily responsible for compromising democracy: "It is our fault and nobody else's that the word 'democrats' is now used either in quotation marks, or accompanied by a 'so-called' or simply in the insulting form of 'der'mokraty.'"[14] And it was also the fault of the democrats if the communists and nationalists had managed to present themselves as the defenders of the people.[15]

Burtin glimpsed signs of this moral bankruptcy in the democrats' propensity to conceive politics in a "pragmatic" way, to the detriment of the imperatives of their conscience: "We have learned that in politics we must above all be 'realists,' that 'politics is the art of the possible' (our 'political scientists' have so often repeated this phrase in recent years!), the pragmatic art of compromise, of weaving, of balance, while honesty, sincerity and human character are naive and childish illusions irrelevant to serious politics."[16]

"Truly democratic politics," he insists, can be "neither amoral, nor 'half moral,' nor indifferent to morality" because "it is the quality of the means and not the ends that ultimately determines the outcome of any political activity."[17] That is why, he continued, "only an honest policy, based on solid moral principles, is capable of being truly effective."[18] From 1992 on, Burtin repeatedly insisted that in politics, "principles" are more important than "programs." Democrats, he said, were far too preoccupied with programmatic issues, such as whether democracy should be Social Democratic or liberal in character, presidential or parliamentary. In his view, these debates overshadowed the essential issue—namely, the principles of political action. He was careful to specify that he meant neither "impersonal" principles such as the division of powers nor the "principles" claimed by communists like Nina Andreeva.[19] The principles that Burtin wanted to see reactivated were, first of all, "ethical self-control" and the ability "to say a decisive 'no' to politicking, verbiage, greed, and careerism." Principles that would be characteristic of people with the "temperament of a dissident," by which he meant in particular Sakharov, whose "shining example" he called on his fellow citizens to follow.[20] These principles, based on the harmony of consciousness and actions, were widely considered by liberal intellectuals as the necessary attributes for self-realization, as we saw in chapter 3. But unlike many of his fellow liberals, Burtin felt that the respect of these principles was also essential for the exercise of power.

In an even more original way for the time, he saw the source of these principles in a sentiment that was clearly inspired by his *narodnik* perspective—a "responsibility toward the people": "The Russian intelligentsia, especially since the time of Chernyshevsky and Pisarev, has always felt a sense of responsibility to the people, an unpaid 'debt' to them, to use Tvardovsky's word. When this feeling, which nourished the spirit of *narodniki* and *zemstvos*, of Chekhov, Korolenko, Tvardovsky, and Sakharov, weakened in us, we lost our immunity and became vulnerable to the virus of immorality, vanity, superficiality, verbiage, and politicking."[21]

For Burtin, this sense of duty to the people necessarily derived from the expression of personal conscience, hence his main recommendation to all democrats to cultivate their "inner being" in such a way as to make moral rules "the natural norm of their behavior."[22] Rather than blaming the communists, the nationalists, or even Yeltsin for the evils that had befallen the country, the democrats must "begin with themselves, by a trial on themselves, by the personal example of their selflessness, their self-limitation, their absence of greed."[23] And it would only be on this condition that they would regain the confidence of the people. This was why, Burtin insisted, the democratic opposition "must above all be a moral opposition," putting forward moral principles before any political program.[24]

Back to Dissidence

We saw in chapter 2 that in 1987 Burtin had criticized nationalist intellectuals for having only a partial view of reality when they attributed the decline of society to personal moral bankruptcy. It is not enough, he wrote back then, to simply "start with oneself" and cultivate one's personal conscience, because such an orientation would not address the social root of all individual moral failures, which he identified as Stalinism and its enduring legacy. After the collapse of the USSR, Burtin continued to denounce the Stalinist system—which, using much broader language, he now referred to simply as "state socialism"—which he said persisted in post-Soviet Russia despite all the ideological and institutional changes, thus demonstrating a remarkable power of metamorphosis: "A snake-system, which can quickly throw off its old skin (Marxism-Leninism in particular) and easily slip into a new one. A lizard-system, which loses its pursuer, leaving only its tail in its hands. A werewolf-system, capable of changing its appearance at will while retaining its essence."[25]

The first generation of democratic politicians, claimed Burtin, was not morally "prepared" to lead the country, precisely because they came from this Stalinist system, in which "morality was, so to speak, illegal and hid in the corners."[26] In 1993, Burtin even stated that this generation of democrats—his own—was already too compromised and that the work of establishing democracy must therefore "start from the beginning, from scratch."[27] Considering the scale of such a task, however, Burtin's preferred means seemed quite modest. While from 1989 to 1991 he had called on his fellow liberals to oppose Gorbachev and the Communist Party by way of a political opposition based on widespread popular mobilization and endowed with its own program, his preferred strategy for ridding the country of "plutocrats" after 1991 was the public expression of personal conscience—an ill-defined moral opposition that lacked any definite program.

This proposal marked a return to the political dissidence of the pre-perestroika years, by which opponents of the regime sought through their moral example and their protest speech to denounce the infractions committed by Soviet power against its own rules and values, without openly calling the larger system into question. Indeed, Burtin hailed those with a "dissident's temperament," those who engaged in moral opposition to the new post-Soviet power, notably in the wake of the first Chechen War.[28] In the absence of permanent political organizations with strong popular legitimacy, however, this principled opposition proved to be quite fragile in the face of repression from the state. The weakness of moral opposition thus gave rise to the counterarguments of those democrats who lamented the impotence of the disarmed conscience and who thought that one should know to bend one's principles in order to better defend democracy.

Batkin and Pragmatic Opposition

In May 1992, Leonid Batkin formulated an analysis of the political situation very similar to Burtin's when he drew a parallel between the failings of Gorbachev and Yeltsin as "enlightened reformers":

> It is becoming more and more obvious that we are reliving a familiar dream. Yeltsin's power is repeating, with the horrifying accuracy found only in dreams, everything that happened recently under Gorbachev. Gorbachev was a Party reformer who personified in the eyes of the country and the world the progressive movement toward reform. Today, Russia is led by a new reformer, Yeltsin. . . . Before, the so-called democrats said: What can we do? We have to support Gorbachev, or else God forbid! Now they exclaim: Let's gather around Yeltsin or else Sterligov, Baburin, Astafyev, Anpilov will come to power and it will be really bad. And in the meantime, B. N. Yeltsin is wavering like Gorbachev before him. While continuing to assert his unflagging commitment to reform, he is drifting more and more to the right. It is not

Yeltsin's personality and subjective intentions that are at stake, but the policy of "privatization" for the benefit of the *nomenklatura* and to the detriment of the population, the concessions to the military-industrial complex and to an international policy that is putting Russia at odds with its neighbors, as well as causing the blossoming "under Yeltsin" of an ideology of [imperial] restoration.[29]

Like Burtin, Batkin denounced democrats' recurrent tendency to seek the consolidation of reform rather than constitute themselves as an autonomous opposition. But unlike Burtin, Batkin was far from thinking that the solution was to be found in a "moral opposition." For Batkin, such an opposition already existed; the problem was precisely that it was *only* moral. Commenting on the actions of the small group he formed with his colleagues and friends, he lamented, "We are obliged, alas, to pass into the opposition. For the moment, this 'we' is only a few isolated people, that is why this opposition has an especially idealistic and moral character."[30] This moral character was in his eyes the sign of its weakness, the root cause of its inability to make itself heard by power. Batkin's critical view on the role of morality in politics stemmed from his original conception of politics as both "pragmatic" and strictly democratic—a rare combination for the time.

The Open Question of Power

Leonid Batkin shared the universalist orientation common to most of the liberal intelligentsia of the time, which held that perestroika must mean an end to the USSR's—and subsequently Russia's—claim to occupy an exceptional place in the world and in history and that it must lead the country toward "world civilization." What made Batkin's view of this question original was his argument that the historical necessity of this modernization did not provide a definite answer to the question of power so much as *raise* this question in a democratic way, such that it remained *open*. This idea of democratic openness, although not subject to any detailed theorization, is found at several points in his writings during perestroika.

For Batkin, the openness of this question of power stems from a clear separation between society, the domain in which economic interests are formed, and politics, the public domain in which such interests are formally expressed and contested. In his long article from 1988, included in the collection *Inogo ne dano*, Batkin celebrates the "return of real and open politics" as the "most important condition of perestroika," made possible by the "destatization of society." It is because the state detaches itself from society, he explains, that politics is now possible: "Since the late 1920s . . . , politics has disappeared from the life of our society. Politics has disappeared as a particular modern sphere of human activity, in which the different interests of classes and groups are manifested and confronted, positions are publicly confronted, and dynamic compromises are worked out. Politics has disappeared and consequently *everything has become political.*"[31]

He proposed in this article a "permanent perestroika of perestroika," which implied not only the radicalization of Gorbachev's program but more broadly the permanent questioning of official politics as a condition for the existence of political life. This might seem obvious, as questioning the government is indeed a daily fixture in the life of an established democracy. As Batkin pointed out, in a society "full of life," the controversy over reforms must continue as long as the reforms themselves—which is to say forever, since society is perpetually changing.[32] However, it should be noted that this idea was highly original among Soviet liberals, who more often than not apprehended political conflict as a threat to the course of reforms and therefore sought to consolidate the reformer's power. Batkin tirelessly denounced this tendency toward consolidation. As early as 1988, he had defended the democratic street activists against the liberal economist Gavriil Popov, who accused them of playing into the hands of the reaction by destabilizing Gorbachev.[33] Batkin's response was primarily strategic: the reformer, he said, had to be pushed to his "left" if he was not to become a hostage to those on his "right," who, for their part, did not hesitate to pressure the leader.[34] But more fundamentally, Batkin also argued that conflicts of interest in the public square should be interpreted not as a symptom of instability but rather as a sign of the emergence of a genuine political life, which democrats must take advantage of to encourage the reformer to implement the promised reforms.

A year later, in the summer of 1989, Batkin offered a scathing rebuttal to Andranik Migranian and Igor Kliamkin's claim that reforms could only be implemented with an "iron fist."[35] Batkin opposed the idea of an authoritarian transition with a theoretical argument that drew on the idea of the "openness" of politics. Thus, Batkin noted that the "question of power"—*who* decides and *how*—having been finally raised explicitly after the first session of the USSR Congress, should from then on remain open because, unlike other social questions, it is beyond the scope of any rational solution: "[The question of power] is not only the most important problem, but one might say it is the only one that really matters. For all other problems, even the most serious ones, can all be solved by rational solutions. And we already know what those solutions are, if only from the experience of other countries. As for the question of the mechanism by which power is transmitted, it can in no way be solved in a rational way in a transitory historical situation like ours."[36]

In the same article, Batkin made clear that this rational indeterminacy was not specific to some "transitional historical situation" but characteristic of the political domain in general, in contrast with the economic domain. As regards the latter, Batkin, like most liberal intellectuals, believed that a market economy simply corresponds to human nature.[37] But as far as politics is concerned, Batkin rejected any determinism that would pretend to solve the question of power once and for all.

This position did not make him a relativist—far from it. There was no doubt in his eyes that the USSR must import the Western model of parliamentary democracy. However, he conceived of democracy in an agonistic perspective, implying that conflict is an irreducible and even desirable aspect of politics: "Historians will write: 'In 1988–1989, political life returned to the USSR.' The question of power, of course, is not resolved, but that is what is remarkable, insofar as since 1918, it was always resolved in an absolutely indisputable way. Today, for the first time, it is in a certain way posed. In the conditions of the democratic choice that has been made, this question—in a preliminary way, however—is rendered normatively open, that is to say, it is effectively a permanent *question*, and in this sense it is *already resolved*."[38]

The rapid pace of events during perestroika left Batkin, like so many other members of the democratic movement, little time to elaborate his ideas beyond the "rapid analyses" he wrote "with feverish speed in response to concrete situations."[39] Two years after the debate on the "iron fist," the denunciation by Marietta Chudakova of Batkin's penchant for engaging in the "depravity of struggle" gave him yet another opportunity to explain his conception of a democracy that would leave the question of power open. He claimed to understand the concerns of his interlocutor about a potential "revenge of reaction" and the country's possible descent into "chaos."[40] He also said that he "[understood] the thirst for social understanding" as well as the need for compromise. But he maintained that the only way to reach an acceptable compromise was through a "healthy political struggle" and not through the consolidation of reformist power. As in 1988, he insisted on the importance of preserving the autonomy of civil society, which he said must not be put at the service of the state in any way, even if it was apparently pursuing the most noble causes. There was no "affinity" that allowed the democratic movement to recognize, as Chudakova says, Russian leaders as "its own":

> This is "our" real cursed habit: either to hate power or to declare our "affinity" with it, our "love" for it. . . . I would answer . . . that "our

power" does not exist. Nowhere! In any case, not in a democracy. Power has its function and its interest; and it is fully understandable and justified in its desire to rule without hindrance. The fetters are us, that is to say society, in which workers, trade unions, the press, entrepreneurs, peasants, etc. each have their function and their interest. "Our democracy" is what corresponds to this whole field of confrontation and convergence of interests, including the particular interest of the executive power. But "our power" does not exist (unless one lives under totalitarianism).[41]

Here is Batkin's main point of divergence from the proponents of consolidation: democracy cannot be embodied in a specific individual or institution, since it resides precisely in the permanent openness of the question of power. This means that the defense of democracy against its opponents involves cultivating political contestation in the public domain, rather than attempting to resolve it in the name of a noble cause.

Chudakova, it should be remembered, advocated for a "moratorium" on criticism against democratic leaders in order to preserve people's confidence in democracy. According to Batkin, this unconditional support for the reformist leadership would undermine the mechanism by which civil society might actually help the political class resist conservative pressures and achieve the promised reforms. Still opting to place his trust in the Russian president, Batkin concluded, "I affirm that we will help the reforms of the Yeltsin government by acting intelligently, democratically, in accordance with our principles and, if necessary, in opposition."[42] Like Burtin, Batkin thus insisted on the need for the democratic opposition to base its positions on "principles." His definition of that term, however, was entirely distinct from any consideration of personal conscience and the moral imperative to "start with oneself." For Batkin, political principles are first and foremost principles of action, and for this reason they are eminently pragmatic.

The Pragmatism of Democratic Principles

In his 1988 article on the "renewal of history," Batkin attacked the conception of glasnost that was then widely held by the liberal intelligentsia. As we saw in chapter 2, public criticism was generally thought to serve democracy by purifying society of its deviant elements and subjecting it to the expression of conscience. This new possibility of expression is eminently valuable, Batkin acknowledged, but it feeds apathy if it does not translate into real change: "If we can tell the truth to the whole country, sure, that's great! . . . But if this hard-won truth, which we are now allowed to shout in the wilderness, doesn't change anything about the barren nature of the landscape (because before we thought: all we have to do is make the truth appear, say it loud and clear for everyone to hear), then it only increases social apathy. 'Okay, it's out there. So what? So nothing.'"[43]

Batkin also warned his colleagues and friends about the moral intransigence that underlies their conception of glasnost. In particular, he attacked the widely held idea that glasnost should put an end to lies and "half-truths," a term often used at the time to describe nuanced judgments that do not meet the supreme criteria of factual and moral truth. But, according to Batkin, such a binary perspective is dangerous because it perpetuates a criterion by which public expression is deemed legitimate or not, and potentially even leads to censorship:

> And so long live glasnost. But what glasnost for what purpose? The answers are not as simple as they seem. It has become a commonplace to consider the half-truth as the worst form of lie. It is understandable that a truth distorted, even if it is "only" 1/100th or 1/1000th, remains a lie, in politics as well as in science. This is the very principle of a distortion. But in politics, it is possible that the problem lies not in the immoral character of this principle but in its institutionalization. . . . For if the authorities forbid the distortion of the truth, this remains terribly dangerous, because it implies that someone is in charge of determining the criteria that make it possible to distinguish truth from its distortions. No, it is better for everyone to be able to lie and for everyone to be able to denounce the lie.[44]

Batkin's position on glasnost is indicative of the role he assigned in democracy to truth inspired by personal conscience. For him, democracy is not the triumph of truth over falsehood but rather the institutionalization of the inevitable public contestation. We saw in chapter 5 that such a rejection of a moral criteria in politics is also characteristic of the advocates of an authoritarian transition to democracy. Andranik Migranian and Igor Kliamkin, for example, both agree with Batkin that morality is in a sense alien to politics and is more properly to be found in the intimate domain of personal conscience and the speculative domain of philosophical or artistic reflection. Likewise, Batkin writes, "Art and spirit are nothing less, but of course nothing more than art and spirit. Man does not live by his mind alone, which is far from being indifferent to his daily bread. The awakening of the Soviet press and culture is in itself remarkable, but it must be the prelude to broader social changes."[45] He thus criticized the typically Romantic idea, widespread among many Soviet intellectuals, that art, as the bearer of higher ideals, must guide political action. We see this idea echoed by, among others, the liberal journalist Andrei Nuikin: "Literature and art in general have a huge responsibility for economic development, for industrial modernization, for increasing the strength of the army, and for many other things. Not in a direct way, but through their influence on public opinion, through the formation of a moral climate in the country and the world."[46]

For Batkin, as for Migranian and Kliamkin, "realism" and "pragmatism" dictated a rejection of the idea that politics should be guided by conscience. For Batkin, however, unlike Migranian and Kliamkin, it does not follow that democracy should be discarded for the sake of reform. As far as he was concerned, democratic principles are not ideals that emanate from the personal conscience but rather principles of action that derive from the very requirements of politics. To those who asked democratic activists to moderate their demands so as not to destabilize the reformist power, Batkin offered the following reply: "There is nothing more *pragmatic* (I consciously leave aside the moral and legal aspects) than to quietly satisfy the nonviolent demands" emanating from society, rather than waiting for them to take illegal form."[47] It is in the practical interest of the reformer, he argued, to welcome the emergence of political life in all its messiness, because it leads more surely to reforms than would a "consolidated" power dominating an obedient society, because popular mobilization helps the reforming power counterbalance the conservative pressure from the establishment.[48]

Batkin took issue with the claims of self-styled political scientists that they could sweep away democratic principles in the name of the historical imperatives of modernization. For him, a politics subjected to a necessity that exceeds it is not even worthy of the name, and even less the epithets "pragmatic" or "realistic"; it is only opportunism. He bolstered this claim with an apologia of the "art of politics," and one cannot help but wonder if it was not inspired by his expertise as a historian of the Italian Renaissance, so reminiscent is this "art" of the concept of *virtù*. Batkin defines it as "the faculty of feeling and realizing at every moment, in every mobile situation, the *new* and necessary *measure* of the possible."[49] For Batkin, the true politician must not make himself the servant of a historical necessity—*fortuna*, to continue the parallel with the Italian Renaissance—that exceeds him and that would be manifested by either the presence or absence of historical preconditions to action. Reflecting on Otto von Bismarck's famous reference to politics as "the art of the possible," he writes,

> We want to be realistic. We were taught from our youth that "politics is the art of the possible." This means that in this sphere of human activ-

ity devoted to the affairs of state, it is bad politics not to take circumstances into account. But what is meant by "the possible"? And why is an "art" required? No art is required to bend to circumstances; it is enough to put down the oars and let yourself be carried by the current. If ignoring circumstances is bad politics, bending to them is no politics at all. It is opportunism, politicking, ruse: anything but politics in the serious sense of the term.[50]

While the practice of politics is often inspired by certain eminent examples—Batkin, as we have seen, has only good words for Western parliamentary democracies—the principles that guide it are not moral or historical imperatives that would justify a definitive resolution of the question of power. This implies, first, that no one leader can embody democracy, regardless of his or her actions. This is why Batkin sought to support Yeltsin only insofar as his actions were deemed democratic, and not, as Chudakova argued, for the president's "honesty" and "courage." Second, it implies that democratic principles are acquired through political action and are therefore potentially intelligible to all, regardless of one's moral dispositions. This is why Batkin, who otherwise did not share the sense of duty to the "people" of a *narodnik* like Burtin, remained resolutely optimistic about the emergence of a democratic political culture in Russia and consistently celebrated any example of democratic popular mobilization. To those liberal intellectuals—and there were many—who worried that irrationality and chaos would accompany the masses' entry into politics, he replied with confidence:

> The people have enough reason and emotion. Not the "people" [*narod*] in its mythological and rhetorical sense, but, to put it without deceptive pathos, the population, we the (various) inhabitants of the country are in the end not so inert, stupid, drunk, and disposed only to the senseless and ruthless riot, but colossally mature politically since . . . last March. . . . It is especially in these "chaotic meetings" (calling for the multiparty system, for an independent press, etc.) that a new democratic conscience and a new spirit of decision are growing in our eyes (though certainly not everywhere and not always). The people have not yet said their last word. If I had to believe in only one thing, I would believe in this.[51]

After Sakharov's death, the liberal intelligentsia unanimously celebrated his moral qualities, eulogizing "our bitter conscience," a "prophet . . . who does not always see around him, but far away," a man of "high morality and spirituality."[52] Yuri Burtin, as mentioned earlier, also considered Sakharov "a shining example" of the unstinting commitment to moral principles in front of the compromises of the "pragmatists." The "pragmatists" also described Sakharov as an idealist, but in their case to better dismiss his proposals. Kliamkin, for example, brushed aside Sakharov's position as "a certain moral benchmark of society, an ideal," but one incapable of arriving at a concrete political mechanism that would steer the country safely toward democracy and the market.[53] Batkin, by contrast, refused to qualify Sakharov's democratic positions as idealism; such a label would be too great a gift to the partisans of the authoritarian transition since it would leave them the monopoly on pragmatism. He replied to Kliamkin as follows: "By basing himself on contemporary realities, Sakharov does not only propose a 'moral' reference point, but a political reference point for this transition period. Dear colleagues, we should not be under any illusion: the authoritarian 'models' are contrary to these benchmarks, both moral and practical."[54] After Sakharov's death, Batkin used his pen to further denounce the late dissident's sacralization as a moral icon:

> It was said of him that he was a "dreamer," a "Don Quixote," an "idealist," that he thought only about what must be and that he did not take into account the reality of the situation. Sakharov was in fact the most realistic, the most practical politician. He didn't base himself only on what is moral, on what must be. He took into account the Russian daily realities on the scale of the twentieth century. . . . That is why he fought for a liberal parliamentary democracy as the form of life that corresponds to contemporary production, contemporary science, the contemporary level of society. He was practical and that is why he saw beyond our present situation. He remained a realist, because he was absolutely foreign to any opportunism.[55]

Thus, both Burtin and Batkin invoked Sakharov's political legacy to encourage their fellow democrats to form a democratic opposition to Yeltsin. But these were two very different images of the former dissident, one "idealist" and the other "pragmatic," and they inspired different arguments. While Burtin called for the creation of a moral opposition based on personal conscience, Batkin refused to endow democracy with a moral imperative: in his eyes, it resided in the guarantee of the practical conditions of the autonomy of society vis-à-vis the authorities and, by the same token, of an open and plural politics.

Beyond the Pragmatism-Idealism Dichotomy

Among the supporters of a democratic opposition to Yeltsin, there was no consensus on the role of morality in politics. If Burtin saw this strategy as based on a restoration of morality in the conscience of each individual person, Batkin insisted on not leaving the monopoly on pragmatism to the supporters of the "iron fist" and conceived of democracy as a wholly practical procedure indifferent to the moral quality of the citizenry. It would therefore be reductive, in this context, to oppose the "idealism" of those who criticized Yeltsin to the "pragmatism" of those who unconditionally supported him. In sum, the dividing line between these two opposing views of the role of morality in politics did not correspond to the one that separated the supporters of consolidation and the supporters of democratic autonomy.

On the one hand, Batkin and the theorists of the authoritarian transition asserted—though for very different reasons—the importance of dissociating the domain of morality from that of politics. For Batkin, the political domain must be autonomous in order to preserve the openness of the question of power, while for Migranian, Kliamkin, Chubais, and other proponents of authoritarian transition, politics must be separated from morality in order to conform to the imperatives of modernization and stability. But the importance of these anti-moralist views within the liberal intelligentsia should not be overstated. For, on the other hand, most of the liberal protagonists in the debate on the relationship of the democratic movement to reformist power, for all their apparent divergences, nevertheless remained within what was essentially a shared moral perspective, one whose ideals, concepts, and postulates they held in common.

For Burtin, as for Chudakova, political life was a binary struggle between those who embody universal values—democracy and the market—and those who, either by interest or by blindness, express dogmatic ideas. The question of power, in their perspective, serves to distract us from a much more fundamental issue: the return to civilization or the restoration of totalitarianism. What is essential, therefore, is not so much the way in which power is exercised and the program it puts forward but the position that power occupies in this binary moral struggle. Like Chudakova, Burtin determined his relationship to power according to a relative moral affinity that knows only two possibilities, "our power" (*nasha vlast'*) or "the power of others" (*chuzhaia vlast'*)—that is, the power of one's opponent in this binary struggle.[56] If they came to advocate diametrically opposed political strategies from 1991 onward, it was not because one was "pragmatic" and the other "idealistic" but rather because they did not give the same priority status to the two moral aspects of the political project of the liberal intelligentsia under perestroika: the purification of social consciousness and self-realization through the sincere expression of personal consciousness. For Chudakova, the victory over the "red-brown" forces required tolerating the undemocratic practices of the reforming power. For Burtin, meanwhile, a power that lacks integrity cannot credibly oversee reform. Both refused to compromise their ideals: the signatories of the "Letter of 42" refused any compromise with the nationalist-communist "vampires," and Burtin denounced Yeltsin's concessions to the *nomenklatura*. Their operative values were fundamentally different—Burtin could be called left-wing for his defense of the interests of "the people," and Chudakova right-wing for her support of a neoliberal government—but their respective reasoning was based on common postulates, concepts, and ideals inherited from the moral perspective on politics shared by most liberal intellectuals during perestroika.

Conclusion

It is hardly the least of the paradoxes of perestroika that a large part of the Soviet liberal intelligentsia, a group whose commitment to democratization was driven by powerful moral aspirations for truth, honesty, and democracy, should come to support the concentration of power in the hands of a reformer who, while he certainly embodied an uncompromising rejection of communism, implemented an authoritarian and technocratic modernization policy that largely abandoned all moral concerns in the name of the laws of the market. In the decade that followed the dissolution of the USSR, while some liberal intellectuals sought to convert their eroding prestige by securing for themselves profitable positions as experts in the service of the new power and others returned to the posture of moral indignation and dissent, liberal ideas saw the esteem they had once enjoyed in the eyes of the public plummet sharply. In their stead came a nationalist and conservative discourse whose ascendance signaled the abrupt end of the golden, if tumultuous, period for liberal ideas that had begun in 1987. Beyond the inevitable conservative backlash that follows any revolution, the liberal intelligentsia's virtual banishment from the public sphere in Russia assumed the character of a drastic decline that has since overshadowed the positive legacy of perestroika.

This tragic fate was not just the result of structural factors exogenous to the action of liberal intellectuals, since a large number of them actively cheered the authoritarian consolidation of Yeltsin's power and thus ensured its democratic legitimacy in the eyes of the Russian population and those of the Western countries. This responsibility is real, but it does not mean that all the thought and action that liberal intellectuals had committed to democratization deserves to be consigned to the dustbin of history on the pretext that it was rooted in a simple lack of constructive ideas, the radicalism allegedly inherent to the Russian intelligentsia, or the perpetuation of secretly Bolshevik attitudes.[1] As we have seen, an in-depth and empathetic study of their political interventions reveals a much more complex picture, one in which the notions of morality inherited from socialist humanism nourished a promising but contradictory horizon of expectation, which in turn collided with the painful experience of irreducible political conflict as the party's control over public life eroded. Troubled by this new reality, which disappointed those who had hopes for the consolidation of society through democratization, liberal intellectuals were faced with a host of strategic dilemmas that illustrated the difficulty of addressing the delicate question of power—of *who* should govern, and *how*—when confronted with imperatives deemed superior, such as the purification of social consciousness or the modernization of society through the market.

At the intersection of ideas and action, hope and disillusionment, this book has insisted on the importance of moral aspirations in understanding the motivations and strategic choices of the Soviet liberal intelligentsia. In their assumed moralism, those intellectuals committed to democratization were indeed different from most of their Western contemporaries. However, it would be simplistic to see this moralism as the sole cause of the liberal intelligentsia's tragic fate, as if it had been enough for Soviet liberals to understand Western liberalism better and to opt for a strictly procedural approach—one based strictly on the guarantee of individual rights and the design of proper institutional mechanisms and devoid of lofty moral purpose—to achieve the desired results. On the one hand, this would be to delude oneself about the alleged neutrality of procedural liberalism, while on the other it would cause one to lose sight of the relevance, in the context of late Soviet society, of fully assuming the moral conditions for the establishment of democracy.

The moralism of Soviet liberalism, in fact, can be seen as a lucid, albeit highly paradoxical, response to the dual challenge confronting liberal ideas in late Soviet Russia. The first challenge aligns with what the Polish sociologist Jerzy Szacki termed the "constructivist" mission of liberalism in eastern Europe. This mission sought not only to justify an established system or to promote sectoral reforms but, above all, to found a new societal order.[2] Such an undertaking extended beyond procedural rules; it required the mobilization of a substantive vision of a better life, capable of inspiring its proponents to break with the status quo. The second challenge was specific to the minority status of liberal ideas in Russia. Despite being championed by influential elites, they were nourished in relative social isolation and political marginality—a predicament that endured from tsarist times through the Soviet era, persisting into the post-Soviet period.[3] Faced with these challenges, Soviet liberal intellectuals lacked the luxury enjoyed by their Western counterparts, who could dismiss moral considerations as incidental or illegitimate aspects of democratic institutions.

Political scientists who have analyzed perestroika as a top-down revolution or as an elite pact have appropriately focused on the institutional dimensions of the transition to democracy: the establishment of a party system, the nature of power relations, and constitutional design. The presumed legitimacy of democracy is seldom considered among the factors influencing its long-term success because of the common assumption that its desirability is self-evident. However, modern democracies invariably rely on a "founding narrative" that connects the new regime to a source of authority beyond itself, transforming the event of its establishment into a proper beginning.[4] The presumed legitimacy of democracy is also evident in the academic literature on the revolutions of 1989 in eastern Europe, which observers at the time assumed to have not brought any new ideas and to be simply about "catching up" with the West.[5] This assumption, which clearly echoes the "triumphalist" historiographical trend in the interpretations of perestroika presented in the introduction of this book, proved shortsighted. The historian James Krapfl's in-depth study of the meanings Czechoslovak citizens gave to their Velvet Revolution reveals a "surprisingly idealistic revolution that was at once social, political, and even religious" in its aspiration to provide nothing less than "blueprints for the refashioning of quotidian human relations and the 'rebirth' of the self."[6]

Likewise, Soviet liberals were fully convinced that democracy is based not only on institutions but on hearts and minds as well. In this perspective, their emphasis on morality stemmed less from political immaturity than from a concern with establishing democratic institutions on a solid normative basis. If society does not overcome its hypocrisy and systemic cynicism, they consistently argued, if it does not sanitize itself on the basis of universal values, then even the best laws will simply "hang in the air," as Sakharov would say.[7] At the same time, liberals believed that the communist system corrupts personal conscience and that a harmonious conscience can fully develop only in a context oriented toward democracy and the market. But then, how can the moral conditions necessary for the success of political and economic reforms be created in Soviet society if it is precisely these reforms that make moral recovery possible?

In this sense, it seems that the moralism of the Soviet liberal intelligentsia, beyond the fact that it was a legacy of socialism, illustrates more fundamentally the inextricable contradictions posed by a classic question of political philosophy: Are there shared moral norms that are prerequisites for the lasting establishment of democracy, and if so, how can they be nurtured? The thoughts and actions of the Soviet liberals, in this respect, carried lessons that are applicable far beyond the framework of Russia or even the post-communist world more broadly. To conclude this book, I propose to bring out the general theoretical significance of this particular experience by relating it to an oft-raised question in political philosophy, especially in its republican tradition: How to establish the necessary moral foundations for freedom?

The Moral Basis of Freedom

Just as freedom is not simply liberation, the transition to democracy is not simply the end of despotism. Democracy is a form of power based on binding laws and durable institutions. However, the creation of democratic institutions inevitably involves an element of arbitrariness, insofar as it interrupts the apparently natural course of the established order and imposes itself at the expense of a plurality of other political options. How can this original arbitrariness be overcome and a lasting democratic power be founded without proceeding in an authoritarian manner and denying the freedom that is its principle?

Soviet liberals faced the classic problem of the aporia that lies at the root of liberty, which Jean-Jacques Rousseau summed up in these terms: "In order that a people in the process of formation should be capable of appreciating the principles of sound policy and follow the fundamental rules of reasons of state, it would be necessary for the effect to become the cause; the spirit of community, which should be the result of the constitution, would have to have guided the constitution itself; before the existence of laws, men would have to be what the laws have made them."[8]

Soviet liberals first attempted to overcome this aporia through persuasion—or, as the sociologist Gil Eyal would describe their Czechoslovak counterparts, through the exertion of "pastoral" power.[9] The constant and passionate involvement of many Soviet liberal intellectuals in the media testifies to their willingness to act as a moral elite whose stated mission, in the context of glasnost, was to denounce lies and reveal the truth in order to help create the moral conditions for a deepening of perestroika. The journalist Len Karpinsky expresses this idea very clearly in an article from 1988, in which he recognizes exactly this aporia: "Who will do perestroika? The people. And who will make the people again? The process of perestroika." But unlike Rousseau, who proposed solving the problem by resorting to deception by way of an instrumental use of religion, Karpinsky thought that it was enough for those who were already "ready" for perestroika—namely, the liberal intellectuals themselves—to "open the doors of perestroika" for the rest of the population.[10] But this persuasion, as we have seen, was only partially successful. The liberals did manage to set the tone of public life on several points—democratization, criticism of Stalinism and the "command administrative system"—but they faced stiff resistance from their opponents, and especially from conservative communists and nationalists, who refused to allow the liberals to wield their monopoly as a putative moral elite. From 1989 onward, it became a commonplace of liberal discourse to recognize the insufficiency of persuasion. As Karpinsky wrote in 1990, "I remember my first illusions . . . with a bitter smile. It seemed to me that all I had to do was reveal the secret truth and everyone would immediately understand and move forward."[11] But how to overcome the aporia described above if not by persuasion? How to create the moral conditions for the functioning of democratic institutions in a society that is considered corrupt?

In the end, the solution favored by many liberal intellectuals was an act of foundational violence: an attempt to establish the legal order through the brutal liquidation of political conflict. The crushing of the parliamentary opposition in the fall of 1993 was indeed the founding act of the contemporary Russian political system; it was supported by most liberals in the hope that reforms, as well as generational renewal, would finally succeed in overcoming the moral corruption inherited from the communist system. In adopting this stance, these liberals followed unwittingly the teachings of Niccolò Machiavelli, who, unlike Rousseau, considered it possible to establish freedom through violence. To be clear, and contrary to Machiavelli's reputation, the Russian liberals who unconditionally supported Yeltsin in 1993 were far from indifferent to moral issues. But like Machiavelli, they came to believe that "a wise understanding [will] ever reprove anyone for any extraordinary action that he uses to order a kingdom or constitute a republic. It is very suitable that when the deed accuses him, the effect excuses him."[12] Unlike Machiavelli, though, these liberals did not seem to foresee that a regime based on violence must regularly resort to such coercive action if it is to ensure the obedience of the people. The authoritarian character of contemporary Russian democracy was thus inscribed at its birth, first and foremost in the choice to concentrate power in the hands of an "enlightened" elite in order to insulate the new power from the corruption of society.

The case of post-Soviet Russia holds for us an important lesson about freedom and its founding—namely, that the establishment of democratic institutions is inseparable from that of the authority that undergirds them. The successful establishment of a democracy, therefore, depends not only on what form it takes—the laws and institutions to which it gives rise—but also on *how* and *why* it is founded. In post-Soviet Russia, democratic forms have often been perverted by those rulers who seek to maintain the regime despite its blatant lack of legitimacy and to make people forget this original flaw.

Does it follow, then, that it is impossible to establish freedom in countries where, like Russia, democratic power cannot be based on a relatively consensual source of authority? Are the defenders of democratic principles condemned, in these circumstances, to a moral opposition like that of the Soviet dissidents, without hope of establishing lasting, real-world institutions? It seems that the ideas espoused by some of the liberal intellectuals presented in this book, in particular those of Leonid Batkin, suggest a way out of this alternative between the brief shelf life of an authority established through violence, on the one hand, and the fact that morality in itself does not suffice to build democratic institutions, on the other. By the same token, they propose a solution to the aporia at freedom's root. This solution, which is reminiscent of Hannah Arendt's reflections on the American Revolution, consists in recognizing that democracy's authority is derived from the very *act* by which it is founded—that is to say, from political action itself.[13] Political conflict, in this perspective, is not an obstacle to the consolidation of democratic power; it is the process by which both freedom and the moral conditions in which it is exercised are constituted. Let us lengthily quote Leonid Batkin:

> It is true that, as we are reminded a thousand times, we still do not have the necessary soil [for a parliamentary democracy], that is to say, a society in which each person would be above all a private owner, either of his forces and capacities, or of the means of production, of real estate, etc. But civil society, for its part, needs democratic freedoms in order to develop. Fortunately, we already have important elements from which democracy, the market economy, and the society of citizens could soon appear, one *thanks* to the other and vice versa, in a *simultaneous* and dramatic permutation of causes and consequences. One cannot but be struck by the fantastic speed with which, from 1989 onward, on a soil that was considered unfavorable, have grown the first

roots (of course, not everywhere and not always deeply) of freedom of speech and of the press, of freedom of association and of strike, but also independent trade unions, the rudiments of a multiparty system, the possibilities of citizen pressure on power and more or less free elections.... Unquestionably, Russia will only achieve democracy through democracy. By deepening its norms and habits.[14]

Learning from the Soviet Liberals

In December 2021, the Supreme Court of Russia ordered the dissolution of the International Memorial Society, dedicated to the defense of human rights and the memory of the crimes of Stalinism. Often considered the flagship of Russian post-Soviet civil society, it was founded in 1987 and legalized in 1990. The creation of Memorial closely paralleled that of the political discussion club Moscow Tribune, involving many of the same individuals featured in this book, notably Sakharov and Afanasyev. Its dissolution, just months before the full-scale invasion of Ukraine in February 2022 and the death of Gorbachev in August of the same year, symbolically brought the curtain down on an era of Russian history initiated with the launching of democratization in 1987.

What remains in Russia of the ideals championed by Soviet liberals at the time of perestroika? Disillusionment is the dominant sentiment, as opinion polls have consistently demonstrated over the last three decades.[15] Yet in stark contrast to the memory of the "wild 1990s" purposefully demonized by Putin's regime and massively rejected by the population,[16] the legacy of perestroika remains relatively open to contrasting interpretations. Strikingly, a 2013 survey indicated that half of Russians believed "perestroika is not over," implying that it remains, for many, unfinished business waiting to uphold its ideals.[17] These mixed sentiments provide the background for recurrent calls within Russia to "continue," "complete," or even "reiterate" perestroika (hence the catchword "perestroika 2") while avoiding the repetition of its mistakes.[18]

Crucial for those who still adhere to its values in Russia is the question of the lessons to be learned from the "original" perestroika. While the most commonly held lessons concern the reformer's strategy in conducting reforms from above so as to avoid the collapse of the state, there are also lessons that directly concern individuals who, like the Soviet liberals at the time, wish to contribute to the cause of democracy in a more modest but decisive way—by taking a stance in the public sphere, in the media, or at the helm of political organizations. For these intellectuals and activists, perestroika supposedly tells a cautionary tale against excessive "radicalism," for failing to support the enlightened leader and indulging in political mobilization. The philosopher and public intellectual Boris Mezhuev expresses this standard view in his book calling for a "repetition" of perestroika. He argues that when Gorbachev unexpectedly offered Soviet liberals the opportunity to lead a movement from below, the "'political awakening' of 1987–1991 became an expression of naive and sometimes irresponsible radicalism. . . . And there were no figures nearby . . . who could help the democratic public take power from the weakening grip of the liberal nomenklatura in a way that would prevent the country from descending into chaos and becoming a semicolony."[19] Consequently, we are told that the tragic experience of Soviet liberals teaches that modernization and democratization should be pursued by building a consensus between the reformer and a constructive opposition led by an enlightened elite.

This book aims to challenge this view. It shows that this conservative established knowledge posing as the hard-learned lesson from retrospective insight on perestroika was actually the dominant view among the supposedly radical Soviet liberal intelligentsia. Their most prestigious members constantly strove for "consolidation" behind the reformer, viewing emerging political conflicts as the prelude to civil war. The vision of democracy that this strategy entailed, as an essence or an outcome entrusted to competent hands, prevailed at the end of perestroika, creating the institutional and symbolic conditions for the erosion of the democratic project.

Perhaps it is time, then, to overcome the long-standing apprehension that conflict is inherently threatening to democracy. To consider the realization, which many Soviet liberals found astonishing when political life reawakened in 1989, that a genuinely democratic approach to the "question of power"—*who* rules and *how*—lies not in definitive resolutions aimed at achieving specific outcomes but rather in the continual raising of the question itself.

Notes

Introduction

1. For ease of reading, I use the term Russia to refer to both the Russian Soviet Federative Socialist Republic (RSFSR) and its successor after the dissolution of the USSR, the Russian Federation.

2. Georges Nivat, "De la Russie libérée à la Russie libre," *Esprit* 223 (July 1996): 97. Unless otherwise noted, all translations are my own.

3. Insofar as it remained attached to socialism for a long time, the Soviet liberal intelligentsia was not "liberal" in the sense generally understood in the West. We will return to this question later.

4. Masha Gessen, *Dead Again: The Russian Intelligentsia after Communism* (London: Verso, 1997), 4.

5. Quoted in Viktor Sheinis, "Uroki avgusta. Demokratam vazhno osmyslit' proschety i oshibki, sovershennye do i posle GKChP," Iabloko, August 18, 2006, https://www.yabloko.ru/Publ/2006/2006_08/060818_mn_scheinis.html.

6. I employ the terms used by anthropologist Janine Wedel to refer to the stages of the aid relationship between Western countries and eastern Europe, including Russia. See Wedel, *Collision and Collusion: The Strange Case of Western Aid to Eastern Europe, 1989–1998* (New York: Palgrave, 2001), 7.

7. Moshe Lewin, *The Gorbachev Phenomenon: A Historical Interpretation* (Berkeley: University of California Press, 1988); Marc Ferro, *Les origines de la perestroïka* (Paris: Ramsay, 1990).

8. Steven Fish, *Democracy from Scratch: Opposition and Regime in the New Russian Revolution* (Princeton, NJ: Princeton University Press, 1995), 28.

9. Michael McFaul, *Russia's Unfinished Revolution: Political Change from Gorbachev to Putin* (Ithaca, NY: Cornell University Press, 2001), 63.

10. Marcia Weigle, *Russia's Liberal Project: State-Society Relations in the Transition from Communism* (University Park: Pennsylvania State University Press, 2000); Robert English, *Russia and the Idea of the West: Gorbachev, Intellectuals and the End of the Cold War* (New York: Columbia University Press, 2000).

11. Leon Aron, *Roads to the Temple: Truth, Memory, Ideas and Ideals in the Making of the Russian Revolution, 1987–1991* (New Haven, CT: Yale University Press, 2012); Steven Fish, *Democracy Derailed in Russia: The Failure of Open Politics* (Cambridge: Cambridge University Press, 2005); McFaul, *Russia's Unfinished Revolution*; Igor Timofeyev, "The Development of Russian Liberal Thought since 1985," in *The Demise of Marxism-Leninism in Russia*, ed. Archie Brown (Basingstoke, UK: Palgrave Macmillan, 2004), 51 118.

12. See, for example, the words of the economist Egor Gaidar, Yeltsin's prime minister in the early 1990s and an architect of post-Soviet economic shock therapy, in *Gosudarstvo i evoliutsiia* (Moscow: Evraziia, 1994).

13. Serguei Oushakine, "In the State of Post-Soviet Aphasia: Symbolic Development in Contemporary Russia," *Europe-Asia Studies* 52, no. 6 (2000): 991–1016; Stephen Hanson, *Post-imperial Democracies: Ideology and Party Formation in Third Republic France, Weimar Germany and Post-Soviet Russia* (Cambridge: Cambridge University Press, 2010).

14. Timur Atnashev, "Transformation of the Political Speech under Perestroika: Free Agency, Responsibility and Historical Necessity in the Emerging Intellectual Debates (1985–1991)" (PhD diss., European University Institute, Florence, 2010).

15. John G. A. Pocock, *The Machiavellian Moment: Florentine Political Thought and the Atlantic Republican Tradition* (Princeton, NJ: Princeton University Press, 1975).

16. Timur Atnashev, "Utopicheskii konservatizm v epokhu pozdnei perestroiki: otpuskaia vozhzhi istorii," *Sotsiologiia vlasti* 29, no. 2 (2018): 12–53.

17. These terms come respectively from Peter Reddaway and Dmitri Glinski, *The Tragedy of Russian Reforms: Market Bolshevism against Democracy* (Washington, DC: United States Institute of Peace Press, 2001); Richard Sakwa, *The Crisis of Russian Democracy: The Dual State, Factionalism and the Medvedev Succession* (Cambridge: Cambridge University Press, 2010); and Vladislav Zubok, *Collapse: The Fall of the Soviet Union* (New Haven, CT: Yale University Press, 2021).

18. On a genealogy of this argument within Russia, see Guillaume Sauvé, "Un libéralisme bolchévique? Histoire conceptuelle du double pouvoir en Russie," *Canadian Journal of Political Science / Revue canadienne de science politique* 53, no. 1 (2020): 117–32.

19. Alexander Lukin, *The Political Culture of Russian "Democrats"* (Oxford: Oxford University Press, 2000).

20. On post-Soviet Russian liberals' retrospective criticism of perestroika, see Guillaume Sauvé, "The Lessons from Perestroika and the Evolution of Russian Liberalism: 1995–2005," in *Dimensions and Challenges of Russian Liberalism*, ed. Ricardo Cucciola (Cham: Springer, 2018), 139–51.

21. Pavel Khazanov, *The Russia That We Have Lost: Pre-Soviet Past as Anti-Soviet Discourse* (Madison: University of Wisconsin Press, 2023), 6.

22. Ilya Budraitskis, *Dissidents among Dissidents: Ideology, Politics and the Left in Post-Soviet Russia* (London: Verso Books, 2022), chap. 5.

23. For a critical appraisal of the Russian liberals' mimicry of Western concepts, see Ivan Krastev and Stephen Holmes, *The Light That Failed: Why the West Is Losing the Fight for Democracy* (New York: Pegasus Books, 2019).

24. Oleg Kharkhordin, *The Collective and the Individual in Russia: A Study of Practices* (Berkeley: University of California Press, 1999); Alexei Yurchak, *Everything Was Forever, Until It Was No More: The Last Soviet Generation* (Princeton, NJ: Princeton University Press, 2006).

25. Among the many great works on this topic, in addition to those mentioned above, see Vladimir Gel'man, *Authoritarian Russia: Analyzing Post-Soviet Regime Changes* (Pittsburgh: University of Pittsburgh Press, 2015); Stephen Kotkin, *Armageddon Averted: The Soviet Collapse, 1970–2000* (Oxford: Oxford University Press, 2008); Michael Urban, *The Rebirth of Politics in Russia*, with Vyacheslav Igrunov and Sergei Mitrokhin (Cambridge: Cambridge University Press, 1997).

26. The use of the "democrat" label can also seem problematic when we consider the overtly authoritarian tendencies of many of the Soviet liberal intellectuals. But Alexander Lukin's solution—namely, to qualify the word with quotation marks each and every time it appears in his book—only makes the reading more cumbersome without solving the problem of conceptual polysemy. See Lukin, *Political Culture of Russian "Democrats."*

27. For a wider study of the evolution of liberalism in Russia, see Paul Robinson, *Russian Liberalism* (Ithaca, NY: Northern Illinois University Press, an imprint of Cornell University Press, 2023).

28. For several accounts in this vein, see Irina Kochetkova, *The Myth of the Russian Intelligentsia: Old Intellectuals in the New Russia* (London: Routledge, 2010), chap. 4.

29. On this phenomenon, see Pierre Bourdieu, *Manet, une révolution symbolique. Cours au Collège de France (1998–2000)* (Paris: Seuil, 2013).

30. Dmitrii Furman, "'Perevernutyi istmat?' Ot ideologii perestroiki k ideologii 'stroitel'stva kapitalizma' v Rossii'," *Svobodnaia mysl'*, no. 3 (1995): 15.

31. To be sure, Andrei Sakharov and Aleksandr Solzhenitsyn enjoy greater fame than their contemporaries, yet in both cases this largely preceded perestroika. Moreover, both played a relatively limited role in the debates of that time: Sakharov because of his death in December 1989 and Solzhenitsyn because of his exile to the United States, which ended only after perestroika. An analysis of the political thought of this period cannot ignore these key figures, but neither can it focus on them to the exclusion of other voices. As for party reformers, such as Gorbachev, his right-hand man Yakovlev, or Yeltsin, their political status was quite different from that of the liberal intelligentsia.

32. For an example of such an approach, see Aron, *Roads to the Temple.*

33. These interviews were conducted as follows: Yuri Afanasyev, Moscow suburbs, October 24, 2013; Anatoly Akhutin and Irina Berliand, Moscow, January 21, 213; Leonid Batkin, by phone, January 21, 2013, then by email; Nadezhda Batkina, Moscow, April 10, 2017, then by email; Elena Burtina, Moscow, April 18, 2014; Marietta Chudakova, Moscow, April 20, 2014; Boris Dubin, Moscow, January 17, 2013; Boris Firsov, St. Petersburg, November 2, 2013; Svetlana Gannushkina, Moscow, April 5, 2014; Valentin Gefter, Moscow, November 9, 2013; Vladimir Gel'man, Helsinki, November 27, 2012; Leonid Gozman, Moscow, April 10, 2017; Abdusalam Guseinov, Moscow, October 16, 2013; Viacheslav Igrunov, Moscow, October 21, 2013; Vladimir Iliushenko, Moscow, April 10, 2017; Igor Kliamkin, Moscow, December 14, 2012; Andranik Migranian, New York, April 23, 2013; Arkady Murashev, Moscow, October 31, 2013; Aleksandra Shaikevich, by Skype, June 11, 2014; Viktor Sheinis, Moscow, November 8, 2013, then by email; Aleksandr Tsipko, Moscow, November 9, 2013; Faina Yablokova, Moscow, April 21, 2014 and Grigorii Vodolazov, Moscow, November 6, 2013.

1. The Moral Challenge of Perestroika

Epigraph: Mikhail Gorbachev, *Perestroika: New Thinking for Our Country and the World* (New York: Harper and Row, 1987), 30.

1. Chapters 1 and 2 partially rely on material that I previously introduced in my article titled "The Apogee of Soviet Political Romanticism: Projects for Moral Renewal in Early Perestroika (1985–1989)," *Europe-Asia Studies* 70, no 9 (2018): 1407–32.

2. Gorbachev himself invoked this phrase in his memoirs to sum up the state of mind in which he first launched perestroika in March 1985. Mikhail Gorbachev, *Naedine s soboi* (Moscow: Grin strit, 2012), 384. This phrase was also the title of a documentary that caused a sensation in 1990, in which the conservative nationalist director Stanislav Govorukhin painted an extremely bleak portrait of Soviet society.

3. The Soviet philosopher Abdusalam Guseinov observed that the term "morality" appeared more often in the 1986 party program than it did in the 1961 program, which already represented a twentyfold increase in the term's use compared to the 1919 program. Abdusalam Guseinov, "Bol'she morali, no ne moralizatorstva," in *Perestroika i nravstvennost'*, ed. M. Iskrov (Baku: Azerneshr, 1988), 24.

4. A classic example of this kind of interpretation can be found in Carl Schmitt's definition of political Romanticism as "subjectified occasionalism," whose complexity is rooted in "the moral deficiency of a lyricism that can take any content at all." "Where political activity begins," Schmitt concludes, "political romanticism ends." Carl Schmitt, *Political Romanticism* (London: Routledge, 2017), 158–60.

5. In the rather condescending words of Anatoly Sobchak, mayor of St. Petersburg, in a retrospective assessment of the democratic movement that brought him to power during the perestroika period. Anatoly Sobchak, *Zhila-byla kommunisticheskaia partiia* (St. Petersburg: Lenizdat, 1995), 40.

6. Michael Löwy and Robert Sayre, *Romanticism against the Tide of Modernity* (Durham, NC: Duke University Press, 2001).

7. Charles Taylor, *Hegel* (Cambridge: Cambridge University Press, 1975), chap. 20.

8. For a similar view, see Mark Sandle, *A Short History of Soviet Socialism* (London: UCL Press, 1999), 313.

9. Richard De George, *Soviet Ethics and Morality* (Ann Arbor: University of Michigan Press, 1969), 111.

10. Aleksandr Bikbov, *Grammatika poriadka: Istoricheskaia sociologiia poniatii, kotorye meniaiut nashu real'nost'* (Moscow: Izdatel'skii dom Vysshchei shkoly ekonomiki, 2014), 195–237; Polly Jones, *Revolution Rekindled: The Writers and Readers of Late Soviet Biography* (Oxford: Oxford University Press, 2019), chap. 3.

11. The *Great Soviet Encyclopedia* is a work of exceptional scope and ambition. As a historian of science explains, it had an essential function in Soviet society: "Similarly to the French *Encyclopédie* of the eighteenth century, *The Great Soviet Encyclopedia* served not merely a descriptive but also a normative function in the Soviet 'Enlightenment': it defined the boundaries of knowledge . . . [and] certified the validity of scientific theories included in its volumes." Slava Gerovitch, *From Newspeak to Cyberspeak: A History of Soviet Cybernetics* (Cambridge, MA: MIT Press, 2002), 103. Politizdat was the main publisher of political literature by the Communist Party of the USSR. The discipline of scientific communism was introduced in 1963 as a mandatory subject for all higher education in the USSR. Scientific communism was considered one of the three branches of Marxism-Leninism, together with Marxist-Leninist philosophy and political economy.

12. *Bol'shaia sovetskaia entsiklopediia*, 3rd ed. (1969–78), s.v. "Moral'."

13. Petr Fedoseev, K. Brutents, and V. Afanas'ev, *Nauchnyi kommunizm: Uchebnik* (Moscow: Politizdat, 1983), 418.

14. Fedoseev, Brutents, and Afanas'ev, 417. We shall see later on the circumstances in which the *Moral Codex* was adopted.

15. Fedoseev, Brutents, and Afanas'ev, 418

16. Fedoseev, Brutents, and Afanas'ev, 415.
17. Fedoseev, Brutents, and Afanas'ev, 411.
18. Fedoseev, Brutents, and Afanas'ev, 261.
19. Fedoseev, Brutents, and Afanas'ev, 422.
20. This is taken from the back cover of one of the titles from this series, Aleksandr Levikov's *Vesy doveriia* (Moscow: Politizdat, 1983).
21. Claude Lefort, *Un homme en trop. Réflexions sur L'archipel du goulag* (Paris: Éditions du Seuil, 1976), 75.
22. The Decembrists were a group of Russian officers who launched an unsuccessful coup attempt in December 1825 aimed at overthrowing the tsarist government and forcing the adoption of a constitution.
23. On "qualitative" individualism, see *The Sociology of Georg Simmel*, trans. and ed. Kurt H. Wolff (New York: Free Press, 1950), 81. On the concept of personality in Russia, see Nikolaj Plotnikov, ed., "The Discourse of Personality in the Russian Intellectual Tradition," special issue, *Studies in East European Thought* 61, nos. 2–3 (August 2009): 71–241.
24. The *Narodniki* defended a version of socialism aimed at combining the collectivism of the traditional peasant commune with the technologies of industrial modernity in order to advance society toward modernity while bypassing the various stages of capitalist development.
25. Karl Kautsky, *Erfurtin ohjelma* (Helsinki: Tammi, 1974), 167, quoted in Pekka Sutela, *Economic Thought and Economic Reform in the Soviet Union* (Cambridge: Cambridge University Press, 1991), 7.
26. Vladimir Lenin, "K kharakteristike ekonomicheskogo romantizma. Sismondi i nashi otechestvennye sismondisty," in *Polnoe sobranie sochinenii* (Moscow: Politizdat, 1969), 2:123–202.
27. Mikhail Heller, *Cogs in the Soviet Wheel: The Formation of Soviet Man* (London: Collins Harvill, 1988).
28. Vladimir Lenin, "Zadachi soiuzov molodezhi," in *Polnoe sobranie sochinenii*, 41:301–18.
29. David Hoffmann, *Stalinist Values: The Cultural Norms of Soviet Modernity, 1917–1941* (Ithaca, NY: Cornell University Press, 2003).
30. Vadim Volkov, "The Concept of kul'turnost': Notes on the Stalinist Civilizing Process," in *Stalinism: New Directions*, ed. Sheila Fitzpatrick (New York: Routledge, 2000), 210–30.
31. Quoted in Hoffmann, *Stalinist Values*, 62.
32. Jochen Hellbeck, *Revolution on My Mind: Writing a Diary under Stalin* (Cambridge, MA: Harvard University Press, 2006), 21.
33. *Bol'shaia sovetskaia entsiklopediia*, 2nd ed. (1949–58), s.v. "Nravstvennost'."
34. Miriam Dobson, *Khrushchev's Cold Summer: Gulag Returnees, Crime, and the Fate of Reform after Stalin* (Ithaca, NY: Cornell University Press, 2009), 146.
35. De George, *Soviet Ethics and Morality*, 106.
36. For a detailed analysis of the *Moral Codex*'s contents, see De George, *Soviet Ethics and Morality*, chap. 5.
37. Oleg Kharkhordin, *The Collective and the Individual in Russia: A Study of Practices* (Berkeley: University of California Press, 1999), chap. 8.
38. Vladimir Shlapentokh, *Soviet Ideologies in the Period of Glasnost: Responses to Brezhnev's Stagnation* (New York: Praeger, 1988), 131.

39. Gorbachev, *Perestroika*, 75–76.

40. Mikhail Gorbachev, "'Interviiu zhurnalu Shpigel' (FRG)," in *Izbrannye rechi i stat'i* (Moscow: Izdatel'stvo politicheskoi literatury, 1990), 4:59.

41. Andrei Zdravomyslov, "O prichinakh negativnykh iavlenii v usloviiakh sotsializma," in Iskrov, *Perestroika i nravstvennost'*, 116.

42. Zdravomyslov, 117.

43. Zdravomyslov, 118.

44. Anna Ivanova, *Magaziny "Berezka": Paradoksy potrebleniia v pozdnem SSSR* (Moscow: NLO, 2017).

45. In the 1950s and 1960s, the most prominent members of this group included Fedor Abramov, Viktor Astafyev, Vasily Belov, Efim Dorosh, Boris Mozhaev, Viktor Likhonossov, Evgeny Nossov, Vasily Shukshin, Aleksandr Solzhenitsyn, Aleksander Yashin, and Sergei Zalygin. See Yitzak Brudny, *Reinventing Russia: Russian Nationalism and the Soviet State, 1953–1991* (Cambridge, MA: Harvard University Press, 1998), esp. chaps. 2 and 3.

46. Samizdat was a clandestine system for the circulation of dissident writings. Aleksandr Sol'zhenitsyn, "Žit' ne po lži," 1974. This text appeared legally for the first time in the USSR in the February 1989 issue of the journal *Vek XX i mir*.

47. Alexander Solzhenitsyn, "Live Not by Lies," *Index on Censorship* 33, no. 2 (2004): 203.

48. Solzhenitsyn, 204.

49. Yitzhak Brudny, "Between Liberalism and Nationalism: The Case of Serguei Zalygin," *Studies in Comparative Communism* 21, nos. 3–4 (1988): 331–40.

50. On the relationship between nationalist literature and the consolidation of a conservative and patriotic ideology within the party, see Nikolai Mitrokhin, *Russkaia partiia. Dvizhenie russkikh natsionalistov v SSSR, 1953–1985 gody* (Moscow: NLO, 2003).

51. Dmitrii Likhachev, "O Russkom," *Novyi Mir*, March 1980, 10–38.

52. Dmitrii Likhachev, "Gomosfera—termin nashikh dnei," *Ogonek*, no. 36 (1984): 17.

53. Dmitrii Likhachev, "Ot pokaianiia—k deistviiu!," *Literaturnaia gazeta*, (September 9, 1987): 2.

54. Dmitrii Likhachev, "Ekologiia kul'tury," *Znanie-sila*, June 1982, 22–24; Likhachev, "Gomosfera—termin nashikh dnei."

55. Likhachev, "Ot pokaianiia—k deistviiu!"

56. Dmitrii Likhachev, "Trevogi sovesti," *Literaturnaia gazeta*, no. 1 (January 1, 1987): 11.

57. Likhachev, 11.

58. Likhachev, 11.

59. Likhachev, 11.

60. Likhachev, 11.

61. Likhachev uses this phrase in the eighth letter of *Pis'ma o dobrom i prekrasnom*, a collection of reflections published in 1985 and composed, according to the preface, of "life advice."

62. Vladislav Zubok, *D. S. Likhachev v obshchestvennoi zhizni Rossii kontsa XX veka* (St. Petersburg: Evropeiskii dom, 2011), 74.

63. Bondarev, quoted in "Perestroika—volia, muzhestvo, ob"ektivnost'. V Sekretariate Pravleniia Soiuza pisatelei RSFSR," *Literaturnaia Rossiia*, March 27, 1987, 3.

64. Less influential in the public sphere than the conservative nationalists who collaborated with *Nash sovremennik*, radical Slavophiles such as Mikhail Lobanov and

Vadim Kozhinov displayed virulent anti-Western, anti-intellectual, and antisemitic views and advocated for a return to the tsarist system. Both groups—the conservative nationalists and the radical Slavophiles—collaborated in the journal *Molodaia gvardiia*.

2. Liberal Moralism in the USSR

Epigraph: Andrei Sakharov, "Neizbezhnost' perestroiki," in *Inogo ne dano*, ed. Iurii Afanas'ev (Moscow: Progress, 1988), 127.

1. On the "party liberals" close to Gorbachev, such as Aleksandr Yakovlev and Anatoly Chernyaev, see Archie Brown, *The Gorbachev Factor* (Oxford: Oxford University Press, 1996), chap. 4.

2. Yitzhak Brudny, "The Heralds of Opposition to Perestroika," in *Milestones in Glasnost and Perestroika. Politics and People*, ed. Ed A. Hewett and Victor H. Winston (Washington: Brookings Institution, 1991), 162.

3. A survey conducted between March 1988 and January 1989 among readers of the journal *Knizhnoe obozrenie*, viewers of the public affairs TV program *Vzgliad*, students at Moscow State University, and Muscovites contacted at random by telephone lists the fifty most popular essayists at the time (the question was "Who should be published in 1989?"). Among the top twenty are fourteen liberal intellectuals (Nikolai Shmelev, Andrei Nuikin, Gavriil Popov, Yuri Karyakin, Fedor Burlatsky, Otto Latsis, Anatoly Strelyany, Arkady Vaksberg, Gennady Lisichkin, Igor Kliamkin, Yuri Afanasyev, Evgeny Evtushenko, Vitaly Korotich, and Yuri Burtin); two liberal nationalists (Vasily Seliunin and Yuri Chernichenko); and one conservative nationalist (Valentin Rasputin, in eighteenth place). In contrast, Gorbachev is in thirty-ninth place. Semen Kliger, "Publitsistika-88 kak ob"ekt issledovaniia," in *V svoem otechestve proroki? Publitsistika perestroiki: Luchshie avtory 1988 goda*, ed. Ninel' Streltsova (Moscow: Knizhnaia palata, 1989), 242.

4. I return to this ideological shift in chapter 6.

5. Gil Eyal, Ivan Szelenyi, and Eleanor R. Townsley, *Making Capitalism without Capitalists: The New Ruling Elites in Eastern Europe* (New York: Verso, 1998), 95.

6. *Bol'shaia sovetskaia entsiklopediia*, 3rd ed. (1969–78), s.v. "Moral'."

7. Iurii Afanas'ev, "Perestroika i istoricheskoe znanie," in Afanas'ev, *Inogo ne dano*, 491–506; Andrei Sakharov, "Pliuralizm—eto konvergenciia," *Vek XX i mir* 1 (1989): 18–20; Leonid Batkin, "Stat' Evropoi," *Vek XX i mir*, July 1988, 29–33.

8. Iurii Afanas'ev, "Sotsial'naia pamiat' chelovechestva," *Nauka i zhizn'*, September 1987, 67. This comparison was inspired by some of the most pressing ecological issues of the time, and in particular the 1985 mobilization against the Soviet state's efforts to reverse the flow of several Siberian rivers, mentioned briefly in chapter 1.

9. Leonid Batkin, "Ostanetsia li vlast' u partii?," in *Vozobnovlenie istorii: Razmyshleniia o politike i kul'ture* (Moscow: Moskovskii rabochii, 1991), 141.

10. Timur Atnashev, "Transformation of the Political Speech under Perestroika: Free Agency, Responsibility and Historical Necessity in the Emerging Intellectual Debates (1985–1991)" (PhD diss., European University Institute, Florence, 2010).

11. Atnashev notes that liberals tend to use the term "natural-historical development," while nationalists speak of "organic evolution." See "Transformation of the Political Speech under Perestroika," 325.

12. In reference to the *Narodniki* movement, in the second half of the nineteenth century, which advocated agrarian socialism.

13. Iurii Burtin, *Ispoved' shestidesiatnika* (Moscow: Progress-Traditsiia, 2003).

14. Burtin, "Akhillesova piata istoricheskoi teorii Marksa," *Oktiabr'* 11 (1989): 3–25; Burtin, "Akhillesova piata istoricheskoi teorii Marksa," *Oktiabr'* 12 (1989): 3–48.

15. Burtin, "Akhillesova piata istoricheskoi teorii Marksa," *Oktiabr'* 12 (1989): 22 (emphasis in original).

16. Burtin, 24.

17. Liudmila Saraskina et al., "Barrikady perestroiki," *Vek XX i mir*, February 1988, 22.

18. Len Karpinskii, "Sotsializm—eto prosto normal'naia zhizn'." *Vek XX i mir* 7 (1987), 41.

19. Karpinskii, "Sotsializm," 43.

20. Iurii Kariakin, *Peremena ubezhdenii: Ot oslepleniia k prozreniiu* (Moscow: Izdatel'stvo Raduga, 2007).

21. Ales' Adamovich, "Dodumyvat' do kontsa. Avtobiografiia—1985," in *Vyberi—zhizn': literaturnaia, publicistika* (Minsk: Mastatskaia literatura, 1986), 348–73.

22. Iurii Kariakin, "Ne opozdat'! (Zametki publitsista)," in *Vopros vsekh voprosov. Bor'ba za mir i istoricheskie sud'by chelovechestva*, ed. Iurii Kariakin and V. Petrovskii (Moscow: Progress, 1985), 216–29.

23. Adamovich, *Vyberi—zhizn'*.

24. Sheila Fitzpatrick, *Tear Off the Masks! Identity and Imposture in Twentieth-Century Russia* (Princeton, NJ: Princeton University Press, 2005), 25.

25. Iurii Burtin, "Vam, iz drugogo pokolen'ia," *Oktiabr'* 10 (1987): 193.

26. In addition to the article cited above, these are Iurii Burtin, "Real'naia kritika—vchera i segodnia," *Novyi Mir* 6 (1987): 222–39; and Burtin, "Izzhit' Stalina!," in *Ispoved' shestidesiatnika* (Moscow: Progress-Traditsiia, 2003), 263–73.

27. Burtin, "Real'naia kritika—vchera i segodnia," 226–27. Nikolai Dobroliubov (1836–1861) was a revolutionary literary critic and democratic publicist.

28. Burtin, "Izzhit' Stalina!"

29. Rybakov was the author of the novel *Children of the Arbat*, which was banned for a long time and finally published in 1987. Simonov is the former director of *Novyi Mir* and the author of a memoir in which he describes his meetings with Stalin, published in 1988.

30. Burtin, "Izzhit' Stalina!," 266.

31. Burtin, 266.

32. Burtin, 266 (emphasis in original).

33. Len Karpinskii, "Pochemu stalinizm ne skhodit so stseny?," in Afanas'ev, *Inogo ne dano*, 648.

34. Burtin, "Real'naia kritika—vchera i segodnia," 232.

35. Leonid Batkin, "Vozobnovlenie istorii," in Afanas'ev, *Inogo ne dano*, 190.

36. Also referred to as the "administrative command system," or simply the "administrative system" or the "command system."

37. The novel *A New Assignment*, written in 1964, was first published in 1986 in the literary journal *Znamia*.

38. Gavriil Popov, "S tochki zreniia ekonomista. O romane Aleksandra Beka *Novoe naznachenie*," *Nauka i zhizn'*, April 1987, 65.

39. Popov, 58.

40. For a criticism of these assumptions, see Anna Krylova, "The Tenacious Liberal Subject in Soviet Studies," *Kritika: Explorations in Russian and Eurasian History* 1, no. 1 (Winter 2000): 119–46.

41. See, for example, Vladimir Shlapentokh, *Public and Private Life of the Soviet People: Changing Values in Post-Stalin Russia* (Oxford: Oxford University Press, 1989).

42. Popov, "S tochki zreniia ekonomista," 59.

43. Popov, 59.

44. Popov, 65.

45. Popov, 56, 59, 64.

46. This is the case, for example, with Andrei Sakharov, who writes that bureaucracy "is accompanied to varying degrees by negative phenomena: an administrative management structure of command with mechanical subordination of intermediate links to higher authorities and disregard for democratic control exercised from below." Sakharov, "Neizbezhnost' perestroiki," 122.

47. "Novye knigi v PIKe," *Demokraticheskaia Rossiia*, June 7, 1991, 16.

48. Igor Timofeyev, "The Development of Russian Liberal Thought since 1985," in *The Demise of Marxism-Leninism in Russia*, ed. Archie Brown (Basingstoke, UK: Palgrave Macmillan, 2004), 60.

49. Andrzej Walicki, *Marxism and the Leap to the Kingdom of Freedom: The Rise and Fall of the Communist Utopia* (Stanford, CA: Stanford University Press, 1995), 539, 546.

50. Political perfectionism should not be confused with moral perfectionism, which is the preserve of moral philosophy and deals with the conditions of individual fulfillment, and even less with the common meaning of the term, which refers to an excessive tendency to seek perfection. The term "perfectionism" is hereafter used to refer to political perfectionism.

51. This tendency can be observed in the writings of American philosophers such as John Rawls and Ronald Dworkin and also in those of French authors such as Pierre Manent and Claude Lefort.

52. Michael Freeden, *Liberal Languages: Ideological Imaginations and Twentieth-Century Progressive Thought* (Princeton, NJ: Princeton University Press, 2005); Martha Nussbaum, "Perfectionist Liberalism and Political Liberalism," *Philosophy and Public Affairs* 39, no. 1 (2001): 3–45.

53. Serguei Oushakine, "The Terrifying Mimicry of Samizdat," *Public Culture* 13, no. 2 (April 2001): 191–214.

3. Opinion and Truth

Epigraph: Grigorii Pomerants, "Son o spravedlivom vozmezdii," *Vek XX i mir*, November 1990, Old.Russ.ru, http://old.russ.ru/antolog/vek/1990/11/spor.htm.

1. A comparison made by George Breslauer in *Gorbachev and Yeltsin as Leaders* (Cambridge: Cambridge University Press, 2002), 236.

2. Archie Brown, *Seven Years That Changed the World: Perestroika in Perspective* (Oxford: Oxford University Press, 2007), 110.

3. Vladimir Sogrin, *Politicheskaia istoriia sovremennoi Rossii 1985–2001* (Moscow: Ves' mir, 2001), 40.

4. Mikhail Gorbachev, *Perestroika: New Thinking for Our Country and the World* (New York: Harper and Row, 1987), 80.

5. *Inogo ne dano* literally translates as "There is no other way." Tellingly, Sakharov's article in this collection is titled "The Inevitability of Perestroika."

6. Len Karpinskii, "Pochemu stalinizm ne skhodit so stseny?," in *Inogo ne dano*, ed. Iurii Afanas'ev (Moscow: Progress, 1988), 663.

7. Karpinskii, 663.

8. Evgenii Ambartsumov et al., "Revoliutsiia: Bolezn' ili istselenie?," *Moskovskie novosti*, December 17, 1989, 13.

9. Quoted in Pekka Sutela and Vladimir Mau, "Economics under Socialism: The Russian Case," in *Economic Thought in Communist and Post-Communist Europe*, ed. Jürgen Wagener (New York: Routledge, 1998), 35–36.

10. The anthropologist Natalia Roudakova refers to this presumption as "epistemological realism," which Soviet journalists inherited from Marxism. Natalia Roudakova, *Losing Pravda: Ethics and the Press in Post-truth Russia* (Cambridge: Cambridge University Press, 2017), 52.

11. Nikolai Shmelev, "Avansy i dolgi," *Novyi Mir*, June 1987, 142–58.

12. Shmelev, 144.

13. Shmelev, 157.

14. Shmelev, 144, 151.

15. Leonid Batkin, "Mertvyi khvataet zhivogo" (September 1989), in *Vozobnovlenie istorii: Razmyshleniia o politike i kul'ture* (Moscow: Moskovskii rabochii, 1991), 124.

16. Liudmila Saraskina et al., "Barrikady perestroiki," *Vek XX i mir*, February 1988, 22.

17. Karl Polanyi, *The Great Transformation: The Political and Economic Origins of Our Time* (Boston: Beacon, 2001).

18. A survey of Soviet and British economists in 1990 showed that the former were much more likely than the latter (95 percent versus 66 percent) to agree that "the market is the best mechanism for regulating economic life." Vincent Barnett, "Conceptions of the Market among Russian Economists: A Survey," *Soviet Studies* 44, no. 6 (1992): 1093.

19. Karpinskii, "Pochemu stalinizm ne skhodit so stseny?," 660.

20. Dmitrii Likhachev, "Trevogi sovesti," *Literaturnaia gazeta*, no. 1 (January 1987): 11.

21. On this conflation of factual and moral truth, see also Timur Atnashev, "Idealy nauchnoi ob"ektivnosti i chestnosti kak obosnovanie politiki glasnosti v perestroiku," Gefter.ru, October 9, 2013, https://gefter.ru/archive/10224. Once again, this attitude was not unique to the Soviet context or exclusive to Russian culture. Eastern European dissidents also shared a similar perspective, where truth was intrinsically linked to virtue. In their case, both notions were "fused beyond recognition in the term 'civility' (in Czech, *kulturnost*)." Gil Eyal, Ivan Szelenyi, and Eleanor R. Townsley, *Making Capitalism without Capitalists: The New Ruling Elites in Eastern Europe* (New York: Verso, 1998), 93.

22. Hannah Arendt, "Truth and Politics," in *Between Past and Future: Eight Exercises in Political Thought* (New York: Viking, 1968), 227–64.

23. Arendt, 264.

24. Arendt, 258.

25. Andrei Sakharov, "Neizbezhnost' perestroiki," in Afanas'ev, *Inogo ne dano*, 127.

26. Arendt, "Truth and Politics," 260.
27. Arendt, 240.
28. Arendt, 239.
29. Quoted in Philip Boobbyer, *Conscience, Dissent and Reform in Soviet Russia* (London: Routledge, 2005), 200.
30. Iurii Afanas'ev, "Govorim o proshlom, no reshaetsia budushchee sotsializma," *Moskovskie novosti*, May 10, 1987, 11.
31. Nina Andreeva, "Ne mogu postupat'sia printsipami," *Sovetskaia Rossiia*, March 13, 1988, 2. For an English version, see Nina Andreeva, "I Cannot Give Up My Principles," in *The Structure of Soviet History: Essays and Documents*, ed. Ronald Grigor Suny (Oxford: Oxford University Press, 2002), 438–45.
32. Andreeva, "I Cannot Give Up My Principles," 443–44.
33. She also denounces, but with less insistence, the "neo-Slavophiles" who seek "to return to the social forms of presocialist Russia." Andreeva, 444–45.
34. Andreeva, 445.
35. Andreeva, 445.
36. "Printsipy perestroiki: Revoliutsionnost' myshleniia i deistvii," *Pravda*, April 5, 1988, 2.
37. "Printsipy perestroiki," 2.
38. "Printsipy perestroiki," 2.
39. Timur Atnashev, "Switching Regimes of Publicity: How Nina Andreeva Facilitated the Transformation of Glasnost into Freedom of Speech," *Social Sciences* 49, no 4 (December 2018): 80.
40. Iurii Kariakin, "Zhdanovskaia zhidkost', ili protiv ochernitel'stva," in Afanas'ev, *Inogo ne dano*, 412–23.
41. Kariakin, 417.
42. Kariakin, 422–23.
43. Karpinskii, "Pochemu stalinizm ne skhodit so stseny?," 668–69.
44. Iurii Afanas'ev, "Perestroika i istoricheskoe znanie," in Afanas'ev, *Inogo ne dano*, 494.
45. Likhachev, "Trevogi sovesti," 11.
46. Igor' Vinogradov, "Mozhet li pravda byt' poetapnoi?," in Afanas'ev, *Inogo ne dano*, 279.
47. Likhachev, "Trevogi sovesti," 11.
48. Quoted in Elena Joly, *La troisième mort de Staline: Entretiens avec des intellectuels gorbatchéviens* (Paris: Actes Sud, 1988), 181–82.
49. Afanas'ev, "Perestroika i istoricheskoe znanie," 279.
50. Afanas'ev, 496. The "records" in question are the exploits sung by Stalinist propaganda, particularly in the context of the Stakhanovite campaign.
51. Afanas'ev, 496–97.
52. As shown by the extensive study of public opinion conducted by a team of sociologists from the Pan-Soviet Center for the Study of Public Opinion (Vsesoiuznyi tsentr izucheniia obshchestvennogo mneniia, or VTsIOM) from 1988. Iurii Levada, ed., *Est' mnenie! Itogi sociologicheskogo oprosa* (Moscow: Progress, 1989).
53. Iurii Burtin, "Vam, iz drugogo pokoleniia," *Oktiabr'* 10 (1987): 196.
54. Iurii Burtin, "Real'naia kritika—vchera i segodnia," *Novyi Mir* 6 (1987): 230.

55. Andrei Razbash, dir., *Deti XX s"ezda* (Moscow: Glavnaia redaktsiia programm dlia molodezhi Tsentral'noe televidenie SSSR, 1988).

56. See the previous chapter, pages 41–45, for more details on the structural approach advocated by Burtin, what he called the "sense of the system."

57. Andreeva, "I Cannot Give Up My Principles," 441.

58. Andreeva, 442.

59. A. Egorov, "Esli po sovesti—*Inogo ne dano*. O dvukh knigakh publitsistiki," *Literaturnoe obozrenie*, October 1988, 3–6.

60. It seems that this criticism did not fall on unhearing ears. The French version of *Inogo ne dano*, unlike the original Soviet one, includes in an appendix an abridged version of Andreeva's letter, "presented to the French reader as a document." Youri Afanassiev, ed., *La seule issue* (Paris: Fayard, 1989), 543.

61. Iurii Afanas'ev, "Neskol'ko slov ot redaktora," in Afanas'ev, *Inogo ne dano*, 6 (emphasis in original).

62. Vassilii Aksenov et al., "Pust' Gorbachev predostavit nam dokazatel'stva," *Moskovskie novosti*, April 12, 1987, 12.

63. Gil Eyal, *The Origins of Postcommunist Elites: From Prague Spring to the Breakup of Czechoslovakia* (Minneapolis: University of Minnesota Press, 2003), 29.

64. Likhachev, "Trevogi sovesti," 11.

65. Iurii Kariakin, "Stoit li nastupat' na grabli? (Otkrytoe pis'mo odnomu Inkognito)," *Znamia*, September 1987, 201.

66. Len Karpinskii, "Nravstvennost' i glasnost'," *Moskovskie novosti*, May 21, 1989, 3. The Russian expression that Karpinsky uses in the original means "measure seven times, cut once."

67. Batkin, "Vozobnovlenie istorii," 163.

4. A Reluctant Opposition (1989)

Epigraph: Leonid Batkin, "Ostanetsia li vlast' u partii?," in *Vozobnovlenie istorii: Razmyshleniia o politike i kul'ture* (Moscow: Moskovskii rabochii, 1991), 127 (emphasis in original).

1. This political pluralism received de jure recognition the following year, in March 1990, with the abolition of article 6 of the Soviet Constitution that established the "leading role" of the Communist Party within Soviet society.

2. Today Nizhnyi-Novgorod. Sakharov was placed under house arrest in 1980, following his condemnation of the Soviet invasion of Afghanistan.

3. Andrei Sakharov, "Neizbezhnost' perestroiki," in *Inogo ne dano*, ed. Iurii Afanas'ev (Moscow: Progress, 1988), 122–34.

4. Andrei Sakharov, "Otkrytoe pis'mo Prezidentu Akademii nauk SSSR A.P. Aleksandrovu (20 okt., 1980)," Sakharov Archive, October 1980, https://www.sakharov-archive.ru/sakharov/works/otkrytoe-pismo-prezidentu-an-sssr-a-p-aleksandrovu-20-okt-1980/.

5. Karl Popper, *The Open Society and Its Enemies* (Princeton, NJ: Princeton University Press, 1994).

6. Niels Bohr was a Danish physicist, one of the principal theorists of quantum mechanics. After the Second World War, he militated for the peaceful use of nuclear energy. René Cassin served as France's representative at the UN; he was one of the

authors of the Universal Declaration of Human Rights and a winner of the Nobel Peace Prize.

7. Andrei Sakharov, "O strane i o mire," Sakharov.Space, June 1975, https://www.sakharov.space/lib/o-strane-i-mire.

8. Sakharov, "O strane i o mire."

9. Sakharov, "Neizbezhnost' perestroiki," 129.

10. Jay Bergman, *Meeting the Demands of Reason: The Life and Thought of Andrei Sakharov* (Ithaca, NY: Cornell University Press, 2009), 222.

11. See, for example, Andrei Sakharov, "Razmyshleniia o progresse, mirnom sosushchestvovanii i intellektual'noi svobode" (1968), in *Trevoga i nadezhda* (Moscow: Inter-Verso, 1991), 11–47.

12. Andrei Sakharov, "O pis'me Aleksandra Sol'zhenitsyna 'Vozhdiam Sovetskogo Soiuza,'" Sakharov.Space, April 3, 1974, https://www.sakharov.space/lib/o-pisme-aleksandra-solzhenicyna-vozhdyam-sovetskogo-soyuza.

13. Andrei Sakharov, "Predvybornaia platforma" (February 1989), in *Vospominaniia* (Moscow: Prava cheloveka, 1996), 570–74.

14. Andrei Sakharov, "Pamiatnaia zapiska," Sakharov Archive, June 1972, https://www.sakharov-archive.ru/sakharov/works/pamjatnaja-zapiska/.

15. Isaiah Berlin, "The Pursuit of the Ideal," in *The Proper Study of Mankind: An Anthology of Essays* (New York: Farrar, Straus and Giroux, 1997), 1–16.

16. Sakharov, "Predvybornaia platforma."

17. Sakharov's opinion on the relative values of socialism and capitalism evolved over the years. In an essay from 1968 ("Razmyshleniia o progresse . . ."), he places the two systems on the same level and sees in convergence the quest for a middle way. In a 1975 essay ("O strane i mire"), convergence is instead presented as the introduction to socialist societies of capitalist elements that should, in time, prevail. This was also his vision of convergence in 1989.

18. Andrej Sakharov, "Pliuralizm—eto konvergentsiia," *Vek XX i mir*, January 1989, 18–20. The "new thought" is the name Gorbachev gave to his approach to politics, and in particular to foreign policy.

19. Sakharov, "Predvybornaia platforma."

20. He wrote about it in his essay "O strane i mire," written in 1975, and then in 1988 in an interview with journalist Zora Safir, quoted in Bergman, *Meeting the Demands of Reason*, 359.

21. Andrei Sakharov, "Gor'kii, Moskva, dalee vezde," in *Vospominaniia*, 397.

22. As a reminder, the soviets had appeared in Russia during the revolutions of 1905 and 1917 as local instances of direct democracy. In subsequent decades, however, they had been transformed into venues for the ritual and unanimous approval of party decisions by the regime that bore their name.

23. Mikhail Gorbachev, "O khode realizatsii reshenii XXVII s"ezda KPSS i zadachakh po uglubleniiu perestroika" (June 1988), in *Izbrannye rechi i stat'i* (Moscow: Izdatel'stvo politicheskoi literatury, 1990), 6:353.

24. So as to differentiate it from the Congress of People's Deputies of the Russian Soviet Federative Socialist Republic, elected a year later (hereafter referred to as the "Russian Congress").

25. Gorbachev, "O khode realizatsii reshenii XXVII s"ezda KPSS i zadachakh po uglubleniiu perestroika," 353.

26. One-third of the seats in the USSR Congress were reserved for representatives of recognized social organizations, such as the Communist Party, as well as the Komsomol (the youth organization) and the Academy of Sciences, among others.

27. On the foundation and the activities of the Moscow Tribune during the perestroika era, see Guillaume Sauvé, "A Reluctant Opposition: Soviet Liberals within the Moscow Tribune," *Slavic Review* 80, no. 1 (2022): 722–44.

28. Sakharov, "Gor'kii, Moskva, dalee vezde," 333.

29. Leonid Batkin, *Episody moei obshchestvennoi zhizni* (Moscow: Novyi khronograf, 2013), 123. (emphasis in original).

30. Petr Filippov, interview by Carole Sigman, *Clubs politiques et perestroïka en Russie. Subversion sans dissidence* (Paris: Karthala, 2009), 133–34.

31. Batkin, "Vozobnovlenie istorii," 475, 484.

32. Howard L. Biddulph, "Protest Strategies of the Soviet Intellectual Opposition," in *Dissent in the USSR: Politics, Ideology, and People*, ed. Rudolf L. Tökés (Baltimore: Johns Hopkins University Press, 1975), 115.

33. "O sozdanii politiko-kul'turnogo obshchestvenogo kluba 'Moskovskaia Tribuna,'" *Biulleten' "Moskovskoi Tribuny,"* no. 1 (1989): 4.

34. "O sozdanii politiko-kul'turnogo obshchestvenogo kluba 'Moskovskaia Tribuna,'" 4.

35. Iurii Afanas'ev et al., "Otkrytoe obrashchenie kluba 'Moskovskaia Tribuna,'" November 12, 1988. Sakharov Archive, F.1, Op.3, Ed.khr.168.

36. "Interv'iu s Iakovom Bergerom," Yeltsin Center, July 12, 2012, http://www.yeltsincenter.ru/decryption/intervyu-s-yakovom-bergerom.

37. See, for example, David Remnick, *Lenin's Tomb: The Last Days of the Soviet Empire* (New York: Random House, 1993), chap. 11.

38. Jiří Pribán, *Dissidents of Law: On the 1989 Velvet Revolutions, Legitimations, Fictions of Legality and Contemporary Versions of the Social Contract* (London: Routledge, 2019).

39. Barbara Falk, *The Dilemmas of Dissidence in East-Central Europe: Citizen Intellectuals and Philosopher Kings* (Budapest: Central European University Press, 2003), 315–16.

40. "Uchreditel'noe sobranie obshchestvenno-diskussionnogo kluba 'Moskovskaia tribuna,'" *Ekspress-khronika*, no. 42(63) (October 1988): 8.

41. Afanas'ev et al., "Otkrytoe obrashchenie kluba 'Moskovskaia Tribuna.'"

42. Stephen Cohen, in Andrei Sakharov et al., "Interpretations and Perceptions of Perestroyka," in *Milestones in Glasnost and Perestroika*, ed. Ed A. Hewett and Victor H. Winston (Washington, DC: Brookings Institution, 1991), 142–43.

43. Ales Adamovich, Yuri Afanasyev, Yuri Karyakin, Roald Sagdeev, Andrei Sakharov, Viktor Sheinis, and Sergei Stankevichwere among those elected.

44. Andrei Sakharov, "Za mir i progress," *Moskovskie novosti*, February 5, 1989, 8.

45. In a letter dated July 27, 1989, and published the following year under the title "Na zlobu dnia," in *Cherez ternii*, ed. A. Protashchik (Moscow: Progress, 1990), 447.

46. Sakharov, "Gor'kii, Moskva, dalee vezde," 415–16.

47. Mikhail Gorbachev, "Narashchivat' intellektual'nyi potentsial perestroiki," in *Izbrannye rechi i stat'i*, 7:246.

48. The episode is narrated by Sakharov in his memoirs: Sakharov, "Gor'kii, Moskva, dalee vezde," 391.

49. On Popov and Shmelev, see chapter 2 of this volume.
50. Sakharov, "Gor'kii, Moskva, dalee vezde," 405.
51. Sakharov, 445.
52. Sakharov, 377.
53. Andrei Sakharov, "V narode vsegda sokhraniaiutsia nravstvennye sily," *Knizhnoe obozrenie*, April 7, 1989, 6.
54. "Stenogramma obsuzhdeniia proektov Zakona CCCP ob izmeneniiakh i dopolneniiakh Konstitutsii CCCP i Zakona o vyborakh narodnykh deputatov CCCP," *Biulleten' "Moskovskoi Tribuny,"* no. 1 (1989): 88–89.
55. Sakharov, "Gor'kii, Moskva, dalee vezde," 378.
56. Boris Kagarlitsky, *Farewell, Perestroika: A Soviet Chronicle* (New York: Verso, 1990), 133.
57. Vladimir Pribylovskii, "Miting v Luzhnikakh," *Panorama*, May 1989, 3. Telman Gdlyan was an investigating judge who became famous in 1988 for his involvement in a campaign against corruption among senior Communist Party figures in Uzbekistan. In 1989, he was himself prosecuted for breaking the law during his investigations, which gave him the reputation of an uncorrupted practitioner of vigilante justice persecuted by the authorities.
58. Leonid Batkin, "Vstrecha dvukh mirov na s"ezde deputatov," *Moskovskie novosti*, no. 24 (1989): 9.
59. Andrei Sakharov, "Vsia vlast' sovetam!," *Vek XX i mir*, August 1989, 9–12.
60. Sakharov, "Gor'kii, Moskva, dalee vezde," 442.
61. Sakharov, "Vsia vlast' sovetam!," 12.
62. Evgenii Ambartsumov et al., "Revoliutsiia: Bolezn' ili istselenie," *Moskovskie novosti*, December 17, 1989, 13.
63. *Pervyi s"ezd narodnykh deputatov SSSR. Stenograficheskii otchet* (Moscow: Izdaniia Verkhovnogo soveta SSSR, 1989), 1:226.
64. Vladimir Pribylovskii, "Mezhregional'naia deputatskaia gruppa (MDG)," in *Slovar' oppozitsii: Novye politicheskie partii i organizatsii Rossii* (Moscow: Postfactum, 1991), 19.
65. *Pervyi s"ezd narodnykh deputatov SSSR. Stenograficheskii otchet*, 1:228.
66. *Pervyi s"ezd narodnykh deputatov SSSR. Stenograficheskii otchet*, 1:229–30.
67. Deputy V. N. Stepanov, a sovkhoz director from Karelia. *Pervyi s"ezd narodnykh deputatov SSSR. Stenograficheskii otchet*, 1:229.
68. Deputy V. S. Obraz, a pensioner from Poltava, Ukraine. *Pervyi s"ezd narodnykh deputatov SSSR. Stenograficheskii otchet*, 1:284.
69. Kuzbass is an industrial region located in southwestern Siberia. Its main administrative center is Kemerovo.
70. Viktor Sheinis, *Vzlet i padenie parlamenta: Perelomnye gody v rossiiskoi politike (1985–1993)* (Moscow: Moskovskii Tsentr Karnegi, 2005), 248.
71. Marietta Chudakova, "Natan Eidel'man, istorik Rossii," *Znanie-sila*, December 1990, 24.
72. Vera Tolz, *The USSR's Emerging Multiparty System* (New York: Praeger, 1990), 227.
73. Iurii Afanas'ev, "Sotsialisticheskaia ideia ostaetsiia putevodnoi" (July 1989), in *Rossiia na rasput'e, t. 1. Ia dolzhen cto skazat'* (Moscow: PIK, 1991), 269.

74. Afanas'ev, 269.

75. Igor' Kliamkin, "Do i posle prezidentskikh vyborov" (June 1990), in *Trudnyi spusk s ziiaiushchikh vysot* (Moscow: Pravda, 1990), 26.

76. Page numbers in each of the following sources—all authored by Iurii Afanas'ev—come from the collection *Rossiia na rasput'e*, t. 1. *Ia dolzhen eto skazat'* (Moscow: PIK, 1991): "Sotsialisticheskaia ideia ostaetsiia putevodnoi," 273; "Imperiia govorit na iazyke khimicheskogo oruzhiia," 276; "Polozhenie v strane," 289; "Preobrazovaniia otstaiut ot tempov raspada," 317.

77. Sakharov, "Gor'kii, Moskva, dalee vezde," 445.

78. Vladimir Tikhonov, quoted in Mark Kramer, "The Collapse of East European Communism and the Repercussions within the Soviet Union (Part 2)," *Journal of Cold War Studies* 6, no. 4 (Fall 2004): 44.

79. James Krapfl coined the term "revolution envy" to describe the aspiration of citizens in Poland, Hungary, and Bulgaria, where changes occurred through deals in elite circles, to replicate the accomplishments of popular mobilization seen in Czechoslovakia and East Germany. James Krapfl, "The Discursive Constitution of Revolution and Revolution Envy," in *The 1989 Revolutions in Central and Eastern Europe: From Communism to Post-Communism*, ed. Kevin McDermott and Matthew Stibbe (Manchester: Manchester University Press, 2013): 271–84. Soviet liberals harbored such mimetic desires toward all eastern European revolutions, with variations based on their preferred reform strategy.

80. Mark Kramer, "The Collapse of East European Communism and the Repercussions within the Soviet Union (Part 1)," *Journal of Cold War Studies* 5, no. 4 (Fall 2003): 178–256.

81. Among the numerous contributors to *Inogo ne dano*, only two authors cited reforms in other socialist countries as examples. Predictably, these were two experts from the Institute of Economics of the World Socialist System, Evgeny Ambartsumov and Andranik Migranian. However, in their articles, eastern Europe is not given any particular focus among communist countries and is still closely associated with the reformist experiments of Yugoslavia and China. Evgenii Ambartsumov, "O putiakh sovershenstvovaniia politicheskoi sistemy sotsializma," in Afanas'ev, *Inogo ne dano*, 77–96; Andranik Migranian, "Mekhanizm tormozheniia v politicheskoi sisteme i puti ego preodoleniia," in Afanas'ev, *Inogo ne dano*, 97–121.

82. Marina Pavlova-Sil'vanskaia, "Pliuralizm dlia obshchestva—Pliuralizm dlia sebia. Pol'sha pered vyborami," *Literaturnaia gazeta*, no. 22 (May 31, 1989): 14.

83. Marina Pavlova-Sil'vanskaia, "Pol'skaia formula," *Literaturnaia gazeta*, no. 29 (July 16, 1989): 9, 14; Marina Pavlova-Sil'vanskaia, "Rech', sochinennaia na lestnitse," *Literaturnaia gazeta*, no. 35 (August 23, 1989): 9; Marina Pavlova-Sil'vanskaia, "Moment istiny," *Moscovskie novosti*, no. 34 (August 20, 1989): 3.

84. On the Soviet liberals' reactions to the 1989 revolutions in eastern Europe, see Guillaume Sauvé, "De la difficulté de rattraper l'Europe de l'Est. Dilemmes des démocrates de Russie face aux révolutions de 1989," *Revue d'études comparatives Est-Ouest* 50, no. 2–3 (2019): 49–82.

85. Afanas'ev, "Imperiia govorit na iazyke khimicheskogo oruzhiia."

86. Andrei Sakharov, "Interv'iu A. D. Saharova v frantsuzskoi gazete 'Le Monde,'" *Russkaia mysl'*, October 6, 1989, 5.

87. Andrei Sakharov, "Vystuplenie na vstreche s kollektivom 'Uralmashzavoda,'" Sakharov Archive, September 15, 1989, https://www.sakharov-archive.ru/sakharov/works/vystuplenie-na-vstreche-s-kollektivom-uralmashzavoda/.

88. The other cochairs were Gavriil Popov and the Estonian deputy Viktor Palm', who received slightly more votes than Sakharov. Pribylovskii, "Mezhregional'naia deputatskaia gruppa."

89. Quoted in Sheinis, *Vzlet i padenie parlementa*, 227–28. Primakov was then president of the Union Council, the upper house of the Supreme Soviet. He would later serve as minister of foreign affairs and prime minister of Russia in the late 1990s.

90. Afanas'ev, "Polozhenie v strane."

91. Afanas'ev, "Polozhenie v strane."

92. Remarks quoted in Sheinis, *Vzlet i padenie parlementa*, 235.

93. Sheinis, 235.

94. See, for example, Aleksandr Verkhovskii, "Na Moskovskoi Tribune," *Panorama*, December 12, 1989, 2.

95. Quoted in Verkhovskii, 2.

96. Sakharov, "Vystuplenie na vstreche s kollektivom 'Uralmashzavoda.'"

97. Sakharov.

98. James Krapfl, *Revolution with a Human Face: Politics, Culture, and Community in Czechoslovakia, 1989–1992* (Ithaca, NY: Cornell University Press, 2013), 14–22, 35–73.

99. Vitalii Iaroshevskii, "Desiat' dnei, kotorye potriasli Pragu," *Moskovskie novosti*, no. 49 (December 3, 1989): 8.

100. Oleg Bogomolov, "Uroki na budushchee," *Moskovskie novosti*, no. 50 (December 10, 1989): 3.

101. Evgenii Ambartsumov, "Ne nervnichat'!," *Literaturnaia gazeta*, no. 52 (December 27, 1989): 10.

102. According to the testimony of Elena Bonner, who was present at the MDG meeting. Elena Bonner, "Mezhregionaly i Sakharov," Sakharovskii tsentr, December 26, 2008, https://www.sakharov-center.ru/news/2008/mezregionsakharov-t.html.

103. The number of participants in this one-off strike is unclear. Michael Urban offers the figure of one million. Michael Urban, *The Rebirth of Politics in Russia. With Vyacheslav Igrunov and Sergei Mitrokhin*. (Cambridge: Cambridge University Press, 1997), 361n109. Popov claims in his memoirs that this figure was inflated by the party apparatus in an effort to scare Gorbachev and that, "according to [their] data," the reality would have been hundreds of thousands. Gavriil Popov, *Snova v oppositsii* (Moscow: Galaktika, 1994), 77.

104. Andrei Sakharov, "Politicheskaia zabastovka," *Demokraticheskaia Rossiia*, no. 12 (December 11, 1991): 2.

105. Andrei Sakharov, "Poslednee vystuplenie" (December 14, 1989), in *Vospominaniia* (Moscow: Prava cheloveka, 1996), 590.

106. Sakharov, 590.

107. We return to these initiatives in chapter 6.

108. Aleksandr Verkhovskii, "'Grazhdanskoe deistvie'—novoe obshchedemokraticheskoe dvizhenie," *Panorama*, no. 2(14) (February 1990): 3; Aleksandr Verkhovskii, "'Grazhdanskoe deistvie' iznutri," *Panorama*, no. 4(16) (March 1990): 3.

109. Popov, *Snova v oppositsii*, 67.

110. Urban, *Rebirth of Politics in Russia*, 163.
111. Urban, 92.

5. Modernization and the Iron Fist

Epigraph: Igor' Kliamkin, Andranik Migranian, and Georgii Tselms, "Nuzhna li zheleznaia ruka?," *Literaturnaia gazeta*, no. 33 (August 1989): 10.

1. Andrei Sakharov et al., "Interpretations and Perceptions of Perestroyka," in *Milestones in Glasnost and Perestroika: Politics and People*, ed. Ed A. Hewett and Victor H. Winston (Washington, DC: Brookings Institution, 1991), 140, 145.

2. Kliamkin, Migranian, and Tselms, "Nuzhna li zheleznaia ruka?"

3. Andranik Migranian, "Dolgii put' k evropeiskomu domu," *Novyi Mir*, July 1989.

4. Kliamkin, Migranian, and Tselms, "Nuzhna li zheleznaia ruka?"

5. The article inspired an argumentative response from the historian Leonid Batkin, as well as hundreds of letters from readers, excerpts of which were subsequently published in the same publication. See Leonid Batkin, "Mertvyi khvataet zhivogo," in *Vozobnovlenie istorii: Razmyshleniia o politike i kul'ture* (Moscow: Moskovskii rabochii, 1991); Georgii Tselms, "Doloi liubogo diktatora!," *Literaturnaia gazeta*, no. 39 (September 1989): 14. Kliamkin and Migranian were offered the opportunity to reply three months later. This reply was itself accompanied by a rebuttal from Evgeny Ambartsumov, which, in the opinion of the paper's editorial staff, closed the debate. Igor' Kliamkin, Andranik Migranian, and Evgenii Ambartsumov, "Oboidemsia bez 'zheleznoi ruki,'" *Literaturnaia gazeta*, no. 52 (December 1989): 10.

6. The debate continued in the MT, where Migranian and Batkin crossed swords during the November 18, 1989, session. It did not go unnoticed abroad either; in the United States and France, for instance, it was the subject of multiple articles. See Vladimir Shlapentokh, "Who's Behind the Coup Talk in Moscow?," *New York Times*, September 23, 1989, 23; Ewa Bérard-Zarzicka, "Quelques propositions pour une perestroïka autoritaire," *Les Temps modernes*, no. 523 (1990): 11–22. This debate has also been the subject of a retrospective study: Barry Sautman, "The Devil to Pay: The 1989 Debate and the Intellectual Origins of Yeltsin's 'Soft Authoritarianism,'" *Communist and Post-Communist Studies* 28, no. 1 (March 1995): 131–51.

7. In political philosophy, perfectionism is the idea that the state must undertake reforms in order to create the conditions for the moral development of its citizens. On the Soviet liberals' political perfectionism, see chapter 2, page 50.

8. Igor' Kliamkin, interview with the author, December 14, 2012, Moscow (hereafter cited as Kliamkin interview).

9. Igor' Kliamkin, "Kakaia ulitsa vedet k khramu?," *Novyi Mir*, November 1987, 150–88.

10. Mikhail Katkov (1818–87) was a writer, editor, and literary critic who strongly supported autocracy and censorship against revolutionaries and also against democratic demands. Liberal conservatism was a current of nineteenth-century Russian liberalism that supported tsarism in order to protect the bourgeois order from the revolutionary threat.

11. The collection *Vekhi* (Milestones) was published in 1909 and includes contributions from Nikolai Berdiaev, Petr Struve, Semen Frank, and Sergei Bulgakov. It contains virulent criticism of the Russian intelligentsia for its worship of the people

and its role in the 1905 revolution. The collection *Smena vekh* (Change of milestones), published in 1921, is less known. It was written by a group of Russian liberals who had emigrated to Prague and proposed reconciliation with the Bolsheviks as the best guarantee of the integrity of the Russian state.

12. Kliamkin interview.

13. First at the Institute of Economics of the World Socialist System, then at the Institute of Economic and Political Research of the Academy of Sciences.

14. Kliamkin, "Kakaia ulitsa vedet k khramu?" All quotations in this and the next four paragraphs are taken from this article.

15. The reference to "real socialism" here is obviously invoked as a superficial sign of conformity to the ideological canons of the moment. Kliamkin did not even bother to explain how these laws were specifically socialist, and in his later articles he no longer used this label.

16. Igor' Kliamkin, "Chto nas zhdet vperedi?," in *Trudnyi spusk s ziiaiushchikh vysot* (Moscow: Pravda, 1990), 3–10. The article is dated by the author to June 1989, but it was first published in *Moskovskie novosti*, July 2, 1989.

17. Igor' Kliamkin, "Desiat' voprosov opponentam i samomu sebe," *Literaturnaia gazeta*, no. 52 (December 1989): 10.

18. Kliamkin stated this openly at a roundtable discussion on freedom and necessity in history organized in reaction to his article "Which Way Leads to the Church?" See Iakov Berger et al., "Istoriia—protsess? Istoriia—drama?," *Znanie-sila*, July 1988, 23–25.

19. Iurii Burtin and Igor' Kliamkin, "Chto mozhet i chego ne mozhet El'tsin," *Demokraticheskaia Rossiia*, no. 17 (July 1991): 9.

20. Andrei Sakharov, "Konstitutsiia Soiuza Sovetskikh Respublik Evropy i Azii" (December 1989), in *Konstitutsionnye idei Andreia Sakharova*, edited by Leonid Batkin (Moscow: Novella, 1990), art. 2, p. 4.

21. Igor' Kliamkin, "Pochemu trudno govorit' pravdu. Vybrannye mesta iz istorii odnoi bolezni," *Novyi Mir*, February 1989, 204. All quotations in this and the following four paragraphs are taken from this article.

22. Or an "ideological perestroika."

23. Abdusalam Guseinov et al., "Perestroika i nravstvennost'," *Voprosy filosofij*, July 1990, 7.

24. Nikolai Shmelev, "Novye trevogi," *Novyi Mir*, April 1988, 175.

25. Guseinov et al., "Perestroika i nravstvennost'," 7–8.

26. Igor' Kliamkin, "Oktiabrskii vybor prezidenta," *Ogonek*, no. 47 (October 1990): 6.

27. Nikolai Travkin et al., "Ot perestroiki k normal'noi zhizni," *Moskovskie novosti*, no. 16 (April 1990): 8.

28. Kliamkin, Migranian, and Tselms, "Nuzhna li zheleznaia ruka?"

29. Kliamkin, Migranian, and Tselms.

30. Kliamkin, Migranian, and Tselms.

31. Kliamkin, "Chto nas zhdet vperedi?," 9. The "impossible," in this case, was the program put forth by radical democrats like Sakharov. As we saw in the previous chapter, it should be remembered that, according to the general terms of perestroika, the left was represented by the reformists during this period and the right by the conservatives, which had the effect of placing the supporters of the market on the left and the communists on the right.

32. Batkin, "Mertvyi khvataet zhivogo," 118.

33. Igor' Kliamkin, "Do i posle prezidentskikh vyborov" (June 1990), in *Trudnyi spusk s ziiaiushchikh vysot*, 36.

34. Political science was first recognized as a discipline by the Soviet state in 1989, with the first doctoral degrees awarded in 1990. The first departments and faculties of political science were established in the second half of 1991.

35. Migranian, "Dolgii put' k evropeiskomu domu," 175.

36. Edward Walker, "Andranik M. Migranyan: A Soviet Machiavelli?," *Soviet Observer* 1, no. 1 (April 1990): 1–4.

37. Alexis de Tocqueville was also among Migranian's favorite authors, above all for his historical reflections on the dangers of revolutionary change. We will come back to this later, on page 129.

38. Andranik Migranian, *Demokratiia i nravstvennost'* (Moscow: Znanie, 1990).

39. Andranik Migranian, interview with the author, April 23, 2013, New York.

40. Andranik Migranian, "Vzaimootnoshcheniia mezhdu individom, obshchestvom i gosudarstvom v politicheskoi teorii marksizma i problemy demokratizatsii sotsializma," *Voprosy filosofii*, July 1987, 75–121.

41. Migranian, *Demokratiia i nravstvennost'*, 48.

42. Migranian, 48.

43. Migranian, 54–55.

44. Migranian, 50.

45. A conservative journalist and political commentator who worked on Ronald Reagan's campaign against Jimmy Carter.

46. Migranian, *Demokratiia i nravstvennost'*, 53.

47. Migranian, 10.

48. Migranian, 60.

49. Migranian, 58.

50. Benjamin Constant, "The Liberty of the Ancients Compared to That of the Moderns," in *Democracy: A Reader*, ed. Ricardo Blaug and John Scharzmantel (New York: Columbia University Press, 2016), 108.

51. In contrast to the English and French systems, which he claimed lacked a sufficiently clear robust separation of powers. Migranian, "Dolgii put' k evropeiskomu domu," 175.

52. Leonid Batkin, "Stat' Evropoi," *Vek XX i mir*, July 1988, 29–33.

53. Batkin, 33.

54. Andranik Migranian, "Legko li stat' Evropoi?," *Vek XX i mir*, December 1988, 22.

55. Migranian, 22.

56. Migranian, 22.

57. Migranian, 22.

58. Andranik Migranian, "Mekhanizm tormozheniia v politicheskoi sisteme i puti ego preodoleniia," in *Inogo ne dano*, ed. Iurii Afanas'ev (Moscow: Progress, 1988), 97–121.

59. Migranian, 99.

60. Migranian's references to Marx and Engels should not obscure the fact that his analysis was completely alien to the Marxist "class approach," which he would go on to explicitly reject in an article published a year later. He explained that totalitarianism cancels out social classes and creates a relationship of individual submission to power, which is why he "considers discussions about which class or social stra-

tum supported the Stalinist regime to be unfounded." This is an implicit criticism of Kliamkin's historical theory. Migranian, "Dolgii put' k evropeiskomu domu," 168.

61. Migranian, "Mekhanizm tormozheniia v politicheskoi sisteme i puti ego preodoleniia," 107–8. The mention of "our socialist ideals" was strictly cosmetic. As mentioned, Migranian's approach had nothing in common with socialism.

62. Migranian, 109.

63. Migranian, "Dolgii put' k evropeiskomu domu," 183.

64. Migranian, 184. Ironically, Migranian later came to support Yeltsin, when the latter emerged in the fall of 1991 as the latest strong leader claiming to preserve society from chaos.

65. Migranian, 184.

66. Migranian, 182.

67. Migranian, "Dolgii put' k evropeiskomu domu," 182; Andranik Migranian, "Plebistsitarnaia teoriia demokratii Maksa Vebera i sovremennyi politicheskii protsess," *Voprosy filosofii*, June 1989, 148–58; Kliamkin, Migranian, and Tselms, "Nuzhna li zheleznaia ruka?"

68. Migranian, "Dolgii put' k evropeiskomu domu," 169–70.

69. According to Daniel Wikler, a philosophy professor at the University of Wisconsin who spoke with Migranian several times in the 1980s, Migranian was a "strong supporter" of Jeane Kirkpatrick, US ambassador to the United Nations from 1981 to 1985. Kirkpatrick had formulated the idea that authoritarian regimes are preferable to totalitarian ones because they can be transformed into democracies. Daniel Wikler, "Marxist Thought Finds an Unlikely Godmother," *New York Times*, October 15, 1989.

70. Migranian, "Dolgii put' k evropeiskomu domu," 177.

71. Migranian, "Mekhanizm tormozheniia v politicheskoi sisteme i puti ego preodoleniia," 119–20.

72. Migranian, 112. That said, Migranian opposed the proposal put forward by Sakharov and other members of the MDG in late 1989 to immediately amend the Soviet Constitution so as to set the framework for future reforms. Migranian considered this initiative "inappropriate" at this "critical stage" of the transition to democracy. Instead, he proposed amendments to the Constitution, a task he wished to see entrusted to a "council of experts." Andranik Migranian, "Demokratiia v teorii i istoricheskoi praktike," *Kommunist*, January 1990, 41.

73. Migranian, "Demokratiia v teorii i istoricheskoi praktike," 37.

74. Migranian, 40.

75. Migranian, 37. In this passage, Migranian presents this necessity as temporary, specific to the "initial stage" of political reform. Yet he suggests at other times that liberal values must *always* take precedence over democratic values. For example, he argues that the "adjustments" that were made in the nineteenth and twentieth centuries in Western countries to ensure greater democratic participation—notably, the extension of the franchise—betray too great a bias in favor of democracy and ignore the values of liberalism, thereby leading to despotism and totalitarianism. As usual, Migranian expresses his opinion by quoting experts, in this case "the vast majority of Western economists, sociologists and political scientists," who, he says, agree that the solution to the current crisis is a "rightward" shift in favor of the core values of liberalism and away from democracy. Migranian, "Demokratiia v teorii i istoricheskoi praktike," 41.

76. Migranian, "Mekhanizm tormozheniia v politicheskoi sisteme i puti ego preodoleniia," 113.

77. Migranian, "Dolgii put' k evropeiskomu domu," 169.

78. Migranian, 169–70.

79. Kliamkin, Migranian, and Tselms, "Nuzhna li zheleznaia ruka?"

80. Migranian, "Legko li stat' Evropoi?," 24.

81. Migranian, *Demokratiia i nravstvennost'*, 56.

82. Migranian, "Mekhanizm tormozheniia v politicheskoi sisteme i puti ego preodoleniia," 117.

83. On the conception of regime building as fabrication, see Hannah Arendt, "What Is Authority?," in *Between Past and Future: Eight Exercises in Political Thought* (New York: Viking, 1968), 91–141.

84. Kliamkin, "Oktiabrskii vybor prezidenta," 4.

85. Kliamkin, "Trudnyi spusk s ziiaiushchikh vysot. Razmyshleniia v kanun vyborov o vtorom S"ezde narodnykh deputatov SSSR i politicheskoi situatsii v strane," in *Trudnyi spusk s ziiaiushchikh vysot*, 15.

86. One journalist combed through these letters and reported that out of the hundreds received, only a few were in defense of Migranian and Kliamkin. Tselms, "Doloi liubogo diktatora!," 14. All the letters excerpted below are drawn from this article.

87. Quoted in Igor Timofeyev, "The Development of Russian Liberal Thought since 1985," in *The Demise of Marxism-Leninism in Russia*, ed. Archie Brown (Basingstoke, UK: Palgrave Macmillan, 2004), 86.

88. Iurii Afanas'ev, "Kolossal'nyi eksperiment zakonchilsia. Gipnoz eshche deistvuet" (April 2, 1990), in *Rossiia na rasput'e, t. 1. Ia dolzhen eto skazat'*, 338.

89. "Zhestkim kursom . . . ," *Vek XX i mir*, June 1990, 15–19.

90. On the intrigues that led Gaidar to become Yeltsin's main economic adviser, see Vladislav M. Zubok, *Collapse: The Fall of the Soviet Union* (New Haven, CT: Yale University Press, 2021), chap. 9.

6. The Dilemma of the Democratic Movement (1990–93)

Epigraph: Iurii Afanas'ev, "Molchanie demokraticheskih 'iagniat'" (1993), in *Rossiia na rasput'e, t. 2. Petlia El'tsina* (Lewiston, NY: Edwin Mellen, 2000), 35. For reasons of clarity, I have opted for "collaborators" as a simple translation of *edinomyshlenniki*, which literally means "those who share the same ideas."

1. For this reason, DR and the democratic movement are often seen as synonymous, including by the authors discussed in this chapter. Although this is not strictly accurate, I maintain a similar usage in this chapter so as not to burden the reader with lengthy descriptions of the fringe democratic organizations that waged their own, parallel struggles during this period—notably, the anarchists, the Socialist Party, the Christian Democratic Union, and the Democratic Union.

2. Yitzhak Brudny, "The Dynamics of 'Democratic Russia,' 1990–1993," *Post-Soviet Affairs* 9, no. 2 (1993): 150.

3. I use the term Russia to refer to both the Russian Soviet Federative Socialist Republic (RSFSR) and its successor after the dissolution of the USSR, the Russian Federation.

4. Such as Viktor Aksiuchits, Mikhail Astafyev, Sergei Baburin, Bela Denisenko, Ilya Konstantinov, Lev Ponomarev, Oleg Rumiantsev, Marina Salye, Sergei Shakhrai, Gleb Yakunin, and Ilya Zaslavsky. On this cohort of activists, see Carole Sigman, *Clubs politiques et perestroïka en Russie. Subversion sans dissidence* (Paris: Karthala, 2009), chap. 2.

5. As noted in the introduction, most of the Soviet liberals studied in this book, whose involvement in perestroika dates back to at least 1987, belong to the Sixtiers generation, those who became politicized in the context of Khrushchevian de-Stalinization in the late 1950s and early 1960s.

6. It is worth emphasizing that rejection of Marxism-Leninism and Communist Party rule did not necessarily mean rejection of the ideology of "Socialism," which still had many adherents, even though they found it difficult to articulate what it might mean in the changed circumstances, as exemplified by the case of Afanasyev.

7. Iurii Afanas'ev, "Perspektivy peremen v Vostochnoi Evrope i v SSSR," in *Rossiia na rasput'e, t. 1. Ia dolzhen eto skazat'* (Moscow: PIK, 1991).

8. This pattern can also be observed within several European Communist movements that gradually migrated toward social democracy in the 1970s and 1980s, a trajectory that Gorbachev himself assumed a few years later. For such a comparison, see Jacques Lévesque, "The Messianic Character of Gorbachev's 'New Thinking': Why and What For?," in *The Last Decade of the Cold War: From Conflict Escalation to Conflict Transformation*, ed. Olav Njolstad (London: Frank Cass, 2004), 159–76.

9. Iurii Afanas'ev, "Perestroika i istoricheskoe znanie," in *Inogo ne dano*, ed. Iurii Afanas'ev, (Moscow: Progress, 1988).

10. Iurii Afanas'ev, "Sotsialisticheskaia ideia ostaetsia putevodnoi," in *Rossiia na rasput'e, t. 1. Ia dolzhen eto skazat'*, 271–72. Jesus Christ is probably mentioned as a humanist, not a religious figure, since religion does not play a significant role in Afanasyev's views.

11. Iurii Afanas'ev, "Istochnik napriazhennosti—oshibochnaia i opasnaia politika" (March 12, 1990), in *Rossiia na rasput'e, t. 1. Ia dolzhen eto skazat'*, 335-36. Afanasyev's speech delivered on March 12, 1990, at the third session of the Congress of People's Deputies; Afanas'ev, "Kolossal'nyi eksperiment zakonchilsia. Gipnoz eshche deistvuet," in *Rossiia na rasput'e, t. 1. Ia dolzhen eto skazat'*, 337. Interview, *Der Spiegel*, April 2, 1990.

12. Iurii Afanas'ev, "Mesto i zadachi politicheskoi oppozitsii v SSSR," in *Rossiia na rasput'e, t. 1. Ia dolzhen eto skazat'*, 368.

13. Iurii Afanas'ev, "Mirazhi vlasti" (May 10, 1991), in *Rossiia na rasput'e, t. 2. Petlia El'tsina*, 126; Iurii Afanas'ev, "'DemRossiia' dolzhna ostat'sia samostoiatel'noi" (July 19, 1991), in *Rossiia na rasput'e, t. 2. Petlia El'tsina*, 168. The term "radical-liberal" was not a common political identity at that time. It seems to have been created by Afanas'ev to signify both his relationship to power (radical and therefore critical) and his ideological orientation (liberal).

14. Igor Timofeyev, "The Development of Russian Liberal Thought since 1985," in *The Demise of Marxism-Leninism in Russia*, ed. Archie Brown (Basingstoke, UK: Palgrave Macmillan, 2004), 91; Peter Reddaway and Dmitri Glinski, *The Tragedy of Russian Reforms: Market Bolshevism against Democracy* (Washington, DC: United States Institute of Peace Press, 2001), 166.

15. See Dmitrii Furman, "'Perevernutyi istmat?' Ot ideologii perestroiki k ideologii 'stroitel'stva kapitalizma' v Rossii," *Svobodnaia mysl'*, no. 3 (1995): 12–25; Vladislav

Zubok, "How the Late Socialist Intelligentsia Swapped Ideology," *Kritika: Explorations in Russian and Eurasian History* 15, no. 2 (May 2014): 335–42.

16. In the autumn of 1990, Gorbachev made several important concessions to the conservatives in the party: he reversed his earlier decision and rejected the economic reform plan—the so-called Five-Hundred-Day Plan—proposed by the Russian government; he dismissed Foreign Minister Eduard Shevardnadze, considered by many a liberal; and he appointed Boris Pugo to the Ministry of the Interior and Gennady Yanayev to the post of vice president. Both were unabashedly conservative figures in the party and would participate in the failed coup of August 1991.

17. According to a March 1991 poll, 53 percent of the Moscow population trusted DR, compared to the 11 percent who trusted the Communist Party. A survey conducted that summer indicated that the coalition had the support of 40 percent of the population nationwide. Brudny, "Dynamics of 'Democratic Russia,'" 154.

18. Yeltsin's dependance on DR at the time can be demonstrated by a concrete example. On March 28, 1991, an exceptional session of the Russian Congress was held, the main item on the agenda being Yeltsin's removal from office as head of the Russian Republic. This initiative came from conservative deputies, with the tacit approval of Gorbachev. On the day of the meeting, DR organized a large demonstration in support of Yeltsin under the walls of the Kremlin, despite Gorbachev's express prohibition and the fact that Moscow was surrounded by the army. Not only did the deputies of the Congress not dare to dismiss Yeltsin but they voted for new special powers for him.

19. So named for the domain in the Moscow region where the signing took place. It is also known as the "9 + 1 agreement" because it was signed by Gorbachev and the leaders of nine Soviet republics.

20. Iurii Afanas'ev et al., "Nikto do sikh por ne smog vniatno ob''iasnit'" (August 8, 1991), in Afanas'ev, *Rossiia na rasput'e, t. 2. Petlia El'tsina*, 145–48.

21. John Dunlop, "Anatomy of a Failed Coup," in *The Rise of Russia and the Fall of the Soviet Empire* (Princeton, NJ: Princeton University Press, 1993), 186–255.

22. Iurii Burtin, "Chuzhaia vlast'," *Nezavisimaia gazeta*, December 1, 1992, 5.

23. Those who left the coalition at that time were the Democratic Party of Russia, led by Nikolai Travkin; the Constitutional Democratic Party, led by Ilya Konstantinov and Mikhail Astafyev; and the Christian Democratic Party, led by Viktor Aksiuchits.

24. Marietta Chudakova, "Blud bor'by," *Literaturnaia gazeta*, October 30, 1991, 3.

25. Leonid Batkin, "Tri dnia dvukh prezidentov," *Literaturnaia gazeta*, October 16, 1991, 4.

26. Chudakova, "Blud bor'by." The quotes in this and the next paragraph come from this article.

27. Emphasis in original.

28. As reported by a journalist attending the discussion at the MT. Galina Koval'skaia, "Intelligentsiia i vlast': Revoliutsionnye demokraty i 'vekhovtsy' na 'Moskovskoi Tribune,'" *Demokraticheskaia Rossiia*, November 3, 1991, 5.

29. A bipolar view that did not do justice to the complexity of the political spectrum. At that time, DR had two reformist rivals in parliament (the Movement for Democratic Reforms, led by Gavriil Popov and Aleksandr Yakovlev, among others, and the Civic Union, led by Aleksandr Rutskoi, a former Yeltsin running mate, and Nikolai

Travkin, a former DR leader, among others) and one direct opponent (the National Salvation Front, led by nationalists, communists, and former DR members such as Ilya Konstantinov and Mikhail Astafyev). DR members tended to see all these groups as pawns of the revanchist forces originating from the Soviet Communist Party.

30. Koval'skaia, "Intelligentsiia i vlast'."

31. Chudakova, "Blud bor'by." The quotations in this paragraph come from this article.

32. Koval'skaia, "Intelligentsiia i vlast'." All quotations in this paragraph are taken from this article.

33. The rapprochement between Yeltsin and the *nomenklatura*, especially those members who represented what is commonly called the "military-industrial complex," was already underway when this debate began. Indeed, as early as the summer of 1991, Yeltsin had chosen General Aleksandr Rutskoi as his presidential running mate, against the advice of DR leaders. From the autumn of 1991, Yeltsin largely favored established members of the *nomenklatura* in his appointments to key state positions.

34. James Krapfl, *Revolution with a Human Face: Politics, Culture, and Community in Czechoslovakia, 1989–1992* (Ithaca, NY: Cornell University Press, 2013), 227.

35. Iurii Burtin, "U dvizheniia est' budushchee, esli ono ne zamknetsia v politike . . . ," *Demokraticheskaia Rossiia*, September 27, 1991, 8–9. This idea was formally proposed by Leonid Batkin at the Second Congress of DR in November 1991.

36. Iurii Afanas'ev et al., "Nam nechego delat' v etoi kompanii," *Demokraticheskaia Rossiia*, January 30, 1992, 18.

37. "Zhestkim kursom . . . ," *Vek XX i mir*, June 1990, 15–19. The quotations in this paragraph come from this source.

38. Aleksandr Tsipko, "Ostorozhno, bol'shevizm!," *Ogonek* 47 (November 1990): 9–11.

39. Tsipko himself reiterated his argument over the years. See, for example, Aleksandr Tsipko, "Ne vozvodite khulu na perestroiku!," in *Proryv k svobode: o perestroike dvadtsat' let spustia*, ed. Viktor Kuval'din (Moscow: Al'pina Biznes Buks, 2005), 334–43.

40. Vladislav Zubok, *Collapse: The Fall of the Soviet Union* (New Haven, CT: Yale University Press, 2021), 210, 116, 66.

41. A third view was the "iron fist" perspective exposed in chapter 5.

42. I previously addressed this point in the conclusion of an article titled "A Reluctant Opposition: Soviet Liberals within the Moscow Tribune," *Slavic Review* 80, no. 1 (2022): 722–44.

43. Gil Eyal, *The Origins of Postcommunist Elites: From Prague Spring to the Breakup of Czechoslovakia* (Minneapolis: University of Minnesota Press, 2003), chap. 5.

44. On the "elective affinity" between dissidents and technocrats in Czechoslovakia during the same period, see Gil Eyal, Ivan Szelenyi, and Eleanor Townsley, *Making Capitalism without Capitalists: The New Ruling Elites in Eastern Europe* (New York: Verso, 1998), chap. 3.

45. Iurii Burtin et al., "Est' li u Rossii nadezhda?" (May 29, 1992), roundtable discussion, in *God posle Avgusta: Gorech' i vybor*, ed. Iurii Burtin (Moscow: Literatura i politika, 1992), 209–56.

46. Burtin et al., 217–18.

47. Burtin et al., 236.

48. Burtin et al., 244. Berger seemed to have changed his mind since the fall of 1991, when he had strongly criticized Chudakova's position, as we saw earlier.

49. Pavel Khazanov, *The Russia That We Have Lost: Pre-Soviet Past as Anti-Soviet Discourse* (Madison: University of Wisconsin Press, 2023), 112. According to Khazanov, the vision of "emergency reformism" served as the common ground upon which the "Stolypinist" coalition of the liberal and conservative wings of the late Soviet intelligentsia was established. The coalition is named after the tsarist prime minister Petr Stolypin, who was widely regarded at the time as a model of an enlightened reformer.

50. This was the case with Aleksandr Rutskoi (Yeltsin's running mate in the 1991 presidential election) and Ruslan Khasbulatov (appointed chair of the Supreme Soviet on Yeltsin's initiative), as well as Sergei Baburin, Ilya Konstantinov, and Viktor Aksiuchits (former DR activists).

51. For an exploration of the concept of "dual power," its Bolshevik origin, and its utilization in liberal discourse during the early 1990s as a historical argument supporting an enlightened dictatorship, see Guillaume Sauvé, "Un libéralisme bolchévique? Histoire conceptuelle du double pouvoir en Russie," *Canadian Journal of Political Science / Revue canadienne de science politique* 23, no. 1 (2020): 117–32.

52. A parallel phenomenon unfolded on the opposite end of the political spectrum, where autonomous nationalist and Communist movements strategically aligned themselves with the congressional opposition to Yeltsin. This alliance was not self-evident, as the opposition in Congress predominantly comprised apparatchiks and former allies of Yeltsin, who did not entirely align with the activists' ideals and principles. For an in-depth analysis of these strategic discussions within the "red-brown" sphere, reminiscent of the debates that reverberated within the liberal intelligentsia, see Juliette Faure, *The Rise of the Russian Hawks: Ideology and Politics from the Late Soviet Union to Putin's Russia* (Cambridge: Cambridge University Press, 2025), chap. 3.

53. The Russian parliament, like the Soviet one disbanded in 1991, was composed of the large Russian Congress and of a smaller and more powerful institution called the Supreme Soviet, whose members were elected among the deputies of the Congress.

54. In answer to the question "Do you trust the President of the Russian Federation?" 57.7 percent of voters answered in the affirmative. To the question "Do you approve of the socioeconomic policy of the President and the government of the Russian Federation?" the yes vote was 53 percent. To the question "Do you think it is necessary to hold early elections of the President of the Russian Federation?" the yes vote was 49.5 percent. The question "Do you think it is necessary to hold early elections of the people's deputies of the Russian Federation?" received a positive answer from 67.2 percent of voters. And yet the Constitution stated that early elections require a turnout of at least 50 percent of the electorate, which was not the case.

55. Other famous signatories of this letter include artists committed to democratization from the beginning of perestroika, Bella Akhmadulina, Viktor Astafyev, Daniil Granin, Bulat Okudzhava, Anatoly Pristavkin, and Lev Razgon; directors of liberal perestroika journals, Anatoly Ananyev and Georgy Baklanov; literary critics and publicists attached to the democratic movement, such as Andrei Nuikin; and academician Dmitri Likhachev.

56. "Pisateli trebuiut ot pravitel'stva reshitel'nykh deistvii," *Izvestiia*, October 5, 1993, 3.

57. "Ne budem blagodushny i nereshitel'ny! Obrashchenie sobraniia demokraticheskoi obshchestvennosti Moskvy k prezidentu Rossii B. N. El'tsinu," *Nezavisimaia gazeta*, October 13, 1993, 5. The quotations in this paragraph are taken from this letter.

58. "The New Times vpervye publikuet otkrovennye interv'iu Borisa Nikolaevicha El'tsina," *New Times*, April 30, 2007, https://newtimes.ru/articles/detail/12855/. The redaction of the new Russian Constitution as Yeltsin came to wield absolute power seems not to have qualified, in his view, as a "decision that would be serious enough to influence the fate of Russia."

59. Among Soviet liberals who condemned Yeltsin's iron fist were Egor Ligachev, former director of *Moskovskie Novosty*, and Vitaly Tretyakov, director of *Nezavisimaia gazeta*. The historian Mikhail Gefter resigned in protest from the Presidential Council. The Memorial organization conducted an independent investigation into the victims of the October events. The protest views of Leonid Batkin and Yuri Burtin are explored in greater detail in the following chapter.

60. Alexis Berelowich and Michel Wieviorka, *Les Russes d'en bas. Enquête sur la Russie post-communiste* (Paris: Éditions du Seuil, 1996), chap. 8.

61. Steven Fish, *Democracy Derailed in Russia: The Failure of Open Politics* (Cambridge: Cambridge University Press, 2005), 219.

62. Quoted in Berelowitch and Wieviorka, *Les Russes d'en bas*, 54.

63. Ol'ga Malinova, *Liberalizm v politicheskom spektre Rossii (na primere partii "Demokraticheskii vybor Rossii" i obshchestvennogo ob"edineniia "Iabloko,"* Yabloko.ru, 1998, https://www.yabloko.ru/Publ/Liber/olga.html.

64. This is also evident in the cross-case comparison conducted by Lussier between two Russian provinces. While citizens in the Krasnoyarsk region witnessed three competitive gubernatorial elections in nine years, declared a high level of personal efficacy, and remained involved in contentious political participation, their counterparts in the Kazan region, who never experienced political turnover, quickly became disillusioned with their ability to influence outcomes and disengaged from electoral struggles. Danielle Lussier, *Constraining Elites in Russia and Indonesia: Political Participation and Regime Survival* (Cambridge: Cambridge University Press, 2016), chap. 6.

65. Lussier, *Constraining Elites in Russia and Indonesia*, 263.

7. Forgotten Democratic Opposition Projects

Epigraph: Iurii Burtin, "Gorbachev prodolzhaetsia," in *Ispoved' shestidesiatnika* (Moscow: Progress-Traditsiia, 2003), 286.

1. Anatolii Sobchak, *Zhila-byla kommunisticheskaia partiia* (St. Petersburg: Lenizdat, 1995); Gavriil Popov, *Snova v oppositsii* (Moscow: Galaktika, 1994).

2. Vladimir Gel'man. "'Liberaly' versus 'demokraty': ideinye traektorii postsovetskoi transformatsii v Rossii," *Mir Rossii* 29, no 1 (2020): 53–79.

3. Iurii Burtin et al., "Est' li u Rossii nadezhda?," in *God posle Avgusta: gorech' i vybor*, ed. Iurii Burtin (Moscow: Literatura i politika, 1992), 254.

4. See chapter 4.

5. Iurii Burtin, "Chuzhaia vlast'," *Nezavisimaia gazeta*, December 1, 1992, 5.

6. Iurii Burtin, "Na zlobu dnia," in *Cherez ternii*, ed. A. Protashchik (Moscow: Progress, 1990), 448.
7. Iurii Burtin, "Gorbachev," *Nezavisimaia gazeta*, January 17, 1991, 4.
8. Burtin, 4.
9. Burtin, 4.
10. Iurii Burtin, "Gorbachev prodolzhaetsia," in *God posle Avgusta: gorech' i vybor*, 65.
11. Burtin, 65.
12. Burtin, "Chuzhaia vlast'," 5.
13. Burtin et al., "Est' li u Rossii nadezhda?," 249.
14. Burtin, "Gorbachev prodolzhaetsia," 66.
15. Burtin et al., "Est' li u Rossii nadezhda?," 252.
16. Burtin, "Gorbachev prodolzhaetsia," 67.
17. Burtin et al., "Est' li u Rossii nadezhda?," 253.
18. Burtin et al., 254.
19. Iurii Burtin, "Printsipy vazhnee programm," *Grazhdanskaia mysl'*, July 1, 1993, 1. On Nina Andreeva's communist manifesto and the Soviet liberals' reaction, see chapter 3, pages 61–65.
20. Iurii Burtin et al., "Est' li u Rossii nadezhda?," 253–54.
21. Burtin, "Gorbachev prodolzhaetsia," 68. Dmitri Pisarev (1840–68) was a literary critic and translator of revolutionary and nihilist orientation. Vladimir Korolenko (1853–1921) was a writer and journalist of *narodnik* inspiration.
22. Burtin, 69.
23. Burtin, 69.
24. Burtin et al., "Est' li u Rossii nadezhda?," 253.
25. Burtin, "Gorbachev prodolzhaetsia," 65. Burtin later devoted an article to "the system's" ability to mutate: Iurii Burtin, "Oboroten'," *Oktiabr'*, November 1994, 172–79.
26. Burtin, "Printsipy vazhnee programm," 1.
27. Iurii Burtin, "Teatr nominal'noi demokratii" (1993), in *Novyi stroi. O nomenklaturnom kapitalizme. Stat'i. Dialogi. Interv'iu* (Moscow: EPITsentr, 1995), 28.
28. Burtin et al., "Est' li u Rossii nadezhda?," 254.
29. Burtin et al., "Est' li u Rossii nadezhda?," 211. German Sterligov, Sergei Baburin, Mikhail Astafyev, and Viktor Anpilov were leading nationalist politicians.
30. Burtin et al., 212.
31. Leonid Batkin, "Vozobnovlenie istorii," in *Inogo ne dano*, ed. Iurii Afanas'ev (Moscow: Progress, 1988), 158 (emphasis in original).
32. Batkin, 189.
33. Popov was already a star of the liberal intelligentsia after publishing an article in the spring of 1987 in which he proposed the concept of an "administrative system of command." This is covered at length in chapter 2, pages 45–48.
34. Batkin, "Vozobnovlenie istorii," 171.
35. See chapter 5.
36. Leonid Batkin, "Ostanetsia li vlast' u partii?," in *Vozobnovlenie istorii: Razmyshleniia o politike i kul'ture* (Moscow: Moskovskii rabochii, 1991), 127 (emphasis in original).
37. Batkin, "Mertvyi khvataet zhivogo," in *Vozobnovlenie istorii*, 124.
38. Batkin, "Ostanetsia li vlast' u partii?," 127 (emphasis in original). An agonistic conception of democracy—from the Greek *agon*, or "struggle"—embraces permanent public conflict as an essential aspect of politics.

39. Leonid Batkin, "Tri stseny iz pervogo akta," in Protashchik, *Cherez ternii*, 402.
40. Leonid Batkin, "Rossiia na rasput'e," *Literaturnaia gazeta*, December 11, 1991, 3.
41. Batkin, 3.
42. Batkin, 3.
43. Batkin, "Vozobnovlenie istorii," 161.
44. Batkin, 163.
45. Batkin, 163.
46. Andrei Nuikin, *Na tom stoiu! Nravstvennye orientiry v sevodniashchnei literature* (Moscow: Sovetskii pisatel', 1991), 23.
47. Batkin, "Vozobnovlenie istorii," 168.
48. Batkin, 171.
49. Batkin, 171 (emphasis in the original).
50. Batkin, 172.
51. Batkin refers in this passage to March 1989, which saw the first large demonstrations during the election for the USSR Congress. He also mocks Pushkin's famous sentence about the Russian riot. As indicated in chapter 4, pages 97–100, it was a common trope of the liberal intelligentsia to express the fear of the masses' entrance in politics. Leonid Batkin, "Eshche odin obeskurazhivaiushchii uspekh," in *Vozobnovlenie istorii*, 154–55.
52. These are, respectively, the words of the editorial staff of *Moskovskie novosti*, Sergei Averintsev and Yuri Karyakin, in the special report the newspaper published shortly after Sakharov's death. "Andreiu Sakharovu—gor'koi sovesti nashei," *Moskovskie novosti*, December 17, 1989, 1–3.
53. Igor' Kliamkin, Andranik Migranian, and Georgii Tselms, "Nuzhna li zheleznaia ruka?," *Literaturnaia gazeta*, no. 33 (August 1989): 10.
54. Batkin, "Mertvyi khvataet zhivogo," 118.
55. Leonid Batkin, "Chto nas zhdet posle smerti Sakharova?" (December 17, 1989), in *Vozobnovlenie istorii*, 297–98.
56. Burtin, "Chuzhaia vlast'."

Conclusion

1. See the critique of these interpretations in the introduction.
2. Jerzy Szacki, *Liberalism after Communism* (Budapest: Central European University Press, 1995), 210.
3. George Fischer, *Russian Liberalism: From Gentry to Intelligentsia* (Cambridge, MA: Harvard University Press, 1958); Paul Robinson, *Russian Liberalism* (Ithaca, NY: Northern Illinois University Press, an imprint of Cornell University Press, 2023).
4. Gilles Labelle, "Le 'Préambule' à la 'Déclaration de souveraineté du Québec': Penser la fondation au-delà de la 'matrice théologico-politique,'" *Revue canadienne de science politique / Canadian Journal of Political Science* 31, no. 4 (December 1998): 659–81; Lynn Hunt, *Politics, Culture, and Class in the French Revolution* (Berkeley: University of California Press, 1984).
5. Jürgen Habermas, "What Does Socialism Mean Today? The Rectifying Revolution and the Need for a New Thinking on the Left," *New Left Review* 183, no. 1 (September–October 1990): 3–22.

6. James Krapfl, *Revolution with a Human Face: Politics, Culture, and Community in Czechoslovakia, 1989–1992* (Ithaca, NY: Cornell University Press, 2013), 7.

7. Andrei Sakharov, "Neizbezhnost' perestroiki," in *Inogo ne dano*, ed. Iurii Afanas'ev (Moscow: Progress, 1988), 127.

8. Jean-Jacques Rousseau, *The Social Contract* (Oxford: Oxford University Press, 1994), 78.

9. As mentioned in chapter 2, page 70. Gil Eyal, *The Origins of Postcommunist Elites: From Prague Spring to the Breakup of Czechoslovakia* (Minneapolis: University of Minnesota Press, 2003), 29.

10. Len Karpinskii, "Pochemu stalinizm ne skhodit so stseny?," in Afanas'ev, *Inogo ne dano*, 663.

11. Len Karpinskii and Iurii Afanas'ev, "Sozdat' poriadok iz khaosa," *Moskovskie novosti*, September 23, 1990, 6.

12. Niccolò Machiavelli, *Discourses on Livy* (Chicago: Chicago University Press, 1996), 29. On this point, my interpretation diverges from that of Timur Atnashev, who describes the end of perestroika as an "anti-Machiavellian moment" characterized by the rejection of the legitimacy of human action in favor of an unquestioning faith in historical *fortuna*. It is true that the rejection of social engineering and the disillusionment with persuasion are important features of the political thinking of this period, but they are accompanied among many liberals by support for the political voluntarism of an "enlightened" reformer. Timur Atnashev, "Transformation of the Political Speech under Perestroika: Free Agency, Responsibility and Historical Necessity in the Emerging Intellectual Debates (1985–1991)" (PhD diss., European University Institute, Florence, 2010), chap. 6.

13. Hannah Arendt, *On Revolution* (New York: Penguin Books, 2006).

14. Leonid Batkin, "Rossiia na rasput'e," *Literaturnaia gazeta*, December 11, 1991, 3 (emphasis in original).

15. Levada-Tsentr, "'Perestroika,'" April 23, 2019, https://www.levada.ru/2019/04/23/perestrojka/.

16. Gulnaz Sharafutdinova, *The Red Mirror: Putin's Leadership and Russia's Insecure Identity* (New York: Oxford University Press, 2021), chap. 5.

17. Fond obshchesvtennoe mnenie, "Istoricheskaia pamiat': vzgliady pokolenii," August 19, 2013, https://fom.ru/Proshloe/11041.

18. See, for example, Boris Mezhuev, *Perestroika-2: opyt povtoreniia* (Moscow: Ves' mir, 2014); Tat'iana Vorozheikina et al., *1985–2015: Tsennosti perestroiki v kontekste sovremennoi Rossii* (Moscow: Gorbachev Fond, 2015).

19. Mezhuev, *Perestroika-2*, 148.

Bibliography

Primary Sources

Adamovich, Ales'. "Dodumyvat' do kontsa. Avtobiografiia—1985." In *Vyberi—zhizn': literaturnaia, publicistika*, 348–73. Minsk: Mastatskaia literatura, 1986.

Afanas'ev, Iurii. "DemRossiia dolzhna ostat'sia samostoiatel'noi." In *Rossiia na rasput'e, t. 2. Petlia El'tsina*, 164–69. Lewiston, NY: Edwin Mellen, 2000.

Afanas'ev, Iurii. "Govorim o proshlom, no reshaetsia budushchee sotsializma." *Moskovskie novosti*, May 10, 1987, 11, 13.

Afanas'ev, Iurii. "Imperiia govorit na iazyke khimicheskogo oruzhiia." In *Rossiia na rasput'e, t. 1. Ia dolzhen eto skazat'*, 275–84. Moscow: PIK, 1991.

Afanas'ev, Iurii. "Kolossal'nyi eksperiment zakonchilsia. Gipnoz eshche deistvuet." In *Rossiia na rasput'e, t. 1. Ia dolzhen eto skazat'*, 336–45. Moscow: PIK, 1991.

Afanas'ev, Iurii. "Mesto i zadachi politicheskoi oppozitsii v SSSR." In *Rossiia na rasput'e, t. 1. Ia dolzhen eto skazat'*, 328–36. Moscow: PIK, 1991.

Afanas'ev, Iurii. "Mirazhi vlasti." In *Rossiia na rasput'e, t. 2. Petlia El'tsina*, 124–28. Lewiston, NY: Edwin Mellen, 2000.

Afanas'ev, Iurii. "Molchanie demokraticheskih 'iagniat.'" In *Rossiia na rasput'e, t. 2. Petlia El'tsina*, 30–40. Lewiston, NY: Edwin Mellen, 2000.

Afanas'ev, Iurii. "Neskol'ko slov ot redaktora." In *Inogo ne dano*, edited by Iurii Afanas'ev, 5–6. Moscow: Progress, 1988.

Afanas'ev, Iurii. "Istochnik napriazhennosti—oshibochnaia i opasnaia politika." In *Rossiia na rasput'e, t. 1. Ia dolzhen eto skazat'*, 333-36. Moscow: PIK, 1991.

Afanas'ev, Iurii. "Perestroika i istoricheskoe znanie." In *Inogo ne dano*, edited by Iurii Afanas'ev, 491–506. Moscow: Progress, 1988.

Afanas'ev, Iurii. "Perspektivy peremen v Vostochnoi Evrope i v SSSR." In *Rossiia na rasput'e, t. 1. Ia dolzhen eto skazat'*, 362–75. Moscow: PIK, 1991.

Afanas'ev, Iurii. "Polozhenie v strane." In *Rossiia na rasput'e, t. 1. Ia dolzhen eto skazat'*, 288–301. Moscow: PIK, 1991.

Afanas'ev, Iurii. "Preobrazovaniia otstaiut ot tempov raspada." In *Rossiia na rasput'e, t. 1. Ia dolzhen eto skazat'*, 317–20. Moscow: PIK, 1991.

Afanas'ev, Iurii. "Sotsialisticheskaia ideia ostaetsia putevodnoi." In *Rossiia na rasput'e, t. 1. Ia dolzhen eto skazat'*, 268–74. Moscow: PIK, 1991.

Afanas'ev, Iurii. "Sotsial'naia pamiat' chelovechestva." *Nauka i zhizn'*, September 1987, 64–72.

Afanas'ev, Iurii, Leonid Batkin, Iurii Burtin, and Bela Denisenko. "Demokraty vyshli iz kavyshek. Nam nechego delat' v etoi kompanii." In *Rossiia na rasput'e, t. 2. Petlia El'tsina*, 179–82. Lewiston, NY: Edwin Mellen, 2000.

BIBLIOGRAPHY

Afanas'ev, Iurii, Arkadii Migdal, Iurii Koriakin [sic], Iurii Chernichenko, Andrei Sakharov, Iurii Burtin, Leonid Batkin, and Iurii Levada. "Otkrytoe obrashchenie kluba 'Moskovskaia Tribuna.'" November 12, 1988. Sakharov Archive, F.1, Op.3, Ed.khr.168.

Afanas'ev, Iurii, Lev Timofeev, Leonid Batkin, Viacheslav Ivanov, Iurii Burtin, Vladimir Bibler, and Elena Bonner. "Nikto do sikh por ne smog vniatno ob"iasnit'." In *Rossiia na rasput'e*, t. 2. *Petlia El'tsina*, 145–48. Lewiston, NY: Edwin Mellen, 2000.

Afanassiev, Youri, ed. *La seule issue*. Paris: Fayard, 1989.

Aksenov, Vassilii, Vladimir Bukovskii, Eduard Kuznetsov, Iurii Liubimov, Vladimir Maksimov, Ernst Neizvestnyi, Iurii Orlov, Leonid Pliushch, Aleksandr Zinov'ev, and Ol'ga Zinov'eva. "Pust' Gorbachev predostavit nam dokazatel'stva." *Moskovskie novosti*, April 12, 1987, 12.

Ambartsumov, Evgenii. "Ne nervnichat'!" *Literaturnaia gazeta*, no. 52 (December 27, 1989): 10.

Ambartsumov, Evgenii. "O putiakh sovershenstvovaniia politicheskoi sistemy sotsializma." In *Inogo ne dano*, edited by Iurii Afanas'ev, 77–96. Moscow: Progress, 1988.

Ambartsumov, Evgenii, Len Karpinskii, Vadim Kozhinov, Mikhail Kozhinov, and Igor' Shafarevich. "Revoliutsiia: Bolezn' ili istselenie?" *Moskovskie novosti*, December 17, 1989, 12–13.

Andreeva, Nina. "I Cannot Give Up My Principles." In *The Structure of Soviet History: Essays and Documents*, edited by Ronald Grigor Suny, 438–45. Oxford: Oxford University Press, 2002.

Andreeva, Nina. "Ne mogu postupat'sia printsipami." *Sovetskaia Rossiia*, March 13, 1988, 2.

Batkin, Leonid. "Chto nas zhdet posle smerti Sakharova?" In *Vozobnovlenie istorii: Razmyshleniia o politike i kul'ture*, 297–300. Moscow: Moskovskii rabochii, 1991.

Batkin, Leonid. *Episody moei obshchestvennoi zhizni*. Moscow: Novyi khronograf, 2013.

Batkin, Leonid. "Eshche odin obeskurazhivaiushchii uspekh." In *Vozobnovlenie istorii: Razmyshleniia o politike i kul'ture*, 142–55. Moscow: Moskovskii rabochii, 1991.

Batkin, Leonid. "Mertvyi khvataet zhivogo." In *Vozobnovlenie istorii: Razmyshleniia o politike i kul'ture*, 108–26. Moscow: Moskovskii rabochii, 1991.

Batkin, Leonid. "Ostanetsia li vlast' u partii?" In *Vozobnovlenie istorii: Razmyshleniia o politike i kul'ture*, 121–41. Moscow: Moskovskii rabochii, 1991.

Batkin, Leonid. "Rossiia na rasput'e." *Literaturnaia gazeta*, December 11, 1991, 3.

Batkin, Leonid. "Stat' Evropoi." *Vek XX i mir*, July 1988, 29–33.

Batkin, Leonid. "Tri dnia dvukh prezidentov." *Literaturnaia gazeta*, October 16, 1991, 4.

Batkin, Leonid. "Tri stseny iz pervogo akta." In *Cherez ternii*, edited by A. Protashchik, 402–33. Moscow: Progress, 1990.

Batkin, Leonid. "Vozobnovlenie istorii." In *Inogo ne dano*, edited by Iurii Afanas'ev, 154–91. Moscow: Progress, 1988.

Batkin, Leonid. "Vstrecha dvukh mirov na s"ezde deputatov." *Moskovskie novosti*, no. 24 (1989): 9.

Berger, Iakov, Iurii Burtin, Leonid Volkov, Renata Galtseva, Aleksei Elymanov, Vladimir Iliushchenko, Igor' Kliamkin, Iurii Levada, Nikolai Razumovich, Leonid Sedov, and Igor' Engel'gardt. "Istoriia—protsess? Istoriia—drama?" *Znanie-sila*, July 1988, 23–25.
Biulleten' "*Moskovskoi Tribuny.*" "O sozdanii politiko-kul'turnogo obshchestvenogo kluba 'Moskovskaia Tribuna.'" No. 1 (1989): 4.
Biulleten' "*Moskovskoi Tribuny.*" "Stenogramma obsuzhdeniia proektov Zakona CCCP ob izmeneniiakh i dopolneniiakh Konstitutsii CCCP i Zakona o vyborakh narodnykh deputatov CCCP." No. 1 (1989): 65–104.
Bogomolov, Oleg. "Uroki na budushchee." *Moskovskie novosti*, no. 50 (December 10, 1989): 3.
Bol'shaia sovetskaia entsiklopediia. 2nd ed., 52 t. Moscow: Bol'shaia sovetskaia entsiklopediia 1949–1958.
Bol'shaia sovetskaia entsiklopediia. 3rd ed., 30 t. Moscow: Bol'shaia sovetskaia entsiklopediia 1969–1978.
Bonner, Elena. "Mezhregionaly i Sakharov." Sakharovskii tsentr, December 26, 2008. https://www.sakharov-center.ru/news/2008/mezregionsakharov-t.html.
Burtin, Iurii. "Akhillesova piata istoricheskoi teorii Marksa." *Oktiabr'* 11 (1989): 3–25.
Burtin, Iurii. "Akhillesova piata istoricheskoi teorii Marksa." *Oktiabr'* 12 (1989): 3–48.
Burtin, Iurii. "Chuzhaia vlast'." *Nezavisimaia gazeta*, December 1, 1992, 5.
Burtin, Iurii. "Gorbachev." *Nezavisimaia gazeta*, January 17, 1991, 4.
Burtin, Iurii. "Gorbachev prodolzhaetsia." In *God posle Avgusta: gorech' i vybor*, 54–69. Moscow: Literatura i politika, 1992.
Burtin, Iurii. *Ispoved' shestidesiatnika*. Moscow: Progress-Traditsiia, 2003.
Burtin, Iurii. "Izzhit' Stalina!" In *Ispoved' shestidesiatnika*, 263–73. Moscow: Progress-Traditsiia, 2003.
Burtin, Iurii. "Na zlobu dnia." In *Cherez ternii*, edited by A. Protashchik, 434–56. Moscow: Progress, 1990.
Burtin, Iurii. "Oboroten'." *Oktiabr'*, November 1994, 172–79.
Burtin, Iurii. "Printsipy vazhnee programm." *Grazhdanskaia mysl'*, July 1, 1993, 1.
Burtin, Iurii. "Real'naia kritika—vchera i segodnia." *Novyi Mir* 6 (1987): 222–39.
Burtin, Iurii. "Teatr nominal'noi demokratii." In *Novyi stroi. O nomenklaturnom kapitalizme. Stat'i. Dialogi. Interv'iu*, 21–28. Moscow: EPITsentr, 1995.
Burtin, Iurii. "U dvizheniia est' budushchee, esli ono ne zamknetsia v politike . . ." *Demokraticheskaia Rossiia*, September 27, 1991, 8–9.
Burtin, Iurii. "Vam, iz drugogo pokolen'ia." *Oktiabr'* 10 (1987): 191–202.
Burtin, Iurii, Leonid Batkin, Vasilii Seliunin, Zoia Krakhmal'nikova, Iurii Afanas'ev, Larisa Piashcheva, Bela Denisenko, Vladimir Lopatin, Leonid Gordon, Vladimir Bibler, Valerii Abramkin, Iakov Berger, and Dmitrii Furman. "Est' li u Rossii nadezhda?" In *God posle Avgusta: gorech' i vybor*, edited by Iurii Burtin, 209–56. Moscow: Literatura i politika, 1992.
Burtin, Iurii, and Igor' Kliamkin. "Chto mozhet i chego ne mozhet El'tsin." *Demokraticheskaia Rossiia*, no. 17 (July 1991): 8–9.
Chudakova, Marietta. "Blud bor'by." *Literaturnaia gazeta*, October 30, 1991, 3.
Chudakova, Marietta. "Natan Eidel'man, istorik Rossii." *Znanie-sila*, December 1990, 24–32.
Demokraticheskaia Rossiia. "Novye knigi v PIKe." June 7, 1991, 16.

Egorov, A. "Esli po sovesti—*Inogo ne dano*. O dvukh knigakh publitsistiki." *Literaturnoe obozrenie*, October 1988, 3–6.
Ekspress-khronika. "Uchreditel'noe sobranie obshchestvenno-diskussionnogo kluba 'Moskovskaia tribuna.'" No. 42(63) (October 1988): 8.
Fedoseev, Petr, K. Brutents, and V. Afanas'ev. *Nauchnyi kommunizm: Uchebnik*. Moscow: Politizdat, 1983.
Fond obshchesvtennoe mnenie. "Istoricheskaia pamiat': vzgliady pokolenii." August 19, 2013. https://fom.ru/Proshloe/11041.
Furman, Dmitrii. "'Perevernutyi istmat?' Ot ideologii perestroiki k ideologii 'stroitel'stva kapitalizma' v Rossii'." *Svobodnaia mysl'*, no. 3 (1995): 12–25.
Gaidar, Egor. *Gosudarstvo i evoliutsiia*. Moscow: Evraziia, 1994.
Gorbachev, Mikhail. *Izbrannye rechi i stat'i*. 7 t. Moscow: Izdatel'stvo politicheskoi literatury, 1990.
Gorbachev, Mikhail. *Naedine s soboi*. Moscow: Grin strit, 2012.
Gorbachev, Mikhail. *Perestroika: New Thinking for Our Country and the World*. New York: Harper and Row, 1987.
Guseinov, Abdusalam. "Bol'she morali, no ne moralizatorstva." In *Perestroika i nravstvennost'*, edited by Mikhail Iskrov, 19–29. Baku: Azerneshr, 1988.
Guseinov, Abdusalam, Igor' Kliamkin, Aleksandr Titarenko, Vladimir Bibler, Genrikh Batishchev, Iurii Sogomov, and Lev Mitrokhin. "Perestroika i nravstvennost'." *Voprosy filosofij*, July 1990, 3–24.
Iaroshevskii, Vitalii. "Desiat' dnei, kotorye potriasli Pragu." *Moskovskie novosti*, no. 49 (December 3, 1989): 8.
Izvestiia. "Pisateli trebuiut ot pravitel'stva reshitel'nykh deistvii." October 5, 1993, 3.
Kagarlitsky, Boris. *Farewell, Perestroika: A Soviet Chronicle*. New York: Verso, 1990.
Kariakin, Iurii. "Ne opozdat'! (Zametki publitsista)." In *Vopros vsekh voprosov. Bor'ba za mir i istoricheskie sud'by chelovechestva*, edited by Iurii Kariakin and V. Petrovskii, 216–29. Moscow: Progress, 1985.
Kariakin, Iurii. *Peremena ubezhdenii: Ot oslepleniia k prozreniiu*. Moscow: Izdatel'stvo Raduga, 2007.
Kariakin, Iurii. "Stoit li nastupat' na grabli? (Otkrytoe pis'mo odnomu Inkognito)." *Znamia*, September 1987, 200–224.
Kariakin, Iurii. "Zhdanovskaia zhidkost', ili protiv ochernitel'stva." In *Inogo ne dano*, edited by Iurii Afanas'ev, 412–23. Moscow: Progress, 1988.
Karpinskii, Len. "Nravstvennost' i glasnost'." *Moskovskie novosti*, May 21, 1989, 3.
Karpinskii, Len. "Pochemu stalinizm ne skhodit so stseny?" In *Inogo ne dano*, edited by Iurii Afanas'ev, 648–70. Moscow: Progress, 1988.
Karpinskii, Len. "Sotsializm—eto prosto normal'naia zhizn'." *Vek XX i mir* 7 (1987): 36–43.
Karpinskii, Len, and Iurii Afanas'ev. "Sozdat' poriadok iz khaosa." *Moskovskie novosti*, September 23, 1990, 6.
Kliamkin, Igor'. "Chto nas zhdet vperedi?" In *Trudnyi spusk s ziiaiushchikh vysot*, 3–10. Moscow: Pravda, 1990.
Kliamkin, Igor'. "Desiat' voprosov opponentam i samomu sebe." *Literaturnaia gazeta*, no. 52 (December 1989): 10.
Kliamkin, Igor'. "Do i posle prezidentskikh vyborov" (June 1990). In *Trudnyj spusk s ziiaiushchikh vysot*, 26–45. Moscow: Pravda, 1990.

Kliamkin, Igor'. "Kakaia ulitsa vedet k khramu?" *Novyi Mir*, November 1987, 150–88.
Kliamkin, Igor'. "Oktiabrskii vybor prezidenta." *Ogonek*, no. 47 (October 1990): 4–7.
Kliamkin, Igor'. "Pochemu trudno govorit' pravdu. Vybrannye mesta iz istorii odnoi bolezni." *Novyi Mir*, February 1989, 204–38.
Kliamkin, Igor', Andranik Migranian, and Evgenii Ambartsumov. "Oboidemsia bez 'zheleznoi ruki.'" *Literaturnaia gazeta*, no. 52 (December 1989): 10.
Kliamkin, Igor', Andranik Migranian, and Georgii Tselms. "Nuzhna li zheleznaia ruka?" *Literaturnaia gazeta*, no. 33 (August 1989): 10.
Kliger, Semen. "Publitsistika-88 kak ob"ekt issledovania." In *V svoem otechestve proroki? Publtsistika perestroiki: Luchshie avtory 1988 goda*, edited by Ninel' Streltsova, 239–44. Moscow: Knizhnaia palata, 1989.
Koval'skaia, Galina. "Intelligentsiia i vlast': Revoliutsionnye demokraty i 'vekhovtsy' na 'Moskovskoi Tribune.'" *Demokraticheskaia Rossiia*, November 3, 1991, 5.
Lenin, Vladimir. *Polnoe sobranie sochinenii*. 56 t. Moscow: Politizdat, 1969.
Lenin, Vladimir. "Zadachi soiuzov molodezhi." In *Polnoe sobranie sochinenii*, 41:301–18. Moscow: Politizdat, 1969.
Levada, Iurii, ed. *Est' mnenie! Itogi sotsiologicheskogo oprosa*. Moscow: Progress, 1989.
Levada-Tsentr. "'Perestroika.'" April 23, 2019. https://www.levada.ru/2019/04/23/perestrojka/.
Levikov, Aleksandr. *Vesy doveriia*. Moscow: Politizdat, 1983.
Likhachev, Dmitrii. "Ekologiia kul'tury." *Znanie-sila*, June 1982, 22–24.
Likhachev, Dmitrii. "Gomosfera—termin nashikh dnei." *Ogonek*, no. 36 (1984): 17–19.
Likhachev, Dmitrii. "O Russkom." *Novyi Mir*, March 1980, 10–38.
Likhachev, Dmitrii. "Ot pokaianiia—k deistviiu!" *Literaturnaia gazeta*, (September 9, 1987): 2.
Likhachev, Dmitrii. "Trevogi sovesti." *Literaturnaia gazeta*, no. 1 (January 1, 1987): 11.
Literaturnaia Rossiia. "Perestroika—volia, muzhestvo, ob"ektivnost'. V Sekretariate Pravleniia Soiuza pisatelei RSFSR." March 27, 1987, 3.
Mezhuev, Boris. *Perestroika-2: opyt povtoreniia*. Moscow: Ves' mir, 2014.
Migranian, Andranik. *Demokratiia i nravstvennost'*. Moscow: Znanie, 1990.
Migranian, Andranik. "Demokratiia v teorii i istoricheskoi praktike." *Kommunist*, January 1990, 33–42.
Migranian, Andranik. "Dolgii put' k evropeiskomu domu." *Novyi Mir*, July 1989, 166–84.
Migranian, Andranik. "Legko li stat' Evropoi?" *Vek XX i mir*, December 1988, 22 25.
Migranian, Andranik. "Mekhanizm tormozheniia v politicheskoi sisteme i puti ego preodoleniia." In *Inogo ne dano*, edited by Iurii Afanas'ev, 97–121. Moscow: Progress, 1988.
Migranian, Andranik. "Plebststitarnaia teoriia demokratii Maksa Vebera i sovremennyi politicheskii protsess." *Voprosy filosofii*, June 1989, 148–58.
Migranian, Andranik. "Vzaimootnoshcheniia mezhdu individom, obshchestvom i gosudarstvom v politicheskoi teorii marksizma i problemy demokratizatsii sotsializma." *Voprosy filosofii*, July 1987, 75–121.
Moskovskie novosti. "Andreiu Sakharovu—gor'koi sovesti nashei." December 17, 1989, 1–3.
New Times. "The New Times vpervye publikuet otkrovennye interv'iu Borisa Nikolaevicha El'tsina." April 30, 2007. https://newtimes.ru/articles/detail/12855/.

Nezavisimaia gazeta. "Ne budem blagodushny i nereshitel'ny! Obrashchenie sobraniia demokraticheskoi obshchestvennosti Moskvy k prezidentu Rossii B. N. El'tsinu." October 13, 1993, 5.

Nuikin, Andrei. *Na tom stoiu! Nravstvennye orientiry v sevodniashchnei literature*. Moscow: Sovetskii pisatel', 1991.

Pavlova-Sil'vanskaia, Marina. "Moment istiny." *Moscovskie novosti*, no. 34 (August 20, 1989): 3.

Pavlova-Sil'vanskaia, Marina. "Pliuralizm dlia obshchestva—Pliuralizm dlia sebia. Pol'sha pered vyborami." *Literaturnaia gazeta*, no. 22 (May 31, 1989): 14.

Pavlova-Sil'vanskaia, Marina. "Pol'skaia formula." *Literaturnaia gazeta*, no. 29 (July 16, 1989): 9, 14.

Pavlova-Sil'vanskaia, Marina. "Rech', sochinennaia na lestnitse." *Literaturnaia gazeta*, no. 35 (August 23, 1989): 9.

Pervyi s"ezd narodnykh deputatov SSSR. Stenograficheskii otchet. 5 vols. Moscow: Izdaniia Verkhovnogo soveta SSSR, 1989–1991.

Pomerants, Grigorii. "Son o spravedlivom vozmezdii." *Vek XX i mir*, November 1990. Old.Russ.ru. http://old.russ.ru/antolog/vek/1990/11/spor.htm.

Popov, Gavriil. *Snova v oppositsii*. Moscow: Galaktika, 1994.

Popov, Gavriil. "S tochki zreniia ekonomista. O romane Aleksandra Beka *Novoe naznachenie*." *Nauka i zhizn'*, April 1987, 54–65.

Pravda. "Printsipy perestroiki: Revoliutsionnost' myshleniia i deistvii." April 5, 1988, 2.

Pribylovskii, Vladimir. "Mezhregional'naia deputatskaia gruppa (MDG)." In *Slovar' oppozitsii: Novye politicheskie partii i organizatsii Rossii*, 19. Moscow: Postfactum, 1991.

Pribylovskii, Vladimir. "Miting v Luzhnikakh." *Panorama*, May 1989, 3.

Razbash, Andrei, dir. *Deti XX s"ezda*. Moscow: Glavnaia redaktsiia programm dlia molodezhi Tsentral'noe televidenie SSSR, 1988.

Sakharov, Andrei. "Gor'kii, Moskva, dalee vezde." In *Vospominaniia*, 241–446. Moscow: Prava cheloveka, 1996.

Sakharov, Andrei. "Interv'iu A. D. Saharova v frantsuzskoi gazete 'Le Monde.'" *Russkaia mysl'*, October 6, 1989, 5.

Sakharov, Andrei. "Konstitutsiia Soiuza Sovetskikh Respublik Evropy i Azii." In *Konstitutsionnye idei Andreia Sakharova*, edited by Leonid Batkin, 4–14. Moscow: Novella, 1990.

Sakharov, Andrei. "Neizbezhnost' perestroiki." In *Inogo ne dano*, edited by Iurii Afanas'ev, 122–34. Moscow: Progress, 1988.

Sakharov, Andrei. "O pis'me Aleksandra Sol'zhenitsyna 'Vozhdiam Sovetskogo Soiuza.'" Sakharov.Space, April 3, 1974. https://www.sakharov.space/lib/o-pisme-aleksandra-solzhenicyna-vozhdyam-sovetskogo-soyuza.

Sakharov, Andrei. "O strane i o mire." Sakharov.Space, June 1975. https://www.sakharov.space/lib/o-strane-i-mire.

Sakharov, Andrei. "Otkrytoe pis'mo Prezidentu Akademii nauk SSSR A.P. Aleksandrovu (20 okt., 1980)." Sakharov Archive, October 1980. https://www.sakharov-archive.ru/sakharov/works/otkrytoe-pismo-prezidentu-an-sssr-a-p-aleksandrovu-20-okt-1980/.

Sakharov, Andrei. "Pamiatnaia zapiska." Sakharov Archive, June 1972. https://www.sakharov-archive.ru/sakharov/works/pamjatnaja-zapiska/.

Sakharov, Andrei. "Pliuralizm—eto konvergentsiia." *Vek XX i mir* 1 (1989): 18–20.
Sakharov, Andrei. "Politicheskaia zabastovka." *Demokraticheskaia Rossiia*, no. 12 (December 11, 1991): 2.
Sakharov, Andrei. "Poslednee vystuplenie." In *Vospominaniia*, 589–90. Moscow: Prava cheloveka, 1996.
Sakharov, Andrei. "Predvybornaia platforma" (February 1989). In *Vospominaniia*, 570–74. Moscow: Prava cheloveka, 1996.
Sakharov, Andrei. "Razmyshleniia o progresse, mirnom sosushchestvovanii i intellektual'noi svobode" (1968). In *Trevoga i nadezhda*, 11–47. Moscow: Inter-Verso, 1991.
Sakharov, Andrei. "V narode vsegda sokhraniaiutsia nravstvennye sily." *Knizhnoe obozrenie*, April 7, 1989, 6.
Sakharov, Andrei. "Vsia vlast' sovetam!" *Vek XX i mir*, August 1989, 9–12.
Sakharov, Andrei. "Vystuplenie na vstreche s kollektivom 'Uralmashzavoda.'" Sakharov Archive. Accessed February 24, 2023. https://www.sakharov-archive.ru/sakharov/works/vystuplenie-na-vstreche-s-kollektivom-uralmashzavoda/.
Sakharov, Andrei. "Za mir i progress." *Moskovskie novosti*, February 5, 1989, 8.
Sakharov, Andrei, Yelena Bonner, Stephen F. Cohen, Ed A. Hewett, and Victor H. Winston. "Interpretations and Perceptions of Perestroyka." In *Milestones in Glasnost and Perestroika*, edited by Ed A. Hewett and Victor H. Winston, 139–52. Washington, DC: Brookings Institution, 1991.
Saraskina, Liudmila, Boris Mozhaev, Iurii Afanas'ev, Leonid Batkin, Len Karpinskii, Grigorii Pel'man, Iurii Burtin, Andrei Nuikin, Grigorii Kunitsyn, and Anatolii Arsen'ev. "Barrikady perestroiki." *Vek XX i mir*, February 1988, 12–27.
Sheinis, Viktor. "Uroki avgusta. Demokratam vazhno osmyslit' proschety i oshibki, sovershennye do i posle GKChP." Iabloko, August 18, 2006. https://www.yabloko.ru/Publ/2006/2006_08/060818_mn_scheinis.html.
Sheinis, Viktor. *Vzlet i padenie parlementa: Perelomnye gody v rossiiskoi politike (1985–1993)*. 2 vols. Moscow: Moskovskii Tsentr Karnegi, 2005.
Shlapentokh, Vladimir. "Who's Behind the Coup Talk in Moscow?" *New York Times*, September 23, 1989, 23.
Shmelev, Nikolai. "Avansy i dolgi." *Novyi Mir*, June 1987, 142–58.
Shmelev, Nikolai. "Novye trevogi." *Novyi Mir*, April 1988, 160–75.
Sobchak, Anatolii. *Zhila-byla kommunisticheskaia partiia*. St. Petersburg: Lenizdat, 1995.
Solzhenitsyn, Alexander. "Live Not by Lies." *Index on Censorship* 33, no. 2 (2004): 203–7.
Travkin, Nikolai, Galina Starovoitova, Mar'iu Lauristin, Igor' Kliamkin, Andrei Nuikin, Viacheslav Shostakovskii, Gavriil Popov, Otto Latsis, and Ales' Adamovich. "Ot perestroiki k normal'noi zhizni." *Moskovskie novosti*, no. 16 (April 1990): 8–9.
Tselms, Georgii. "Doloi liubogo diktatora!" *Literaturnaia gazeta*, no. 39 (September 1989): 14.
Tsipko, Aleksandr. "Ne vozvodite khulu na perestroiku!" In *Proryv k svobode: o perestroike dvadtsat' let spustia*, edited by Viktor Kuval'din, 334–43. Moscow: Al'pina Biznes Buks, 2005.
Tsipko, Aleksandr. "Ostorozhno, bol'shevizm!" *Ogonek* 47 (November 1990): 9–11.
Vek XX i mir. "Zhestkim kursom . . ." June 1990, 15–19.

Verkhovskii, Aleksandr. "'Grazhdanskoe deistvie' iznutri." *Panorama*, no. 4(16) (March 1990): 3.
Verkhovskii, Aleksandr. "'Grazhdanskoe deistvie'—novoe obshchedemokraticheskoe dvizhenie." *Panorama*, no. 2(14) (February 1990): 3.
Verkhovskii, Aleksandr. "Na Moskovskoi Tribune." *Panorama* no. 12 (December 1989): 2.
Vinogradov, Igor'. "Mozhet li pravda byt' poetapnoi?" In *Inogo ne dano*, edited by Iurii Afanas'ev, 277–96. Moscow: Progress, 1988.
Vorozheikina, Tat'iana, Vasilii Zharkov, Andrei Zakharov, Andrei Kolesnikov, Aleksei Levinson, Nikolai Petrov, and Andrei Riabov. *1985–2015: Tsennosti perestroiki v kontekste sovremennoi Rossii*. Moscow: Gorbachev Fond, 2015.
Yeltsin Center. "Interv'iu s Iakovom Bergerom." July 12, 2012. http://www.yeltsincenter.ru/decryption/intervyu-s-yakovom-bergerom.
Zdravomyslov, Andrei. "O prichinakh negativnykh iavlenii v usloviiakh sotsializma." In *Perestroika i nrvastvennost'*, edited by Mikhail Iskrov, 115–20. Baku: Azerneshr, 1988.

Secondary Sources

Arendt, Hannah. *On Revolution*. New York: Penguin Books, 2006.
Arendt, Hannah. "Truth and Politics." In *Between Past and Future: Eight Exercises in Political Thought*, 227–64. New York: Viking, 1968.
Arendt, Hannah. "What Is Authority?" In *Between Past and Future: Eight Exercises in Political Thought*, 91–141. New York: Viking, 1968.
Aron, Leon. *Roads to the Temple: Truth, Memory, Ideas and Ideals in the Making of the Russian Revolution, 1987–1991*. New Haven, CT: Yale University Press, 2012.
Atnashev, Timur. "Idealy nauchnoi ob"ektivnosti i chestnosti kak obosnovanie politiki glasnosti v perestroiku." Gefter.ru, October 9, 2013. https://gefter.ru/archive/10224.
Atnashev, Timur. "Switching Regimes of Publicity: How Nina Andreeva Facilitated the Transformation of Glasnost into Freedom of Speech." *Social Sciences* 49, no 4 (December 2018): 71–90.
Atnashev, Timur. "Transformation of the Political Speech under Perestroika: Free Agency, Responsibility and Historical Necessity in the Emerging Intellectual Debates (1985–1991)." PhD diss., European University Institute, Florence, 2010.
Atnashev, Timur. "Utopicheskii konservatizm v epokhu pozdnei perestroiki: otpuskaia vozhzhi istorii." *Sotsiologiia vlasti* 29, no. 2 (2018): 12–53.
Barnett, Vincent. "Conceptions of the Market among Russian Economists: A Survey." *Soviet Studies* 44, no. 6 (1992): 1087–98.
Bérard-Zarzicka, Ewa. "Quelques propositions pour une perestroïka autoritaire." *Les Temps modernes*, no. 523 (1990): 11–22.
Berelowich, Alexis, and Michel Wieviorka. *Les Russes d'en bas. Enquête sur la Russie post-communiste*. Paris: Éditions du Seuil, 1996.
Bergman, Jay. *Meeting the Demands of Reason: The Life and Thought of Andrei Sakharov*. Ithaca, NY: Cornell University Press, 2009.
Berlin, Isaiah. "The Pursuit of the Ideal." In *The Proper Study of Mankind: An Anthology of Essays*, 1–16. New York: Farrar, Straus and Giroux, 1997.

Biddulph, Howard L. "Protest Strategies of the Soviet Intellectual Opposition." In *Dissent in the USSR: Politics, Ideology, and People*, edited by Rudolf L. Tökés, 96–115. Baltimore: Johns Hopkins University Press, 1975.
Bikbov, Aleksandr. *Grammatika poriadka: Istoricheskaia sociologiia poniatii, kotorye meniaiut nashu real'nost'*. Moscow: Izdatel'skii dom Vysshchei shkoly ekonomiki, 2014.
Boobbyer, Philip. *Conscience, Dissent and Reform in Soviet Russia*. London: Routledge, 2005.
Bourdieu, Pierre. *Manet, une révolution symbolique. Cours au Collège de France (1998–2000)*. Paris: Seuil, 2013.
Breslauer, George. *Gorbachev and Yeltsin as Leaders*. Cambridge: Cambridge University Press, 2002.
Brown, Archie. *The Gorbachev Factor*. Oxford: Oxford University Press, 1996.
Brown, Archie. *Seven Years That Changed the World: Perestroika in Perspective*. Oxford: Oxford University Press, 2007.
Brudny, Yitzhak. "Between Liberalism and Nationalism: The Case of Serguei Zalygin." *Studies in Comparative Communism* 21, nos. 3–4 (1988): 331–40.
Brudny, Yitzhak. "The Dynamics of 'Democratic Russia,' 1990–1993." *Post-Soviet Affairs* 9, no. 2 (1993): 141–70.
Brudny, Yitzhak. "The Heralds of Opposition to Perestroika." In *Milestones in Glasnost and Perestroika. Politics and People*, edited by Ed A. Hewett and Victor H. Winston, 153–89. Washington, DC: Brookings Institution, 1991.
Brudny, Yitzak. *Reinventing Russia: Russian Nationalism and the Soviet State, 1953–1991*. Cambridge, MA: Harvard University Press, 1998.
Budraitskis, Ilya. *Dissidents among Dissidents: Ideology, Politics and the Left in Post-Soviet Russia*. London: Verso Books, 2022.
Constant, Benjamin. "The Liberty of the Ancients Compared to That of the Moderns." In *Democracy: A Reader*, edited by Ricardo Blaug and John Scharzmantel, 108–10. New York: Columbia University Press, 2016.
De George, Richard. *Soviet Ethics and Morality*. Ann Arbor: University of Michigan Press, 1969.
Dobson, Miriam. *Khrushchev's Cold Summer: Gulag Returnees, Crime, and the Fate of Reform after Stalin*. Ithaca, NY: Cornell University Press, 2009.
Dunlop, John. "Anatomy of a Failed Coup." In *The Rise of Russia and the Fall of the Soviet Empire*, 186–255. Princeton, NJ: Princeton University Press, 1993.
English, Robert. *Russia and the Idea of the West: Gorbachev, Intellectuals and the End of the Cold War*. New York: Columbia University Press, 2000.
Eyal, Gil. *The Origins of Postcommunist Elites: From Prague Spring to the Breakup of Czechoslovakia*. Minneapolis: University of Minnesota Press, 2003.
Eyal, Gil, Ivan Szelenyi, and Eleanor R. Townsley. *Making Capitalism without Capitalists: The New Ruling Elites in Eastern Europe*. New York: Verso, 1998.
Falk, Barbara. *The Dilemmas of Dissidence in East-Central Europe: Citizen Intellectuals and Philosopher Kings*. Budapest: Central European University Press, 2003.
Faure, Juliette. *The Rise of the Russian Hawks: Ideology and Politics from the Late Soviet Unionto Putin's Russia*. Cambridge: Cambridge University Press, 2025.
Ferro, Marc. *Les origines de la perestroïka*. Paris: Ramsay, 1990.

Fischer, George. *Russian Liberalism: From Gentry to Intelligentsia*. Cambridge, MA: Harvard University Press, 1958.
Fish, Steven. *Democracy Derailed in Russia: The Failure of Open Politics*. Cambridge: Cambridge University Press, 2005.
Fish, Steven. *Democracy from Scratch: Opposition and Regime in the New Russian Revolution*. Princeton, NJ: Princeton University Press, 1995.
Fitzpatrick, Sheila. *Tear Off the Masks! Identity and Imposture in Twentieth-Century Russia*. Princeton, NJ: Princeton University Press, 2005.
Freeden, Michael. *Liberal Languages: Ideological Imaginations and Twentieth-Century Progressive Thought*. Princeton, NJ: Princeton University Press, 2005.
Gel'man, Vladimir. *Authoritarian Russia: Analyzing Post-Soviet Regime Changes*. Pittsburgh: University of Pittsburgh Press, 2015.
Gel'man, Vladimir. "'Liberaly' versus 'demokraty': ideinye traektorii postsovetskoi transformatsii v Rossii." *Mir Rossii* 29, no. 1 (2020): 53–79.
Gerovitch, Slava. *From Newspeak to Cyberspeak: A History of Soviet Cybernetics*. Cambridge, MA: MIT Press, 2002.
Gessen, Masha. *Dead Again: The Russian Intelligentsia after Communism*. London: Verso, 1997.
Habermas, Jürgen. "What Does Socialism Mean Today? The Rectifying Revolution and the Need for a New Thinking on the Left." *New Left Review* 183, no. 1 (September–October 1990): 3–22.
Hanson, Stephen. *Post-imperial Democracies: Ideology and Party Formation in Third Republic France, Weimar Germany and Post-Soviet Russia*. Cambridge: Cambridge University Press, 2010.
Hellbeck, Jochen. *Revolution on My Mind: Writing a Diary under Stalin*. Cambridge, MA: Harvard University Press, 2006.
Heller, Mikhail. *Cogs in the Soviet Wheel: The Formation of Soviet Man*. London: Collins Harvill, 1988.
Hoffmann, David. *Stalinist Values: The Cultural Norms of Soviet Modernity, 1917–1941*. Ithaca, NY: Cornell University Press, 2003.
Hunt, Lynn. *Politics, Culture, and Class in the French Revolution*. Berkeley: University of California Press, 1984.
Ivanova, Anna. *Magaziny "Berezka": Paradoksy potrebleniia v pozdnem SSSR*. Moscow: Novoe literaturnoe obozrenie, 2017.
Joly, Elena. *La troisième mort de Staline: Entretiens avec des intellectuels gorbatchéviens*. Paris: Actes Sud, 1988.
Jones, Polly. *Revolution Rekindled: The Writers and Readers of Late Soviet Biography*. Oxford: Oxford University Press, 2019.
Kharkhordin, Oleg. *The Collective and the Individual in Russia: A Study of Practices*. Berkeley: University of California Press, 1999.
Khazanov, Pavel. *The Russia That We Have Lost: Pre-Soviet Past as Anti-Soviet Discourse*. Madison: University of Wisconsin Press, 2023.
Kochetkova, Irina. *The Myth of the Russian Intelligentsia: Old Intellectuals in the New Russia*. London: Routledge, 2010.
Kotkin, Stephen. *Armageddon Averted: The Soviet Collapse, 1970–2000*. Oxford: Oxford University Press, 2008.

Kramer, Mark. "The Collapse of East European Communism and the Repercussions within the Soviet Union (Part 1)." *Journal of Cold War Studies* 5, no. 4 (Fall 2003): 178–256.
Kramer, Mark. "The Collapse of East European Communism and the Repercussions within the Soviet Union (Part 2)." *Journal of Cold War Studies* 6, no. 4 (Fall 2004): 3–64.
Krapfl, James. "The Discursive Constitution of Revolution and Revolution Envy." In *The 1989 Revolutions in Central and Eastern Europe: From Communism to Post-Communism*, edited by Kevin McDermott and Matthew Stibbe, 271–84. Manchester: Manchester University Press, 2013.
Krapfl, James. *Revolution with a Human Face: Politics, Culture, and Community in Czechoslovakia, 1989–1992*. Ithaca, NY: Cornell University Press, 2013.
Krastev, Ivan, and Stephen Holmes. *The Light That Failed: Why the West Is Losing the Fight for Democracy*. New York: Pegasus Books, 2019.
Krylova, Anna. "The Tenacious Liberal Subject in Soviet Studies." *Kritika: Explorations in Russian and Eurasian History* 1, no. 1 (Winter 2000): 119–46.
Labelle, Gilles. "Le 'Préambule' à la 'Déclaration de souveraineté du Québec': Penser la fondation au-delà de la 'matrice théologico-politique.'" *Revue canadienne de science politique / Canadian Journal of Political Science* 31, no. 4 (December 1998): 659–81.
Lefort, Claude. *Un homme en trop. Réflexions sur L'archipel du goulag*. Paris: Éditions du Seuil, 1976.
Lévesque, Jacques. "The Messianic Character of Gorbachev's 'New Thinking': Why and What For?" In *The Last Decade of the Cold War: From Conflict Escalation to Conflict Transformation*, edited by Olav Njolstad, 159–76. London: Frank Cass, 2004.
Lewin, Moshe. *The Gorbachev Phenomenon: A Historical Interpretation*. Berkeley: University of California Press, 1988.
Löwy, Michael, and Robert Sayre. *Romanticism against the Tide of Modernity*. Durham, NC: Duke University Press, 2001.
Lukin, Alexander. *The Political Culture of Russian "Democrats."* Oxford: Oxford University Press, 2000.
Lussier, Danielle. *Constraining Elites in Russia and Indonesia: Political Participation and Regime Survival*. Cambridge: Cambridge University Press, 2016.
Machiavelli, Niccolò. *Discourses on Livy*. Chicago: Chicago University Press, 1996.
Malinova, Ol'ga. *Liberalizm v politicheskom spektre Rossii (na primere partii "Demokraticheskii vybor Rossii" i obshchestvennogo ob"edineniia "Iabloko")*. Yabloko.ru, 1998. https://www.yabloko.ru/Publ/Liber/olga.html.
McFaul, Michael. *Russia's Unfinished Revolution: Political Change from Gorbachev to Putin*. Ithaca, NY: Cornell University Press, 2001.
Mitrokhin, Nikolai. *Russkaia partiia. Dvizhenie russkikh natsionalistov v SSSR, 1953–1985 gody*. Moscow: NLO, 2003.
Nivat, Georges. "De la Russie libérée à la Russie libre." *Esprit* 223 (July 1996): 94–112.
Nussbaum, Martha. "Perfectionist Liberalism and Political Liberalism." *Philosophy and Public Affairs* 39, no. 1 (2001): 3–45.
Oushakine, Serguei. "In the State of Post-Soviet Aphasia: Symbolic Development in Contemporary Russia." *Europe-Asia Studies* 52, no. 6 (2000): 991–1016.

Oushakine, Serguei. "The Terrifying Mimicry of Samizdat." *Public Culture* 13, no. 2 (April 2001): 191–214.
Plotnikov, Nikolaj, ed. "The Discourse of Personality in the Russian Intellectual Tradition." *Studies in East European Thought* 61, nos. 2–3 (August 2009): 71–241.
Pocock, John G. A. *The Machiavellian Moment: Florentine Political Thought and the Atlantic Republican Tradition.* Princeton, NJ: Princeton University Press, 1975.
Polanyi, Karl. *The Great Transformation: The Political and Economic Origins of Our Time.* Boston: Beacon, 2001.
Popper, Karl. *The Open Society and Its Enemies.* Princeton, NJ: Princeton University Press, 1994.
Priban, Jiri. *Dissidents of Law: On the 1989 Velvet Revolutions, Legitimations, Fictions of Legality and Contemporary Versions of the Social Contract.* London: Routledge, 2019.
Reddaway, Peter, and Dmitri Glinski. *The Tragedy of Russian Reforms: Market Bolshevism against Democracy.* Washington, DC: United States Institute of Peace Press, 2001.
Remnick, David. *Lenin's Tomb: The Last Days of the Soviet Empire.* New York: Random House, 1993.
Robinson, Paul. *Russian Liberalism.* Ithaca, NY: Northern Illinois University Press, an imprint of Cornell University Press, 2023.
Roudakova, Natalia. *Losing Pravda: Ethics and the Press in Post-truth Russia.* Cambridge: Cambridge University Press, 2017.
Rousseau, Jean-Jacques. *The Social Contract.* Oxford: Oxford University Press, 1994.
Sakwa, Richard. *The Crisis of Russian Democracy: The Dual State, Factionalism and the Medvedev Succession.* Cambridge: Cambridge University Press, 2010.
Sandle, Mark. *A Short History of Soviet Socialism.* London: UCL Press, 1999.
Sautman, Barry. "The Devil to Pay: The 1989 Debate and the Intellectual Origins of Yeltsin's 'Soft Authoritarianism.'" *Communist and Post-Communist Studies* 28, no. 1 (March 1995): 131–51.
Sauvé, Guillaume. "The Apogee of Soviet Political Romanticism: Projects for Moral Renewal in Early Perestroika (1985–1989)." *Europe-Asia Studies* 70, no. 9 (2018): 1407–32.
Sauvé, Guillaume. "De la difficulté de rattraper l'Europe de l'Est. Dilemmes des démocrates de Russie face aux révolutions de 1989." *Revue d'études comparatives Est-Ouest* 50, no. 2–3 (2019): 49–82.
Sauvé, Guillaume. "The Lessons from Perestroika and the Evolution of Russian Liberalism: 1995–2005." In *Dimensions and Challenges of Russian Liberalism*, edited by Ricardo Cucciola, 139–51. Cham: Springer, 2018.
Sauvé, Guillaume. "A Reluctant Opposition: Soviet Liberals within the Moscow Tribune." *Slavic Review* 80, no. 1 (2022): 722–44.
Sauvé, Guillaume. "Un libéralisme bolchévique? Histoire conceptuelle du double pouvoir en Russie." *Canadian Journal of Political Science / Revue canadienne de science politique* 53, no. 1 (2020): 117–32.
Schmitt, Carl. *Political Romanticism.* London: Routledge, 2017.
Sharafutdinova, Gulnaz. *The Red Mirror: Putin's Leadership and Russia's Insecure Identity.* New York: Oxford University Press, 2021.

Shlapentokh, Vladimir. *Public and Private Life of the Soviet People: Changing Values in Post-Stalin Russia*. Oxford: Oxford University Press, 1989.
Shlapentokh, Vladimir. *Soviet Ideologies in the Period of Glasnost: Responses to Brezhnev's Stagnation*. New York: Praeger, 1988.
Sigman, Carole. *Clubs politiques et perestroïka en Russie. Subversion sans dissidence*. Paris: Karthala, 2009.
Simmel, Georg. *The Sociology of Georg Simmel*. Translated and edited by Kurt H. Wolff. New York: Free Press, 1950.
Sogrin, Vladimir. *Politicheskaia istoriia sovremennoi Rossii 1985–2001*. Moscow: Ves' mir, 2001.
Sutela, Pekka. *Economic Thought and Economic Reform in the Soviet Union*. Cambridge: Cambridge University Press, 1991.
Sutela, Pekka, and Vladimir Mau. "Economics under Socialism: The Russian Case." In *Economic Thought in Communist and Post-Communist Europe*, edited by Jürgen Wagener, 33–79. New York: Routledge, 1998.
Szacki, Jerzy. *Liberalism after Communism*. Budapest: Central European University Press, 1995.
Taylor, Charles. *Hegel*. Cambridge: Cambridge University Press, 1975.
Timofeyev, Igor. "The Development of Russian Liberal Thought since 1985." In *The Demise of Marxism-Leninism in Russia*, edited by Archie Brown, 51–118. Basingstoke, UK: Palgrave Macmillan, 2004.
Tolz, Vera. *The USSR's Emerging Multiparty System*. New York: Praeger, 1990.
Urban, Michael. *The Rebirth of Politics in Russia*. With Vyacheslav Igrunov and Sergei Mitrokhin. Cambridge: Cambridge University Press, 1997.
Volkov, Vadim. "The Concept of kul'turnost': Notes on the Stalinist Civilizing Process." In *Stalinism: New Directions*, edited by Sheila Fitzpatrick, 210–30. New York: Routledge, 2000.
Walicki, Andrzej. *Marxism and the Leap to the Kingdom of Freedom: The Rise and Fall of the Communist Utopia*. Stanford, CA: Stanford University Press, 1995.
Walker, Edward. "Andranik M. Migranyan: A Soviet Machiavelli?" *Soviet Observer* 1, no. 1 (April 1990): 1–4.
Wedel, Janine. *Collision and Collusion: The Strange Case of Western Aid to Eastern Europe, 1989–1998*. New York: Palgrave, 2001.
Weigle, Marcia. *Russia's Liberal Project: State Society Relations in the Transition from Communism*. University Park: Pennsylvania State University Press, 2000.
Wikler, Daniel. "Marxist Thought Finds an Unlikely Godmother." *New York Times*, October 15, 1989.
Yurchak, Alexei. *Everything Was Forever, Until It Was No More: The Last Soviet Generation*. Princeton, NJ: Princeton University Press, 2006.
Zubok, Vladislav. *Collapse: The Fall of the Soviet Union*. New Haven, CT: Yale University Press, 2021.
Zubok, Vladislav. *D. S. Likhachev v obshchestvennoi zhizni Rossii kontsa XX veka*. St. Petersburg: Evropeiskii dom, 2011.
Zubok, Vladislav. "How the Late Socialist Intelligentsia Swapped Ideology." *Kritika: Explorations in Russian and Eurasian History* 15, no. 2 (May 2014): 335–42.

Index

activity (*aktivnost'*), 19
Adamovich, Ales, 40–41, 82, 147, 151, 161, 169
administrative command system, 45–48, 109, 131
Afanasyev, Yuri: on administrative command system, 48; on Andreeva's letter, 65; career of, 69, 76, 170; Civic Action movement, 107; criticism of presidency of the USSR, 138; on democratic opposition, 102, 169, 171; evolution of political discourse of, 144–45; Gorbachev and, 143; on half-truths, 66; influence of, 170, 192, 201; Interregional Group of Deputies and, 95, 97, 101; on loss of historical consciousness, 36; on market economy, 36, 145; on perestroika, 54, 70; political activism, 13, 140, 154; pressure on the Russian president, 148; radicalism of, 102, 145, 157; on revolutions in Poland and Hungary, 100; on "Russian riot," 98; on Scandinavian model of socialism, 145; on Solidarność, 144; speeches, 98; on Stalinism, 66–67; on USSR Congress deputies, 88; vision for the Democratic Russia coalition, 153
Ambartsumov, Evgeny, 105, 210
Andreeva, Nina: attitude to perestroika, 62, 70, 72–73; criticism of, 62–63, 69; debate initiated by, 63–65, 94; desire for absolute truth, 68; "I Cannot Give Up My Principles" letter, 62; "principles" claimed by, 173
Andropov, Yuri, 25, 26
Anglo-American political philosophy, 50
aporia, 189, 190
Arendt, Hannah, 60, 61, 191
Article 6 of the Soviet Constitution, 92, 95, 97, 101, 102, 108
Astafyev, Mikhail, 30, 175, 200
Atnashev, Timur, 6, 37, 63
August Coup of 1991, 148, 150

authoritarianism, 12, 113, 114, 132–33, 134–35

Baltic states, 142, 143
Batkin, Leonid: academic career, 170; on art, 180–81; on autonomous opposition, 169; "Becoming Europe," 129; criticism of Chudakova, 151; criticism of Gorbachev, 150; criticism of state apparatus, 103; on democracy, 178–79, 180, 191–92; on democrats, 176, 177; "depravity debate" and, 152–53, 178; on direct and universal election, 89; on glasnost, 179–80; on Gorbachev, 175; on idea of democratic openness, 176–77; on idea of the "iron fist," 177–78; influence of, 170; on market economy, 58, 178; on morality, 45, 184; Moscow Tribune and, 82, 83; on notion of political realism, 83, 85; on opposition, 108, 125, 176, 178; on perestroika, 36–37, 177; polemic with Kliamkin, 125; on "Polish model," 91; political activism of, 13, 140, 154, 157; pragmatism of, 177, 181, 184; pressure on the Russian president, 148; on progress, 36; on "red-brown" threat, 152; on Sakharov, 182, 183; on self-censorship, 71; support for Yeltsin, 175–76, 179, 182; on truth, 180; view of politics, 181–82, 184; vision for the Democratic Russia coalition, 153
Belinsky, Vissarion, 20, 22
Belov, Vasily, 30, 70, 200
Berezka stores, 27–28
Berger, Yakov, 84, 87, 103, 152, 159
Bibler, Vladimir, 103, 152, 154
Bogomolov, Oleg, 55, 105
Boldyrev, Yuri, 102, 152, 169
Bondarev, Yuri, 30, 32, 70
Bonner, Elena, 154
Brezhnev, Leonid, 24, 42, 43, 52, 67
bureaucrats, 46, 47

INDEX

Burtin, Yuri: background of, 38, 171; on capitalism, 38; on citizens' committees, 153; criticism of Soviet system, 38, 40, 43–44, 48; on cultivating a "sense of the system," 43, 44; democratic activism, 154; on democrats, 173, 174; "depravity debate" and, 158; on Dobroliubov, 43; election as head of DR, 140; on goals of Soviet reforms, 171; on Gorbachev, 172, 175; on half-truths, 67–68; on image of Stalin, 67; influence of, 13, 115, 168, 170, 201; on Kliamkin, 120; on morality, 45, 171–75, 183; on nationalist intellectuals, 174–75; on opposition, 169; on perestroika, 39, 87, 171–72; on plutocrats, 172, 175; on politics, 184; on popular mobilization, 175, 182; pressure on the Russian president, 148; on question of power, 184–85; on Rasputin, 44–45; recollections of August events of 1991, 149; on responsibility toward the people, 173–74; on Sakharov, 182–83; on social criticism, 42–43; on socialist revolution, 38–39; on Stalinism, 43, 174; view of progress, 37–38; vision of Soviet society, 171–72; writing of, 42; on Yeltsin, 172

censorship, 11, 72, 115
Central Control Commission, 22
Chechen Wars, 3, 165, 175
Chernichenko, Yuri, 30, 105, 161, 169
China, 114, 125–26, 132, 210
Choice of Russia (political party), 166
Chubais, Anatoly, 138–39, 154, 158, 159, 163, 184
Chudakova, Marietta: on affinity between democrats and Russian leaders, 150–51; critics of, 151–52; on dissolution of Parliament, 161; on freedom of expression, 151; "Letter of 42," 161; on "moratorium" on criticism against democratic leaders, 179; on politics, 184; on question of power, 184–85; radicalism of, 157; on "red-brown" threat, 184; support for Yeltsin, 169, 182; support of idea of "iron fist," 177, 178; "The Depravity of Struggle" speech and article, 149–50, 151, 156, 158; on USSR Congress, 97
Civic Action movement, 107
civility, 22, 24, 127
civil society, 113, 125, 127, 133, 134, 135–36, 139

coal miners' strikes, 97
Cold War, 1, 7–8
Communist Bloc: collapse of, 73
communist morality: conception of, 21, 23–24, 40, 41–42; internalization of, 18; perestroika and, 25–28; Romantic sensibility of, 19; social determinants of, 18–19, 21–22
Communist Party of the Soviet Union: 1961 program, 23; abolition of monopoly on power, 79; ban of factions, 96; Central Committee plenums, 53, 79–80; civilizing mission of, 21–22; collegial bodies, 81; democratic opposition to, 2, 141; de-Stalinization program, 22–23, 42; dissolution of, 148; educational mission of, 18; Interregional Group of Deputies and, 101; monopoly on power, 36, 73, 80, 92; monopoly on truth, 55; moral leadership of, 23–24, 28; Nineteenth Conference (June 1988), 53, 80; Twentieth Congress of, 43; Twenty-Eighth Congress of, 144
Congress of People's Deputies of the USSR. *See* USSR Congress
conscience (*sovest'*), 44, 45, 59, 60
consciousness (*soznatel'nost'*), 18, 19, 28, 29, 121
conservative nationalists, 29–30, 32, 70, 220
Constant, Benjamin, 128
Constitutional Court, 163
Czechoslovakia: moral project, 10; transition to democracy, 140, 158, 189; Velvet Revolution in, 104–105, 188

democracy: *vs.* democratization, 132, 189; exported, 129; institutionalization of, 153; legitimacy of, 188; as liberation, 136; mechanisms of, 134; moral basis of, 158, 188; parliamentary, 133; political action and, 152, 191; popular sovereignty and, 128, 133; under rule of the "iron fist," 124; in Russia, character of, 190; transition to, 113–14, 129–30, 132, 133–34; as work of fabrication, 136
Democratic Choice of Russia (political party), 166
democratic movement, 12, 146, 154–55, 170, 216
Democratic Platform, 107, 144, 145, 147
Democratic Russia coalition (DR): anti-communism of, 147–48; autonomy strategy of, 152–54, 156; Communist Party and, 146–48; debates about political

role of, 149; demonstrations organized by, 141, 147; "depravity debate," 149–50, 152–53, 154, 158–59; dissident wing of, 170; dissolution of, 165–66; election of Coordination Council of, 153; electoral successes, 143, 148–49; formation of, 140; ideological shifts, 142–46; leaders of, 140–41, 142, 148, 153–54; national liberation discourse, 143; opposition to Gorbachev, 141, 142, 156, 157; pragmatic course of, 168; proponents of consolidation of, 147; purpose of, 141; "radicals" and "moderates" factions, 141, 156–58; Russian government and, 155–56; Second Congress, 149, 153; split in, 149, 154; support for Yeltsin, 147, 148–49, 151, 154, 155, 157, 160–61, 164, 169–70; Third Congress, 154

Democratic Union, 83, 216

democratization: consequences of, 56; consolidation of power and, 11; criticism of, 118, 124; vs. democracy, 132, 189; liberal intelligentsia and, 45; official launch of, 49; promotion of, 80; resistance to, 53

democrats: Burtin's recommendations for, 174; criticism of, 165, 174–75, 176; generational and intellectual divide, 169; label of, 197; moral bankruptcy of, 173; popular opinion of, 165; Soviet ideology and, 6–7

"depravity debate," 149–50, 151–53, 154, 158–59

de-Stalinization, 13, 22–23, 34, 36, 42, 54

Dissidents: in eastern Europe, 35, 104, 204; in the Soviet Union, 51, 60, 69, 75, 133, 175, 191

Djilas, Milovan, 38, 171

Eastern Europe: "constructivist" mission of liberalism, 187; post-communist parliamentary elections, 155; revolutions of 1989, 100, 104–105, 113, 144, 188

East Germany, 10, 104, 143

ecological movement, 31

economic romanticism, 21

education: socialist project of, 18, 19, 22–23

Estonian Popular Front, 107

Eyal, Gil, 35, 70, 158, 189

factual truth, 57, 59–61, 180, 204

freedom, 50, 189, 190

Furman, Dmitri, 13

Gaidar, Egor, 139, 155, 158, 159

Gdlyan, Telman, 91, 209

Gefter, Mikhail, 82, 221

glasnost, 25–26, 30, 53–54, 57, 60, 179–80

Gorbachev, Mikhail: August Putsch and, 148; cadre policy, 26; campaign against illegal income, 26; Communist Party and, 81; confrontation between Sakharov and, 87, 88, 91–92; death of, 192; decree on "public offense" to the organs of state power, 87–88; democratic pressure on, 112–13, 146; Democratic Russia coalition and, 156, 157; economic reforms, 81–82; as "enlightened reformer," 175; glasnost policy, 25–26, 30; Interregional Group of Deputies and, 101, 143; liberal intelligentsia and, 52, 53, 54, 87, 141, 142, 146–48; Nineteenth Party Congress, 80; opposition to, 69, 87, 97, 101, 110, 125, 172; perestroika, 1, 52, 53, 54, 80, 114; political program of, 79–81, 109–10; popular support, 81, 100, 108; prohibition campaign, 25; rapprochement with the West, 54; resignation of, 172; USSR Congress and, 113

Gordon, Leonid, 89, 159

Granin, Daniil, 61, 169

Great Soviet Encyclopedia, 17, 23, 35, 198

half-truth, 65, 66, 67–68

Havel, Vaclav, 104, 158

Hungary, 99, 104, 113, 125–26, 143–44

Independent Civic Initiative, 154

individualism, 40, 47

informal organizations, 73, 83, 85, 90–92, 134

Inogo ne dano (There is no other way) publication, 13, 55, 65, 69, 75–76, 82, 99, 130, 135, 176

International Memorial Society, 192

Interregional Group of Deputies: creation of, 94, 96, 101; decline of, 107; elections of March 1990 and, 142–43; fear of social unrest, 97–98, 100; Gorbachev and, 143; members of, 95; "radicals" and "moderates" factions, 102–3; political demands, 102, 142; radicalization of, 102, 103, 107; reformist agenda of, 73, 95; refusal to act as opposition, 109; role in Soviet political life, 73, 95; Soviet leadership and, 101

"iron fist": idea of, 113–16, 119, 137–38, 159, 177–78, 190

Karpinsky, Len: background and career, 39; criticism of the *nomenklatura*, 39; on debates against Andreeva, 64–65; on Gorbachev, 147; influence of, 13, 115; on market economy, 39, 58; on moral law, 59; Moscow Tribune and, 82; on perestroika, 44, 64–65, 190; on plurality of opinions, 56; on Romantic ideals of self-realization, 39, 40; on self-censorship, 71; on socialism, 39–40; on Soviet society, 39; on Stalinist system, 44, 55
Karyakin, Yuri: background of, 40; on debates against Andreeva, 64; "depravity debate" and, 151; on human progress, 41; on individualism, 40; influence of, 13, 39, 115, 201; involvement in peace movement, 40; moralism of, 40–41, 91; Moscow Tribune and, 82; on parliamentary elections, 164; radicalism of, 157; on self-censorship, 71; support for Yeltsin, 169
KGB (Committee for State Security), 115, 148
Khrushchev, Nikita: bureaucratic apparatus and, 52; critique of the "cult of personality," 43; de-Stalinization efforts, 42, 159; ouster of, 24, 62; reforms, 122; "Secret Speech," 23
Kis, Janos, 85
Kliamkin, Igor: on authoritarian transition to democracy, 114, 124–26, 157, 184; critics of, 119–20, 137; defense of the "present," 122; determinism of, 120; disagreement with Migranian, 125; education and career, 115; on historical necessity, 119–20; idea of the "iron fist," 115, 116, 119, 125, 177; interview on "iron fist", 137–38; on Khrushchev's reforms, 122–23; lectures and publications of, 116; on liberation, 136; on lying to oneself, 121; on market economy, 123, 124; moral discourse of, 122, 123, 180; on objective social laws, 117–18; on pace of economic reforms, 98; on perestroika, 113, 118–19, 121, 122–23; as political commentator, 116–17; on political reform, 136–37; on politics and morality, 114–15; positivist method of, 118; on pragmatism, 181; on Sakharov, 183; on social development, 124; on Soviet society, 121; on Stalinism, 116, 118, 120, 121–22; on transition to democracy, 113; on truth, 121; on USSR Congress, 113; "What Lies Ahead?," 119; "Which Way Leads to the Church?," 115–17, 118; "Why It Is Difficult to Tell the Truth," 121
Komsomol (communist youth organization), 24
Krapfl, James, 153, 188

Latsis, Otto, 3, 115, 201
Lefort, Claude, 19, 203
Lenin, Vladimir, 21, 23, 37, 39, 52, 145
Leningrad Association of Socioeconomic Sciences, 138
"Letter of 42," 161–62, 185
liberal economists, 154
liberal intelligentsia: anti-Stalinism of, 34, 35, 36, 41; attitude to Marxism-Leninism, 16, 40; contradictory expectations of, 10–11; debates with Andreeva, 63–64; democratization and, 8–9, 45, 49; disillusionment scholarship on, 4, 5–6, 7; division within, 149; drift toward opposition, 87; Gorbachev and, 73–74; ideal of freedom and, 50; ideology of, 7, 41, 145–46; influence of, 2–3, 34, 52–53, 190; intellectual pluralism of, 61; "iron fist" idea and, 159; isolation from ordinary citizens, 90, 188; marginalization of, 3, 165, 166, 186–87; moralism of, 10, 11, 15–17, 33, 35–36, 40, 42, 44, 45, 49, 50–51, 70, 187, 188–89; movement for peace and, 40; national liberation discourse and, 142; opposition to nationalists and communists, 3, 44, 94, 110, 146; perestroika and, 36, 37, 41, 98–99; polarization within, 54; political evolution of, 51, 73, 74, 75, 167; popular mobilization and, 11, 112; aporia of the founding of liberty, 189, 190; prominent figures of, 13; *publicistika* of, 4–5, 14; question of power and, 11, 187; radicalism of, 7, 91, 141, 170, 187; "red-brown" threat and, 149, 151, 152, 159; "revolution envy" toward Eastern Europe, 99, 210; rise of, 1–2, 9, 34; Romantic sensibility of, 36, 48, 49, 58; self-censorship, 35; social gap between apparatchiks and, 158; strategy toward the Soviet regime, 49, 74–75; struggle for truth, 60, 67, 68, 110; support for the "enlightened leader," 7, 94, 106, 108, 157–58; support for Yeltsin, 148–49, 159; triumphalist vision of, 4–5, 7, 12; view of

dictatorship, 158, 159; view of economy, 58, 124; vision of progress, 36, 37–38, 49; vs. Western liberals, 50
liberalism, 2, 9–10, 187; *See also* Soviet liberalism
liberal nationalists, 29–30
liberal press, 34
Ligachev, Egor, 25
Likhachev, Dmitri: on democracy, 30–31; influence of, 30, 40, 41; on lies in Soviet society, 31; moral discourse of, 30–31, 32, 59; nationalist views of, 30; on social consciousness, 70–71; Soviet Cultural Foundation and, 32; "Stoic" position of, 45; support for Yeltsin, 169, 220; "The Pangs of Conscience," 31; on truth and half-truth, 59, 65
Lithuania, 3, 147, 160
Lukin, Alexander, 6–7
"lying to oneself" (*samoobman*), 120–22

Machiavelli, Niccolò, 190, 224
Manual of Scientific Communism, 18–19
market economy: controversial ideas about, 58–59; as mode of economic regulation, 124; objective laws of, 57–58; vs. planned economy, 123; scientific validity of, 59; socialism and, 145
Marxism-Leninism: abandonment of, 6, 9; decline of, 4, 41–42; doctrinal framework of, 23; "ideological monism" of, 78; liberal intelligentsia and, 16, 40; moral doctrine of, 17–19, 35, 48; technocratic character of, 18
mass politics, fear of, 7, 97, 101, 113, 131–32, 134, 138, 157, 182, 223
MDG (*Mezhregional'naia deputatskaia gruppa*). *See* Interregional Group of Deputies
Mezhuev, Boris, 193
Michnik, Adam, 85, 97
Migranian, Andranik: background and education of, 126–27; on bureaucratic "totalitarianism," 130; call for an "iron fist", 115, 133; on civil society, 113, 125, 127, 133, 134, 135; critics of, 137, 177; on democratization, 132; disagreement with Kliamkin, 125; ideas of Western political science and, 126; on independent legislative bodies, 132–33; influence of, 113, 133, 168; inspiration by American political system, 130, 132; interview on "iron fist", 137–38; on legislation on civil disobedience, 134; Machiavellianism of, 126; on Marxism, 128; moral discourse of, 128–29, 130–31, 135, 180; on National Salvation Committee, 135; on opposition, 125; on paternalism, 136; on perestroika, 113, 126; on political participation of the masses, 131, 134–35; political reform proposed by, 136; on politics and morality, 114–15; on populist leaders, 131; on pragmatism, 181; publications of, 127, 129, 130, 210; on relationship between the individual, society, and the state, 127–29; on social polarization, 131; on Stalin, 130; on task of political science, 126; on task of the reformer, 135, 136; technocratic program of, 136, 137; on totalitarianism vs. authoritarianism, 132, 133, 134–35; on transition to democracy, 113, 114, 129–30, 131, 133–34, 135–36, 157, 184; on USSR Congress, 113, 131–32
Moral Codex of the Builder of Communism, 18, 23, 24
morality: conservative conception of, 48, 49; democracy and, 188–89; economy and, 123; environmental factors of, 22; as foundation of culture, 30; freedom and, 128, 189; internalization of, 18; Marxism-Leninism and, 17, 26–27, 30; "objective factors" of, 18; perestroika and, 15–16; personal conscience (*sovest'*) and, 28, 44, 45, 122, 172; politics and, 10, 23, 35, 48, 114–15, 123, 183–84; as private disposition, 135; question of power and, 11; reformist conception of, 48, 49; revolutionary conception of, 42, 48–49; scientific literature on, 17; Soviet doctrine of, 15, 17, 18–20, 21–22; universal values and, 21, 35–36, 42
moral monism, 55–56, 78, 98, 102
moral opposition, 170, 175, 176
moral truth, 57, 59, 60, 61, 65, 102, 158, 180, 204
Moscow Popular Front, 91
Moscow Tribune (MT): foundation of, 13, 82, 83–84; gap between ordinary citizens and, 90–91; informal organizations and, 91; lack of political influence, 84–85; leaders of, 73, 82, 140; political actions, 84, 85, 90; radicalization of, 86; refusal to act as opposition, 109; reputation of, 82; session on constitutional reform, 89; support for Gorbachev, 85

INDEX

Narodniki (populist movement), 20, 21, 37–38, 171, 174, 199
nationalist intellectuals: anti-Western views, 32–33, 48; national liberation discourse, 142; environmental projects and, 31; liberal intelligentsia and, 32, 44, 174–75; moral discourse of, 31; perestroika and, 31–33; promotion of Russian culture, 32
naturalization of socialist ideals, 41
neoliberal economists: reform program of, 138–39
New Economic Policy, 37, 99
nomenklatura (bureaucratic elite), 1, 27, 38, 39, 70, 130, 153, 171–72
Novodvorskaya, Valeriya, 83
Novo-Ogarevo agreement, 147–148, 152
nuclear disarmament, 40
Nuikin, Andrei, 181, 201, 220

open society, 76–77, 93
opposition: debates on the relevance of, 83, 86, 98, 102–9; formation of, 140–141, 142; meaning of, 74; Sakharov's view of, 101, 106, 157; Soviet liberals' resistance to the idea of, 75, 94–95; to the system *vs.* opposition to the government, 74, 109–10, 149
organized lying, 60

Pavlova-Silvanskaya, Marina, 100
peasant masses, 28, 44, 121
perestroika: authoritarian rule and, 113–14; "brake mechanisms" of, 54; critical analysis of, 118–19, 121, 176–78, 190; democratization and, 49; end of, 6; Gorbachev's statements on, 52, 53; historiography of, 6, 9, 156, 169; individualism and, 46; launch of, 1; legacies of, 7, 167, 192–93; liberal turn of, 9, 61; moral dimensions of, 12, 15–16, 25–28, 37, 41, 46, 55–56; obstacles to, 44; opponents of, 61–62, 72–73, 93; outcomes of, 1–2; pace of reforms of, 98; as perfectionist project, 115; political dimensions of, 12, 112; popular views of, 123, 192; progressive nature of, 51; purpose of, 48; as revolution, 52, 188; scholarship on, 4, 6, 8; shift in the reform strategy, 47; skepticism about, 5–6, 69–70; supporters of, 63, 72–73, 93; variants of, 56–57, 94
Perestroika Club, 83
personal conscience (*sovest'*), 28, 44, 45, 174

personality realization (*lichnost'*), 20
"petit bourgeois" vices, 38
pluralism, 76, 77–78, 93, 94, 141, 160
Poland: civil society, 85, 113; economic reforms, 160; mobilizational model, 91, 140, 144, 148; moral project, 10; political reform, 99, 140; revolution, 99, 100, 113; social discontent, 160; Solidarność movement, 91, 97, 99, 156
political perfectionism, 50
political pluralism, 9, 72, 73, 78, 79, 107–108, 110
political realism, 83, 85
political Romanticism, 16, 50
politics: Bismarck's statement on, 181; morality and, 114–15, 184; pragmatism of, 181–82
Politizdat (publishing house), 18, 19
Ponomarev, Lev, 153, 154, 217
Popov, Gavriil: on administrative system of command, 45–46, 48; call for political strike, 105; conciliatory strategy, 109, 177; critique of systemic duplicity, 46–47; Democratic Russia coalition and, 140; on expansion of Gorbachev's authority, 138; Interregional Group of Deputies and, 94, 95–96, 97–98, 211; on moral decline of society, 46; on opposition, 108; on perestroika, 47; political career of, 138, 141; pragmatism of, 168, 198; on socialism, 47; at USSR Congress, 88
Popper, Karl, 76, 126
popular mobilization, 11, 97, 112, 160, 164
popular sovereignty, 80, 128, 133
positivism, 20, 57, 117–18
Pozsgay, Imre, 99
pragmatism, 16, 168–70, 181–82
Prague Spring, 41, 115
prohibition campaign, 25
Public Committees for Russian Reforms, 153, 155
publicistika (committed essay), 14
Pushkin, Aleksandr, 97, 98
Putin, Vladimir, 3, 5, 7, 12, 192

question of power, 11, 73, 79, 86, 92–93, 110, 171, 176–82, 193

Rasputin, Valentin, 30, 31, 32, 44–45, 70, 201; *The Fire*, 44–45
"red-brown" threat, 149, 151, 152, 155, 159–65, 168, 184–85
referendum of April 1993, 161

Romania, 104
Romanticism, 10, 16–17
Rousseau, Jean-Jacques, 189, 190
Russian Congress, 155, 159, 160, 218
Russian Federation: anti-revolutionary sentiment, 7; authoritarianism, 190–91; concentration of power, 12; Constitution of 1993, 163, 164, 165; cultural atavism, 5; democratic erosion, 5, 166–67; economic recession in, 5; emergence of, 1; international support, 161; invasion of Ukraine, 192; moral corruption of population, 5; nostalgia for Soviet Past, 6; parliamentary elections of 1993, 164; political parties, 166; political pluralism, 141, 160; "shock therapy," 159–60
Russian intelligentsia, 7, 20, 22, 156, 187, 212
Russian peasantry, 28, 44, 121
Russian Soviet Federative Socialist Republic (RSFSR): economic reforms in, 139; nationalist discourse in, 142–43; parliamentary elections in, 155; political strikes in, 147–48

Sakharov, Andrei: call for political strike, 105, 106; conciliatory strategy, 109; contribution to *Inogo ne dano*, 75–76; death of, 107, 146, 182, 183; debate against Solzhenitsyn, 77; "Decree on Power" speech, 88, 91–92, 93, 97, 114; defense of human rights, 75, 76; on democratization, 77, 125, 140; draft for new Soviet constitution, 103, 120–21; electoral program, 78–79; elitism of, 77; evolution of political thought of, 36, 75, 79, 93, 207; Gorbachev and, 79, 82, 87, 88, 91–92; house arrest of, 75; idealism of, 183; idea of social control, 77; influence of, 13, 174, 182–83, 192, 197; inspiration by the American political system, 132; Interregional Group of Deputies and, 95, 103, 105–7; legacy of, 183; on Marxism-Leninism, 78; on morality, 89; Moscow Tribune and, 82; notion of open society, 76; on opposition movement, 106, 142, 157; on perestroika, 90, 100–101, 106, 112; on pluralism, 76, 77–78; political strategy of, 103; posthumous celebration of, 107; on question of power, 79, 86; radicalization of, 75, 79, 86, 103, 106–7; on revolutions in Poland and Hungary, 100; on truth telling, 60; USSR Congress and, 88–89; vision of world politics, 77

self-censorship, 35, 70–71
Seliunin, Vasily, 30, 158–59, 161, 169
Seventiers (*semidesiatniki*), 169
Sheinis, Viktor, 103
Shmelev, Nikolai, 57–58, 59, 88, 123, 201; "Advances and Debts," 57
"shock therapy," 159–60
Shubkin, Vladimir, 89–90
Siberian rivers diversion project, 31, 201
Sixtiers (*shestidesiatniki*), 13, 22, 115, 126, 143, 169
Slavophiles, 20, 32, 54
Smena vekh (Change of milestones), 116, 212
Sobchak, Anatoly, 141, 168, 198
social conscience: *vs.* economic and political reality, 99; quest for purification of, 61, 70–71
social criticism, 42–43
Social Democratic bloc, 154
socialism, 2, 20–21, 38, 144
"socialism with a human face," 41, 145
socialist humanism, 10, 35, 38, 50, 187
socialist personality, 18, 19
Solidarność movement, 91, 97, 100, 144, 156
Solzhenitsyn, Aleksandr: arrest of, 28; call for preservation of "spiritual independence," 29; condemnation of Western capitalism, 38; debate against, 77; influence of, 38, 40, 41, 197, 200; "Live Not by Lies" manifesto, 28–29, 31; "Stoic" position of, 45; on truth, 29
Soviet Cultural Foundation, 32
Soviet liberalism: socialist humanism and, 10, 50; moralism of, 10, 187–88; political perfectionism of, 50; popularity of, 9; *vs.* Western liberalism, 49–50
Soviet modernity, 19, 20, 28
Soviet society: class division, 39; Communist Party role in, 36, corruption, 24–25; ideology, 5–7; moral discourse of, 15–16, 22, 24–25, 28, 31, 33, 130–31; "negative phenomena" of, 27, 42; "petty-bourgeois" mentality, 27; political regime, 19–20; rational organization of, 20–21; universal attributes, 41; "vestiges" (*perezhitki*) of capitalism in, 21
Soviet Writers' Union, 54
Stalin, Joseph: attempt at moral rehabilitation of, 67; criticism of, 23, 43–44; literary depictions of, 43; peasantry policy, 28; role in the Great Patriotic War, 67

Stalinism, 22–23, 41, 42, 43, 116, 121–22
Stalinist neo-Romanticism, 23, 25
Supreme Soviet of the Soviet Union, 81, 161
systemic duplicity, 46–47

Taylor, Charles, 17
Timofeev, Lev, 154
Tocqueville, Alexis de, 129
totalitarianism, 46, 132, 134–35
truth: conscience and, 59; debates on, 65–66; despotic character of, 61; moral discourse of, 29, 121, 180; politics and, 60, 61; totalitarian regimes and, 60
truth telling, 60–61, 69
Tsipko, Aleksandr, 115, 156

Ukraine: Russia's invasion of, 192
Union of Right Forces (political party), 166
Union of Soviet Socialist Republics. *See* USSR
Union of Writers of Russia, 32–33
United Russia (political party), 166
United Workers' Front, 101, 103
universal values, 35–36, 44, 53, 55–57, 78
USSR: bureaucracy, 130; censorship, 115; cognitive revolution in, 145–46; democratic reform, 104, 130, 131; disintegration of, 1, 4, 145, 148; economic policy, 121; elections of 1989, 74; elections of 1990, 142–43; first legal opposition in, 95; nationalist movements in, 142–43; political system, 72, 73; post of president of, 138; prevalence of heroic individualism, 47; relationships with the West, 32, 52; resistance to reform, 52; social polarization, 130, 131; stagnation period, 24–25, 42; *See also* Soviet society
USSR Congress: aggressively obedient majority of, 88, 96; confrontation between Gorbachev and Sakharov at, 87, 88, 91–92, 104; criticism of, 131; disbandment of, 148; election campaign, 81, 86; factions, 96; media coverage of, 93–94; political debates, 88, 142; radical deputies, 113; Soviet liberals' view of, 93

Vekhi (Milestones), 116, 156, 212
village writers, 28, 29, 30
Vilnius January Events of 1991, 147

Wałęsa, Lech, 156
Westernizers, 54

Yabloko (political party), 165, 166, 169
Yakovlev, Aleksandr, 57, 62–63, 101
Yakunin, Gleb, 153, 168, 217
Yeltsin, Boris: backroom deals, 147; consolidation of power, 139, 163, 187; delay of parliamentary elections in 1991, 155; Democratic Russia coalition and, 147, 151, 154, 155, 160–61, 218; economic policy, 139; election as president of Russia, 148; as "enlightened reformer," 175–76; Gorbachev and, 143; international support, 161; Interregional Group of Deputies and, 95, 101; liberal intelligentsia and, 3, 12, 162, 169–70, 172, 190; parliamentary support of, 155; political crisis of 1993, 165; protest vote against, 164; reputation of, 91; rise to power, 3, 141, 142, 148–49; Russian Congress' vote on removal from office, 160; union strikes and, 148; at USSR Congress, 88

Zalygin, Sergei, 30, 31, 200
Zaslavskaya, Tatyana, 55
Zdravomyslov, Andrei, 27
Zhigulin, Anatoly, 65–66

www.ingramcontent.com/pod-product-compliance
Lightning Source LLC
Chambersburg PA
CBHW031353230426
43670CB00006B/528